OPERA AS THEATER

BOOKS BY GEORGE R. MAREK

OPERA AS THEATER

THE WORLD TREASURY OF GRAND OPERA

A FRONT SEAT AT THE OPERA

PUCCINI

THE GOOD HOUSEKEEPING GUIDE TO MUSICAL ENJOYMENT

GEORGE R. MAREK

OPERA
AS
THEATER

HARPER & ROW, PUBLISHERS, NEW YORK AND EVANSTON

To Erich Leinsdorf, in friendship

CONTENTS

FOREWORD

If you like it you like it very much. If you don't like it you can't stand it. Of the popular arts opera is the one which boils up the hottest partisanship—or freezes to the coldest indifference.

To me opera is one of the most satisfying of the arts. It is a tandem which couples the free-roaming power of music to the animated and three-dimensional power of drama. It is a combination and a form, indeed, where two great arts did seem to set their seal.

I become angry when somebody whose judgment I respect derogates opera.

Are there such derogators? Indeed there are. Charles Lamb felt "inexplicable anguish" sitting through an Italian opera. Mark Twain thought that *Lohengrin*'s "banging and slamming and booming and crashing were something beyond belief." We have all met the bespectacled music lover who will listen to Scarlatti or to Bartók but is unable to endure the rudeness of *Rigoletto*. We are acquainted with the young woman who would like Wagner if only the singing were eliminated. Proust seems to have known her: the Guermantes' friends discuss *Tristan* and reduce what is worthwhile in the score to the few measures for the hunting horns in the second act. But the garden variety of operaphobe is to be found among those who smile a superior smile as they speak of the old-fashioned and puerile stories which serve as vehicles for operatic music.

The indictment is false. To be sure, there are good operas the librettos of which could hardly be classed as literature. (But then, they are not supposed to be literature.) The best operas, those which give us our strongest and most enduring satisfaction, must have and do have librettos of remarkable vitality, all the more remarkable when we consider that works for the stage age more rapidly than works of music. *Hedda Gabler* seems more dated than Strauss' *Don Juan*; both were created about 1890.

The trouble is that quite often we do not understand—*really* understand—what is going on on the stage, that we fail to grasp the intention of composer and librettist. Language difficulties are one obstacle, but they are not the only obstacle. We judge a libretto with too modern an ear, though we are quite willing and indeed eager to judge the music with an ear that is well tempered to the composer's language. The reason is not difficult to define: what happens on the stage is corporeal, what happens in music is free, not bound by pictorial realism. Music need not "make sense" except in musical terms.

Yet the best operas do make sense. They disclose their sense and admit us to the circle of enjoyment and wonder, when we understand, *really* understand, the play. Then we are free to be moved by the music.

It is the ambition of this book to aid the reader in such understanding. Though the music of ten popular operas is discussed—without, however, musical quotations, since I believe that such quotations are not valuable to a sufficient number of readers—the stress of discussion is laid on the drama. Wagner felt this was the proper preparation: "While listening to a good—a rational—opera, people should, so to speak, not think of the music at all, but only feel it unconsciously, while their fullest sympathy should be occupied by the action represented."

This book, this essay in affection, hopes to demonstrate with the detailed example of these works the belief, already expressed, that a successful work for the lyric stage demands a high degree of integrated and closely meshed skill, and that it must be successful on two counts: its dramatic presentation and its musical content. An opera with an out-and-out shoddy libretto cannot be properly considered of the first rank. There are one or two exceptions—I am as familiar with *Il Trovatore* and *Madama Butterfly* as the next man—but by and large the restriction applies, because an opera is not wholly a musical experience.

What is a good libretto? It is one which offers the composer the opportunity to permeate words with music, so that from the fusion may emerge a work of art the two components of which are no longer separable, just as color and line are no longer separable in a painting. An opera is not a play set to music; it is not words onto which music has been grafted, or words titivated with music. It is drama expressed *through* music. It follows that the music itself must contain the drama which is inherent in the words. There must take place a complete amalgamation between plot and song, between action on the stage and action in the music, between the characters as conceived by the librettist and the characters as we sense them in tonal expression.

Not all good stories, plays, or novels lend themselves to musical treatment. As a rule, neither a work of absolute introspection nor a plot which ranges far and wide will serve. Prokofiev's attempt to set *War and Peace* to music is a failure (though one scene, the death of Prince Andrew, is extraordinarily effective). A modern composer has set *Madame Bovary* to music; nothing of Flaubert's subtle portrait of a woman remains. We get instead a few isolated stagy scenes such as Emma visiting the pawnbroker. Emma is too complex a creation to be able to live behind the footlights.

Is simplicity then the criterion? Not altogether. This book attempts to show that the verbal half of the venture is neither so raw nor so ingenuous as we are sometimes led to expect. Certain it is that every successful opera composer (except Rossini) has labored diligently over his libretto. There exists much biographical evidence, ranging from Mozart to Richard Strauss, of the punctilious care and the word-by-word worry which the composer has bestowed upon the text. Charles Burney, the eighteenth-century musical historian, reported this about Gluck:

He studies a poem a long time before he thinks of setting it. He considers well the relation which each part bears to the whole; the general cast of each character, and aspires more at satisfying the mind than flattering the ear. This is not only being a friend of poetry, but a poet himself; and if he had language sufficient, of any other kind than that of sound, in which to express his ideas, I am certain he would be a great poet: as it is, music, in his hands, is a most copious, nervous, elegant, and expressive language. It seldom happens that a single air of his operas can be taken out of its niche and sung singly with much effect; the whole is a chain, of which a detached single link is but of small importance.

That an operatic work must be a dual combination is as true of what we call "old-fashioned" opera as it is of the psychologically finer products such as *Otello* or *Don Giovanni*. Surely *Lucia di Lammermoor* seems at first to be nothing but an exercise in singing, grafted onto a naïve plot. Yet in discussing Joan Sutherland's performance, the critic Peter Stadlen wrote that it "was a living repudiation of the belief that in pre-Verdian Italian opera the action is merely a peg on which to hang the music and singing. In the Mad Scene in particular it became clear that one was primarily being subjected to a dramatic experience." (London *Daily Telegraph*, September 4, 1961.) This is an extreme example; *Lucia* is in truth pretty primitive stuff.

A final test of a good opera is popularity. Perhaps the test is applicable to any art, though it must be particularly applicable to a work designed for the theater. If the popular element is altogether missing, something is wrong. Something may be wrong with Debussy's *Pelléas et Mélisande,* an opera which contains superb music but music couched in such nonpopular, nontheatrical terms that it cannot hold the stage, not even in its native France.

"Popular," needless to say, does not mean cheap. In reviewing a recent performance of *Carmen,* Paul Henry Lang wrote that "the popular element is present everywhere but always informed with the most tasteful, original, and attractive refinements that make the work into one of the most sparkling scores ever conceived."

If opera is all its enthusiasts claim it to be, then it must be self-explanatory. Why read a book and do homework? That a work of art is completely self-revealing is true in theory only. In practice what is needed is a modest guide who will point once, and then let the listener do the rest. A listener's imagination is reinforced not only by suggestions as to where to listen, but also by hints which may help to elucidate the work's plan and design. It is additionally reinforced by knowledge of the sources from which the opera has been derived, be they as rich as Shakespeare or as meager as Sardou.

Perhaps I will make no new converts. At the least I hope to kindle some who are half-converted to new enthusiasm, to help them sense more acutely the heady odor of the opera house, a mixture of grease paint and violin varnish.

GEORGE R. MAREK

December, 1961

P.S. I have followed accepted usage in titling the operas, grammatically inconsistent though this may be. We do not call *La Traviata* "The One Who Has Strayed," and conversely, few people say *Le Nozze di Figaro*. High points of the music I have given both in the original language and in translation, especially when they are something like a set piece.

INTRODUCTION

Beaumarchais, that witty and skillful writer of comedies, who was the originator though not the author of two of the most cherished libretti of all time, was also responsible for a maxim which, although no doubt unknown to most opera fans, might well express the secret belief of a large number of them. In his *Le Barbier de Séville* there occurs a phrase which has it that *"ce qui ne vaut pas la peine d'être dit, on le chante."* Now, conversely, if whatever is not worth saying is to be sung, it follows—if not by the rules of strict logic, certainly by those of sloppy argument—that whatever is being sung must be pretty imbecilic.

That, I submit, is how many people feel about the words in an opera libretto. "Everybody knows" (so they say) "that an opera text is the lowest kind of literary production, and anyhow—all that counts in opera is the music." So just settle back in your seat, let the sound of music float over you, wait for *"Celeste Aïda"* or *"Vissi d'arte"* to come around, and, if there is some recitative—that needless bore that only serves the plot—then do as the chic snobs did in the early Venetian opera houses: go back to the ante-room of your box and play a few moves of chess.

What? you have no box? or you have one, but there is no chessboard in it? Well, relax and give some thought to your income tax, or any other agreeable subject, until that fool on stage has finished his vain attempt to elucidate what is going on, and the next hit tune approaches, which is after all what opera is for and about.

I can hardly deny that opera can be enjoyed in this fashion. If I

were to deny it, the facts of life in the lyric theater would rise to
fly in my face. Many opera buffs (and in my gloomier moments
I tend to think: most opera buffs) go to an opera performance in
precisely that frame of mind, or—more correctly—mindlessness.

Whether opera can be pleasurably consumed in this sybaritic
way is really quite immaterial. What is essential is whether opera
was meant to be nothing more than a cornucopia of alluring tunes,
a tightrope walk in the neighborhood of high C, and the trapeze
art of coloratura. The answer is an unqualified *no*.

You do not have to be a historian or a musicologist (and I
surely am neither) to remember that, in its beginnings, opera was
an art entirely of and for the theater. Its very name (long before
the term *opera* was ever used) proves it: *dramma in musica*. Its
early theorists, as well as its first practitioners, intended it to be a
drama heightened by music, by the emotional impact of music,
and not a conglomeration of sound and fury, signifying nothing
much, with words added only by way of regrettable necessity, because one cannot sing *la, la, la* all evening long.

Opera, then, is supposed to flow from the union of text and
music, a drama or a comedy told in song, with—later on—a strong
dosis of symphonic comment added onto it. And while it is true
that this dramatic principle of opera has suffered more violations
than you can shake a baton at, while it is a well-known fact that
opera has time and time again fallen into the hands of the star
singer, to whom nothing matters but the beauty of his voice, and
possibly that of his legs, it is also true, and rather comforting, that
within the three and a half centuries of opera's existence time and
time again the dramatic essence of the musical theater has asserted
itself and opera has returned to its original mission.

Whenever a batch of mindless, soulless, meaningless scores had
lorded it over the lyric stage, a musician would come along who
once again took opera seriously as a dramatic entity and, therefore,
insisted on collaborating with a writer to whom a libretto was
more than a string of singable words. This is the way, the only
way, masterpieces in opera are created.

Popular opera may subsist on a silly book; great opera cannot.
I defy anybody to name a truly great opera that has a bad libretto.
Let me hasten to add that I do not imply that the text of Bizet's
Carmen, splendid though it is, can boast the same literary level

as that gem of twentieth-century comedy writing, Hugo von Hofmannsthal's *Der Rosenkavalier*. What I will claim is that no theatrically valid opera can be written without a cogent book. If you think I am wrong, just turn the pages. Read George Marek.

If all Mr. Marek set out to do was to point up the bare bones of the plots, he need not have bothered; books doing just that come by the dozen. Quite apart from giving his readers valuable, and sometimes invaluable, insight into the background of both the operas and their creators, he has outlined for you not only what happens in opera, but also how it happens, why it happens, and (if you have a bit of imagination of your own) how it could have happened quite differently. It is all so deftly done, so unpedantic and yet so well ordered, that I should not be surprised if even a person tone-deaf and severely nonoperatic in his tastes would be thrilled by following the intricate meanderings of these libretti. And one thing surely no one can any longer believe, after reading Mr. Marek's analyses (which on occasion could almost be called psychoanalyses), and that is: that all libretti are the outpourings of feeble-minded hacks.

The listener who expects from opera no more than a musical bath will always be with us, and especially in this country where opera is largely sung in the original; while the large majority of the public does not understand more than five words of the language sung, the theatrical aspect of opera is often grievously neglected. This, I fear, applies on both sides of the footlights. A Scarpia who never bothered to find out what happened to Tosca after his demise, or a Wotan who does not know *Götterdämmerung*, is hardly likely to be an ideal representative of his role. Similarly, a stage director who considers it his only function to put the soprano and the tenor in a position comfortable enough for the belting out of the next duet, and an impresario who believes to have done his duty once he has signed up the best vocal talent available do not serve the best interests of opera as a powerful and unique art form. Anyone who has ever attended an operatic performance that was dramatically gripping as well as musically great will, I think, agree.

What happens *in* opera George Marek is telling us in great and fascinating detail. What happens *to* opera when nobody cares what happens in opera can still be seen all too often on the lyric stage. If this book, in addition to being entertaining, urbane, and frequently erudite, helps make the opera lover more demanding as to the dramatic values of operatic performances, Mr. Marek will have achieved more than just telling us what Baron Ochs said to Mariandel.

RUDOLF BING

THE MARRIAGE OF FIGARO

COMPOSER:	Wolfgang Amadeus Mozart
LIBRETTIST:	Lorenzo Da Ponte
FIRST PERFORMANCE:	May 1, 1786 Burgtheater, Vienna
RECEPTION:	Success, but soon forgotten

CHARACTERS:

Count Almaviva, Grand Corregidor of Andalusia	Baritone
Figaro, his valet and major-domo of the château	Bass
Dr. Bartolo, a physician of Seville	Bass
Don Basilio, music master to the Countess	Tenor
Antonio, gardener of the château and Susanna's uncle	Bass
Don Curzio, counselor-at-law	Tenor
Cherubino, head page to the Count	Soprano
Countess Almaviva	Soprano
Susanna, head waiting woman to the Countess	Soprano
Marcellina, Dr. Bartolo's housekeeper	Mezzo-soprano
Barbarina, Antonio's daughter	Soprano

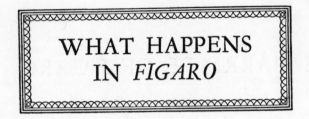

WHAT HAPPENS
IN *FIGARO*

J. Dover Wilson, the editor of *The Cambridge Shakespeare,* wrote a book called *What Happens in Hamlet.* *Time* magazine said it was as entertaining as a detective story. It is.

With due deference, we propose to borrow Mr. Wilson's idea and examine what happens in *Figaro.* To be sure, our examination will not be as learned as his; yet if it clears up some puzzling points in the plot it may enhance our enjoyment and consequently our admiration of the work as a whole. The opera is one of those works of art which seem inexhaustible. There is always something new to be gleaned in it and mined from it. The better you know *Figaro,* the better you treasure it.

On the other hand, it is possible—indeed it has been possible for over a hundred and fifty years—to enjoy *Figaro* without really knowing the plot, or at least without following the convolutions of its intrigue. What, for example, is it that the villagers thank the Count for in such melodious terms (Act I)? What is the position Figaro holds in the Count's household? If he is a servant, how may he roam the palace as freely and impudently as he does? What is the relationship of Susanna to the gardener Antonio and his to Figaro? Why does the Countess dictate a letter to Susanna instead of writing it herself and why does she dictate the words so unhesitatingly (Act III)? What do the two ladies intend by dressing Cherubino in women's clothes and why and how do they change their plan? Are there any grounds for the Count's jealousy or is he acting as the conventional husband of the comedy?

The answer to none of these questions is, as I say, essential to a great deal of the pleasure one derives from the music. All music lives a detached life, detached from the obligation of explaining itself in terms other than musical ones. But there is more! *Figaro* is more than glorious music, flowing from throats and orchestra pit and touching us with magic. It is a great psychological comedy, perhaps the greatest of all such comedies. Mozart has delineated each of his characters in the music, has in fact created each character through the music, has presented with music their traits, foibles, attractive and equivocal characteristics. He has done so in a subtle and light-footed language. Once we understand this idiom, once we "hear" these characters well, we will "see" them in the round. How very much this acquaintance will enrich us! In *Figaro* we meet some of the most interesting protagonists to be found on any stage. The wider vision brings us the sense of fulfillment that we derive from the greatest art. Finally Mozart has offered us here the challenge of following intricate action, by creating large and dexterously knit ensembles, such ensembles as even he was never to duplicate. Neither *Don Giovanni* nor *Così fan tutte* nor *Die Zauberflöte* contains musical tapestry of comparable complexity.

To accept this challenge, to retrace the psychological strokes, and to participate fully in the hide-and-seek of the comedy, it will help us if we understand more precisely who everybody is, what it is they are doing and why, and what kind of comedy librettist and composer were attempting to set before their audiences. We shall not waste our time if we examine *Figaro* afresh from the original, from Mozart's and Da Ponte's, point of view.

To do this we must go back to the original comedy by Beaumarchais. As usual when an operatic libretto is based on a spoken play, compression and condensation necessary for musical purposes have taken place. Obscure points are elucidated by the more explicit theater piece, and a knowledge of its background. Da Ponte claimed creative credit for his libretto. In point of fact he did nothing much more than to translate and adapt. We are safe in relying on Beaumarchais. It is probable that Mozart himself worked on the libretto.[1] Both men had the text of the play before them. Both men

---

[1] "The fact that da Ponte gives almost no information about the composition of the libretti he wrote for Mozart perhaps indicates that the composer contributed a great deal to them; da Ponte was not the man to acknowledge such help, even from Mozart. It

could take for granted that many in the eighteenth-century audience knew the play. We no longer do. That is fortunate, wrote the prudish Henry Krehbiel, for he thought the play "a moral blister."

The author of the play was an indigenous product of the eighteenth century. Pierre Augustin Caron was born in Paris in 1732 as the son of a simple watchmaker. But the tradesman's neighborhood of St. Denis did not long satisfy the young man. After serving briefly as an apprentice to his father, he left the shop to make his way in the Parisian world. He learned to play the harp, an instrument which in those days had all the charm of novelty, and by this skill he was able to ingratiate himself with the four daughters of Louis XV, "Mesdames of France." He made music for them and even conducted some small family concerts at court. Thus sponsored, he obtained at the age of twenty-three the office of *Controleur Clerc d'Office de la maison du Roi,* which meant that on state occasions he carved and served the meat course to His Majesty. The court official through whom Caron obtained this office soon afterward died, and Caron married his widow. He now dropped the name of Caron and took on the name of "Beaumarchais," which may have been the name of a small property owned by the widow or may have been a purely fictitious "ancestry by purchase." A self-made aristocrat, he was soon able to grant favors for various people at court. One of them returned the favor by passing on some valuable financial hints which allowed Beaumarchais to earn enough money to purchase further titles. Consequently, in 1761 he bought the title of "Secretary to the King" and only two years later that of *Lieutenant-Général des Chasses à la Capitainerie de la Varenne du Louvre.* These titles, indicating his rise, enabled him to participate ever more efficiently in the general corruption of the court, and to consolidate his own fortunes.

In the course of his career he became banker, manufacturer of paper, wholesaler of wood, shipbuilder—as such he furnished a warship to the American Colonies in the War of Independence—secret agent of Louis XV and his successor, intrigant for (and oc-

---

may be, too, that one of the reasons why none of da Ponte's libretti for other composers —with the possible exception of *Una Cosa Rara* for Martin—ever had such lasting success as those he wrote for Mozart, is that Mozart himself contributed more to his libretti in the form of suggestions and advice than we know." *The Libertine Librettist* (a biography of Lorenzo da Ponte) by A. Fitzlyon.

casionally against) Madame Pompadour and Marie Antoinette, publisher (he published a complete edition of Voltaire), smuggler of weapons from Holland, and organizer of a union of playwrights. He built several grand edifices, the grandest of them being his own palace on the Boulevard Beaumarchais. In the tradition of the speculator, he had his downs as well as his ups. Three times he was arrested in Paris, once in Vienna; he was banished to Hamburg, his fortune was confiscated and then regained; and over and over again he was to be seen in the law courts for one reason or another, but most often for seducing the wife of some worthy citizen. When he did not win in court, he inundated his adversary in a flood of pamphlets bristling with wit and malice. He died at the age of sixty-seven in 1799, having witnessed and outlived the first bloody days of the French Revolution and seen himself become one of its main celebrities. He died, to be sure, as plain Citizen Beaumarchais.

He began to write merely for amusement—*"par délassement"*—and after creating one successful and one unsuccessful serious play in the bourgeois style he turned to farce, rather to operetta, and produced *The Barber of Seville,* a play interpolated with Spanish folk songs. Later he revised this, eliminating the music; in this version *The Barber* was produced in 1775 at the Comédie Française. It took him another five years to follow *The Barber* with its sequel, *The Marriage of Figaro.* The manuscript of this comedy was finished in 1780. It was accepted by the Comédie the following year. But it took three years to get the dangerous piece past the five censors who successively turned it down, three years and all of Beaumarchais' ability for intrigue.[2] He enlisted in his cause princes, duchesses, dukes, and ministers, marshaling their aid against the king, Louis XVI, to whom the play had been read and who declared it "detestable and unplayable." The very dislike of the king favored the play in the opinions of the king's retinue. The Duke of Provence, later Louis XVIII, became its sponsor. Several times the performance was announced but canceled, once at the last moment when the carriages had already begun to roll to the theater. The more repeated the obstacles, the greater became the desire of the pro-Beaumarchais faction to see themselves lampooned, to feel the pricks of the barbs hurled against their own skins. The people

---

[2] A contemporary critic wrote: "It took more wit to get it performed than to write the piece."

who had most reason to fear the effect of the play wanted most to
see it performed.

Finally the day arrived: on the twenty-seventh of April, 1784,
the performance took place. From early morning on, the doors of
the theater were beleaguered. The guards were called but the
crowds overwhelmed them, forced the entrance, broke the iron
gate, and overflowed into the corridors. The ladies of the nobility
took their dinner in the dressing rooms of the performers in order
to be sure of getting a place.

Figaro was given many times that season and the next, was performed on many stages, and was printed in innumerable editions.
Though Joseph II had forbidden its performance in Vienna, the
play was known to every educated man and woman in that city by
the time Mozart had chosen the subject.

Did Beaumarchais know, when he wrote *Figaro*, that he was to
become the petrel of the French Revolution? Did he write *Figaro*
with the purpose of giving voice to the problems of the times? Did
he wish to incite, to make propaganda? Hardly. Nothing in Beaumarchais' career or character indicates that he was a didactic writer,
intending to mount the barricades. What he created was an autobiographical play: Figaro is Beaumarchais himself in Spanish costume, the man of lowly origin who by his wits gets the better of
his betters. We have reviewed the author's personal history in some
detail in order to point this parallel. Whatever Beaumarchais' intentions, the ideas he expressed were the ideas which hovered in the
air. Through the lens of his dramatic skill he focused them to the
burning point. So it happened that *Figaro* became one of the two
propaganda pieces which best served the French Revolution, the
other being *Charles IX* by Marie Joseph de Chénier. Danton sum-
marized it: "*The Marriage of Figaro* has killed aristocracy, *Charles
IX* has killed royalty."

Mozart must have been perfectly aware of the controversial nature of the play, though he was little interested in the political
world around him. Alfred Einstein, in his book *Mozart, His Character, His Work,* stresses this lack: "There is not a word in his
letters, or in the accounts of him in the reminiscences of those who
knew him, about the French Revolution, which began while he
was still alive; it did not touch him."

On the other hand, not only must Mozart have known of the

Emperor's prohibition of the play, a production of which had been planned by the very Schikaneder group for which Mozart was later to write *Die Zauberflöte*, but he must instinctively have felt not only the long range but the immediate advantages of the subject, the limelight advantages. To quote Einstein once more, "Mozart was much more than a mere professional musician. Just as he saw through people, despite the fact that he was continually taken in by them, so his deep intuition pierced the cultural tendencies of his time, without the help of a single lecture on esthetics." Beaumarchais' play was one recent, vital, much discussed expression of the time's cultural tendencies. Was it not advantageous to use a current subject for an opera?

Perhaps another feature of the comedy which attracted Mozart was the opportunity to give a leading role to a singer he admired, Francesco Benucci, who was to score a triumphant success in the role of Figaro. Two years before he chose the play, he had written to Salzburg: "The Italian *opera buffa* has made its reappearance here and is extremely popular. The *Buffo* is particularly good, his name is Benucci. I've certainly read through a hundred, if not more, libretti. Unfortunately there wasn't a single one with which I was completely satisfied."

In the year in which he wrote this letter, he became acquainted with Paisiello's setting of *The Barber of Seville*. The success of this opera may have further inclined him toward Beaumarchais. Yet we may safely conjecture that the most potent reason for his decision must have been the play's timeliness, offering the opportunity to capture the Viennese public with something they hadn't seen but knew all about, something controversial about which curiosity was rampant.

THE REAL CONFLICT

Before tracing the plot in detail, it will help us to define the conflict which motivates the play. A conflict it is, though on light and nontragic terms. Is it merely a servant-master battle?[3] On the surface it would appear so. But a closer understanding of Figaro's

---

[3] The theme of the clever servant is ancient: it stretches from Plautus to Ben Jonson to James Barrie.

character may teach us better. He is not an enigmatic character—yet we are likely to misunderstand him. Whether we will or no, we now remember Figaro as the barber from Beaumarchais' previous play—rather, from Rossini's opera—in which he is a jolly good-for-nothing, a practical joker, a lover of horseplay, a somewhat harmless and naïve intriguer, making trouble for the sake of trouble, or rather for the sake of a good tip. That is not what he is in the later play. Being an autobiographical figure, he, like his author, has come up in the world. He is still a delightful fellow, still ready to pursue any scheme as long as it promises entertainment, still as keen for money as long as it can be earned without undue work, still proud of his cleverness. He adores Susanna, and this gay love, laced with humor, represents the best part of him. But with all his gaiety he has become more philosophical and, in the play at least, more intellectual. He has even added to the good humor which he has never lost a dash of bitterness. He speaks now the language of an educated man. He has acquired considerable eighteenth-century cynicism. In short, he has grown older. He is of course no longer a barber, his former trade being hardly alluded to, nor the factotum of the city. It may be just as well that we forget the earlier play, if we are to understand him and his adversary correctly.

Almaviva, too, has changed. His love for Rosina has cooled, that is obvious, but altogether the domineering and self-important Count of *The Marriage* is not the lighthearted man-about-Seville who could disguise himself as Lindoro or as a tipsy soldier. Count Almaviva is now an important government official. He is, in fact, "Grand Corregidor of Andalusia," the governor of a large province. He is about to be appointed Spanish Ambassador to England, a post relatively as important in the eighteenth century as ambassador to Russia would be today. He intends Figaro to accompany him and to become his confidential courier, or "confidential secretary." To be sure, Figaro's appointment is part of the Count's scheme for seducing Susanna. Nevertheless, the fact that Figaro could be appointed to a diplomatic post shows that this is a different Figaro from the erstwhile barber. In the castle of the Count, called by Beaumarchais *Aguas Frescas* (Fresh Waters)—the title is to be read ironically—Figaro is the major-domo, or steward. He runs the place. (I presume this rank enables him to enter the

Countess' boudoir without knocking, a bit of stage business in the second act which has always puzzled me and to which I shall return.)

Both protagonists, then, are persons of substance within their spheres. The spheres are poles apart. If we think of the Count's establishment in eighteenth-century terms, if we consider the absolute power he holds over his subjects, if we remember that here he makes his own laws, and if we then contrast him with Figaro, the *arriviste* who has "arrived" thanks to his superior brain, we will understand what Beaumarchais' and Mozart's audiences understood: the conflict is not so farfetched as Count versus barber, but is a conflict of man-to-the-manor-born versus self-made man. Such a conflict possesses verisimilitude. *The Marriage of Figaro* is not a farce, but a comedy. What happens in *Figaro* could have happened in life. It was about to happen in history.

ACT I—PARALLEL PLOTS OF PLAY AND OPERA

Da Ponte's libretto follows Beaumarchais' play remarkably closely, for long stretches merely translating the French text into Italian. Certain significant alterations we shall discuss presently. The first act, however, is almost a word-for-word translation.

After the Overture, which is champagne of the finest vintage, the curtain rises to show us an almost empty room. In it, however, stands a large armchair, which is to play an important role later, and a dressing table. The door on the left leads to the Countess' rooms, one on the right to Almaviva's. An entrance in the back leads to a garden.

The opera begins, as does the play, with a scene between Figaro and Susanna ("*Cinque, dieci*"—"*Five, ten*"), in which Figaro measures the room which the Count has "generously" assigned to them. Full of enthusiasm, he figures where the furniture is to be placed. But Susanna, fussing at her dressing table with her wedding veil, dampens his enthusiasm precipitously by telling him the true reason for the Count's generosity: the chamber is adjacent to his bedroom. What may happen some morning, once the Count has rung for Figaro and dispatched him on a far errand, is expressed graphically by Susanna in a duet ("*Se a caso madama*"—"*If your lady were to call you*"), while Figaro is genuinely scandalized.

"How stupid clever people are occasionally!" Susanna teases Figaro.
We learn the several obstacles to Figaro's and Susanna's impending
union. First, though the Count has voluntarily abolished the ancient *droit du seigneur*[4] which made it lawful for him to spend the
first night with the bride of a vassal, he hopes to obtain the same
result by other means: he has employed Basilio, Rosina's former
music master, as a go-between, and through him he has promised
Susanna a large sum of money, thus changing a *droit* to an *achat*.
Second: the Count wants the young couple to accompany him to
London, where Figaro, as he himself foresees, will be sent on various
official missions, Susanna remaining with the Count. Third: Marcellina, Dr. Bartolo's old housekeeper, has some kind of a claim on
Figaro's hand. She may appear any moment, summoned by the
Count. It is up to Figaro, says Susanna, to thwart the Count's
schemes. Does he dare? He not only does, but relishes the prospect!
In a soliloquy equivalent to, but more explicit than, Figaro's song
in the opera *"Se vuol ballare"* ("If the Count wants to try a
dance, I'll furnish the tune"), he sketches his task in the play: "No
rashness! Concealment and care! First let me try to hurry the marriage before the Count can interfere. Second, remove Marcellina,
who wants to grab poor Figaro as the Devil grabs a poor soul.
Third, to collect as many dowries and wedding gifts as possible.
And above all to spoil the Count's and Basilio's little game. Work
aplenty!"

There follows a scene between Bartolo and Marcellina, in which
Marcellina enlists the fat doctor's help, tells him she means to press
her claim against Figaro, and unfolds her own pretty intrigue: she
intends to spread the rumor that Susanna is being courted by the
Count. Susanna will then deny it, his excellency will take offense,
forbid the marriage, and support Marcellina's claim. In the play,
Marcellina mentions in the course of this conversation Bartolo's old
promise to marry her and refers to little Emanuel, "the fruit of our
forgotten love." Da Ponte reserves that surprise for later and here
gives Dr. Bartolo the opportunity to sing his aria, *"La Vendetta,"*
in which he trumpets forth the joys of vengeance, the intended
victim being of course Figaro. Susanna enters, is goaded by Marcel-

---

[4] This is one of Beaumarchais' impudent touches which Da Ponte retains. We can
imagine how it titillated the first-night audience!

lina into trading polite insults, in a short scene which serves Mozart for the satiric and staccato *duettino, "Via resti servita"*—"Your servant, madam."[5] After this display of cattiness, Marcellina takes her leave and we are now introduced to Cherubino. The figure of the boy is a creation of Beaumarchais'. And a very unusual and successful creation he is in the play. Through Mozart's music the figure has become one of transcendental beauty, the very posture of youth, the delicate embodiment of the state of being in love with love. Mozart draws him with Botticellian grace. But even in the prose version Cherubino is poetic, and we have reason to be eternally grateful to the French author.

Cherubino tells Susanna that the Count is angry at him, having surprised him yesterday alone with Barbarina, the gardener's daughter. (Fanchette in the original. Da Ponte changed the name probably to give it a more Italian sound.) He is now in danger of being sent away. If that happens, he can no longer visit Susanna. But Susanna knows that it isn't from her that he dreads being separated. Is he no longer pining for her mistress? she asks the boy. Indeed, he is; he envies Susanna her good fortune. Is she not able to be near her "beautiful and lofty" mistress morning, noon, and night? Cherubino snatches a ribbon belonging to the Countess and gives Susanna in exchange a love poem he has written. "Poor little Cherubino," Susanna sighs, "he's in a bad way." Cherubino describes his forlorn feeling—in the *"Non so più."* Listen to his confession, as he stammers it out in the play:

CHERUBINO: I no longer know who I am. . . . My heart trembles if I but look at a woman. The very words "love, tenderness" confuse me. To be able to say to somebody, "I love you," has become for me a necessity. I speak the words aloud when I walk in the park. I speak them to your mistress, to the trees, the clouds, and to the wind which carries my sighs away. Yesterday I met Marcellina . . .
SUSANNA: (*Laughing*) What! Even she?
CHERUBINO: Why not? She is a woman, a girl. Woman! Girl! What sweet words! How they thrill me!
SUSANNA: He's lost his head!

[5] In the recitative which follows, Susanna calls Marcellina "old pedant" and "arrogant lady-doctor" because "she has read two books." This ought to give a hint to the singer playing Marcellina not to portray her merely as the ignorant old woman of the farce. The comedy is enriched if Marcellina is played as a haughty old schoolmarm.

Cherubino's aria, a musical expression of his amorous bewilderment, as unsteady as a butterfly, runs along hardly pausing for breath, till the melody lands on a final sigh, Cherubino concluding that even if none were to listen to him he'd still discourse on love.

The Count is heard outside; the frightened Cherubino hides behind the armchair; the Count enters and makes the expected proposal that "Susanna can have anything she wants," is disturbed by the sound of Basilio's voice, in turn hides behind the chair while Cherubino scrambles into it and Basilio enters to gossip with Susanna and to plead the Count's cause. Basilio is running true to form: he insinuates that something is going on between Cherubino and Susanna. Or perhaps not Susanna, perhaps the Countess herself. Isn't it obvious that Cherubino couldn't take his eyes off the Countess during dinner? The whole castle, the whole town is discussing the boy's behavior.

This is too much for the Count. He reveals his presence, to the considerable delight of Basilio. The scandal is bubbling juicier. The Count declares he simply must get rid of that impudent little page. The boy is always underfoot. Why, only yesterday, calling on Barbarina, he found her flustered and embarrassed; and, looking around, whom should he discover behind a curtain but this selfsame Cherubino! Suiting the action to his words, the Count draws the cloth from the armchair. There, again, is the page.

All this is treated by Mozart in a trio (*"Cosa sento?"*—"What do I hear?") of marvelous comic expressiveness. First each of the three has his and her say, *solo,* the vocal writing being stormy and imperious for the Count, sly for Basilio—we seem to see the curved back and the oily smile—and agitated for Susanna, who is the object of all the plotting. Then the voices are contrasted with one another in varied combinations. Then—the touch of genius!—the Count relates the episode with Barbarina in a suspenseful recitative, perhaps to create musical contrast, perhaps so that the audience may understand the incident clearly and have time for a laugh. The recitative section ends with a spiteful cadence by Basilio (*"Ah! Meglio ancora!"*—"Better and better!"), and the trio resumes its fast pace.

After a little further sparring between Count and Cherubino, Figaro reappears, bringing with him a group of villagers. (In the play the Countess herself enters as well, while Da Ponte reserves her for the second act, giving Mozart the opportunity to present her in an aria.)

The reasons for Figaro's entrance are brought out more clearly in the play than in the opera. He brings along the bridal veil and wreath and asks the Count to hand them to Susanna, thus committing him to his consent before witnesses. At the same time the villagers thank their lord for having abolished the *droit du seigneur*, again committing him to a course of action which he is half-regretting. In the opera the villagers sing a short chorus, offering flowers. The Count cleverly sidesteps Figaro's move and spars for time, hoping Marcellina will appear. Then, under the guise of pardoning Cherubino's indiscretions, he actually gets rid of him; he gives the page a commission in his regiment on the condition that he depart at once. In the play the Countess takes leave of Cherubino with a few kindly words which reveal her sympathy, and possibly a little more than sympathy, for the boy. In the opera, the farewell belongs to Figaro. He sings the famous *"Non più andrai"* ("Good-bye, now, to playing"), which hymns the glories of the military life; it is obviously ironic, as the music, with its mock martial strain, makes clear. But in the play the irony is made even clearer: Figaro at once determines to best the Count. He instructs Cherubino to saddle his horse, to pretend to leave, but to return secretly to the castle and to hide himself away. Figaro will contrive, somehow or other, to change the Count's decision once the marriage ceremony has taken place. Once again the playwright tells us that the issue to be joined lies between the Count and the commoner.

ACT II

The Countess' boudoir. Like most boudoirs in French comedies this is liberally furnished with exits and entrances and—what is more important—with hiding places. There is an alcove separated by a large screen; at the left a closet, at the right a door and a window which gives into the garden. When the curtain rises the Countess is alone.

No counterpart exists in the play for the Countess' self-revealing cavatina[6] (*"Porgi Amor"*—"Grant, oh, God of Love"). This

---

[6] A cavatina, in Mozart's terminology, is a short aria.

soliloquy, so delicate, so gently grieving, limns the character of the
Countess and recommends her at once to our affection. She prays
that her husband's love be restored to her or, failing that, she may
be allowed to die. So serious has the onetime flighty Rosina become
—but only in Mozart's imagination. In Beaumarchais, we find
nothing but a few of the usual complaints against the faithlessness
of men in general and the Count in particular. Not that the author
of the play was averse to soliloquies—but he gave them to Figaro
and to the Count, the Countess being a secondary character. The
figure we know and love is the creation of Mozart, and we can
give music, Mozart's music, the credit for setting her before us
with such charm and beauty as to make her not only equal in importance to the other protagonists in this opera, but an immortal
inhabitant of the entire lyric stage.

The soliloquy being over, Da Ponte again follows Beaumarchais
closely. It is time now to knot the threads of the plot. Susanna
enters, and presently Figaro appears in the boudoir[7] and proposes
his master plan. Through Basilio he has sent the Count an anonymous note warning him that the Countess has granted an assignation to an admirer in the park that very night. This, Figaro
calculates, will confuse and occupy the Count, so that, in his
jealous rage and suspicious search for the culprit, he will forget to
oppose Figaro's marriage. The Countess, shocked, protests: this is a
dangerous game, indeed. But Figaro airily waves her fears aside. As
Beaumarchais puts it: "With ninety-nine out of a hundred women
I would not have dared, fearing that with my lie I might have told
the truth." It is significant that Figaro should even consider so impudent a scheme. Let us evaluate it in eighteenth-century terms:
The Count has designs on Susanna. Very well, Figaro crosses these
designs by throwing suspicion on the Countess. But how dare
Figaro plan a revenge on his master, and one which enlists the
Countess herself? Is it not clear that the audience is to think that
Figaro has put himself on an equal plane with Almaviva?

Figaro proposes still another bait with which to trap the Count:

[7] He enters without knocking and, familiar though he be, this is probably a mistaken
or careless bit of staging. He trills a *"la, la, la,"* and it is not Mozart's habit to write
snatches without words. It is probable that Figaro is meant to be heard offstage. Susanna
then says, *"Eccolo, vieni, amico."* She hears him and says to the Countess, "There he is."
Then, *opening the door,* she turns and bids Figaro, "Come, my friend." (I owe this suggestion for staging to Erich Leinsdorf.)

he suggests that Susanna pretend to meet the Count in the garden, that the women dress up Cherubino in girl's clothes, and that he be sent to the rendezvous in place of Susanna. My lord is to be caught red-handed at this rendezvous. Figaro, who leaves little to chance when he is concocting his plots, has Cherubino standing by. Having explained his scheme and reasserted that "if the Count wishes to try a dance, I'll furnish the tune," Figaro makes his exit. Presently the page enters.

Then follows in the play and in the opera the scene of the disguising of Cherubino and the teasing in which the two women indulge at the expense of the young boy. In the play as well as in the opera, Cherubino has written a little song for the Countess. In the play as well as in the opera the page sings it, accompanied on the guitar by Susanna. In the play he sings his poem to the melody of "*Marlborough se va-t-en guerre*"; in the opera it is the "*Voi che sapete*" ("You who know what love is"). The little song is a counterpart to Cherubino's effusive confession in the first act. It is a song more quiet, more lyric, more "contained." Its orchestration suggests that it could be sung under a Spanish balcony, but the lady would have to be as beautiful as the Countess. The stage grouping of the Countess listening, Susanna accompanying Cherubino on the guitar, and Cherubino singing his heart out is meant to represent a well-known eighteenth-century painting by Van Loo entitled "Spanish Conversation."

Susanna locks the door. Cherubino doffs his coat. The paper which bears Cherubino's appointment falls to the ground, and the Countess discovers that the seal is missing from the commission. She hands the paper back to him, and Susanna, pleading with him to hold still, attempts to fit Cherubino in one of her dresses. The teasing mood continues and is expressed by Susanna in her delicious little aria ("*Venite inginocchiatevi*"—"Come here and kneel down"). Here again Da Ponte follows Beaumarchais almost word for word—with one important difference. In the play it becomes clear that the Countess is attracted to Cherubino, if only a little, and that she is not averse to a small flirtation with him. Her feelings hover somewhat between those of a protector—she is Cherubino's godmother—and of a woman intrigued by a young boy's ardent admiration. Twice the Countess sends Susanna away in order to snatch a few moments alone with Cherubino. All this is treated quite lightly by Beaumarchais but is almost altogether suppressed in the opera, probably because Mozart, in deepening and mellowing the character of the Countess, had little use for flirtation. In the opera, as in the play, she discovers that Cherubino is wearing a ribbon belonging to her and that this ribbon is now soiled with blood, Cherubino having accidentally scratched himself and bound the wound with the ribbon. She takes back the ribbon and comforts Cherubino, who is in tears, as best she can, covering the scratch with a piece of "English plaster." The implication that she would like to comfort him further is omitted in the opera. Yet —most of us who hear the scene find in it a restrained but unmistakable aura of eroticism. It is not being too fanciful to say that the audience guesses the attraction which the Countess feels for the page. We get this impression—and savor it—even if we are unable to follow the text. Is it merely the situation and the setting which convey it? Or is the suggestion hidden in the music of the recitative? (Though Mozart could not have known it, Beaumarchais wrote a third Figaro play, *La Mère Coupable*. This was staged in 1792, the year after Mozart's death. Here the Countess, while the Count is on an official journey to the Spanish colonies, finds herself unable to resist Cherubino.)

Now begins the longest and most carefully composed finale of any Mozart created. I say this, though the real finale does not commence until two numbers later. Yet the action from this moment on is so packed and swift and the music so copious and rich—a fast trio being followed by a faster duet with hardly time for recitative until the finale proper begins—that we must look for the starting point of this extraordinary, artfully accelerated, artfully intensified music as being the moment when the Count knocks at the door.

Knock he does, and most inopportunely. The Countess barely has time to hide Cherubino in the closet, when she must admit him; entering, he finds her as confused and embarrassed as he found Barbarina yesterday. He shows her the letter and asks the cause of her discomfiture; before she can reply he hears a noise in the adjoining closet. "Who is it?" he wants to know. "It is Susanna," stammers the Countess. "If it is," he replies in mounting rage, "let her come out." "She can't," objects the Countess lamely. "She is trying on her wedding dress." There follows the *terzetto,* "*Susanna, or via sortite*"—"Come out, Susanna, at once," in which the Count orders Susanna, or whoever may be hidden in that closet, to give a sign of life, while the Countess with equal emphasis bids her stay and keep quiet. But where, in fact, is Susanna? She slipped out of the room before the Count entered, to fetch another ribbon for Cherubino. As she returns, she at once sizes up the situation, hides behind the screen, unseen by both Count and Countess, and from this vantage point observes the quarrel.

The Count's patience, at best none too compliant, is at an end. If the Countess continues to refuse to open the door to the cabinet, he'll call the servants and have it forced. The Countess appeals to his self-esteem: a scandal in front of his servants? She is right, he responds; he himself will fetch the necessary tools. In the meantime he will lock the doors of the room, to make sure that no one can escape. With the elaborate courtesy of sarcasm he offers the Countess his arm; she has no choice but to go with him.

All this follows the play exactly, as does the lightning scene in which Susanna, springing into action, liberates Cherubino from his hiding place. The boy jumps from the window and escapes and Susanna takes his place in the closet. In Beaumarchais it is but a few whispered words and one quick kiss which Cherubino manages to steal from Susanna. In Mozart, it is an enchanting duet (*"Aprite, presto, aprite"*—"Open up, open up quickly") chirped by two darting birds.

The Count returns with the now very agitated Countess. It is probable that his first line, "Everything is just as I left it," brought a laugh from the audiences at the Comédie, as it does from opera audiences today. Now the Countess can prevaricate no longer. She must make her confession. It isn't Susanna who is in that cabinet, but somebody else, somebody quite harmless really, a mere boy, a child . . . yes, Cherubino. The Count starts in rage; Cherubino, indeed, that ubiquitous little rascal! He becomes the avenging husband, he threatens to kill. In vain does the Countess protest that she had planned but a harmless masquerade with Cherubino, in vain does she plead for mercy for the boy. He takes the key and (in a phrase typical of Mozart when he expresses fury) commands Cherubino to step forth. Here begins the finale itself (*"Esci o mai, garzon malnato"*—"Show yourself, you impudent boy"), the Count storming, the Countess pleading. The Count draws his sword, opens the door, and finds—Susanna! The

phrase which mirrors his and the Countess' speechless astonishment
is given to the orchestra; it is but a single phrase but so expressive
that we can "see" the Count deflated before our eyes. Count and
Countess, equally taken aback, manage to exclaim, "Susanna!" and
at once she becomes mistress of the situation. "Why are you so
amazed?" she asks ironically. "The page—that was I." The situation is used by Mozart for an *andante* (to contrast with the preceding and subsequent *allegros*) of such sweet mockery that one is
tempted to cite it as the very summit of comedy!

But perhaps Susanna wasn't alone in the cabinet? The Count
plunges in, and the moment his back is turned Susanna apprises
her mistress of Cherubino's safe escape. It is now her turn to take
advantage of the situation, and with Susanna's aid she reproaches
her husband, shedding the expected tear or two. The Count is all
apologies, all humbleness. He calls her "Rosina" (a fine psychological touch in the play which Da Ponte retained but which is hardly
noticed in the opera), and swears he will reform. After sufficient
time, in the opera for Mozart to develop his trio musically, in the
play for Beaumarchais to launch a few philosophical quips on the
war between the sexes, Rosina forgives Almaviva. All is well.

But only for a brief moment. Figaro enters, self-confident, full
of bonhomie—and of course ignorant of everything that has just
passed. The musicians are ready, he announces, the wedding guests
assembled, the wedding can proceed. Not so fast, interposes the
Count. In the preceding trio, when the Count had inquired about
the letter, the two women had told him the truth: it was Figaro
who wrote it and slipped it to Basilio. Now the Count confronts
the author of his troubles, the cause of his making a fool of himself. "Do you recognize this paper, Signor Figaro?" inquires the
Count in a melody prickly with menace.

To Ernest Newman, "Dramatically and musically this is the
greatest scene in the opera." One may hesitate to choose any one
scene in *Figaro* as the greatest. One need not hesitate to agree that
"from now until the end of the act, indeed, we are in the presence
of one of the miracles of operatic music."[8]

Figaro, the infallible, now makes a blunder. Not knowing that
the two women have tattled, he denies all knowledge of the letter.

8 From *Seventeen Famous Operas* (Alfred A. Knopf, Inc., 1954).

Susanna and the Countess implore him to tell the truth and the Count takes the opportunity to call him a liar. Once again the trump card passes into the hands of Almaviva, the balance of power changes, Figaro is in danger. At this crucial moment there enters the gardener, Antonio.

A word about this seemingly incidental character: he is not incidental in the play. He is Susanna's uncle and nearest living relative. He is the one therefore whose consent is requisite for Susanna's marriage. This consent he has not so far given. Antonio is a snob and, as the Count says in a subsequent soliloquy in the play's third act, "proud as a peacock." The Count means to use Antonio: "He'll never consent that his niece take a man without family as husband. I will exploit our gardener's ancestor worship. All is fair in love and war."[9]

Figaro knows Antonio's objections and it is partly for this reason that he treats the gardener so rudely in the next scene of the opera. More important, in the play an additional bit of irony is introduced in that a gardener, drunk, ignorant, and gross, apes the ideas of the aristocracy with their insistence on family connections.

In a voice thick with wine Antonio explains that somebody jumped out of the window and smashed his flowerpots. He is used to all kinds of things being thrown out of the window, but a man —that is really too much. At once Susanna and the Countess are aware of renewed danger for all of them. They whisper to Figaro for help. Figaro has become Figaro again and has regained his customary insouciance. "It was I," he admits with a loud laugh. "I was frightened when I heard the Count arrive; I had a guilty conscience over that letter." "Then it was you," growls Antonio, "who dropped this piece of paper." It is the page's commission. The Count takes it and asks Figaro what it is, the orchestra all the while insisting on a ticking figure which heightens the tension. The Countess manages to get a glimpse of the paper, whispers to Susanna who in turn passes the information to Figaro. "Why, of course," he responds with equanimity, "it is the page's commission." "And why did he give it to you?" Again the same play— Countess whispering to Susanna, Susanna to Figaro. "Because— well, because—the seal was missing." The three conspirators (and the orchestra) heave a musical sigh of relief. Once again the Count

---

[9] A passing mention is made of this later, in the Count's third-act aria.

is duped, unable to prove guilt or to resolve doubt. His only hope remains that Marcellina, long overdue, will arrive soon and protest against the marriage. That hope is fulfilled. She, Bartolo, and Basilio now come on the scene, and confusion becomes confounded as they demand Marcellina's lawful rights. Figaro, explains Marcellina, had signed a contract to espouse her if he could not repay a certain sum of money. He cannot—therefore she claims Figaro for herself. Bartolo and Basilio support her in a chatter of great speed; Figaro, the Countess, and Susanna oppose them; the Count, pretending impartiality, insists that the complaint be sifted. In a final *prestissimo* burst the act ends.

In the play one additional twist occurs. Basilio puts forward a plea for Marcellina's hand, for whose money he undoubtedly finds a warm spot in his heart. All these complications require ten scenes in Beaumarchais, for they have to be explained one by one. Mozart combines them in the one finale, sacrificing explicitness to musical design. In his *Memoirs*, Da Ponte outlines the principle on which such a finale was built. It should, according to him, show a relationship to the rest of the opera and be a kind of comedy within a comedy. No recitative is to interrupt the full flow of the music. In accordance with the old operatic custom, all the singers of the play had to appear on the stage, whether they were needed by the plot or not. If they were not needed, the librettist had to find some excuse to bring them on. But Da Ponte violates his own precepts: Cherubino is, of course, not among those present. Mozart's design has remained the admiration of all operatic composers and listeners. As we have just seen, the convolutions of the plot are not only manifold, but change rapidly. Neither complexity nor speed fazes Mozart. They challenge his genius to arrive at a solution, one which is uniquely successful. There is not one moment in which the musical interest flags, nor does any one of the participants lose his identity, so superbly are the archness of Susanna, the angry masculinity of the Count, the slipperiness of Figaro, and, floating above all, the dignity of the Countess, characterized in the music. The finale is so constructed as to bring the cast on the scene successively, so that we receive the impression of one long crescendo of excitement, beginning with the Count and Countess, presently joined by Susanna, then by Figaro, then Antonio, and finally and together the unsavory triumvirate of Marcellina, Bartolo, and Basilio. Mozart seemed determined to use almost every form of ensemble, from the duet to the final septet, in which two groups of three voices each are ranged around the authoritative baritone of the lord of the manor.

ACT III AND DIFFERENCES

With Act III, the libretto begins to differ from the play. Having drawn the main lines of the plot, and having tightened these lines sufficiently, Beaumarchais now can afford to slacken the movement, to let action stand still, and to concentrate on the cerebral side of the duel between the Count and Figaro. For the moment, at least, nobody has to hide in a closet or masquerade in women's clothes or force locked doors. What we do get at the beginning of Act III is the Count and Figaro standing face to face, thrusting and parrying. Here, then, the author seizes the opportunity to introduce sociophilosophical comments and to launch revolutionary barbs at his audience. There is a long scene in which the Count tries to find out how far Figaro has guessed the Count's designs to win Susanna, and Figaro in turn evades all straight answers. In this wary conversation they discuss how easy it is to get along in the English language—one expression, "God damn!," suffices—and what is required for a successful diplomatic career. The Count thinks Figaro has the necessary qualifications: wit and adroitness. On the contrary, Figaro rejoins, only mediocrity and obsequiousness mark the good diplomat. All this, though it brings the play to a standstill, makes for the kind of talk the audience relished, repartee laced with Figaro's impudence, of which these excerpts may serve as sample:

COUNT: Why did you appear so late when I had you summoned?
FIGARO: I had to change my clothes. They got soiled in the garden.
COUNT: For that you needed an hour?
FIGARO: At any rate, a little time.
COUNT: Nowadays the servants change their clothes more slowly than their masters.
FIGARO: That is because they have no servants to help them.

And:

COUNT: Is it not true that you are always pursuing crooked paths?
FIGARO: Yes—and on these paths I regularly meet my lord.

Nothing of this is left in the libretto, as such interchange could not serve musical ends. But in the opera as well, the beginning of the third act gives us a moment of rest. It begins quietly with a recitative.

We are in one of the large halls of the palace. The Count is there alone, pacing to and fro. He puzzles over all that has just happened, doubts his wife, yet doubts her not, and plots his further course: he will send Basilio to Seville to ascertain if Cherubino has arrived there. Susanna and the Countess enter at the rear of the stage. From their whispered conversation we learn that the Countess herself has decided to go to a rendezvous in the garden, impersonating Susanna in Susanna's clothes, Cherubino now being unable to serve their purpose. No one, not even Figaro, is to know of this new plan.[10] Susanna is fearful; urged by her mistress she consents, however, and immediately approaches the Count. As pretext she gives out that she was sent by her lady to borrow the Count's smelling salts. At first she receives but a suspicious welcome. Had Susanna not up to now refused to "understand" him and his desire? Yet it takes not much more than a flirtatious glance on the part of Susanna, and the Count, the male fish, snaps at the bait. She will meet him in the garden. He believes her and merely reproaches her for letting him dangle for so long. The Count's joy gives Mozart the opportunity for a duet with Susanna (*"Crudel! Perchè finora"*—"Cruel girl, why have you let me languish up to now?"), a *tour de force* in which the yes and no of consent and denial become confused, Susanna answering the Count's question now to his satisfaction, now blurting out the wrong answer, which she needs must correct. The *"sì"* and *"no"* duet is a Da Ponte-Mozart invention; no counterpart exists in Beaumarchais. Some commentators have cited it as an early example of Freudianism. We needn't go as far as a psychoanalytical interpretation to observe once again how right psychologically the two lines of melody are: Susanna's coquettish, a frail bright thread to wind around the Count, and the Count's ardent, astonished, and replete with self-satisfaction.

[10] The reason for this new plan is explained later. See page 26.

The recitative which follows the duet is a contraction of a bit of dialogue from the play:

SUSANNA: My first duty toward my lord is obedience.
COUNT: Exasperating girl, why did you not say so before this?
SUSANNA: It is never too late to give the better answer.
COUNT: Then you will come to the garden this evening?
SUSANNA: I take a walk in the garden every evening.
COUNT: And why did you treat me so coldly in your room this morning?
SUSANNA: My lord, the page behind the chair—
COUNT: She is right. (*Once more suspicious*) Why, then, your stubborn refusals when I sent my messages with Basilio?
SUSANNA: What need is there of a Basilio between us?
COUNT: She is right again. (*Once more dubious*) And Figaro—you'll tell him everything?
SUSANNA: Everything—except what I *won't* tell him.
COUNT: Excellent. But if you were not to keep your word! Let's understand each other, my treasure: Without the garden, no dowry. Without dowry, no marriage.
SUSANNA: And vice versa: Without marriage no privileges for my lord.

They do understand each other, or so the Count thinks. As Susanna leaves, Figaro hurries by—all this entering and exiting is clumsy dramatically—and Susanna imprudently whispers to him, "We have won our case without a lawyer!" The Count overhears this. He is outraged by what he hears. Here begins, introduced by a stormy recitative made more turbulent by the use of the full orchestra, the great aria of the Count (*"Vedrò, mentr'io sospiro"* —"What! While I suffer a servant mocks me?"). It is the longest solo aria in the opera, possibly the longest which Mozart wrote. It seems to be conceived and composed with such weight and seriousness as to fit better into a tragedy. No doubt Mozart wanted a strong contrast; no doubt he wished to mix a drop of bitterness into the brew. Yet we cannot help feeling that the aria's sincerity, a wounded rage altogether different from that shown by the Count in the second act, is a line in the psychological portrait which is too heavily drawn. It is frustrated desire, duped in the pursuit of love's game, which calls forth so serious a display of emotion. Is this convincing coming from a man for whom love is a game? Parenthetically we may observe that we find a similar instance in another masterpiece of comedy, the *Falstaff* of Verdi, in which Ford's monologue hovers near the tragic and again is set on a different plane from the rest of the music.

In the play the remainder of the act is occupied with the court proceedings, which Beaumarchais treats in what now appears to us tiresome detail, but which gave him the opportunity to satirize the law. We meet a justice of the peace, stuttering, stupid, pedantic, and at every turn making the wrong pronouncements. We are familiar with these caricatures from such figures as Justice Shallow and Dogberry. Several legal hairs are split and a quantity of Latin is used, even as in Shakespeare's comedies. Marcellina forces her claim on Figaro by presenting his promissory note. The Count pronounces judgment against Figaro; Figaro then protests that he cannot marry without the consent of his parents. He does not know who his parents are. He is a foundling, and, judging from the finely embroidered swaddling clothes and a certain tattooed mark on his right arm, it is certain that his progenitors must have been noble or at least rich people. The mark is a rose. (Why did Da Ponte change this to a *spatola*?) To everybody's astonishment, excepting possibly the audience's, Marcellina recognizes in Figaro her and Dr. Bartolo's long-lost child, the fruit of her youthful indiscretion, her Rafaello (Emmanuel in the play).

The marriage plot has come apart at the seams, the Count's scheme has torn, and Figaro is saved from sharing the fate of Oedipus. Beaumarchais takes the opportunity to put into Marcellina's mouth a preachment against the cruelty of men toward women, the double standard, the social injustice which permits no rehabilitation to a woman who has once sinned. "Ungrateful men," she says, "who despise the object of your passion, your victims! It is you who should bear the punishment for your youthful sins, you and the social structure which robs us . . . of the possibility of becoming honorably self-supporting." And much more to that effect. As we expect, all this social discussion is cut away in the opera. The court proceedings are merely hinted at, the revelation of Figaro's paternity, which even in the eighteenth century was one of the oldest and stalest devices of comedy, is made into a very funny, brief recitative. And Susanna's astonishment, Figaro's delight, the Count's anger, Don Curzio's (the lawyer's) inane comments, and Marcellina's and Bartolo's rueful admissions—all these are compressed into one sextet. And what a sextet! *"Riconosci in questo*

amplesso una madre," Marcellina begins. ("Know by this embrace
your own mother.") What wit flashes from the repeated *"Sua
madre? Suo padre?,"* tossed from one to the other. It is in the ensemble, above all, that opera has the advantage over the spoken
play. We know little about Mozart's opinion of his own music; but
by rare good fortune we do know that this sextet was his favorite
number in the opera.[11]

With the resolution of the court proceedings, Beaumarchais' act
ends. Da Ponte took the fourth act of the play and combined it
with the third act. A major compression, in which several bits of
comic and not-so-comic byplay are eliminated; on the other hand,
several points necessary to the main structure either fall under the
table (the librettist's table) or are so summarily dismissed as to
become unclear. We willingly forego the complication ensuing
from Bartolo's obstinacy in not wanting to marry Marcellina, Antonio's refusal to give his consent to his niece's marriage to somebody who "hasn't even got a father," and Bartolo eventually being
bullied and forced to marry Marcellina so that he can act as lawful
spouse and father. We are similarly inclined to dispense with Basilio's part in the action: only when he learns that Figaro is Marcellina's son does he renounce his effort for the hand of the woman
who now turns out to be the mother of "such a good-for-nothing."

The important passages which are stunted in the libretto concern chiefly the events leading up to, and the dramatic reason for,
the famous letter scene between the Countess and Susanna. Before
discussing this scene, let us review the action of the opera following
the "recognition scene": Barbarina brings in Cherubino and we
learn that Cherubino did not go to Seville but that Barbarina is
hiding the young page in her house, using her own clothes as a
disguise for him.[12] Then follows a soliloquy by the Countess, her
second self-revealing aria, equally as beautiful as the first. While
waiting for Susanna, she muses on her own misfortune, on the lost
love of her husband, on her grief in the recollection of past happiness (*"Dove sono?"*—"Where are the moments of sweetness and
peace I used to know?").

---

[11] At least, so we are told by Michael O'Kelly in his reminiscences, written many years
later. Perhaps his statement is biased by his own participation in the premiere: he played
Don Curzio (and Don Basilio).

[12] The page is *twice* disguised in women's clothes, a serviceable device since Cherubino
is a female role.

This is followed by a short scene in which the meddling Antonio assures the Count that he will prove to him that Cherubino is still among those present and indeed in his own house, excellently being taken care of by Antonio's daughter. Once again the Countess and Susanna enter, and once again it is obvious that all this coming and going is weakly constructed. Whether the changes in the play here were made by Mozart or Da Ponte we have no means of ascertaining. The internal evidence seems to indicate that Da Ponte was trying to satisfy the musician. Probably Mozart wanted to follow the full and lively sextet with a slow and contemplative aria, contrast that aria with a duet (the Letter Duet), and end the act with a strong ensemble number. If these indeed were his intentions, he succeeded, though at the cost of a certain letdown in the continuity of interest, due to the long recitatives between the sextet and the "*Dove sono?*" and again between the latter and the Letter Duet. Once we are there—ah! then we are "transported into a better world" (to quote the words of Schubert's tribute to music).

The Letter Scene

Dramatically, however, the scene needs explanation. For if it is permissible to apply logic to a comedy, what is the purpose of the letter? Isn't the plot unraveled? Figaro has won his case, the Count must now give his consent to the double marriage of Figaro and Susanna, Bartolo and Marcellina, and there is no further need to trick him, no further need for Figaro's plan of sending somebody like Cherubino to a rendezvous with the Count, to surprise him in such circumstances, and thus to shame him into consent. Why then the letter that the Countess dictates, why the change of clothes between Susanna and the Countess (hinted at earlier—see page 22), why in short the entire plan, which was originally designed to secure Figaro's wedding? To be sure, we need misunderstandings and complications for the final act, the fifth in Beaumarchais, the fourth in Da Ponte, but that is hardly sufficient motivation. The answer lies in a fine scene between the Countess and Susanna in the play. The Countess wishes to go through with the original plan of the exchange of clothes, not to aid Figaro, but *to help herself*, to try to recapture her husband's love. An unexpected obstacle arises: Susanna now refuses, for "Figaro no longer wishes it." Misunder-

standing Susanna's refusal and in her hurt and grief interpreting
it as Susanna's having come to an understanding with the Count,
she turns away sadly. Susanna, falling to her knees before her
adored mistress, protests that the Countess does her an injustice.
The latter in turn apologizes and kisses her Susanna. And now the
Countess makes it clear that she herself wants to meet the Count,
disguised as Susanna, that she hopes "in the hour of twilight" to
win him. So she conceives the idea of summoning the Count to the
rendezvous by writing him a billet-doux. She must, she says, hark
back to past times; she must take recourse to Rosina's former
tricks. "A little note to Lindoro . . ." But since her husband would
recognize her handwriting, somebody else must write the note.
That somebody else is of course Susanna. As a further precaution,
the note must be apparently noncommittal and yet be quite explicit: the Count must understand, but if the letter should fall into
hands for which it is not intended, it must not be compromising.
And so Rosina conceives the idea of using for her message to
Lindoro a "*romanza* by Moratin," an existing poem. Moratin was
a contemporary Spanish playwright who was particularly interested in French drama, having made translations into Spanish of a
number of French plays. Presumably then Beaumarchais was paying a compliment to a fellow worker. Much of this is not even
hinted at in the opera—neither Susanna's refusal, nor the Countess' mistrust, nor the fact that the letter is not one composed
freshly by the Countess. In the opera she merely says that she wants
to fix the location of the appointment in the garden more precisely, that she will therefore dictate instructions, and that she herself will take the whole responsibility of the trick that is to be
played on the Count.

The Letter Duet, a "*canzonetta sull'aria*," a song floating on a
zephyr, is one of Mozart's supreme inspirations. Am I guilty of
reading something into it that isn't there when I say that it has the
quality of a quotation? The melody flows so smoothly, the dictation
proceeds so evenly that I felt, long before I had studied the play,
that the Countess was reciting by heart. We cannot know whether
Mozart intended this, whether it was an instinctive expression of a
unique musical dramatist, or whether it is just an accident and my
supposition is erroneous. In any case, the Countess bids the receiver
of the letter to appear in the pine grove this evening, and Susanna,

taking down her words, repeats them and echoes the Countess' melody. Then the two voices unite in close harmony at the point when the two women have finished the letter and assert, one to the other and no longer as dictation, that "the Count will understand the rest."

After the letter is written, it needs to be sealed. The Countess decides to seal it with a pin[13] and asks Susanna to write on the back of the letter, "Send the seal back as an answer." Susanna laughingly suggests that this seal is more "bizarre" than the seal on the page's commission. And that ends the pivotal scene—except that in the play we find a further subtle touch: the Countess draws the pin from her kerchief, and lets fall the ribbon which the page had originally appropriated and which the Countess had taken back. Beaumarchais hints once again that the Countess is not indifferent to Cherubino's admiration, since she now wears the ribbon, soiled as it is, on her person.

We might mention one final point, perhaps of interest only to musicologists. In some editions of the score of *Figaro,* the Countess' words when she dictates are printed in quotation marks, thus acknowledging that these are words not by Da Ponte but by somebody else: Da Ponte did no more than to translate the French text by Moratin word for word, changing however the "chestnut alley" to which the Count is bidden in the original to a pine grove, probably because "*pini*" is an easier word to sing than "*castagni.*"

Barbarina now enters with the peasant girls and with Cherubino dressed as one of them. They sing a tribute to the Countess and bring her flowers. The Countess singles out Cherubino and wants to know who that pretty and demure girl might be. The Count and Antonio steal in, Antonio catching Cherubino by taking off his headdress and substituting for it his soldier's hat. Now the fat is in the fire. When Figaro enters he is at first made to repeat his story and then is confronted with his lie. Impudently he brushes the whole matter aside. "If the page says that he jumped out of the window, well, then he did. If he, Figaro, could jump, anyone else could do the same thing. Why not? He wasn't going to call anybody a liar." Since luck is usually on the side of Figaro, he is saved from the Count's wrath by the beginning of the wedding proces-

[13] Sending a love letter with a pin denoted "danger" in eighteenth-century usage.

sion (finale). The Count and Countess take their place, the villagers pay their respects and dance a fandango. During the dance
Susanna slips the letter to the Count, the Count opens it and pricks
his finger with the pin. The action is adumbrated humorously by
the orchestra. Figaro observes to Susanna: "Somebody must have
slipped a love note into his hand." The Count surreptitiously looks
for the pin and cannot find it. Then he turns to the assembly and
announces that this evening the marriage of the two happy couples,
Figaro and Susanna, Bartolo and Marcellina, will be formally celebrated with pomp and feasting, a supper and a ball. This inspires
the chorus to a final burst of enthusiasm as the curtain falls.

ACT IV—THE TWO SOLILOQUIES

The last act plays in the garden, near the pine grove. There are
rustic pavilions right and left. It is night. Barbarina enters with a
lantern; she is searching for something.

The beginning of this last act has aggrieved more than one commentator. So staunch an admirer of the opera as Ernest Newman
felt that not only the librettist but Mozart himself "wrought his
own undoing," that the opera "declines sadly for a time, not only
in dramatic vigor but in musical interest," and that only with
Figaro's second entrance does all the fumbling end. Similarly,
though less harshly, Edward J. Dent, in his critical study of Mozart
operas, sees in the opening of Act IV "a complete change of temper. Hitherto the whole intrigue has been hardly more than a game
of scoring points, with a game-player's amused satisfaction at every
trick won; and now Barbarina—the last character one would expect to do so—sets the tone of sinister anxiety with the strange key
of F minor." (If you can hear a tone of sinister anxiety in the little
aria by Barbarina, you are a better listener than I am.) It is perfectly true that, after Barbarina's plaintive little song (*"L'ho per-
duta"*—"I have lost it") which opens the act, both libretto and
music represent less than the best of Da Ponte or the best of
Mozart. But perhaps things aren't quite so bad as all *that*. They are
not in stage performances; Marcellina's and Basilio's arias are invariably omitted and we arrive at Figaro's second entrance without
too much delay.

The dramatic purpose of Barbarina's *arietta*—its music is quite as diminutive as she is—is to let us know that she has been commanded by the Count to find the pin he has lost—she *is* looking for it in a most unlikely spot, the garden!—and that she has met with no success so far. Figaro and Marcellina come upon her and she lets the cat out of the bag by telling Figaro that she is looking for the pin which the Count wants to return to Susanna. Figaro pumps her for more information and learns that the Count has asked Barbarina to be cautious; in bringing the pin back to Susanna she is to say that "Here is the key to the pine grove." Figaro immediately puts the most jealous possible interpretation on this, and substitutes one of Marcellina's pins, giving it to Barbarina in order to get rid of her. Alone with his mother, he bewails his fate, the fate of the husband betrayed even before the wedding night. Marcellina, whose character seems to have bettered itself since the first act—she is now a sensible and sympathetic mother—counsels moderation. Figaro won't hear of it. He suspects, he will watch, and should his suspicions be well founded, he will revenge not only himself but the whole race of husbands! With these words he stalks away.

Marcellina, left alone, determines to warn Susanna, of whose innocence she is convinced. Anyway, women ought to stick together and protect one another from these ungrateful men! Cue for an aria, one in the form of a minuet. Mozart could not free himself of the convention of giving even his minor characters a solo piece to sing. So now it is Marcellina's turn and soon Basilio's. Her aria is a poor piece of work, offering with considerable coloratura the thought that women are more to be pitied than to be blamed (*"Il capro e la capretta"*—"The goat and his mate").

Re-enter Barbarina, bringing a little light supper for Cherubino, with whom she has a rendezvous; then Bartolo and Basilio, whom Figaro has bidden to be witnesses to the scandal he is about to discover. Figaro asks them to wait while he searches about the garden. When he whistles the two are to come forward. (Barbarina in the meantime has made herself scarce.) Again for no better reason than that he has to have his moment close to the footlights, Basilio holds up the proceedings by singing his aria, *"In quegl'anni"*—"In the years of my youth." This is a curious one. It is a better piece of music than Marcellina's and contains near its end a march theme which to Dent and Einstein[14] sounds "like a deliberate quotation of some well known tune." What the tune is or what the purpose of the quotation has not been ascertained.

Now Figaro comes into view again. He is half-concealed in a conspirator's cloak and a broad-brimmed hat. For once he is quite sorry for himself and has a few plaintive things to say about his ungrateful Susanna. His recitative, like the recitative which precedes the Count's aria in Act III, is accompanied by the orchestra and for the same reason, to lend additional weight to the ensuing aria. We may compare Figaro's aria, *"Aprite un po' quegl'occhi,"* to Figaro's soliloquy in the last act of the play; it epitomizes the difference between the playwright's and the composer's point of view. The difference is significant. The aria is a free invention by Da Ponte, undoubtedly made to Mozart's measure, and we may draw our inferences from the fact that the librettist set aside his model, to which up to now he has been largely so faithful. Beaumarchais' soliloquy would not serve. Why not? First, what does Figaro sing in the aria?

FIGARO: Open your eyes, you foolish, incautious men and observe what women are! Those creatures you call goddesses, who enfeeble reason and on whose altar you burn incense—what are they? They are witches who enchain us to make us suffer, they are sirens who sing to drown us, they are birds[15] who decoy with their plumes. They are comets who shine with a borrowed light. They are roses with thorns, sleek foxes, benign bears and malicious doves, masters of trickery, friends who play false. They feel neither love nor pity. No, no, no! But I simply won't complete my story: every man knows it.

Even with the handicap of a more or less literal translation, it may be apparent that Da Ponte here shows considerable poetic ability, a comic conceit not without charm, which must have amused and pleased Mozart, as did Leporello's catalogue recital in *Don Giovanni*, to which Figaro's aria bears a musical affinity. It is a patter song, light in tone, with a mocking glint peeping through Figaro's genuine vexation. The music makes it clear that we need not take Figaro's jealousy too seriously and that all will come out right in a short while. Figaro is addressing the audience,[16] at least

---

[14] Alfred Einstein, one of the greatest of the Mozart scholars.

[15] *Civette*, meaning in Italian both "owls" and "flirts."

[16] Pinza used to put his foot on the prompter's box and point straight at the audience.

the men in the audience. He is stepping out of the framework of the play, a convention which has its origin in the *commedia dell'arte*. But no matter how he does it, his subject is the old subject of woman's wiles, *così fan tutte*.[17] It is all in the name of love. And nobody would really think that Figaro—or Mozart—damns love.

How different is the soliloquy in the play! How different, how serious! Little laughter here, little love. It is a long monologue, in which Beaumarchais steps out of the framework of the play, but without directly addressing the audience, and pours out his autobiography as well as the thoughts, thoughts unruly, bold, and bitter, which hovered in the air and were to spawn the shattering revolution. Figaro speaks not to the men in the theater, but to the Count.

FIGARO: Because you are a great lord you think you are a great genius! Birth, riches, rank, and position have made you proud. What have you ever done to deserve your fortune? You took the trouble to be born: that was the only work you ever did. From then on you spent your life as an ordinary man and wasted it. I, on the other hand, I, the foundling child of the people, made my own way. To earn my bread, hard, dry bread, I have employed in one day more ingenuity than the entire government of the kingdoms of Spain and Navarre used in a hundred years. And you dare to measure yourself with me? You—with me?

He then proceeds to tell the story of his life, and while he doesn't quite speak of the anthropophagi and men whose heads do grow beneath their shoulders, he does embroider a fantastic tale of how at first he "sought an honest, decent profession," but soon, finding all doors barred to him, he began "to stroll through Spain, a guitar on my back, singing Moorish ditties at the country fairs." Up and down the ladder of fortune he climbed, now affluent, now poor, now deep in debt, making his way as a street singer, a waiter, a gambler, a barber, and, most unfortunately for him, as an author, a journalist who told the truth. Because a sultan objected to his songs, he was arrested and thrown into prison.

FIGARO: Had I but one of those mighty moguls here before me, who so lightheartedly mistreat a man whose only crime it was to have spoken the truth! Tired of feeding me, they threw me out at last. Once again I take up my pen: I become a journalist. I was told that in Spain I

---

17 In *Così* Guglielmo addresses the women of the audience on the same subject.

would enjoy freedom of the press. I could write what I wanted, provided only that I would submit it to two or three censors and that of course I would say nothing against the state, the court, the church, against good manners or bad officials, nor against certain privileged ballet girls. To use this extraordinary liberty, I founded a newspaper and called it "Useless Leaves." . . . I have come to understand that to get along in the world, knowledge is less important than good manners. Everyone around me lived by cheating. Yet I was supposed to be honest. That was my undoing. What a curious fate! . . . I have seen everything, done everything, tasted everything. I have lost all illusions.

All this begins to sound more like Voltaire than Beaumarchais and is, needless to add, miles removed from *The Barber of Seville*.

To return to the opera: As Figaro, his aria ended, hides in the darkest corner of the grove, the Countess and Susanna enter, each wearing the other's clothes, an exchange which disguises them effectively only in operatic librettos. Marcellina is of the party, and it is hinted that she has told the tale of Figaro's anger to her new daughter-in-law and has been let in on the entire secret. She now acts as a friendly co-conspirator with the women against the men.

So Susanna decides to teach Figaro a lesson. That "rascal spy" is going to get what's coming to him. She asks her mistress' permission to remain alone for a half-hour among the pine trees, and having obtained that permission, her mood changes to gentle introspection, to sweet anticipation. We are not used to this from her; this new phase endears her to us all the more. At last, she says, the moment has come when she will be permitted to enjoy her love, to delight in her desires. The starry night has filled her soul with happiness; yet she is vaguely troubled, she knows not why. This recitative— again Mozart uses the orchestra here—has a subtle, dual purpose. Musically it sets the mood for the *"Deh vieni, non tardar"*—"Oh, come, do not tarry"—which is the dearest jewel of all Susanna's music; dramatically, it heaps fuel onto Figaro's flame and fans the irony. For Figaro, hidden in the corner of the garden unseen but overhearing, and acting still as we expect a jealous lover to act, thinks that the sentiment of the soliloquy is meant for the Count. As to this aria, the distillation of the magic that is Mozart, I shall quote a few words by Gerald Abraham, the Mozart scholar:

Susanna is happy in her love, for she knows everything will soon be put right; she is moved by the stillness and beauty of the night; and she pours out her natural feelings. We have been allowed plenty of musical glimpses of her better self already; we know quite well that she is not merely a pert, heartless soubrette; but here for the first time—it is the crown of the opera before the final hurly-burly—all her real sweetness is disclosed. There is no flummery, no exaggeration, nothing outside the part; Mozart never for a moment forgets himself and allows her to become the Countess.[18] It is all very simple. Yet we know from the composition sketches that, whereas Mozart could do the most difficult-seeming things apparently without effort, this very "simple" piece cost him infinite pains; the end, in particular, was rewritten again and again before he could get it right.

From this point on the complications become absurd. Everybody fails to recognize everybody else or mistakes one for the other. You will have to follow closely to understand what is going on. But if you do not, it is no matter. For by this time the disguises become as implausible as the mixed-up identities in *Twelfth Night*.

Figaro, we are asked to believe, has recognized Susanna in the Countess' clothes,[19] though a scene or two later he will mistake her again for the Countess. Now he thinks he knows his course: to expose Susanna's perfidy. He is interrupted by Cherubino, who enters trilling a song. The boy is on his way to the pavilion where Barbarina is waiting for him with food and love. The figure of another woman is perceived and, as usual, Cherubino stops to inquire who it is. It is the Countess dressed as Susanna. Cherubino takes her to be Susanna and, again as usual, at once tries to make love to her. The duet between them forms the first part of the finale (*"Pian, pianin"*—"Softly, softly"). Cherubino cannot understand why his Susanetta acts so distant and constrained, the point being that the Countess, who has lost what courage she had, is shaking with fear as to what might happen if the Count were to surprise her once again in a compromising situation with the boy. Sure enough, the Count's voice is heard, happy over the prospect of being at last able to enjoy his tête-a-tête with Susanna. He enters and at once sees another man is with the object of his desire, for he, too, takes the disguised Countess to be Susanna. Who is the man? By his voice, this must be Cherubino.

So now we have the five protagonists together, all at cross purposes, and all combined in a piquant ensemble of error. Susanna,

[18] Yet one musicologist—it is perhaps unnecessary to mention that he was a German—gave birth to the theory that Mozart originally intended *"Deh vieni"* for the Countess!

[19] Stage managers try to help the situation by having Susanna during the *"Deh vieni"* lower the hood she wears as the Countess.

too, recognizes the page's voice and knows that his presence has rather gummed the whole plot. Cherubino continues to woo the supposed Susanna. The Countess urges him to leave her. When Cherubino tries to kiss the girl before him, the Count steps between them and, not at all to his pleasure, receives Cherubino's kiss. The page, recognizing the Count, flees in terror. Figaro in turn, who has crept forward better to see what is happening, receives the blow which Almaviva had intended for Cherubino. Susanna and the Countess break out into loud laughter, while Figaro retires once again into the corner of the stage, having gained nothing but a smarting ear.

The Count begins his wooing of the girl he thinks is Susanna. The Countess leads him on charmingly. He fulfills his promise and gives the false Susanna a ring as her dowry. But his pleasure is destined to be a short one: as he leads the girl toward the pavilion— where they need no light, since it isn't to read that they are going there—Figaro stomps boldly forward and the Count has to slip away, promising to return soon.

Now Susanna takes over. In a voice imitating the Countess' she commands Figaro to be silent. Figaro thinks it *is* the Countess: Susanna's disguised voice has fooled him. But of a sudden Susanna forgets and uses her natural voice. The truth now dawns on Figaro; in a joyful aside, he exclaims, "Susanna!" and immediately decides that he will dole out his own special kind of punishment to Susanna for having so thoroughly fooled him and made him miserable. He pretends that he believes that it is indeed the Countess who is with him. So the point of this scene is that Figaro knows that it is Susanna but Susanna does not know that he knows. When she hears his impudent advances, she cannot restrain herself and clouts him a fine box on the ear. It is the second he has received, but how gladly does he receive it!

Mozart changes tempo and tonality as both of them drop their pretense. Figaro sues for forgiveness in a wonderful melody (*"Pace, pace, mio dolce tesoro"*—"Peace, peace, my sweet treasure"), and tells Susanna that he recognized her by her "adorable voice."

The Count re-enters, searching for Susanna. He searches for her in the pavilion, and while he is offstage, Susanna whispers to Figaro that it is now time to end all misunderstanding. But first let them play out the scene for the benefit of her "bizarre lover." Immedi-

ately Figaro throws himself at the feet of the pseudo Countess and
makes love to her with exaggerated gestures (as Leporello does to
Elvira and as the two "Albanians" do in *Così;* one recognizes one
of Mozart's favorite devices). The Count, re-entering, comes upon
them; once again all his distrust is reawakened. No doubt about it,
his wife is betraying him. Seizing Figaro, he shouts for his people.
Figaro simulates terror, the Susanna-Countess darts off into the
pavilion. Responding to the cries, Basilio and Curzio (a later addition, for, as the reader may remember, at the premiere one actor
played both parts), Antonio and Bartolo, as well as a number of
servants, rush in with appropriate exclamations of curiosity. The
Count will expose his wife publicly. He calls for her to show herself. Since she does not, he himself goes into the pavilion and drags
forth—not whom he expected to find but an unexpected bevy of
malefactors—first Cherubino, then Barbarina, then Marcellina, and
finally the Susanna-Countess, begging for pardon. Pardon is refused in no uncertain terms until there emerges from the opposite
pavilion the true Countess, who asks with a smile, "Won't you
pardon them if I wish it?"

For the second time in the comedy, the Count is deflated. He has
lost the game, scoring no points. What is there left for him to do?
To ask the Countess in turn for pardon, which he does in the
penultimate section of the finale, a chorale-like *andante*, in which
all the others join. In woman's way, she grants pardon to her husband. The mad day, the *folle journée*, at last comes to an end with
a merry short ensemble (in D major, the tonality with which the
Overture began).

REFRAIN

Having transversed the incidents of the *journée* in Almaviva's
castle, having compared libretto to play, what general view may
we assume, what conclusion may we reach?

If the narrator has done his task, it will have become apparent
that we have dealt with two works of art, one spoken, one sung,
which, alike though they superficially may appear, differ not in
detail alone.

The differences rise to the surface only when we scrape both
works of the patina of history which now so richly overlays them.

Perhaps we cannot do this entirely; as time progresses our view of
any work of art can never recapture its pristine freshness. Not only
is our subsequent view influenced by current ideas but, what is
more important, it is influenced by later works of art. Art inter-
acts; not only forward, one artist learning from his predecessor,
but backward, later generations interpreting the work with knowledge unavailable to the contemporary. In these particular two
works, we are further confused—"we" meaning the opera audience
—by the other Figaro, the Figaro of *The Barber of Seville*.

While we cannot entirely recreate the mental conditions prevail-
ing in the Paris of 1784 or those in Vienna in 1786, we can, as I
have suggested, profit by attempting to do so. We can then take
stock of what we have here.

We have here a double accomplishment, perhaps unique in the
history of dramatic art. What other example could we cite of the
same plot being responsible for two works of such different conception and purpose? We have first an intellectual, satiric, bitter,
searing play of enormous vitality and of the very greatest consequence, the subject of which is man's inequality with man. At the
end of Beaumarchais' play, the characters step forward and, in old
theatrical tradition, address a rhymed refrain to the audience. In
this epilogue both Figaro and Susanna sum up the play's central
theme:

FIGARO: Man's destiny—whether he is to sit on a regent's throne or live
in a peasant's hut—is determined from the cradle. Blind accident decides. Yet genius can upset fate. So it happens that many a king, in
spite of his deeds in war and peace, is forgotten while Voltaire remains
immortal. . . .

SUSANNA: Many a deep truth is hidden in our merry, mad play. Pardon,
therefore, for the sake of the fun, its serious moments, even if by
chance you dislike them. . . .

Had Mozart used an epilogue (as he did in *Don Giovanni*), Da
Ponte could not have made use of these words. His epilogue would
have been variations on one word: love. The opera is a comedy of
love. Its theme is not man's inequality, but the quality which binds
man and woman. It presents, often in subtle and always in psychologically adroit terms, various aspects of the propulsive motive:
love's awakening and lack of discrimination (Cherubino); its give-

and-take and understanding between two people no longer naïve
or unaware (Susanna and Figaro); its pure ecstasy (Susanna); its
childishness (Barbarina); the deep disappointment of its loss and
the never-ending hope for its reawakening (the Countess); the
humor of its jealousy (Figaro); and its insatiable, uninhibited sexual force (the Count).

All these it offers for our contemplation and our enchantment,
in music of almost unreasonable beauty.

DON GIOVANNI

COMPOSER: Wolfgang Amadeus Mozart

LIBRETTIST: Lorenzo Da Ponte

FIRST PERFORMANCE: October 29, 1787
National Theater, Prague

RECEPTION: Success

CHARACTERS:

Don Giovanni, grandee of Spain	Baritone
Donna Anna, daughter of the Commendatore	Soprano
Don Ottavio, fiancé of Donna Anna	Tenor
Don Pedro, the Commendatore	Bass
Donna Elvira, a noble lady of Burgos	Soprano
Leporello, servant of Don Giovanni	Bass
Zerlina, a peasant girl	Soprano
Masetto, her suitor	Bass

DON GIOVANNI

In my small-boyhood, I by good luck had an opportunity of
learning the Don thoroughly, and if it were only for the
sense of the value of fine workmanship which I gained from
it, I should still esteem that lesson the most important part
of my education. Indeed, it educated me artistically in all sorts
of ways, and disqualified me only in one—that of criticizing
Mozart fairly.

BERNARD SHAW

What happened some time or other during the period of seven
months in which Mozart and Da Ponte worked on *Don Giovanni*?
Between the day that Mozart accepted the old tale of the libertine
as his next operatic subject and the day in Prague when Da Ponte
completed his scrivening, did any change of plans occur? Was the
libretto substantially rewritten at a given moment? We suspect
that it was. We suspect that at a point in the development, perhaps
rather earlier than later, there was a swapping of Pegasus in mid-
stream. We suspect that the final is not the same libretto it started
out to be.

We suspect—but we do not know. How dearly we would love
to know!

Our desire to know goes beyond the worshipful wish to ferret
out every detail which circumstances a masterpiece; it goes beyond
the desire to learn what Keats had for breakfast. If we could know,
we could determine whether certain equivocal characteristics of

the libretto are what most Mozart scholars claim they are, that is weaknesses, or whether the puzzle is a purposeful puzzle. Is the lack of clarity of which many in the audience complain (though with a pardoning smile) due to ineptitude or was it done on purpose to allow a roaming and imprecise ramble to our imagination? If the latter, was it Mozart who wished it so, to serve his music? Some sort of explanation does seem necessary for this libretto. How did it come about that Da Ponte, highly experienced in the making of dozens of librettos, who had just completed the excellent *Figaro* and was later to fashion for Mozart the meritorious original comedy *Così fan tutte*—a man who knew the operatic craft—should turn out something as unclear as *Don Giovanni?*

Let us suppose that Da Ponte delivered a libretto, that it did not satisfy Mozart, that Mozart suggested changes, and that Da Ponte grafted these changes on. Let us suppose so—but, really, we are guessing!

We are before a tantalizing mystery. The opera is one of the supreme manifestations of the human spirit, a work of such profundity and power as to have excited the envy and intense love of virtually all musicians. It has been called "one of the half dozen greatest works of *any* art"; one could fill a fair-sized book with the professional tributes which have been written to it.[1] And the nonprofessional audience is deeply and personally involved in this music. *Don Giovanni* is not something that one merely "enjoys"; if one is at all sensitive to art, one feels that *Don Giovanni* is one of the experiences that make life worthwhile. Yet it is hardly disputable that confusion reigns; at times it seems as if the opera could not make up its mind whether it is a comedy or a tragedy, horseplay or myth, knockabout farce or subtle sermon. Mozart and Da Ponte called it a *"dramma giocoso."* This sobriquet in itself does not mean much: it was a widely used designation in the eighteenth century and was applied to some out-and-out farces. Still, there must have been a reason why the label was selected. The

[1] Gounod, who admired the work so much that he had himself painted holding the score of *Don Giovanni* in his hand, did write a book about it. "It dominated my life like a luminous apparition," he said. Haydn, Rossini, Berlioz, Tchaikovsky, Wagner, Richard Strauss, Brahms, Mahler, Mendelssohn, Chopin (who at the age of seventeen composed his celebrated variations on *"La ci darem la mano"*), and Grieg are some of the composers who were vocal in their praise.

trouble is that the *"dramma"* runs into the *"giocoso"* and we can't always sort the elements. The lack of central clarity harms one of the three female characters, Donna Elvira. Are we supposed to laugh at her attempts to recapture her husband or are we supposed to pity her? Is she a comic or a tragic figure? Is the scene in which the disguised Leporello makes love to her to be taken in the spirit of good, unclean fun or are our sympathies to be engaged and our scruples raised against such callousness?

Nor is Donna Anna clearly drawn. Was this intentional? The portrait is so hazy that it has been possible to spin abstruse and fantastical theories about the lady. We will mention these theories later. Let us just note here that of the three women surrounding the Don, only one, the one simply comic or comically simple, is secure. That is Zerlina.

The libretto has other faults, chief among them that most laggard of lovers, the static Don Ottavio, who seeks revenge but never finds it; he just stands around, his hand on the hilt of his sword, until it is time for him to sing two of the most beautiful of all tenor songs.

The work is so loosely constructed that occasionally it seems to us that it was cut in pieces and the pieces were then stitched together, whether they fitted or not. Inconsistencies of time, uncertainties in the sequence of events spot the action.

In short, Da Ponte's *Don Giovanni* is not nearly so good nor so direct nor so explicit as his *Marriage of Figaro*. No doubt the models which he used for the later opera (mainly a libretto by one Giovanni Bertati) are inferior to Beaumarchais' comedy. But it may also be that the task proposed by Mozart proved too difficult for him and that he could not quite bring off the fusion between a morality play and a masquerade, especially if somewhere along the way the signals were changed.

Is it then correct to say, as one critic has said, that the libretto of *Don Giovanni* is a "botched-up affair"? Are we to assume that Mozart triumphed, though he was dragged down by an insensitive collaborator? No, not at all, certainly not! Any such claim tips the scale unwarrantedly. There is skill in this libretto. There are scenes which are dramatically and psychologically effective. There are wit and charm. There is demonstrated in more than one verse a poetic ability surpassing that which Da Ponte had shown in *Figaro*. The moment after one is ready to condemn, one is forced to admire. Shifting our point of view, we can assert that the very vacillation of the libretto, its swing from one style to another, its roving from the saturnine to the jocund, its ambiguity of fun and fright—all this is the very quality which helps to make *Don Giovanni* challenging. Was this the quality which stimulated Mozart to plumb, deeper than e'er plummet sounded, the well of his talent? Did this libretto give him the opportunity to bring to the stage the kind of music which distinguishes him in symphony and chamber works, music the upper layer of which is gay, while sadness lies underneath? That is why one would dearly love to know who was responsible, who was the libretto's real architect. We shall never know.

Let us see, therefore, what we do know. We do know that about February, 1787, Mozart returned from a visit to Prague, where he had had the pleasure not only of seeing his *Figaro* performed and of conducting one of the performances, but also of tasting the sweet experience of success, and, for a little while at least, the surcease of financial worries. He returned to Vienna with a contract and a hundred ducats in his pocket; the contract was for a work to be specially composed for the Prague theater the next season. After the success of *Figaro*, it was understood that Mozart would turn once again to Da Ponte as his collaborator. Da Ponte was a busy man, never busier than at this moment when the new commission came along. He was official "Poet for the Italian Theater" in Vienna, and as such it was his task to furnish librettos to composers in the vanguard of Viennese theatrical life. Just then he was at work on two projects, an opera for Salieri, *Tarare,* for which he didn't have to do much more than adapt a libretto by Beaumarchais previously produced in Paris; and one for the Spanish composer Martin, *Diana's Tree,* which was an original work. He accepted the third commission; according to his *Memoirs,* it was he who suggested the subject of *Don Giovanni,* and Mozart joyfully concurred. Da Ponte explained his plan of procedure to the Emperor, who was skeptical that his court poet, prolific though he was, could work on three librettos at once. Da Ponte replied that he planned to work for Mozart at night, which would be like reading Dante's

Inferno; for Martin in the morning, and that would be like studying Petrarch; and for Salieri in the evening, which would remind
him of Tasso.

We may disregard these fanciful literary allusions. According to
his own testimony, Da Ponte's working habits were something less
than scholarly:

> I sat down at my desk and stayed there for twelve hours at a stretch. A
> bottle of Tokay was at my right, the inkstand in the middle, and a box
> of Seville tobacco at my left. A lovely young girl of sixteen (whom I
> would like to have loved as a daughter . . . but . . .) was living in the
> house with her mother, who was the housekeeper; she would come to my
> room whenever I rang the bell which, truth to tell, was pretty often,
> especially when it seemed that my inspiration was beginning to cool: she
> would bring me sometimes a biscuit, sometimes a cup of coffee, and some-
> times nothing but her own pretty face, always gay, always smiling, and
> made to inspire poetic fancy and witty ideas. With only brief breaks, I
> continued to work twelve hours a day for two months, and for the whole
> of this time she stayed in the next room, either with a book in her hand
> or with her sewing, so as to be ready to come to me as soon as I rang
> the bell.

Here again we may suspect one of these anecdotes neatly
wrapped to be posted to posterity, though there is probably enough
truth in all this for us to conclude that the libretto of *Don Giovanni* was written under pressure and in haste.

We have one piece of evidence which *is* significant. Many years
later, Da Ponte, living in New York, told Dr. John Francis, a repu-
table American physician and a man of letters, who was one of
the few Americans who saw Da Ponte's value as a source of information about Mozart and so questioned him closely, that "Mozart determined to cast the opera exclusively as serious and had
well advanced in the work. He, Da Ponte, remonstrated and urged
the expedience of the introduction of the comic element in order
to assure the work's success." This is the only external indication
we have of a change of plan. . . .

Mozart worked on the composition during the spring and summer of 1787. It was an eventful year for the composer. He met the
young Beethoven. He composed *"Eine Kleine Nachtmusik."* In
May his father died. (Did Leopold's death echo in Wolfgang's
thoughts, as he worked on the opera?) At the beginning of Sep-

tember, or at the latest toward the middle, he left for Prague accompanied by his wife, Constanze. A portion of the complete manuscript was in his luggage. He continued to work on the score in Prague, whether merely writing down ideas which he had thought out in Vienna or composing fresh material, we have no means of ascertaining. We know, at least, what he wrote down in Prague: the manuscript is written on two different papers: a broader format of Viennese manufacture and a smaller one, made in Prague.[2]

Da Ponte followed Mozart after a few days. Mozart was ensconced in an apartment in the Three Lions Inn,[3] while Da Ponte stopped at a hostelry across the street. The windows of Mozart's and Da Ponte's rooms faced each other, and it is probable that the two men often conferred without leaving their rooms. Did any passer-by remark these two men, both young men (Mozart was thirty-one, Da Ponte thirty-eight), leaning out of their windows and discussing verse and aria? Whenever Mozart could, he went out of the city to visit his friends the Duscheks at their country estate, the Bertramka. There, legend has it, he worked while around him the company played at ninepins. To this day the visitor is shown the stone table in the garden where Mozart worked.

Mozart found the cast available to him in Prague "not as adept as that in Vienna." Undoubtedly the weight and complexity of the opera created particular difficulties. One of the singers fell ill, and since no substitute was available, the premiere had to be postponed. Moreover, Mozart complained, the singers could not be made to rehearse on the days when they had to give a performance. Still, Mozart seems to have gone about his business with great good hu-

---

[2] Mozart's widow sold the manuscript to the publisher Johann André in Offenbach. On his death, André's daughter inherited it. She married a piano manufacturer in Vienna by the name of Streicher. He in turn offered the manuscript for sale to the libraries of Vienna, Berlin, and London, but in vain. The pianist Emil Paur bought it and later put it up for sale at the price of two hundred pounds (one thousand dollars). Pauline Viardot, the daughter of Manuel Garcia, herself a famous Donna Anna, finally bought it for £180, selling part of her jewelry to raise ready cash. She bequeathed the manuscript to the Paris Conservatoire, where it now is. It is too bad that the manuscript is not readily available in a facsimile edition. I enjoyed the privilege of examining it; it affords several interesting clues to the progress of the work. For example, while Mozart's manuscripts are usually neat, *Don Giovanni* bears the trace of great hurry toward the end. The second act finale is full of ink blots and erasures.

[3] It was stipulated in his contract that he was to be provided with proper lodging.

mor and energy. He was a practical man of the theater. He had, so the story goes, difficulty in making Zerlina utter a properly agitated cry during the finale of the first act. Mozart sneaked from the orchestra onto the stage and pinched the actress so hard and unexpectedly that she screeched to everybody's satisfaction.

Thus at least the legend. One other legend must be mentioned: that the Overture was not written until the night before the performance. Mozart asked Constanze to prepare a punch to keep him awake, and while he was working she entertained him by telling him her own version of several fairy tales, from Aladdin to Cinderella. He laughed and kept on writing, but finally he could not hold his head up any longer, and Constanze permitted him to fall asleep on the couch. She promised to wake him after an hour, but he slept so soundly that she didn't have the heart to wake him until five o'clock in the morning. At seven the copyists were due. In an extra burst of speed Mozart finished: at seven the Overture was ready. The story was told by Nissen, who married Constanze after Mozart's death, and who wrote one of the first of the Mozart biographies. Whether it be truth or fable, it is probable that Mozart had thought out the Overture completely and merely postponed the writing down until the last moment.[4]

The impresario Bondini had originally intended to perform the opera as a special tribute to Prince Anton of Saxony and the Duchess Maria Theresia, sister of Joseph II, who were visiting Prague on their wedding trip. The troupe not being ready, Mozart conducted *Figaro* instead, again with great success. *Don Giovanni* was postponed two weeks, then twice again, the premiere finally taking place on the twenty-ninth of October. These postponements no doubt benefited the performance, giving Mozart more time to rehearse.

The performance seems to have been a good one, the local newspaper reporting that "nothing like it had ever been heard in Prague." It was certainly an unqualified success. A friend at the theater reported to Da Ponte in Vienna (Da Ponte had found it necessary to return there before the premiere): "*Evviva* Da Ponte, *evviva* Mozart! . . . As long as such men live, there will be no question of the theater perishing!" The opera was repeated several

---

[4] The manuscript of the Overture gives no evidence of undue haste.

times, and Mozart, basking in the atmosphere of popularity, postponed his departure for some weeks.

In the middle of November he returned to Vienna, and the following May the Emperor commanded a performance of *Don Giovanni* in Vienna. For this performance Mozart made certain changes in the score. He cut the final sextet and he composed a new aria for Don Ottavio, *"Dalla sua pace,"* omitting *"Il mio tesoro"* because the tenor felt that aria was too difficult. For Elvira, sung by Catarina Cavalieri,[5] who had "an accomplished larynx," he added *"Mi tradi,"* while Zerlina and Leporello were presented with an additional duet. The cast consisted of illustrious singers who wanted more and more solo numbers. Perhaps that was the reason for the supplementary music. Perhaps there was another reason, though it seems heresy to mention it: Mozart wanted another fee. In the eighteenth century the composer and the librettist were paid only for the first performance by whatever theater had commissioned the work. By making changes the authors did earn an additional stipend: Mozart 225 gulden, Da Ponte 100 (approximately half of the usual fee).[6] The success of *Don Giovanni* in Vienna was not comparable to its success in Prague, the Viennese public, accustomed to the Martins and the Salieris, finding the work "indigestible."

It is customary, in writing an essay on *Don Giovanni*, to trace the history and development of the dramatic legend, beginning with a play by a seventeenth-century Spanish monk, Tirso de Molina, and following its many guises and adaptations through Molière, Thomas Shadwell, Goldoni, down to Pushkin, Byron, and Bernard Shaw. Like Faust, Oedipus, or Till Eulenspiegel, Don Juan is one of those universal themes which can be used by anybody who has anything new to say. There will probably never be an end to Don Juans. In music too the subject has been treated many times and in many different ways, from the ballet by Gluck to the unfinished opera by Dargormizsky to the tone poem by Richard Strauss. Yet it seems hardly useful to indulge here in a centuries-long genealogy. We know that Raphael copied a certain Roman statue for his "Jonah" in the Chigi Chapel. What of it? It is still a Raphael.

[5] She was the first Konstanze in *The Abduction from the Seraglio.*
[6] The receipt is in the Vienna State Archive.

We can ignore the family tree as we contemplate with astonishment the work itself. Its uncertainties, perhaps due to Da Ponte's
borrowing from many authors, may not have worried Mozart in
the slightest. On the contrary (as I have suggested), they may
have been admitted purposely in the process of shaping the work,
to bestow on it a mystery which it did not possess at birth, but
which was necessary for the expression of Mozart's ideas. There is
something "unreal" about this opera; a dreamlike fantasy pervades
it. The action rushes along in a trance, to be relieved by shafts of
daylight and flashes of sky-blue wit. It begins in darkness; the
time stipulated for most of its scenes is night.[7] It ends in a dubious
dawn, after its hero has perished at the very witching time of
night, when graveyards yawn.

But whether by night or day, now demonic, now luminous, *Don
Giovanni* is always as vital as art itself.

ACT I

A series of unadorned chords opens the Overture. Much later in
the opera we shall hear these chords again, in that terror-laden moment when Don Giovanni opens the door of the palace and sees
confronting him the statue which he had invited to supper. The
effect of this opening is still as strong as if the later orchestra, twice
the size of Mozart's orchestra, had never been invented, as if Wagner and Berlioz had never marshaled the platoon of brass. The mood
of supernatural foreboding continues, expressed in gliding figures
by flutes and violins, alternating between loud and soft. All of this
music is associated with the scene of the visit of the statue in the
last act. It cannot be without significance that Mozart chose for
the opening of his opera material which is lifted from its dark content, not its gay scenes.[8]

But now Mozart breaks away from the musical material of the
opera and writes a fast section which, with several repetitions, con-

[7] Time and place indications of the libretto are uncertain. But it is probable that
eight, possibly nine, of *Don Giovanni's* ten scenes play at night.

[8] Opening statements, I suggest, are as revealing in opera as they are in literature,
though they are less readily analyzed. *Don Giovanni's* beginning may be compared to
Macbeth's first lines:

> "When shall we three meet again
> In thunder, lightning, or in rain?"

tinues to the end of the Overture. One may put any interpretation one wishes on this remarkable *allegro;* very likely Mozart was expressing the devil-may-care insouciance of Don Giovanni's character. Even here we find nothing gay, nothing which would indicate the *buffo* part of the opera.

Scene One

That part begins as soon as the curtain rises. The scene is night in a garden in front of Donna Anna's house. Leporello is standing guard while his master is within. Leporello, in the tradition of Sancho Panza and all the servants before and after, is bemoaning his lot (*"Notte e giorno faticar"*—"Slaving away day and night"). Too much work, too little to eat, and not enough pay! He himself would like to be master, but at the very least he would like to get away from his present employer, a man without scruples or consideration, who is even now toying with some woman inside the house while sleepless Leporello must stand here like a watchdog. Who can bear such ignominy? He's had enough of it. Of a sudden he stops grumbling. He hears something. Somebody is coming. Whatever the cause of the commotion, he wants no part of it. His most prudent course is to hide.

As the music changes from the comically staccato complaints of the servant to an agitated trio, the cause of the disturbance becomes apparent. Donna Anna and Don Giovanni rush from the house, in a violent dispute. It is important to observe that she is dragging him forth, not he her. He is ready to flee, but she, determined and forceful, is holding him in her grip. How curious! This is not the introduction we would have expected to the Great Seducer. He appears more victim than victor.

The first situation in which we find Don Giovanni becomes significant of all that happens to him in the succeeding action. In words, words, words we are assured again and again that the Don is irresistible to women, his triumphs countless, his seductions easily accomplished, his appetite insatiable, his conscience nonexistent, his nerves as steely as his rapier. Yet here we find him first as the ineffective captive. And later what do we find? Throughout the opera he is remarkably unsuccessful. Indeed the only woman in the opera whom he has possessed is Donna Elvira, who, at least according to her own testimony, was his legitimate wife, now abandoned. He fails with Anna, he fails with Zerlina. He fails even with Donna Elvira's maid, whom he serenades, the serenade being interrupted. Later he relates another escapade: disguised as Leporello he picks up a girl who caresses and kisses him, thinking he *is* Leporello. On recognizing his identity, "she creams . . . and I fled the field." One more interruption, one more frustration. Hardly an adequate record for a libertine! We know from Leporello's list the number of the Don's conquests in Europe and in Turkey; they add up to 2,065, though Leporello does not bother to give us the total. In the "Champagne Aria," just before the ball, Don Giovanni declares that before the night is over he will make some ten additions to the list, a fairly ambitious undertaking even for a Don Giovanni. Is all this an empty boast? Is he just talking? Is Leporello's list a lie? Why the discrepancy between the hero's reputation and the action itself? Are we to ascribe the contradiction solely to an accident of plot-making? That seems hardly possible. It is to be assumed that Da Ponte, who himself would have liked nothing better than to be a second Don Giovanni and whose own life could have furnished ample autobiographical material, would have been glad to show his hero triumphant and to present samples of success. It cannot have been delicacy which made the authors skirt demonstration and deprived the Don of a single fulfillment. We know that the one thing Mozart was *not* was a prude. We cannot free ourselves of a suspicion that the Don's ineffectiveness as a lecher is a purposeful device. What was the purpose? We can only guess: perhaps Mozart wished to heighten the dualism of the work by this irony of contradiction, a *giocoso* touch for the chief protagonist, a joke to be played on the hero who is a villain. Perhaps the Prague audience understood the joke: the seducer without seduction. Perhaps that claim of ten women a night is meant to be a ridiculous boast. But, to repeat, this is sheer speculation.

While we have been speculating, the two figures have remained frozen at their very entrance. Having kept them immobile for a time, we might as well keep them so a moment longer to glance at Giovanni's adversary, the magnificent Donna Anna.

On the surface her role is just that, the adversary of the hero. Assaulted and insulted, she stalks through the opera seeking revenge. She enlists her bridegroom, Don Ottavio, in her peregrinations. But for many spectators, analytical or not, this is not enough. Donna Anna is too attractive a woman, her music too evocative, to be content to regard her merely as a Nemesis. There must be more to her and the key to the interpretation of her character must lie in her strange, cold treatment of the man who is constantly in her company, the selfsame Don Ottavio.

Nineteenth-century admirers of the opera, immersed in its mystery, have evolved interpretations of Donna Anna for which there is hardly a shred of evidence either in the words or in the music. Chief among these fanciful interpreters was E. T. A. Hoffmann, a writer of fantastic tales—he influenced Edgar Allan Poe—himself a musician[9] and worshiper of Mozart (the "A" in his initials stands for Amadeus), who wrote a short story, "Don Juan—A Curious Incident which Happened to an Enthusiast on a Journey." This story made an impression not only on the public but on other writers. The narrator of the tale—it is told in the first person— the "Enthusiast on a Journey" is present at a performance of *Don Giovanni* in a provincial theater. He is seated in a box in the theater; after the performance he remains and presently falls asleep. Donna Anna appears to him. She discloses to him that Don Giovanni had taken her by force; but though he killed her father and destroyed not only her own happiness but that of her bridegroom, she is burning with love for him. That passion she can never deny, never subjugate, never extinguish. She feels that it is she who was destined to lead the unfortunate seducer to salvation, it is she who could teach him the beauty of morality. One thing is certain: she can never belong to Don Ottavio. The year's grace which she has asked so that the wedding may be postponed is but an excuse. There is only one course left to her: to die and be united with Don Giovanni. Thus the talk goes on through the night. In the morning the traveler, making ready to proceed on his journey, learns that the singer who had sung Donna Anna the night before had died during the night.[10]

From this view, typical of nineteenth-century romanticism, grew the theory that not only is Donna Anna in love with Don

[9] He composed several operas, his best-known one being *Undine*.

[10] Offenbach, in *Tales of Hoffmann*, pays a tribute to Hoffmann's interest in Mozart. Stella, with whom Hoffmann is in love, is singing Donna Anna at the opera house, while Hoffmann spins his stories. Offenbach quotes the "*Notte e giorno*" theme.

Giovanni but that—piling the Pelion of supposition on the Ossa of inventiveness—Don Giovanni himself feels that Anna is the one woman who can redeem him and set to rest his eternal restlessness.

What is the cause of this restlessness? It appears in some interpretations that it is all the fault of Don Giovanni's mother, for whom Donna Anna serves as a substitute. That mother was either too tender (Gobineau) or too stern (Byron) or all too passionate (Holtei). Still another interpretation has it that Don Juan is a genius, though a genius of the sensual, as Faust is of the spirit. He betrays because he searches; he searches, seeking and never finding, because he is driven by the demonic force of the creative spirit. This view was advanced by the Danish philosopher Sören Kierkegaard.

There is about as much validity to most of this as there is to the theory that Hamlet hated his father. Admitting that we are perfectly at liberty to let our imagination play across these two portraits, we had better adopt the more prudent course of accepting the two for what they appear to be: Don Giovanni as the insatiable lover, ruthless, aristocratic, cynical, sure of his power, giving no thought to consequence, uninterested in the tomorrow, a man who sleeps soundly when he sleeps alone; Donna Anna, beautiful, haughty, a woman brought up in the Spanish tradition, which teaches the integrity of the family and demands revenge should personal integrity or family honor be breached.

It is high time now to liberate them and to follow their fortunes as Mozart and Da Ponte have prescribed them.

The scene between the two is a passionate outburst. "You shall not escape me unless you kill me," Donna Anna cries, while the Don calls her a foolish woman and assures her that she will never learn his identity. While they are struggling with each other, Leporello, safe in his hiding place, joins in to observe sarcastically that his master seems to be once again in a scrape. Leporello's voice forms a sort of ground swell against the two other voices; the serious and the comic are set before us and we experience that "unity in variety" which Winckelmann thought to be the nature of art.

Donna Anna, feeling her strength waning, calls for help, for her servants, for whoever might be within earshot, for anybody except the one who does appear to help her, her own father. Pre-

ceded by threatening upward runs of the orchestra, the Commendatore enters to challenge the intruder to a duel. At the sight
of him, Donna Anna escapes to obtain further help for her father.
Again using ominous scales—the music of the duel bears a subtle
relationship to that of the reappearance of the Commendatore in
the final scene—Mozart graphically describes the swordplay, until
the orchestra comes to the *fermata* at which the Commendatore
receives the mortal thrust.

And now occurs what is one of the supreme moments in the
musical dramatic structure. The tempo from the very beginning of
the opera has been *allegro*, becoming stormier as the scene proceeds.
Now it changes to a hushed and mysterious *andante*, a section of
but eighteen bars long, during which the Commendatore dies,
Leporello admits that he is scared but only of the consequences that
might befall him, not his master, and Don Giovanni observes with
truculent bravado the ebbing of his antagonist's life. The *andante*
is suffused with fear. The lights are dimmed by a shadow, the
shadow of death's messenger, and one has the feeling expressed by
the music only, not by the words, that even Don Giovanni regrets
the deed.

After the Commendatore's death, the orchestra ends the trio of
the three dark voices with a short elegiac strain, and a recitative
begins. "Where are you, Leporello?" Don Giovanni whispers. "Who
is dead?" Leporello asks in turn. "You or the old man?" "What a
stupid question! The old man, of course." "Two master strokes!"
Leporello comments. "Ravish the daughter and murder the father!" "Hold your tongue," Don Giovanni commands, "and let us
get away."

The stage is left empty for a moment; then Donna Anna re-
enters, accompanied by Don Ottavio and several servants carrying
torches. Seeing the body of her father, she flings herself on the
corpse and bursts into lamentations. Stabbing accents in the orchestra accompany Anna as she sees her father's wound, her father's blood, her father's face ashen in death. What a poignant
recitative it is! With a cry, "I die!" Anna faints away. Don
Ottavio dispatches some servants into the house for smelling salts
and cordials. He bids the other servants carry the body away
and addresses words of comfort to his beloved. Reviving, Donna
Anna gives vent to the enormity of her grief, while Don Otta-

vio continues his efforts to console her. She extracts from Ottavio
the solemn promise that the blood here shed will be revenged.
She makes him swear by all the gods that retribution will be
theirs. They reaffirm their oath in a closely linked duet, solemn
and strong (*"Che giuramento, oh Dei!"*—"The vow, oh, gods!"),
as the scene ends.

Scene Two

A street in Seville. At the right is a tavern. It is still night, just
before dawn. Don Giovanni and Leporello seem to be continuing a
lively conversation. Leporello is mustering up courage to tell his
master something that is very much on his mind. He exacts the
promise that Giovanni will not punish him for what he is about to
say and obtains that promise, provided the subject is not the
death of the Commendatore (an indication that this death has disturbed the Don more than is apparent). After several hesitations,
Leporello comes out with it: he thinks that the life his master leads
is nothing short of that of a profligate. As usual when Don Giovanni is crossed by Leporello, he threatens bodily punishment,
promise or no promise. That is the last of Leporello's present effort
to reform his master.

Don Giovanni then confides his objective. He is in love with a
beautiful woman and is certain that this very night she will come
to his summerhouse. Suddenly he stops. "Sh!" he exclaims. "I seem
to sense the perfume of femininity." "What a well-developed sense
of smell," Leporello exclaims, as, looking around, they perceive a
lady approaching. Don Giovanni decides to step aside and unob-
served to observe the newcomer. The newcomer is Donna Elvira.
She enters in a traveling dress and proceeds to pour out her heart
in the aria *"Ah! Chi mi dice mai"*—"Ah! Who can ever tell me
where I will find that monster." To her shame, she confesses, she
has loved him. He has broken faith. And now she means to find
him if for no other than the feminine reason of wanting to tear his
heart out.

Don Giovanni, observing her from afar but not realizing who
she is, is overjoyed at the prospect of being able to console a forsaken woman in her distress. Once Elvira's bravura aria has run its
course, he approaches—and discovers, to his consternation, that

this woman is Donna Elvira, of whom he tired long ago after a brief spell of happiness. Immediately Elvira begins to berate him and recalls to him how he had entered her house by stealth, had through flattery managed to capture her heart, had declared that she was to be his wife, had traveled with her to Burgos, and had then deserted her, leaving her a prey to tears.[11]

She is talking like a book, comments Leporello with obvious glee. Don Giovanni replies to the flood of Elvira's accusations that he had his own good reasons for acting as he did. These reasons will be explained to her by his excellent and trustworthy servant, whose word is as good as gold. With that, he flies off, leaving Leporello and Elvira alone.

He also leaves a problem on the hands of the actress and the stage manager. Elvira's part is a most difficult one to act, and an adequate Donna Elvira is an even rarer occurrence than an adequate Donna Anna. While excoriating Don Giovanni, she must yet enlist our sympathies and stimulate our pity. She is a tragic figure, yet all too often she strikes us as nothing more than a shrew, a Mozartean Fricka. We are not even sure that we are not supposed to laugh at her (see page 42). Only at the very end of the opera do we fully realize the nobility of her nature.

At this moment the scene is set for Leporello's famous Catalogue Aria, to which Elvira has to listen in its entirety. The Catalogue Aria is purely comic, and because Elvira has to be a silent partner to it, the impression given to the audience is that Elvira is part of the *buffo* element of the opera and that her plight need not be taken too seriously. The problem for the stage director is this: What is Elvira supposed to do during the long aria? Is she to sit there in stony dignity? Is she to make an attempt to get away from it all? Is she to listen more or less attentively to Leporello's recital? Or, most apt but most difficult to get across, is she to sink into a trance of contemplation, reviewing to herself the indignities which she is suffering?

Leporello confines his attempt to explain Don Giovanni's be-

---

[11] Da Ponte never makes it clear whether Donna Elvira actually is Don Giovanni's wife. She does refer to him several times as her husband. In Molière's play, the two were actually married, and it is reasonable to assume that Mozart and Da Ponte did consider them so. Elvira's plight becomes sharper if she is in fact his wife.

A glance at the map of Spain will show that the lady has traveled several hundred miles in search of the Don. From Burgos to Seville means traversing most of Spain.

havior by stating the obvious: that she is neither the first nor the last to be betrayed by his master (*"Madamina, il catalogo è questo"* —"Madame, here is the catalogue"). Let her look here, on this book in which Leporello has kept a careful account of the names of all his women, in every city, in every province, in every country. His master's taste is nothing if not international. In Italy, six hundred and forty are recorded; in Germany, two hundred and thirty-one; in France, one hundred; ninety-one in Turkey. But in Spain, ah! in Spain, the catalogue lists no fewer than a thousand and three. All kinds, all sizes, all shapes, all stations, princesses and marquises, baronesses, countesses, ladies' maids and housewives; blondes, old and young; in the winter plump ones, in the summer slim ones. Whoever they may be, he knows how to handle them: with blondes he praises their gentleness, with brunettes their faithfulness. As the music rises to a pompous fanfare, Leporello speaks of statuesque women, to recall, the next moment, accompanied by tiny figures in the violins, all the fluffy little creatures. Petite or big, stately or dainty, it is the same to him. In short, he concludes, as the aria reaches a comic cadenza with the bassoon, "as long as the creature wears skirts, one can be sure what his course will be." This is one of Mozart's most successful patter songs, a marvel of wit and ingenuity, for the full appreciation of which an understanding of the words is desirable.

Having finished this piece of buffoonery, Leporello disappears. Elvira is left alone on the stage, once more to commiserate to herself that she has been traduced. The only feeling left in her heart now is thirst for vengeance.

Scene Three

One is not quite sure where the scene takes place. It may be in the open country near Don Giovanni's house, and in most productions of the opera such is the case. We are in the midst of a group of villagers who are singing and dancing and celebrating the engagement of two of their friends, the pretty Zerlina and her swain, the sturdy Masetto. Zerlina warbles some gay ditty, with the usual refrain that life is made for love, time is fleeting, and ye must gather rosebuds while ye may. Masetto and the others join the song (*"Giovinette, che fate all'amore"*—"Young girls are ripe for love").

Into this innocent idyl appear Don Giovanni and Leporello, having obviously escaped from Elvira. "What pretty girls!" Don Giovanni remarks at once. "What is going on here? Is it a wedding?" On being introduced to the bride and the bridegroom, he assures them that they can both count on his protection. A sudden commotion among the girls is explained away by Leporello, who says that one or two of them are under *his* protection. Don Giovanni invites the whole company to his palace and promises them such treats as chocolate, coffee, wine, and ham. Masetto is to be conducted there at once, while Zerlina may remain behind to be escorted by the cavalier himself. Masetto, who is by no means as stupid as he is usually portrayed, understands the situation and tries to protest, but is soon cowed by the nobleman's threats. All he can do is to vent his rage in an aria (*"Ho capito, signor, sì"*—"I understand, sir, yes indeed"). He calls Zerlina a few uncomplimentary names, spars for time with Leporello but soon enough is hustled off.

Don Giovanni assures Zerlina that she is far too pretty and too refined to be the wife of such a boor as this Masetto is. "But I gave him my word," rejoins Zerlina, all too ready to be convinced of the contrary. "That word is worth nothing. A better fate is in store for somebody who has such sparkling eyes. . . . Let us not lose time. I myself will take you as my wife. Yonder is my house. There we can be alone. And there, my darling, we can be married."

The recitative is an example of the unique skill which Mozart shows in this form of carrying the drama forward. It is full of flattering insinuations, proving Don Giovanni's practiced technique, while Zerlina's replies are short and simple. Don Giovanni's last words—"There we can be married"—are given a particularly seductive turn of phrase and are the cue for the famous duet *"La ci darem la mano"*—"There our troth will be pledged."[12] Zerlina's part in this exquisite little play within the play is a hesitation—*"Vorrei e non vorrei"*—"I want to and yet I do not"—with the *"vorrei"* winning out.

[12] The duet had to be sung three times at the premiere.

As Giovanni and Zerlina, arm in arm, turn to go to the castle, the interfering Fury in the person of Donna Elvira appears from nowhere. She bids them halt. She is just in time, she says, to save the miserable girl. Zerlina is understandably perturbed by this incident. "Is it true, what she claims?" she asks Don Giovanni, whose skill for the moment is put to a severe test. "The poor woman is madly in love with me," he whispers to Zerlina, "and out of pity and the goodness of my heart, I humor her." But Elvira is not to be fobbed off; she proceeds to tell Zerlina what kind of man this lover is. She does so in the aria *"Ah, fuggi il traditor!"*—"Flee the traitor!"—at the end of which she firmly leads the girl away.

Don Giovanni takes his disappointment philosophically. Everything seems to be at sixes and sevens today. The Devil himself seems to be in league against him. Nor is he at the end of his troubles. As he turns, he finds himself face to face with Don Ottavio and Donna Anna. Obviously, the three know one another. Anna turns to him and asks him for proof of his friendship; she needs him now in her distress. "You have only to command," Don Giovanni assures her. "My arm, my sword, my very life are at your service. But why do you weep, fair Donna Anna? What villain has dared to offend you?" Before she has time to answer and to explain the cause of her misery, the watchful Elvira returns. (It is obvious that Elvira's double popping onto the scene, each time with a loud accusation, is particularly awkward. Indeed, her second appearance often causes an unfortunate snicker among the audience.)

Elvira is brought back to take part in the great quartet *"Non ti fidar"*—"Do not trust this stony heart." "He has betrayed me," she tells the astonished Anna, "and he will betray you as well." Both Donna Anna and Don Ottavio, watching Elvira, are much impressed by this strange woman with her "noble aspect and sweet gentleness" (again it is clear how Mozart saw Elvira), "her pale face with its trace of tears." Don Giovanni's reply, given in a confidential whisper, is that the woman is demented and that they had best leave him alone with her so that he may try to calm her. Donna Anna and Don Ottavio do not know whom to believe and whom to doubt. The situation is expressed in a musical grouping, the voices of Anna and Ottavio forming one unit, Elvira's the other, while the dark voice of Don Giovanni swings from one to the other, menacing Elvira, placating the other two. Finally the Don manages to lead Elvira away. It is his intention, he asserts, to follow her closely, to see that she does not harm herself. His parting words are: "So forgive my leaving you, beautiful Donna Anna. If I can be of service to you, I shall await you at my house."

Something in the sound of his voice as he sings these last words strikes a chord of memory in Donna Anna. With a shock she perceives the truth: the man who had attacked her, the man who is responsible for her father's death, he is none other than Don Giovanni. (It is no accident that at this crucial point Don Giovanni calls the lady *"bellissima Donna Anna"*; the interpreter of the Don must make it clear in singing those three words that Giovanni has fallen into his professionally caressing tone.)

We have arrived at the great explanatory scene. Anna must impart to Ottavio the event which led to her father's death. She must break her silence. The explanation is carried on wholly in recitative, though, as was Mozart's custom in consequential situations, that recitative is accompanied by the whole orchestra, here handled with exceptional power. In fact, Anna's first exclamation is preceded by an agitated cry of the orchestra. She breaks out into, "Don Ottavio, I die!"—meaning, as she makes clear in a moment, that she is overcome by the horror of the realization that "This man is my father's murderer!" On being pressed for details by Ottavio, she sketches the incidents of that fateful night, with the orchestra suggesting the night's darkness. The night, she says, was well advanced when she saw a man enter her apartment. Thinking it was Don Ottavio, she did not at first realize that this was a stranger. (Here we must wonder why Donna Anna, the lady brought up in Spanish strictness, was not surprised that her betrothed should be calling on her in the middle of the night. Nothing in the opera indicates that Ottavio and Anna were premarital lovers.) Silently the man approached her and tried to embrace her. She cried out, but in vain. No one came. He pressed his hand over her mouth and choked her cries, while he endeavored to possess her. Struggle as she might, she could not free herself. Thinking herself overcome, a sudden pain and horror infused her with new strength. Twisting and turning, she wrenched herself free and redoubled her cries for help. At this the intruder, taking fright, attempted to flee. But having refound her courage, she went after him, follow-

ing him into the street, and turned "from the assailed to the as-
sailer." Her father awoke, challenged the man, with the result that
the unknown criminal capped his crime by killing the old man.

Thus Donna Anna, in an almost continuous recital which is
broken only by inconsequential remarks by Don Ottavio. Da Ponte
and Mozart could hardly have been more explicit, and it is possible that the scene was set in recitative to make sure that the
audience fully understood the motive which sets the play into
motion. It is the more ironic that this scene of all scenes has been
misunderstood, not only by the fanciful romanticists such as Hoffmann, but by serious Mozart scholars, even by the redoubtable Alfred Einstein. Perhaps the scholars know too much of antecedent history. Bertati makes it quite clear that Don Giovanni has possessed
Donna Anna. So they assume that Da Ponte planned it likewise.
Not the slightest evidence to that effect exists—unless one were to
adduce a bit of recitative dialogue after the killing of the Commendatore (see page 53):

LEPORELLO: Bravo! Two master strokes! Ravish the daughter and murder
the father!
DON GIOVANNI: He asked for his fate!
LEPORELLO: And Donna Anna? Did she ask for it, too?
DON GIOVANNI: Hold your tongue! Don't aggravate me, but come with
me, unless you, too, want something you didn't bargain for.

Even if we were to take Leporello's spitefully jocular remark
seriously, the fact remains that he wasn't there. Don Giovanni
does not say that Leporello is stating a fact. The Don is always
only too ready to narrate his affairs in detail to his servant, but
at no time does he boast of the conquest of Donna Anna. Yet
the theory will not be downed that Don Giovanni was successful.
This makes a liar of the noble Donna Anna. That is dramatically
impossible. No, we must and can believe Donna Anna.

The theory persists because we try hard to find a satisfactory
companion to the leading lady. Don Ottavio isn't such a one, and
never less so than in this scene and immediately after. His two-
word comment at Donna Anna's revelation that she escaped un-
harmed is, "*Ohimè respiro!*"—"Ah, I breathe again!"

Having completed her explanation, Anna launches into the first

of her two great arias, *"Or sai chi l'onore"*—"Now you know who
would have robbed me of my honor." The aria is a restatement of
what she has previously said in recitative, as well as a passionate
renewal of her demand to Don Ottavio to aid her in her quest for
vengeance.

Don Ottavio, left alone, voices a remarkable reflection: "How
am I to believe that a gentleman (*un cavaliere*) could be capable of
so black a crime?" He must do everything in his power either to
undeceive Donna Anna as to the identity of the man in the night—
the poor fellow can't get himself to believe that anybody of his
own social milieu could be guilty of such perversity—or, if indeed
it was Don Giovanni, he must avenge her. He comforts himself
with the serene aria—composed for the Vienna production—
"Dalla sua pace"—"On her peace of mind my own depends."
After hearing it we have no choice but to forgive Don Ottavio for
being Don Ottavio.

Scene Four

Presumably Don Giovanni's palace. Leporello is discovered mut-
tering once again that at all cost he must leave the service of this
madman. Don Giovanni enters, blissfully ignorant of the fact that
his identity has become known to Donna Anna, and strutting with
anticipation of the pleasures of the evening before him. Leporello's
report is all on the pessimistic side: he took the peasants home,
he fed them food and drink, he tried to placate Masetto; and just
when he had everything going well and all the men and women
more than half-drunk, who should walk in but Donna Elvira!
With what Leporello considers great tact, he allowed her to vent
her spleen, and when it seemed to him that her anger was spent, he
led her from the palace, closed the door firmly behind her, and left
her standing in the street. "Excellent!" replies Don Giovanni. "It
could not have been managed any better. The way is smoothed for
me. I am very fond of these country girls." Raising a glass[13] and
making himself ready for the evening, he dashes off the *presto*
bravura aria *"Fin ch'han dal vino"*—"While their spirits are
warmed by wine, let us prepare a grand feast. Invite any pretty girl

[13] This is traditional business, and that is why the aria is known as the "Champagne
Aria."

you find in town, let the dancing be informal. I will toy first with one and then with the other, until by morning our list is augmented by ten more names." Musically, here is the apex of the Don's triumph. The aria is appropriately named—it *is* champagne.

Scene Five—*The Palace Garden*

Several country people are lounging about. They have been invited to Don Giovanni's party and they want to be sure to be on hand when it begins. Among them are our two young friends, the charming Zerlina and the now not so charming Masetto. He is in a righteous huff, thoroughly tormented by jealousy. To entertain another man on the very day of their wedding—it is just too much! Zerlina, trying to make peace, protests that he is mistaken, that there is no cause for anger, that Don Giovanni never so much as touched the tip of her finger. He won't believe her? She is ready to prove her innocence. Let him do anything he wishes to vent his bad temper, let him scold her, even beat her, anything, as long as they will then kiss and make up. The logic is not very valid, but it is the cue for Zerlina's aria, "*Batti, batti*"—"Beat your poor Zerlina—I'll endure it as meek as a lamb." This expression of feminine guile, half-naïve, half-sophisticated, through which runs the figuration of a cello obviously in league with Zerlina—well, Masetto cannot resist it any more than the audience can.

The little witch, as Masetto calls her, has just about succeeded when Giovanni's voice is heard offstage. Zerlina immediately reacts. "Masetto, did you hear the voice of my lord?" This suffices to reawaken his suspicions, and he determines presently to hide himself in a niche nearby and to eavesdrop on everything that might go on between Zerlina and Don Giovanni.

Now begins a hurried duet, a lover's quarrel ("*Presto, presto*"—"I'll quickly hide myself"), in which Zerlina vainly tries to dissuade Masetto from his plan of opposing Don Giovanni's wishes, partly because she is afraid of what the nobleman may do to the poor peasant and partly because she is still titillated and flattered by Don Giovanni's interest.

Masetto slips into a recess as Giovanni enters with some of his servants. They conduct the rest of the country people into the house while he and Zerlina are left alone on the stage. The scene between the two, and indeed all that follows until the beginning of the ball scene, is to be counted among the highest achievements of the musical-dramatic art. (We keep saying this, but how can we help it when we discuss Mozart?) The music, constantly changing and constantly apposite, leads us from one situation to another, the first being a usual enough seduction scene, the latter a bold and original dramatic concept.

Zerlina, having made a halfhearted attempt to hide from Don Giovanni, readily enough comes close to him. Here, almost the only time in the opera, he is convincing as a seducer. With an infinitely caressing turn of phrase and suave manner, Don Giovanni steers Zerlina toward an alcove in the garden. It is his bad luck that it is the very alcove that Masetto has chosen as his place of concealment. As he appears,[14] sour-faced and truculent, Don Giovanni is for a moment thrown into confusion. For a moment only. Regaining his poise, he assures Masetto that his Zerlina has been lonesome for him right along. He leads them both to the feast, as from within the house the musicians hired for the occasion begin to sound their instruments.

A short pause—then enter Donna Anna, Donna Elvira, and Ottavio. All three are masked. It is their purpose to enter the Don's house and confront him with their knowledge of his crime. Since they are all well known to Don Giovanni, they must hide their identities. Da Ponte, as a Venetian, must have been quite familiar with the use of masks; the device presented him with an opportunity to create a visually effective moment of which Mozart took full advantage. The stage tableau and the music convey an impression which seems to make the protagonists grow taller than life. We see them as the advocates of retribution, tremendous figures, universal and eternal.

The most courageous of the three is Elvira, while Don Ottavio concentrates on keeping up Donna Anna's nerve, she being apprehensive of the fate which may befall Ottavio when he challenges the man who killed her father. As the three plot in the darkness, the window of the house is opened. We hear the strains of the famous minuet from within. It is to play an important part in the next scene and links the two scenes together.

---

[14] For his appearance Mozart uses the same device—a drop in tonality—that he used for Susanna's emergence from the closet in *Figaro*, Act II.

Leporello appears on the balcony; turning to Don Giovanni within, he points out the three masked figures. They seem to be persons of quality. Giovanni orders him to invite them,[15] while the three, singing softly in unison, proclaim the Don an unscrupulous traitor. Leporello calls to the three masks and extends the invitation, which is accepted. Through all of this the rhythm of the minuet persists.

Leporello having shut the window and disappeared, Anna, Elvira, and Ottavio doff their masks for a moment and in a solemn trio they pray that heaven protect them in their mission ("*Protegga il giusto cielo*"). The scene which began with a lovers' quarrel ends with a prayer. Music which is an invitation to the dance is closely followed by music expressing high purpose and resolve. If Greek tragedy "is nothing less than pain transmuted into exaltation by the alchemy of poetry,"[16] here is pain transmuted into exaltation by the alchemy of music.

Scene Six

From the darkness of the three masked figures we change to brightest light. We are in the ballroom of Don Giovanni's palace. The promised party is in full swing, the hall is crowded, the candles shed a pleasant glow, servants pass refreshments, and no fewer than three separate orchestras minister to the guests' desire to dance. In the midst of the jollity, Don Giovanni loses no time in paying extravagant compliments to the "enchanting, sparkling Zerlina," much, of course, to the discomfiture of Masetto. The music rushes along at a party pace, until, at the entrance of the three masks, it changes. Heralded by trumpet and wind instruments, the mysterious newly bidden guests are greeted politely by Leporello, while Don Giovanni assures them that his house is open to all. Then the dancing, still to the strains of the minuet, is resumed. As is to be expected, Giovanni selects Zerlina as his partner, while Don Ottavio chooses Anna, being constrained to join the dance so as not to betray himself prematurely. Giovanni now bids Leporello to "take care" of the troublesome Masetto. Here the second orchestra

---

[15] It does not seem to have occurred to commentators that Don Giovanni invites the avenging force *twice* to his house.

[16] Edith Hamilton, *The Greek Way*.

plays a *contredanse,* and after a little while the third orchestra, which has been tuning up, is heard in a waltz. The feat of having three different dances going at once, playing a different tune in a different rhythm, is an ingenious one, and its technical challenge must have delighted Mozart. There is a dramatic purpose as well to this triple dance: the minuet is obviously a dance for the nobility, the *contredanse* for the peasants (though Don Giovanni and Zerlina dance it as well), and the waltz is used for that ill-assorted couple, Leporello and Masetto.[17] Poor Masetto! Leporello practically forces him to dance; being thus engaged he has no opportunity to prevent Giovanni from leading Zerlina, who is hardly resisting, into an adjoining room.

As soon as they have disappeared, Leporello comments that "something rotten is going on" and follows them. In a moment a cry for help is heard from backstage. It is Zerlina's voice. The effect is electric. Masetto hurls himself against the locked door. The three orchestras cease abruptly. The company breaks up in confusion, and the three masks declare that they must save "the innocent girl." Zerlina emerges, still crying, and is followed by Don Giovanni, who drags Leporello after him. "Here," says Giovanni, "here is the scoundrel who has offended you. I shall punish him properly. I shall kill him." But he fools no one. Ottavio produces a pistol and challenges Don Giovanni. All three unmask, and Don Giovanni, now confronted, must recognize them. The storm is about to break over the hero's head.

But it does not. Don Ottavio does nothing more with the pistol than flourish it,[18] and Donna Anna and Donna Elvira do nothing more than call Don Giovanni names, among which the words "traitor" and "tremble" are heard repeatedly. For the moment at least dramatic sense goes to pieces, though Mozart manages to build up a crescendo of excitement by waves of increasing intensity in

[17] In the Champagne Aria, when Don Giovanni describes the arrangements for his feast, he mentions that there will be opportunity for three kinds of dances: specifically, the minuet, the *follia,* and the *alemana.* The *follia* is a Spanish dance in three-four time, which may well be equivalent to the waltz; while the *alemana* is the German *contredanse.* Perhaps we may regard this cross-reference as another bit of evidence that Da Ponte did not handle the libretto as casually as is generally supposed.

[18] The gesture is so ineffective that to save face the pistol business is eliminated in most modern productions, and Ottavio draws his rapier and fences with the Don, though without harming him.

the orchestra and the voices. (The chorus, curiously enough, is silent throughout.) It is straining the credulity of the audience to
let Don Giovanni escape from a situation in which he is completely
cornered. Yet there is a second act to think of, and it would obviously not do to cut the principal protagonist's life short at the finale
of the first act. So escape Don Giovanni does. Crying that he has
not lost one jot of his courage, he draws his sword and hacks his
way through the crowd and out of the palace.

ACT II

Scene One

The setting is a street, on one side of which stands the house in
which Elvira is lodged. Once more we find Don Giovanni and
Leporello deep in conversation, but this time the conversation proceeds not in recitative but in a duet of great verve (*"Eh via buffone, eh via buffone, non mi seccar"*—"Hold on, you clown, stop
bothering me"). We are familiar with the subject they are discussing: Leporello wants to leave the Don's service and the Don
cannot understand why in the world he should even think of it.
Once more Leporello cannot bring himself to take the decisive step,
particularly when Don Giovanni bribes him with a little extra
money. Leporello is mollified, but insists on continuing his moralizing. "Will you not leave women alone?" he asks. The Don: "Leave
women alone? Madman! Do you not know that they are more
necessary to me than the bread I eat, the very air I breathe?" Leporello: "Is it your intention then to deceive them all?" Giovanni:
"The man who is faithful to one alone is cruel to all the others."
At present his enthusiasm is centered on the pretty maid of Donna
Elvira. He wants to try his luck with her, and to do so he aims to
appear before her in Leporello's clothes. Why not in his own? Because the clothes of a gentleman are apt to intimidate a servant
girl. So Giovanni and Leporello exchange cloaks and hats.

The Don, disguised as his own servant, is now ready to approach
Elvira's maid, when, unexpectedly, not the maid but Elvira herself appears on the balcony. Believing herself to be alone, she confides her thoughts to the night air. Sad thoughts they are, for
though she is aware of Don Giovanni's perfidious nature, though

she knows him to be a traitor, she cannot help longing for him (*"Ah! taci, ingiusto cuore"*—"Be silent, my unjust heart"). Though the scene presently develops into a comic one, Mozart could not help giving Elvira music of tenderness and dignity. He must have felt for her deeply to compose such an aria.

Don Giovanni takes it into his head that as long as Elvira has appeared, he might as well revenge himself for her persecution of him and play a trick on her. Placing himself behind Leporello, he addresses words of passion to her, while Leporello executes the appropriate gestures. The time being night and the place being the theater, Elvira is as thoroughly fooled as was to be Roxane when Cyrano stood behind her tongue-tied lover. Elvira *wants* to believe the ardent protestations which float up to her. Responding to the pseudo Giovanni's entreaties, she descends, ready to throw herself into his arms.

Before she appears, Giovanni instructs Leporello that he is to overwhelm her with caresses, imitating his master's voice as best he can. Then he is to lead her off to a remote spot, leaving the house free for Don Giovanni's visit to the servant girl.

Leporello carries out his mission under the observation of his master, who has hidden himself. In most productions the scene is clowned beyond all semblance of taste. Overacting on the part of Leporello only heaps excessive ridicule on Elvira, who would be more of a fool than in fact she is if she could not recognize the difference between the Don's expert love-making and Leporello's crudity. If, however, Leporello presents a fair copy of the Don, the irony of Elvira's guying becomes sensible and effective. Irony is a tool of tragedy as well as of comedy.

The Don, still hidden, pretends to be a brigand and utters a few threatening noises, at which Elvira and Leporello take fright and quit the scene, leaving Giovanni on the stage to sing to a mandolin accompaniment the serenade *"Deh! vieni alla finestra"*— "Oh! come to the window, my treasure." It is the very model of a serenade and really ought to have a worthier object than an unseen serving maid who never takes part in the action.

Once more Don Giovanni is destined to be thwarted. Out of the darkness there now appears Masetto, armed to the teeth and accompanied by a group of his friends. It is obvious that they are searching for Don Giovanni. Sure enough, Masetto dimly espies the figure of a man. To his loud "Who is there?" the man answers, "Do you not know me? I am the servant of Don Giovanni." The false Leporello willingly joins Masetto in denouncing the Don and eagerly seconds his plan for catching and destroying that fine cavalier. In fact, he takes over and instructs Masetto and his friends how to proceed: they are to search until they come upon a man and a young woman on the piazza or underneath a window. The man will be wearing a hat with white plumes, a great cloak over his shoulders, a sword at his side. All this he details in the aria *"Metà di voi qua vadano"*—"Half of you go this way, the rest are to disperse in the other direction." The aria is impudent and very much in character.

But Masetto is to remain with him, the pseudo Leporello. When the two are left alone, Masetto by a simple trick is made to hand over his musket, his pistol, and the rest of his weapons. The Don simply asks if Masetto is sufficiently armed. The trusting fellow shows what he carries on his expedition. Once Don Giovanni has him unarmed, he turns on the poor lad, beats him roundly, and runs off.

There he is, crying for help, every bone in his body hurting him. Fortunately Zerlina hears the cries and traipses to the rescue. Masetto tells her the whole story of his misadventure, how suddenly and without any provocation he was attacked by Leporello or some devil who looked like him. "This is the result of your mad jealousy," Zerlina lectures him. "But where does it hurt you?" Everywhere: his foot, his arm, his hand all pain him. But Zerlina knows the remedy, and she gives her prescription in that gem of a song *"Vedrai carino"*—"You'll see, my darling, what a fine remedy I will apply." What the remedy is is made clear by Da Ponte: it is the natural consolation that a woman can bring to a man. It doesn't taste bitter, this balsam which cannot be purchased at the apothecary's, but which she carries about on her own person. Would he like to know where she keeps it? Let him feel her heart and listen to its beating. As she sings this phrase—*"Sentilo battere!"*—the woodwinds indicate a gentle beating, a theme which is then used by the orchestra for a beautiful postlude.

Supporting Masetto, she leads him away.

So Masetto gets his Zerlina after all. Simplicity triumphs over sophistication.

Scene Two

For reasons known only to Da Ponte and Mozart, Leporello and Elvira have strayed into an unlikely spot, "a dark courtyard before the house of Donna Anna." Elvira is still under the misapprehension that her companion is Don Giovanni, while Leporello has had quite enough of the whole masquerade and is doing his best to get away before worse should befall. In the dark the servant is groping his way around the wall, looking for an escape. As he is about to find the door, it opens, and Donna Anna and Don Ottavio emerge, he continuing his efforts to comfort her while her tears still keep flowing. Once more Leporello fumbles for his escape, but his flight is now cut off by the entrance of Zerlina and Masetto who, believing that Leporello is Don Giovanni, cry out, "Stop, you scoundrel!" This then is the situation for the great sextet. We suspect that the six were brought together for musical reasons, for the scene gives Mozart an opportunity to delineate both pairs of lovers as well as Elvira and Leporello in music which is as psychologically right as it is effective as a whole.[19]

There is a dramatic purpose to the scene as well, contrived though the coincidence is by which they all meet in a given spot. The two couples—one of aristocratic station, the other simple people—are united in their determination to see justice done. Standing between them is Elvira, the woman who loves the culprit. But the man on whom they descend is the false Don Giovanni, and all this emotion, all this seriousness, is wasted on a comic figure. Once again we find here a touch of the irony in which this work abounds.

As the four, singing together, threaten action against the cornered man, Elvira steps forward and exclaims in a voice full of tears, "It is my husband. Have pity on him!" All are astonished to find Elvira in their midst and to hear her defend the man who has so mercilessly injured her. Yet her pleading avails nothing, as in decisive accents they proclaim, "He must die!" As Don Ottavio lifts his sword, Leporello sinks to his knees, throws off his disguise, and in music which comically describes his fright whines for pardon. A united cry goes up: "Leporello—what trick is this?" And the sextet comes to a halt at a firm *fermata*. Then it gathers new

[19] See the discussion of the third-act sextet in *Figaro*, page 25.

speed and momentum, as "a thousand troubled thoughts" assail the
participants. On and on the music tosses and rages, until Donna
Anna turns and leaves the scene.

The others vie for the privilege of punishing the valet. Leporello,
drawing on his reserve of trickery and slyness, first pleads, *"Ah!
Pietà, signori miei"*—"Ah! Pardon, ladies and gentlemen"—implores mercy of each in turn, effectively bamboozles them all, finds
the right door, and runs out. The others would pursue him, but
Don Ottavio holds them back. He has a more important task on
his mind than the punishing of Leporello. There can be no doubt
any more, he tells them, that the murderer of the Commendatore
is indeed Don Giovanni. What has now convinced him he does not
tell us; certainly Giovanni's trick on Elvira could not be considered
fresh evidence. He will have recourse to the proper authorities
(spoken like a hero!) and he promises them that before long they
will all be avenged. Once again, just as we find Don Ottavio at his
lowest in dramatic vitality, he cancels our irritation by his second
aria, *"Il mio tesoro"*—"Go to my treasure meanwhile and console
her."[20]

There follows a mixed-up scene which Mozart wrote for the
Vienna version. Zerlina drags in Leporello, binds him to a chair;
they sing a duet, *"Per queste tue manine"*—"By these dainty hands
of yours"—and Leporello once more escapes, dragging the chair
with him. This scene is invariably omitted in performance, and
need not bother us here.

What follows in performance is Elvira's soliloquy and her aria
"Mi tradì quell'alma ingrata"—"The ungrateful soul has betrayed
me." Before the aria there is a rich recitative[21] accompanied by the
orchestra, in which Elvira for the first time appears at her full
stature. She is torn between her desire to see justice done and the
love that she cannot deny nor tear from her soul. "Unhappy Elvira! What conflicting passions rage in your heart! Why these
sighs? Why such anguish?"

The faults of the libretto are most pronounced in the part of the

---

[20] The aria, with its beautiful, long-breathed phrases, is so difficult that hardly anybody today can do it justice. It is no wonder that the tenor at the Viennese premiere did
not want to sing it. In days gone by, John McCormack made a noteworthy recording
of it.

[21] In my opinion the recitative is finer than the aria.

work we have just traversed. With the beginning of Act II things slide downhill and, all the musical beauties notwithstanding, the drama loses cogency. The comic element comes to the fore in such scenes as the mock serenade to Elvira, the roughhouse with Masetto, and Leporello's sneaking off under the eyes of four watchful people, surely as unconvincing a trick as can be found in opera. It is tempting to put the blame on Da Ponte for all this. But on what evidence?

Now, however, change is imminent. From here to the end of the opera the serious element predominates, and in the very next scene we find both the poet and the composer at their apex.

Scene Three

Night. A churchyard. The moon is high in the sky and sheds its light over the gravestones and monuments. Imposing among these tributes to the dead is the equestrian statue of the Commendatore, Anna's slain father.

A man leaps over the wall of the cemetery. It is Don Giovanni, hiding from somebody or other. He could not be in better spirits. The night seems perfect for roaming about; it is made for amorous hunting. He wonders what might have happened in the little affair of Leporello and Donna Elvira. Just then Leporello himself lumbers into view, not quite in such high spirits, since he is still smarting in body and soul from his recent experience. Exchanging cloaks and hats, they resume their proper attire, while Don Giovanni can hardly wait before he blurts out his latest adventure. Somewhere on some street he saw a young damsel; needless to say, she was pretty and flirtatious. He accosted her, and after some hesitation she responded. She showered him with caresses, all the while murmuring, "My darling Leporello!" It was as his servant, then, that the Don found a complaisant partner. (Is this a further stroke of intended irony?) But all of a sudden the girl realized her mistake. She screamed; passers-by threatened to intervene; he took to his heels, and that is why he has hidden himself here behind this wall. "And you tell me all this quite calmly?" asks the much tried Leporello. "Supposing she had been my wife?" "The adventure would have been better still," Giovanni laughs uproariously.

It is this moment which marks the turning point of Don Gio-

vanni's career and divides the Don triumphant from the dissolute
punished. The story he has just told is the last of the little episodes
that he is so fond of confiding. After the churchyard scene, we
shall lose track of him for a while, that is, until Donna Anna has
had her aria. We then meet him once more. In these two final
scenes a curious alchemy takes place: Don Giovanni, though he
does not change—or perhaps because he does not change—manages
to win from us a measure, if not of approbation, then of admiration. There is something positive and jubilant in his bravado, there
is fire in his consistency. With every fiber of his being he holds fast
to his creed, one which he gave us in the initial scene of the second
act and which he is to express once more in the finale. Nothing, not
even ghostly voices in the night, nor a dead corse revisiting the
glimpses of the moon, nor a last chance at redemption generously
offered him, swerves him from his natural course. He does not ask
for pity. The libertine's liberty is preserved.

Yet in the cemetery scene, as in the scene of the death of the
Commendatore, we cannot help sensing an undercurrent of fear.
We cannot but feel that Don Giovanni is not quite so callous
toward the statue nor quite so unaffected by the atmosphere of the
graveyard as he asserts. Nothing is said in so many words. The
mood of the music, specifically that of the duet which we are
shortly to hear, conveys it.

This large-scaled music, truly "monumental," which fills the
scene is preceded by the lightest kind of parlando recitative, in
which Don Giovanni tells the anecdote of the girl in the street.
When Leporello protests that it could have been his wife and Don
Giovanni answers with a loud laugh, at this moment the dry recitative stops and we hear the voice of the statue: "Your laughter
shall cease ere dawn." The words are accompanied by three trombones, used here for the first time in the score. To one sensitive
listener,[22] these notes sounded as if they were "borne from the or-
bits of far distant stars . . . ice-cold, piercing heart and marrow."

"Who spoke?" Don Giovanni demands. "It must be," says Leporello, shaking from head to foot, "some spirit from the other
world." Giovanni impatiently silences him and again cries, "Who
is there?" as he slashes with his sword at one of the tombs. The

[22] The poet Mörike, who wrote a charming short story, "Mozart on the Journey to
Prague."

voice of the Commendatore bids him leave the dead in peace. Giovanni turns to the statue, recognizes the Commendatore's effigy, and instructs Leporello to read the inscription on the statue. "I did not learn to read by moonlight," Leporello puts forward. But he does read aloud, deciphering these words: "Here I await the villain who has dragged me to this extremity."

"What a silly old fool!" Don Giovanni exclaims. "Tell him that this evening I expect him to supper at my house." What! To face this terrible apparition with such a message—it is more than anybody can ask. As usual Leporello has to be threatened—this time with death—before he obeys. Obey he does, approaching the "most distinguished statue" with many a scrape and bow.

Then begins the duet *"O statua gentillissima,"* one of the masterpieces of the score, contrasting Leporello's terror with Don Giovanni's impudence. The duet has two parts, first the invitation extended by Leporello to the statue and given with the lackey's heart beating against his ribs. When Leporello has finished his invitation, the statue inclines its head but utters no sound. "Look, just look!" stammers Leporello, in an interpolation which serves as a point of rest in the swiftly moving musical current; "its marble head went like this." Giovanni repeats the phrase with Leporello. In the second part Giovanni himself addresses the statue: "Speak if you can. Will you come to supper?" This time the statue does reply. The reply is a monosyllable: "Yes." A cold terror emanates from that word.

The scene ends with Giovanni hurrying away to give orders for the preparation of the feast, Leporello accompanying him, still in a paroxysm of fear.

Scene Four

Donna Anna's house. Once more we meet Don Ottavio at his task of comforting Donna Anna. "The scoundrel's crimes will be punished." He proposes marriage on the morrow to her. She refuses, though protesting that she desires nothing better than to be united with him. She repudiates Ottavio's charge of being "cruel." As she does so, there develops in the orchestra a phrase of great tenderness, a phrase which Mozart uses presently in Donna Anna's aria. She is afraid of what the world might think if they were to

be married so soon. As we have seen, it is this reluctance on Donna
Anna's part which has given support to the theory that she does
not love Ottavio. Yet she now addresses to him her famous aria
"Non mi dir, bell'idol mio"—"Do not protest, my adored one, that
I am cruel to you"—which is plainly a love song.

The aria has been both a source of puzzlement and of irritation
to admirers of the opera. Its first part constitutes a haunting expression of womanly sweetness. But there follows its second part—
the tempo changes from a *larghetto* to an *allegretto,* and Donna
Anna bursts into bravura song, strewing the stage with difficult
scale passages, including a shower of high notes. Berlioz found these
pages "shameful." Being less exigent, let us just note that for once
Mozart failed at the task at which he was egregious, that of supplying his singer with music which demonstrates the singer's
prowess and yet stays within the psychological framework of the
character.

The scene concludes with a brief monologue by Don Ottavio:
he will follow her and share all her sufferings.

Scene Five

Don Giovanni's palace. A table is laid for supper. Leporello is
busily serving this supper, and, as befits a nobleman, there are
present several musicians to entertain him during his repast.

Don Giovanni bids the musicians play. He has paid them well
and wants value to be delivered. At once they strike up a melody
which Leporello recognizes as a tune from *Una Cosa Rara* (*A Rare
Piece*), an opera by Martin, one for which Da Ponte had written
the libretto and which had become so popular in Vienna that it
drove *The Marriage of Figaro* from the boards. (We can guess that
Mozart was cracking an intramural joke, particularly when we
consider the two following lines: "How do you like this concert?"
asks Don Giovanni. "It conforms to your worth," Leporello answers—surely an equivocal remark!)

Don Giovanni praises the flavor of the dish he is tasting, while
Leporello comments on his master's "barbarous appetite." The
musicians sound a new tune, one from Sarti's opera, *I Due Litiganti*
(*The Two Litigants*). Mozart liked Sarti personally—he called

him "an honest good man"—and used this same melody for a set
of variations.

The feast continues, with Leporello pouring the wine and serving the pheasant. He himself snitches a bite of the succulent bird.
Don Giovanni observes him and commands the servant, while his
mouth is full, to speak up plainly. He cannot, he protests; he has a
cold. Then he is to whistle. Now he must confess that his master's
cook is such a wizard that he couldn't resist the temptation of trying the dish. Previous to this bit of traditional master-servant play,
the band has offered still another sample of its repertoire. That
melody "I know only too well," Leporello tells us, for it is the
"Non più andrai" from Figaro. (We may imagine the amusement
of the Prague audiences when this quotation was set before them.)

Suddenly the merrymaking is interrupted. Distraught and desperate, frenzied with grief, Elvira runs in. The music becomes
feverish as Elvira pleads with Don Giovanni. It is the last proof
of her love. She no longer remembers his cruelty. She feels only
pity for him. Let him not mock her suffering.

What is it she wants? That he change his life? That he is unable
to do. But if she cares to, let her join him and have supper with
him. "He must have a heart of stone or no heart at all, if he is not
touched by her grief," murmurs Leporello; while Don Giovanni, in
a glorious phrase, sums up his creed: "A toast to women, a toast
to wine; these are the sustenance and the glory of humanity."
What Elvira has to offer he has spurned. Sadly she turns away, to
walk out of his life forever. As she opens the portal, she utters a
horrible cry, recoils, and flees out of a door on the other side.

Why that cry? Investigate, Don Giovanni commands Leporello.
What is the cause? At once Leporello returns, pale and shaken.
"For pity's sake, my lord, do not stir outside. The man of stone,
the man in white—oh, master, I tremble! He is coming up the
stairs, clump, clump, clump!"

Someone is knocking at the door. Open! But for once the Don
cannot command his servant. Leporello refuses. Taking up a lamp
and drawing his sword, Don Giovanni himself goes to the entrance
and throws the door open. There stands the Commendatore. Like
the trumpets of the Last Judgment, the whole orchestra, including
the trombones, intones the theme we have heard in the Overture.

"Don Giovanni, you have invited me to supper. I have come!" Here are the murderer and the murdered man confronting each other in stark confrontation, Leporello having prudently hidden himself under the table.

Supernatural though the apparition is, it has not bled Don Giovanni of his courage. "I would never have believed it," he answers, "but I will do what I can to entertain you. Leporello, have another plate brought at once." "I do not feed on mortal food," rejoins the statue. "A different need has brought me here." "What do you want?" "Brief must I be. You invited me. Now it is your turn. Answer me—will you come to sup with me?" Throughout this colloquy we hear Leporello's frantic side appeals, a comic counterpoint to the nocturnal scene, in which all three voices heard are dark voices.

"I have made up my mind," responds Don Giovanni. "My heart is firm within my breast. I will come."

"Give me your hand in pledge," the statue demands. As he does so, Don Giovanni cries out in pain. The icy cold of that deadly grip overwhelms him. Now the statue commands what Elvira has pleaded for: "Repent, change your life. It is your last chance." The statue's repeated *"Pentiti!"*—"Repent!"—strike like blows. Freeing himself with an enormous effort, Don Giovanni remains true to his creed. He will not. "No, you foolish old man, I do not repent." "Ah!" replies the statue, as he turns to go, "there is no longer time." A hush comes upon the orchestra as the statue disappears. A moment after, flames shoot out from all sides, the earth trembles, the spirits of Hell assail the Don—we hear their muted chorus from below—and with a cry of pain and at last of terror Don Giovanni is swallowed by the fire. His palace falls into ruins.

In the Epilogue, Elvira, Zerlina, Anna, Ottavio, and Masetto assemble to inquire what has happened to the scoundrel for whom they are still searching. Leporello appears and assures them that they will never find him. He relates in brief the visit of the man of stone and the circumstances of Don Giovanni's end. Don Ottavio turns to Donna Anna. "Now that heaven has avenged our wrong, grant me my desire, let me not languish in vain." Once more Anna pleads for a postponement. She wants yet a year wherein to spend her grief. The others make plans for the future. Elvira will retire to a convent to end her days. As for Zerlina and Masetto, they will go home to sup together. Leporello will hie himself to an inn to find himself a worthier master.

The opera ends with a sextet ("*Questo è il fin di chi fa mal*"), to the sentiment that such is the end of all evildoers. The sextet is clearly a musical coda to the great score. At one time it was the fashion to omit the final scene, ending the opera with Don Giovanni's death. Fortunately we have now thought better of the practice. It is as impossible to omit the Epilogue as it is to snip an inch from the corner of a canvas. The sextet is a return to the "*giocoso*" and reminds us that Mozart encompassed both the supernatural and the conventional, that the demonic elements meet the life of the day, that the work contains the sinner, the sinned-against, and the indifferent, that in its music the flirtatiousness of a Zerlina, the gentleness of an Elvira, the fatty conceit of a Leporello, and the lean pride of the man who would not or could not conform to morality are vividly realized. Mozart created a world: it is a world of contrasts.

FIDELIO

COMPOSER:	Ludwig van Beethoven
LIBRETTISTS:	Josef Sonnleithner
	Georg Friedrich Treitschke
FIRST PERFORMANCE:	November 20, 1805
	Theater an der Wien, Vienna
RECEPTION:	Mild success in its revised version of 1814

CHARACTERS:

Jacquino, a young turnkey	Tenor
Marzelline, his betrothed	Soprano
Rocco, a jailer	Bass
Leonore (Fidelio)	Soprano
Don Pizarro, governor of the prison	Baritone
Florestan, husband of Leonore	Tenor
Don Fernando, Minister of Justice	Bass

FIDELIO

In 1902 I was surprised to learn, when I wrote the programme notes for the Meiningen Concerts, that it showed "paralysis of mind" to speak of Fidelio as if it were a good opera. My surprise was caused by no doubts as to the defects of Fidelio, which had been as obvious to me as to any intelligent child of my age when I first heard it in Berlin in 1888. And, lest I should miss them or be misled by them then, they were explicitly pointed out to me by certain spiritual pastors who worshipped every note of the music and almost every word of the text. What surprised me was that, even in 1902, anybody should still be so unused to the defects of Fidelio as to suppose that they mattered. We know that Paradise Lost conspicuously fails in its purpose to "justify the ways of God to man." That failure is a defect, just as many features in the music and libretto of Fidelio are defects. But we also know that blank verse will not rhyme, that heroic couplets will not make Miltonic verse-paragraphs, and that the first irruption of spoken dialogue into music produces a disagreeable shock if you do not expect it. The old-stager school of critics does not always show that it can distinguish the working hypotheses of art-forms from defects of execution.
DONALD FRANCIS TOVEY, *Essays in Musical Analysis*

Fidelio is an opera which does not live and cannot die. It has a difficult time maintaining its place in the repertoire, each attempt ending in failure. Yet it does not altogether drop out of the repertoire, each failure being succeeded by a new attempt. Musicians, critics, and the public are divided in their opinion. One learns that Beethoven simply could not write for the voice, that neither here nor in the *Missa Solemnis* nor in the last movement of the Ninth Symphony nor in his songs could the composer find proper vocal projection of his ideas. One is told that *Fidelio*'s music is not true music for the stage, that it expresses the action but haltingly and illuminates the characters but dimly. What better clue than Beethoven's several revisions and reworking of the opera? Does this not prove that the composer himself was dissatisfied? Does not the fact that he never again attempted an opera show his essential incompatibility with this art form? To many an unanalytical music lover the matter is even simpler: *Fidelio* is a work which must be regarded reverently but which, to speak plainly, is a bore. They'd exchange the whole opera for the one overture, the Leonore No. 3.

But there are others. Yes, there are others to whom *Fidelio* is a treasurable opera. For them, it is a work apart, to be set above an evening's entertainment, a moving experience, a restorative of faith, a fresh estimate of moral capacity. Acknowledging certain weaknesses of the opera, those of us who love *Fidelio*—and we number the learned Donald Francis Tovey among our company—feel that Beethoven knew very well what he was doing, that the music is in a high sense stageworthy, that Leonore's aria can be sung without a vocal rupture, and that mastery is to be found in most of the ensembles and choruses. Quite recently a French critic, discussing an imminent revival of *Fidelio* at the Paris Opera, wrote: "France, which idolizes Beethoven as a composer of symphonies, quartets, and sonatas, has never acknowledged the dramatic genius which nonetheless he possesses. We admit that the opera contains some good tunes, a trio full of life, a fine quartet, and some effective choruses, but we remain insensible to the strength of the drama which is set before us."

What is the cause of this insensibility? What are the obstacles which block understanding?

Let us first note that *Fidelio* does not "play itself." It is by no means easy to perform. It either comes off—or it is intolerably tedious. The demand for exceptionally fine interpreters is severer here than in most operas—severer than in Verdi, Puccini, Bizet, and perhaps even Wagner—and these must include a conductor who understands *both* opera and Beethoven, and a Leonore who can sing, act, and speak the spoken lines. That is quite a bill of particulars. Consider: She must be able to sing her great aria, the vocal demands of which are cruel and even a little impractical (that much must be conceded). She must be able to handle lines which are something less than deathless dialogue but which must be spoken with conviction. She must combine in herself both the power of dominating the dramatic climaxes and the womanly sweetness which is the essence of Leonore's character. Let her lack either, and Leonore becomes either a virago or a ninny. Lastly, the opera demands that she give the illusion of being able to carry off her male disguise.[1] Let her be of mammalian amplitude, and, on her first appearance as a boy in the service of Rocco, the irreverent are bound to snicker. Wagner tells us in his autobiography of the searing impression Schroeder-Devrient, the first of the famous Leonores, made on him. Berlioz, too, was inspired by Mr. Schroeder-Devrient not only was an exceptional artist, but at the time Wagner first heard her she was a young girl in her twenties. Alas, young sopranos usually cannot sing the part, older sopranos cannot look it.

A further difficulty lies in the sequence of music alternating with spoken text, a combination usual enough in Beethoven's time but now a form to which we have become unused.[2] Unlike *Carmen*, *Fidelio* is not given with recitatives which somebody has added later. No doctoring is possible; one attempt was made years ago at the Metropolitan, with disastrous results. The alternation of song and dialogue creates some extraordinary effects. But it is irritating if one does not understand German. Even if one does, one has to get used to it.

Yet, as we said at the beginning, with all these difficulties the work refuses to remain among those operas by famous composers —Schubert, Schumann, Mendelssohn, Berlioz—which are shelved for good and all. Sooner or later an opera manager, a conductor, a new soprano tries once again, knowing in advance that the new presentation may turn out, like the last one, to be only a labor of love. Among the audience hearing this presentation there will be some who will go home sensing that they have come in contact

---

[1] "Most Leonores look like the Soviet women competitors in the Olympic games." Vincent Sheehan.

[2] We accept it in musical comedy. It bothers us in serious opera.

with a work of great art. If many of the lines and a little of the music are naïve, that naïveté can be forgiven; it springs not from ineptitude but from a man's occupation with an ideal world.

No documents exist to show what it was that attracted Beethoven to the subject so strongly that he chose it knowing that it had been set to music three times previously. Its original treatment had been, in France at least, a popular opera; it was called *Léonore, ou l'Amour Conjugal,* with a libretto by J. J. Bouilly,[3] the music composed by Pierre Gaveau. The opera, which premiered in 1798, was a success, and Beethoven must have known about it. A second treatment was made by Ferdinand Paër, another well-known composer. This opera, *Eleanora,* was produced in Dresden in 1804, at a time when Beethoven was already occupied with his own *Fidelio.* A third version, by Simon Mayr, was given the following spring in Padua. Why this general popularity of the subject? Because in the period succeeding the French Revolution of 1789 and the ensuing Reign of Terror the theme of political subjugation was as much in the air as it is today. According to Bouilly, his libretto was based on an actual incident which occurred in France during the Reign of Terror. As a precaution, however, he transferred the scene to the Spain of the sixteenth century. The play belongs to the type of drama then known as "Rescue Drama." Sonnleithner, who adapted Bouilly's libretto for Beethoven, was an official of the Burgtheater (the Viennese repertory theater), and as such was quite familiar with currently popular plays and what made them so.

Though we cannot prove what interested Beethoven in the theme, we may conjecture that there were two aspects. The first was his belief in freedom, his abhorrence of any form of oppression, his hatred of political tyranny. The second may have been a compensatory reason, a desire to express in music a condition he had never experienced, a feeling he had never known. Conjugal love, with the loyalty, the order, the calm which such love implies, may have represented to this man forever in conflict with the world around him an ideal which he knew to be for him unobtainable.

The high moral tone of the libretto made an appeal to him. He looked for a didactic uplift in all the subjects which he was considering—and he did consider many—and he confessed that as far

[3] He was the librettist of Cherubini's *The Water Carrier,* an opera Beethoven admired.

as he was concerned, he would not have been able to set *Don Giovanni* to music as Mozart did, the subject being too "immoral" for him. Was this, too, compensation? Did he subconsciously wish to atone in his art for a certain moral dubiousness which made him as a human being less than admirable? Can we read into *Fidelio* a self-apology for his meddling quarrel with his sister-in-law?

We are on more certain grounds when we state that he took the greatest pains with the composition of the opera, proceeding with the scenes in order, as if to assure himself of dramatic continuity. He made eighteen attempts at Florestan's aria before he found what he wanted. The final chorus was arrived at after many sketches. From internal evidence it is clear that Beethoven's deepest interest belonged to the figure of Leonore. As the opera unfolds, we can see how Beethoven coasted along with pretty but fairly conventional music; the two opening numbers are no doubt better music than that produced by the average operatic practitioner of the turn of the century but hardly what we expect from Beethoven. The moment Leonore enters, the moment she steps on the stage carrying a physical burden which proves almost too much for her woman's strength and a mental burden at the heaviness of which we can as yet only guess—from that moment on we feel that Beethoven was moved to the very center of his heart. The other characters in the opera are conventional or, worse, nothing at all. Pizarro is simply black villainy incarnate, Rocco the foolish father who, as usual, gets everything wrong, and Jacquino and Marzelline are stock *"Singspiel"* (literally "a play with songs," a musical comedy) figures who owe their existence to the wish of the composer to use two light voices for contrast. Even Florestan, whose music lies on a higher plane, is but a background figure. But Leonore is a great, a truly Beethovian creation.

This is not the place to detail at length the revisions to which Beethoven subjected the opera after its first performance, nor the complicated chronology of the four overtures. (There is some evidence that he was considering a fifth.) Suffice it to say that the early stage history of the opera was not a happy one. Beethoven had finished the work in the summer of 1805. It was produced on the twentieth of November of that year; a less propitious time could hardly have been found. The week before, Napoleon had occupied Vienna and was now ensconced in the summer palace of

Schönbrunn. The boom of French cannons was still to be heard in the city. Those Viennese citizens who could afford it had fled from the city. Those who could not thought it best to stay unobtrusively at home. The audience consisted therefore mostly of French soldiers and officers who no doubt wandered into the theater for want of something to do, as soldiers away from home will, and were confronted by a stage work of which most of them could not have understood a word. It was as if *The Cherry Orchard* were to be presented to an audience of British Horse Guards. In addition, the performance seems to have been a poor one, inadequately rehearsed. The opera failed, and after two more performances Beethoven withdrew it.

But it was hardly conceivable that a major work by the most eminent composer of Vienna, if not of all Europe, should be forgotten. As early as the following month a meeting was held in the house of Beethoven's patron Prince Lichnowsky, at which such friends were present as Treitschke (of whom more in a moment), Sebastian Meier, the baritone who had sung Pizarro (he was Mozart's brother-in-law), Clement, leader of the violins, and the young tenor Röckel, newly arrived in Vienna, to whom we owe many a valuable Beethoven reminiscence. As, for example, an account of this meeting, the purpose of which was the saving of the work through revisions:

As the whole opera was to be gone through, we went directly to the work. Princess Lichnowsky played on the grand piano from the great score, and Clement, sitting in a corner of the room, accompanied with his violin the whole opera by heart, playing all the solos of the different instruments. The extraordinary memory of Clement having been universally known, nobody was astonished by it except myself. Meier and I made ourselves useful by singing as well as we could, he the lower, I the higher parts. Though the friends of Beethoven were fully prepared for the impending battle, they had never seen him in that excitement before, and without the prayers and entreaties of the Princess, an invalid, who was a second mother to Beethoven and acknowledged by himself as such, his united friends were not likely to have succeeded in an enterprise they had undertaken without confidence. . . .

When after their efforts from seven until after one o'clock, the sacrifice of the three members was accomplished, and when we, exhausted, hungry and thirsty, went to revive ourselves with a splendid supper—then none was happier and gayer than Beethoven. His fury had been replaced by exhilaration. He saw me, opposite to him, intently occupied with a French dish and asked me what I was eating. I answered: "I don't know," and with his lion's voice he roared out: "He eats like a wolf without knowing what! Ha, ha, ha!"

The revised *Fidelio,* in two acts instead of three, was put on the stage on the twenty-ninth of March, 1806, and it was on that occasion that the Overture played was the tremendous one we now know as Leonore No. 3. The second version of the work fared better and might have broken through to success. At this moment, however, Beethoven suffered one of those attacks of mistrust to which he was prone. He thought he was being cheated of his share of the receipts and he accused Baron Braun, the intendant of the theater. The Baron protested, pointing out that only the higher-priced seats had thus far been sold, the galleries being empty.

"I do not write for the galleries," said Beethoven.

"No?" replied Braun. "My dear sir, even Mozart did not disdain to write for the galleries."

That was the end of that. Beethoven took back the score. "There will be no more performances."

It was the last of *Fidelio* for eight years.

During those eight years Beethoven's fame had grown even more. In view of his popularity, three members of the Court Theater who were entitled to a benefit performance conceived the idea that the most lucrative box-office draw and attractive novelty they could bring forward for their benefit would be a revival of *Fidelio.* They approached the composer, who agreed, provided that the libretto should once more be recast and that this work should be entrusted to the aforementioned Georg Friedrich Treitschke, an experienced poet and stage manager, in whom Beethoven had confidence. Treitschke suggested a number of changes. One of them was the conversion of the last scene to a scene of bright daylight; in the previous versions the whole of the concluding action took place in the dungeon, and the continuous dark must certainly have been hard on the audience. Beethoven for once proved himself tractable and was delighted by the changes Treitschke suggested. So the opera was given in its third and final form on the twenty-third of May, 1814. On that occasion, at last, the opera was a success.

Much more could be said of the early history of the opera.

Enough has been said to render plausible Beethoven's remark (as reported by Schindler, who is not always reliable) that no work of his caused him greater pangs, yet no work did he love more. *Fidelio* belongs to a period in the composer's creative career in which some of his best-loved children were born, the period of the "Waldstein" and the "Appassionata" sonatas, the "Eroica" Symphony, the Fourth Piano Concerto, and the Fourth and Fifth Symphonies.

If what we have written will be interpreted as a piece of special pleading—that is what it is meant to be. *Fidelio* richly rewards the expenditure of a little imagination, a little predisposing affection on our part.

ACT I

After the *Fidelio* Overture, which is a beautiful, succinct piece of music, appropriate to its purpose, the curtain rises to show us the courtyard of the state prison near Seville. At the back is the main entrance, with a postern gate and a porter's lodge; the cells of the prisoners on the left are behind heavily barred iron doors. The jailer Rocco's house is near the foreground. On the right are the trees of the castle garden and a gate opening on the garden.

Marzelline, Rocco's pretty daughter, is busy ironing the household linen. The young porter of the prison, Jacquino, is at the moment interrupting his work for the purpose of enjoying a confidential chat with Marzelline, with whom he is in love. "At last we are alone" (*"Jetzt, Schätzchen, jetzt sind wir allein"*), he begins. But Marzelline is quite obviously bored with him. To his question "Why cannot things be as they used to be?" she gives him an evasive reply. She is relieved when there is a loud knock at the door and Jacquino has to hurry away to attend to the opening of it. In an aside she tells us that she feels sorry for the suffering she causes Jacquino, but what can she do? She has fallen head over heels in love with Fidelio. When Jacquino returns, her part of the conversation becomes ever more snippish, though he won't take no for an answer.

The little duet is followed by a short spoken dialogue, interrupted by Rocco's voice summoning Jacquino. Reluctantly he goes off once more, leaving Marzelline alone. She now sings a solo aria, expressing her longing to be united with Fidelio—*"O wär' ich schon mit dir vereint.*" It is a pretty enough aria, the orchestral accompaniment in the section in which she plunges into visions of happiness being particularly attractive. All in all, though, the two opening numbers are more or less of a stage wait.

At the conclusion of the aria Rocco enters, inquiring whether Fidelio has returned. He is due back with the dispatches which the jailer is to deliver to the Governor. As soon as the words are spoken there is a knock at the door and Leonore enters. It is she who is "Fidelio." She is disguised as a boy and calls herself by that name (the name is of course symbolic). She wears a simple costume—dark trousers and a red doublet. In addition to the letters, she is carrying the purchases which Rocco commissioned her to make. It appears that she buys well, cheaper than he himself could. Rocco attributes the young man's zeal to a desire to make himself agreeable in Marzelline's eyes. Leonore protests that it is not for the sake of a reward that she performs her duty, but Rocco replies that he cannot be fooled: he knows how to read Fidelio's thoughts.

The situation is now becoming clear: Marzelline is infatuated. Leonore, playing a dangerous game of disguise, has acted so as to give the young girl cause for hope. She could hardly have acted differently. We will learn in a moment that, at whatever cost to herself, Leonore must penetrate the secret of the prison, probe whether the man she loves is still alive, whether a ray of hope, however feeble, remains for the safety of her husband Florestan. As for Rocco, not only does he genuinely like the young "man," but he finds in Fidelio a convenient assistant.

At this dramatically right moment the four characters begin a quartet ("*Mir ist so wunderbar*"—"How strange I feel"), each voicing his own thoughts. Marzelline continues to dream of winning Fidelio's love; Leonore considers the peril which surrounds her on all sides; Rocco expresses his satisfaction at the young couple's future happiness; and Jacquino, who has reentered, wonders if there is anything he can do in a situation which has gone so much against him. Beethoven cast the quartet in canon form, a form in which each voice is committed to sing precisely the same melody. Yet we can hear that these four people are each guided by feelings and motives belonging to him- or herself alone. How this effect is achieved we cannot tell; but it is achieved, and the sum of the four we can call sublime music. The mood is set by a quiet orchestral preamble, grave and intense, which foreshadows the Beethoven of the last quartets. The voices are blended with unparalleled beauty.

The quartet having come to an end, we descend once more to a lower plane. The spoken dialogue is resumed, with Rocco declaring at once, much to Marzelline's pleasure and Leonore's confusion, that Fidelio shall become his son-in-law the day after the Governor's departure. But as a practical father he warns them that more than true love is requisite to happiness. Something else is indispensable. What that something is he tells us at great length in the "Gold" aria. The aria is pulled in by the hair, and neither its text—which vents the surprising philosophy that poverty is not agreeable—nor its music is distinguished. We may surmise that Beethoven, buckling under the necessity of giving the leading bass something to do, could not find the right inspiration and wrote a typical old-fashioned *arietta*. If not he, then certainly his advisers saw its clumsiness, for they persuaded him to omit it from the second version of the opera; it was later restored in the third version.[4]

Leonore replies that for her there exists something even more precious than gold; that is, her employer's confidence. Does she as yet enjoy this confidence? How often has she not noticed Rocco returning breathless and exhausted from the subterranean dungeons. Could she not accompany him and help him in his work? That is difficult; Rocco's orders are that no one is to be admitted to the political prisons. "Think of yourself," begs Marzelline, and the old man admits that sooner or later he will have to ask the Governor's permission to let his assistant enter the secret prisons, the work proving too strenuous for him alone. There is, however, one cell to which no one but himself can be admitted. "That," remarks Marzelline, "must be where the prisoner lies of whom you have spoken several times." "Has he been there long?" Leonore asks. "More than two years." "Two years!" The cry escapes Leonore's lips. But she regains her self-control at once. "He must be a great criminal." "Or he must have powerful enemies, which comes to the same thing," Rocco replies. He does not know the name of the prisoner nor does he want to know. It is dangerous for simple people to be privy to secrets. At any rate, the man will not trouble him much longer. "Oh, God!" exclaims Leonore under her breath.

---

[4] The aria is sometimes omitted today, as for example in the Salzburg performances under Karajan.

Marzelline begs her father not to subject Fidelio to the ordeal of
seeing this unfortunate man. Leonore interposes hastily, "Why not?
I have courage and strength." This is the cue for a trio in which the
orchestra at the very outset indicates the force of Leonore's resolution. Indeed, she has courage and strength, all the courage that
is required (*"Gut, Söhnchen, gut"*).

It is time now for Rocco to take the dispatches to Pizarro, the
Governor. (As the first scene is sometimes played in a small room,
it is customary in some productions of *Fidelio* to change the scene
here to a courtyard. An uninterrupted flow of action, as originally
intended, is preferable.) A military march is heard; a group of
soldiers go through the business of presenting arms. Pizarro enters.
He enters scowling and barks his orders: three sentries are to mount
the wall, six to guard the drawbridge, another six the garden. Anyone approaching the fortress is to be brought to Pizarro at once.
He then peruses the dispatches which Rocco has brought him.
Suddenly he starts. Among the papers he finds an anonymous
letter, though Pizarro thinks he recognizes the handwriting. The
letter reads: "The Minister has been apprised of the fact that in
the state prisons over which you preside there languish several victims of arbitrary force. He is setting out tomorrow to surprise you
with a visit of inspection. Be on your guard!" For a moment Pizarro
quakes. If it were to be discovered that one of the prisoners was
Florestan? No—there must be a way out. There is. A bold deed
will resolve the situation. The man must die—and at once. And he
launches into the famous "Revenge" aria (*"Ha! Welch' ein Augenblick!"*—"What a moment is this!").[5] Now that he has determined his course of action, Pizarro foretastes the bitter pleasure of
slaking his hatred. He shall plunge the dagger into his adversary's
heart. Watching him die, he shall cry "Triumph!" in his ear. The
aria is as turbulent as a sudden thunderstorm, with the orchestra
supplying the thunder and Pizarro's phrases flashing like lightning

---

[5] We owe to Schindler a charming anecdote about this aria. Sebastian Meier, who, as
we have mentioned, was the first Pizarro, boasted that he could sing anything, no matter
how difficult. Just to take Meier down a peg, Beethoven composed a passage in the aria
in which the voice moves over a series of scales played by the strings in such a way as
to form minor seconds with the melodic line. The interval being difficult, Meier lost the
pitch, the more so as the orchestra, understanding the joke, maliciously emphasized the
minor seconds. Snorting with rage, Meier hurled at the composer the accusation: "My
brother-in-law Mozart would never have written such damned nonsense!"

through the murk. The violence of the aria is heightened by contrast: as Pizarro unleashes his wrath, a group of soldiers ask in whispered wonder what is the cause of their leader's distracted behavior.

Everything must be readied for the deed to be done before the Minister arrives. Pizarro calls the captain of the guard and instructs him to climb to the lookout of the tower, taking a trumpeter with him. He is to fix his eyes on the road leading from Seville. As soon as he sees a carriage approaching, the trumpeter is to give a signal. Does he understand? He is to obey on pain of death!

As his next measure, Pizarro summons Rocco; without the old man's help, or at least compliance, nothing can be done (*"Jetzt, Alter!"*). The curious duet between Pizarro and Rocco, a duet for two deep voices, juxtaposes Pizarro's mania with Rocco's scruples. The colloquy is overheard by Leonore, hidden from the two men. At first Pizarro attempts to bribe Rocco. He will be rich if he carries out orders. To the question, "What would you have me do?" Pizarro replies, "Murder!" Rocco protests in shock. Murder? Murder is no part of his duty. But his protest cannot swerve Pizarro's course. "Very well. If your courage fails you, I myself will do the deed. You are merely to go down to the cell and dig a grave. This done, I shall enter, my face concealed: one blow, and it is over." It is understood that they are both speaking of the man, hardly more than a ghost, who lies in the deepest dungeon. Rocco comforts himself with the thought that after the endless suffering this man has undergone, death would be a boon.

The assignation fixed, the two men depart, and Leonore bursts onto the stage. In her great recitative and aria, one of the greatest conceived by any composer, she reveals herself and her purpose, and shows us the stature of her nobility.

An agitated figure for the strings precedes the aria: *"Abscheulicher! Wo eilst du hin? Was hast du vor?"*—"Loathesome being! Whither are you bent? What is your purpose?" She pours out her horror of Pizarro, who is deaf to the call of pity, deaf to the voice of humanity. His mind seems to her like the furious sea, tossing in a paroxysm of evil. Yet to Leonore, confronted with so much evil, all is not dark; she sees the light of a rainbow, rising above dark clouds. Old memories, thoughts of peace, recollections of former tranquillity, are awakened in her. There follows a short *adagio* orchestral introduction, in which the horns play a famous (very difficult) passage; then Leonore begins to pay tribute to hope, "the last star of tired souls." Let not that star fade in the sky! Let it continue to shine with its mild light so that it may guide her way, illumine her goal. However far off that goal, her love will reach it. There is nothing love cannot accomplish. In that thought lies the essence of the aria; in it lies the essence of Beethoven's feeling. Then the tempo changes to *allegro,* and Leonore's soliloquy veers from prayer to resolve. She will remain true to her inner impulse. She is able to bear any burden, suffer all pain, for the sake of the one she loves and who now lies in chains. As she sings of her husband, the music gains strength and fire, to end in a jubilant climbing scale.

As Leonore leaves the stage, Marzelline and Jacquino run in. They quarrel, the subject being once again this strange youth, Fidelio, who came from no one knows where, and now seems to have charmed everybody. Rocco and Leonore re-enter from the garden, and Rocco cuts the quarrel short. Leonore once more attempts some way of gaining access to the prisoners. She now suggests that, the weather being clement, it would be just the right day to grant the wish she has expressed so often, to allow the prisoners a short sight of sunlight, a little respite in the garden. Rocco hesitates. Could he grant this mercy without Pizarro's express permission? Marzelline slyly suggests that her father's interview today with Pizarro seemed long. Could it be that Pizarro asked her father for a favor? If so, then it is likely that he'd be less exacting. "Quite right," replies Rocco. "Very well, then, Jacquino and Fidelio, open the upper cells. Meanwhile I myself will go to Pizarro and engage him in conversation to detain him." Jacquino and Leonore at once carry out his orders.

Slowly and hesitantly, blinking in the unaccustomed light, hardly daring to believe in their unwonted fortune, the prisoners emerge. They exclaim over the sight of daylight; they marvel at the experience of breathing fresh air, while the orchestra surrounds their timid song with tender phrases (*"O welche Lust!"*). One of the prisoners ventures to utter a hope for the future: with God's help, perhaps one day they will be set free. But another admonishes him to speak low; all around them hostile eyes and ears are watching and listening. A simple and a moving paean! Gradually the prisoners move toward the garden, while Leonore eagerly scans their faces in the hope of recognizing her husband among them.

Rocco returns with remarkable news: not only has Pizarro given his permission to Fidelio's marriage to Marzelline, but he has consented to Fidelio's being allowed to descend into the dungeon. This very day he may do so. Leonore cries out, "This very day! This very day! What happiness!" "Yes," continues Rocco, "in a moment or two we shall go down to where lies the man who, for many weeks now, has been given less and less nourishment." "Will he be set free?" asks Leonore. "On the contrary! Within an hour his grave is to be dug." "Are you, Rocco, going to kill him?" "Not I. It is the Governor who will do the deed. You and I will merely prepare the grave." "Perhaps my husband's grave," Leonore murmurs distractedly.

Leonore's exclamation, "This very day!"—"*Noch heute?*"—begins a duet to which are later joined two other voices, then still another, and finally the chorus. The practice of building the close of an act through a successive increase in the number and mass of voices is one which Beethoven may well have learned from Mozart. It is significant that, now that the characters have been introduced, the situation laid bare before the audience, now that the moment of action is drawing nearer, Beethoven relies solely on music. From the prisoners' entrance to the fall of the curtain there is no spoken dialogue.

Rocco details the help he requires from Leonore. Though inwardly she is trembling, she puts up a fine show of confidence: "I shall follow you wherever you wish." Yet she cannot altogether hide the fear of what she is to discover, the shudder before uncertainty. Adept as she is at disguise, this time she cannot prevent her eyes from filling with tears. Rocco notices it and at once determines to spare her the ordeal; he will go down by himself. Against this suggestion Leonore remonstrates so earnestly that the old man agrees to revert to the original plan. Such is the substance of the duet.

At this moment Marzelline and Jacquino break in with the agitating report that Pizarro, having learned of Rocco's indulgence to the prisoners, is on his way here, storming and menacing and swearing that he will punish the jailer. He enters hard upon this announcement. To his question, by what right did Rocco extend such leniency, Rocco answers that today being the name day of the King, a little mercy might be considered a good stroke of diplomacy. Drawing nearer to Pizarro, he whispers that the man destined for death is not among those who were permitted to leave their cells. This quiets Pizarro somewhat. But Rocco is never again to arrogate to himself a similar liberty. The prisoners are to be returned to their captivity at once; Rocco is to go below and dig the grave.

With a sad farewell to the sunlight, the prisoners slink back. How brief was their taste of happiness! In the last section of the finale, each of the principals joins the chorus, Marzelline pitying the prisoners, Jacquino still being sorry for himself, Pizarro reiterating his commands to Rocco, Rocco assuring him that he shall not delay to carry out his wishes, and Leonore asking whether justice has departed from the world. After the concerted climax, the act ends with a few quiet chords in the orchestra; after the tension, the clock seems to run down.

ACT II

Scene One

We now come to the scene which from both a musical and a dramatic point of view is the most stirring of the opera. All that can be said of Beethoven's power as a dramatist can be attested to by the excitement, the vitality of participation which the scene evokes. The progression of the scene from deepest dark and sepulchral despair to the strong light thrown into the dungeon by the open door and the flood of hope suddenly admitted, that progression is at once theatrically telling and symbolic. The dungeon scene passes the test on two levels: as a piece of entertainment behind the footlights it is successful; yet it shares with other works of high art the task of clarifying for us the positive side of man's soul. This ethical function lies beyond entertainment, yet is compatible with it.

The quality of the scene is foreshadowed by an orchestral introduction, one which I think has been insufficiently appreciated because it is overshadowed by the fame of the overtures. All the same, it is an extraordinary piece of mood painting. After four harsh chords, we hear an anguished, low, chromatic phrase which rises into several outbursts of grief. A repeated figure in the strings, combined with the throb of the kettledrum, further accentuates the gloom.

We are in the deepest part of the prison. At the back a flight of steps leads upward; at the left there is a mass of ruins and stones; at the right Florestan is sitting, chained to the wall.

Florestan breaks his silence with the cry, "Oh, God, what darkness here! How awful is this silence, how cruel my ordeal!" Like Leonore in her aria, he too has not abandoned hope. A just God exists. Again like Leonore, he recalls former days, his mind dwelling on the cause of his imprisonment. *"In des Lebens Frühlingstagen"*—"In the springtime of life"—he dared to speak the truth; these chains were his reward. Yet in all his misfortune the one thought that consoles him is the thought that he did his duty. Then, as the tempo of the aria quickens, he seems to fall into a light-headed ecstasy. He senses a sweet air filling this room, a bright light surrounding him on the threshold of death. That air, that light, emanate from an angel. Leonore is that angel. She shall stand by his side and conduct him to the freedom of the heavenly realm. After this vision, he sinks down exhausted.

It is this aria which gave Beethoven no end of trouble. He recast it for the 1814 version, with the help of Treitschke, because he was persuaded that a more solid aria was needed for the tenor than the one he had originally written. (Some critics believe that the original [1805] version of the aria is superior.) [6]

---

[6] This is the story of the revised aria according to Treitschke: "The second act offered a great difficulty at the very outset. Beethoven at first wanted to distinguish poor *Florestan* with an aria, but I offered the objection that it would not be possible to allow a man nearly dead of hunger to sing bravura. We composed one thing and another; at last, in my opinion, I hit the nail on the head. I wrote words which describe the last blazing up of life before its extinguishment.

"What I am now relating will live forever in my memory. Beethoven came to me about seven o'clock in the evening. After we had discussed other things, he asked how matters stood with the aria. It was just finished, I handed it to him. He read, ran up and down the room, muttered, growled, as was his habit instead of singing—and tore open the pianoforte. My wife had often vainly begged him to play; today he placed the text in front of him and began to improvise marvellously—music which no magic could hold fast. Out of it he seemed to conjure the motive of the aria. The hours went by, but Beethoven improvised on. Supper, which he had purposed to eat with us, was served, but —he would not permit himself to be disturbed. It was late when he embraced me, and declining the meal, he hurried home. The next day the admirable composition was finished."

Rocco and Leonore now enter. What follows was technically known as a "Melodrama," the term denoting the use of music with spoken dialogue (melo-drama). "How cold it is in this underground vault!" Leonore exclaims. Rocco points out to her the man who is lying there quite without a sign of life. Perhaps he is dead. Drawing nearer, Rocco ascertains that he is merely asleep. They must get to work at once. Leonore tries in vain to distinguish his features. "God help me if it is he!"

Rocco finds the old well and explains to Fidelio that they shall not have to dig far to clear the opening of rubble. Looking at Fidelio, he observes that he is trembling. "Are you afraid?" Leonore replies: "No, no. But it is so cold in here!" All of these short spoken phrases are not so much accompanied by as set against short phrases by the orchestra, merely a bar or two long and without definite melody. The orchestra whispers, as do the two people, oppressed by silence and darkness.

Then, as Leonore and Rocco start the digging of the grave, the duet begins ("*Nur hurtig fort, nur frisch gegraben*"—"Let's set to work and dig in haste"). The muted strings sound a reiterated dull throb, under which we hear a dark figure for the double bassoons, the whole suggesting the digging work, without in any way being "descriptive." Rocco urges speed, as it cannot be long before Pizarro will enter. Leonore assures him that he will have no cause to complain of her zeal. She helps him as best she can to dislodge a heavy stone. But even while she is working with all her might, Leonore cannot cease for an instant remembering her true task. She swears to herself that her husband shall not become a sacrifice to Pizarro's hatred.

The dialogue is resumed. "He is awake," says Rocco. "Undoubtedly he will plague me with a thousand questions. I must speak to him alone." He clambers out of the grave and turns to Florestan to ask him if he has rested well. "Rested?" Florestan replies. "How can I ever find rest?" Weak as his voice is, Leonore seems to recognize it. If she could but see his face for a moment! A glimmer from Rocco's lantern does illumine his face. Recognizing it, Leonore falls senseless at the foot of the grave.

Florestan begs Rocco once more for information. Who is the man in charge of this prison? Rocco feels that now he can safely answer the question. On learning the dread truth, Florestan implores the jailer to send a messenger to Seville to find Leonore, his wife, and tell her that he lies here in chains in the power of his enemy. That wish Rocco cannot grant. "It will only ruin me, without helping you." "Then," begs Florestan, "if I am destined to end my life here, let me at least die quickly." "This passes all endurance," Leonore murmurs. "For pity's sake," the prisoner continues, "give me a drop of water."

Rocco, his compassion getting the better of his caution, bids Leonore bring a sip of wine from the bottle he has brought along. "Here it is, here it is!" urges Leonore, as she hurries to Florestan's side. At the sound of her voice, Florestan looks at her. "Who is this?" "My helper," Rocco replies, "and in a few days my son-in-law." He notices that Leonore is strangely moved. "Who can fail to be moved? You yourself, Master Rocco—" "It is true," admits the old man. "There is something in his voice . . ." "Yes, oh, yes—something that penetrates deep into your heart."

There follows a trio in which Florestan hopes that the two will, in a better world, earn their reward—*"Euch werde Lohn in bessern Welten."* Rocco asserts that he did what he could for this poor sufferer; and Leonore, alternating between joy and pain, questions the outcome of her enterprise. Placed in the center of this marvelous trio, there occurs an episode which fills one's heart to overflowing. Leonore asks leave to hand the prisoner a morsel of bread which she has carried with her for two days. Rocco hesitates at first, but soon consents. Leonore, offering the bread to Florestan, sings a slow, intense phrase, "Take this bread, you wretched, wretched man." To which Florestan replies with five exclamations of thanks, as if his gratitude could not arrest itself. The trio is then resumed.

After the trio, there is a moment's silence. Rocco then blows a whistle, the signal that all is ready. Guessing the meaning of the signal, Florestan starts up to cry, "Is that my death knell?" Leonore begs him to remain calm and to remember, whatever he may hear or see, that there is a Providence which watches above. Pizarro enters, muffled in his cloak. He orders Fidelio to leave, whereupon she retreats to the darkest corner of the cell. Pizarro whispers to himself that he shall have to get rid not only of Florestan but of the two witnesses to the deed, to make certain that no trace of the secret shall ever sift through. Throwing aside his cloak and drawing his dagger, he now breaks out into a shout of triumph. This is the beginning of the turbulent quartet—*"Er sterbe!"* He shall die, exults Pizarro. But first he shall know who it is who has planned this vengeance. Let him die in the fullness of knowledge that it is Pizarro, the same Pizarro whom Florestan attempted to topple. It is Pizarro, whom he ought to have feared. It is Pizarro who now stands before him. Scornfully Florestan hurls at him the epithet "assassin." Raising his dagger, Pizarro is about to plunge it when, with a rush out of the darkness, Leonore flings herself forward, covering Florestan with her body. Furiously, Pizarro attempts to push her aside. In a voice made strong by despair, she utters the great climactic cry, "Kill first his wife!"

"His wife!" both Pizarro and Rocco exclaim. "Yes, his wife. I have sworn to bring consolation to him and perdition to his enemy." Leonore draws a pistol and with firm purpose but with a trembling hand she points it at Pizarro, with the words, "One more attempt and you will die!"

At this there comes from without, still distant but completely audible, a trumpet call; it is the signal from the tower that the Minister has been sighted on the Seville road. This trumpet fanfare is of course the one we hear in the Leonore Overture No. 3. Here too the immediately following orchestral phrase is one which seems to dispatch a prayer floating to heaven. The four voices unite in wonder and astonishment. Once more, now nearer and louder, the signal sounds. Florestan is saved!

The door of the dungeon is flung open, and Jacquino appears at the top of the stairs accompanied by men carrying torches. "Master Rocco," Jacquino shouts in great excitement (his words are spoken), "the Minister has arrived. His escort is at the very gate of the fortress." "Praised be God!" replies Rocco. "We will come, we will come at once. Let the men with the torches descend and light the way for my lord the Governor." Here the spoken words, set in the middle of a musical number and immediately following the trumpet call, have an electrifying effect. The quartet resumes, or rather its second part begins, in which Leonore and Florestan express their joy, Pizarro calls down curses on this hour, and Rocco is torn between fear for his own future and relief at being released from servitude to a madman.

The torchbearers escort Pizarro from the dungeon, Rocco and Jacquino following him. Leonore and Florestan are left alone. "Oh, my Leonore, what have you done for my sake!" exclaims Florestan. Leonore replies, "Nothing, my Florestan." These are two of the most moving lines of the dialogue, because they are so simple.[7] Returning to music, the two pour out their love for each other in the duet "*O namen-, namenlose Freude!*"—"Oh, unspeakable, unspeakable joy!" Thus ends the great dungeon scene.

It is customary to interpolate here, after the fall of the curtain, the Leonore Overture No. 3. Gustav Mahler is generally credited with inaugurating this custom, though some evidence exists to indicate that the practice antedates him. It has been debated whether the Overture, a mighty music drama in itself, overtowers the opera, and therefore belongs solely in the concert hall. The fact remains, however, that it *is* played in the opera house and that the audience would feel cheated were it not to be presented.

Scene Two

The scene changes to an open space outside the prison. A march-like orchestral introduction leads into a chorus sung both by the people of Seville and the liberated prisoners, who praise the dawn of justice and mercy. During the chorus, the long-awaited Minister of State, Don Fernando, enters. Simultaneously Pizarro is escorted into his presence by a guard of soldiers. The Minister explains his mission: "The best of kings has sent me here to end the night of evil which has enveloped all of you. No longer need you kneel in slavish fear. No tyrant shall you find in me. Let brother seek brother, one aiding all." These sentiments were undoubtedly an expression of Beethoven's convictions, and it is perhaps not too wild a guess that he himself wrote or suggested the words.

Rocco makes his way through the crowd, accompanied by Leonore and Florestan. Don Fernando is astonished to find in this emaciated man standing before him his old friend whom he had long thought dead. He is equally astonished to see Leonore. It is Rocco's task to explain briefly what has happened, how she had come to him dressed as a boy, entered his service, and ingratiated herself so well that he had chosen her for his son-in-law. The disclosure of Fidelio's sex naturally fills Marzelline with confusion.

[7] They do not appear in all editions of the *Fidelio* score and are occasionally omitted in performance, for what reason I cannot fathom.

Pizarro, Rocco continues, was on the point of murdering Florestan and was prevented from the fell deed only by Fernando's arrival.

The people loudly call for Pizarro's punishment. Fernando, turning to Rocco, sets things to right, like a good *deus ex machina*: "You dug this man's grave. Now, you may unfasten his fetters. . . . But stay! That privilege belong to you, Leonore, the noblest of women." And Leonore answers in a phrase into which Beethoven concentrated the last measure of feeling: "Oh God! What a moment is this!"—"*O Gott! O Gott! Welch' ein Augenblick!*"—Florestan echoes her. With this begins the final ensemble, the greatest in the opera, in which all participate to give thanks for their deliverance. Slowly this song mounts to a climax of lucent beauty, as if it were to embrace the better part of all humanity. It is the summation of the work, Leonore's reward—and ours.

The second section of the finale is a jubilant hymn to Leonore in particular and to womanhood in general. "Let all who have won a gracious wife join in our song." These lines are taken, with a small alteration, from Schiller's "Ode to Joy," the text of which was to serve Beethoven again in the Ninth Symphony.

We first met Leonore in bourgeois surroundings. We descended with her into an airless cell. We then climbed the stairs with her into the sunlight. At the last, she has become a symbol of liberation, a standard-bearer of the freedom without which no sunlight is possible, nor any joy.

Yet, though at the end the scene becomes political and "No longer need you kneel" seems dominant in Beethoven's thought, he has not forgotten Leonore as woman, the wife so strong in her love that she dares to throw herself between a dagger and her husband's body. Here then we find a double idealism. It is easy enough to scoff at such a heaping helping of morality, or at least to find it unconvincing. It is easy enough to say that nobody as noble as Leonore could exist. Nor, as we move about the drama, does it require great perspicacity to observe its awkward corners—the impossible disguise, the obtuseness of Rocco, the highly convenient arrival of the Minister, the pale coyness of the two subsidiary characters.

These defects do not matter if we understand the work aright. There is an art which functions with disregard of probability, with unconcern for the touch of reality, with lack of apology for being naïve. The naïveté one finds in *Fidelio* is akin to the naïveté of the Pastoral Symphony with its bird calls and its thunderstorm and its village bassoonist. It can be quickly guyed if we are not prepared to take the art on its own pure terms.

If, however, we are prepared and willing, then Beethoven's legacy, his only opera, becomes infinitely valuable.

CARMEN

COMPOSER:	Georges Bizet
LIBRETTISTS:	Henri Meilhac Ludovic Halévy
FIRST PERFORMANCE:	March 3, 1875 Opéra-Comique, Paris
RECEPTION:	Neither a success nor a failure

CHARACTERS:

Don José, a brigadier	Tenor
Escamillo, a toreador	Baritone
Zuniga, a captain	Bass
Moralès, a brigadier	Baritone
Le Dancaïre	Tenor
Le Remendado	Tenor
Micaëla, a peasant girl	Soprano
Frasquita⎱ gypsies, friends of Carmen Mercédès⎰	Soprano Soprano
Carmen, a cigarette girl, and a gypsy	Mezzo-soprano

CARMEN
THE "PERFECT OPERA"

It is as easy to quote praises for *Carmen* as it is to gather clichés for the guest of honor at a testimonial dinner. *Carmen* is praised by practically everybody because it pleases practically everybody. It pleases the man who "doesn't know anything about music but knows what he likes": he likes a good tune. It pleases the steadfast operagoer, be he a Wagnerian or a Verdian. It is admired by the professional musician, *avant-garde* or conservative. It has been lauded by composers of all nations; in fact, some of the earliest and some of the most generous tributes have come from other than French sources. Brahms went to hear *Carmen* twenty times and asserted, in that gruff voice of his, that he would have gone to the ends of the world to embrace Bizet. Wagner, whose acknowledgment of his contemporaries' deserts was something less than unstinting, exclaimed, "Here, thank God, is someone who for a change has ideas!" Hans von Bülow found the music of *Carmen* "bewitching" and called it his *"Lieblings-Oper."* Tchaikovsky, in a letter to Mme. von Meck, termed it "a masterpiece in every sense of the word." Sibelius or Debussy, Richard Strauss or Gustav Mahler, one would be hard put to it to find a dissenting voice. Nietzsche, in his polemic, *The Case of Wagner*, held *Carmen* up as the example of what an opera ought to be. Contrasting Bizet to Wagner he felt that "All that is good is easy, everything divine runs on light feet." This was the first principle of his new aesthetic. He became a better man after he listened to *Carmen*. It was not only a salutary, it was a perfect artistic experience. In short, *Carmen* was the perfect opera.

The superlative stuck. It was repeated by critic after critic— was there ever one who did not contribute his own *Carmen* essay to the general accolade, from James Huneker to Paul Bekker?— and we still come across it, even in this deprecating age. Yes, the perfect opera. Not just great, not just inspired, not just successful, but perfect.

But it is not perfect. *Carmen* is the strongest and most lifeworthy product of the French operatic tradition, a tradition which it both represents and offends. This form of opera suffers certain weaknesses. Bizet could not altogether free the form, could not entirely unshackle himself from the polite conventions of the Paris Opéra-Comique, could not always replace the *"vous"* with the *"tu"* which the subject called for.

Carmen is a compromise. Probably had Bizet had a free hand and certainly had he written the opera twenty years later in a France which had begun to accept Manet's "Olympia,"[1] he would have created an even more searing work from the original story by Prosper Merimée.

From the very first Bizet fought for this story; he won the battle but he lost one or two skirmishes. The impact of the story on Bizet must have been tremendous. It must have uprooted him and filled him with a fiery enthusiasm, new to him. We know that he revolved the project in his head for several years before he set notes on paper. He must have been aware of the breach of etiquette which so tattery a tale would produce in the theater of his time, which loved to display fancy finery. It was a courageous *faux pas* which turned into a true step forward. There lies as great a distance in daring between the subject of *Djamileh*, Bizet's preceding opera, and that of *Carmen* as between Jane Austen's *Emma* and the Emma Bovary of Flaubert.

Carmen lured him irresistibly. The curious and fortunate result was that once he made the decision, once he was induced to leave

---

[1] Manet's painting, first exhibited in 1865, bears certain similarities to *Carmen*, if comparisons between the two arts are permissible. Here, too, the subject is "shocking," the treatment forthright, the style new, the effect one of life fiercely held fast. The scurrilous terms heaped on "Olympia" were shouted again at *Carmen*. "A plague on these females vomited from Hell!" wrote one critic after the premiere of *Carmen*.

the salon and to explore the back alley, Bizet found within himself
such strength as—judging by his other music—he himself did not
know he had. Again, there is enormous difference between the music of Bizet's other operas and the music of *Carmen*. Prettiness
turned into flame and charm into conviction.

Bizet's friends—there were many—must have been astonished.
Who would have suspected from this gentle man such an opera?
A tale of gypsy life composed by a composer who had never been
to Spain? The ragged theme treated by this rather dandified person, who dressed with care in the finest of linens and protected his
beautiful hands with soft buttonless suede gloves which he would
slip off and throw down with a careless gesture when he sat down
to play the piano? This often bitter-tasting music from the pen of
a man who had such a passion for sweets and cakes and *petits fours*
that he would gobble up the entire contents of a bonbon dish at
one sitting?

The story by Prosper Merimée had been published twenty-six
years before Bizet began his work. By this time Merimée was dead
(he died in 1870; *Carmen*'s premiere occurred in 1875) and his
short novel had come to be accepted as a minor classic. It was all
right to read it, but it was a different matter to use the subject for
a flesh-and-blood presentation in the theater and still quite another
matter to do so in a family theater. A family theater—that was
what the Opéra-Comique was. Bourgeois parents brought their
bourgeois daughters, fathers their sons in search of harmless culture, middle-aged government officials their aunts from the provinces. Marriages were arranged in the theater, "five or six boxes
being taken every night for that purpose." The operas composed
for such an audience were products which nicely dovetailed lachrymose librettos with pretty melodies. The librettists who collabo-
rated with the composers reached high, to the summit of literature,
to Goethe and Shakespeare and Corneille. But by the time they and
the composers got through, *Faust* or *Hamlet* or *Le Cid* came out as
nothing much more than agreeable *triste* love stories.

The librettists for *Carmen* were Henri Meilhac and Ludovic
Halévy, both experienced craftsmen of the spoken as well as of the
lyric theater. Halévy was a cousin of Bizet's wife Geneviève and
a nephew of the famous Fromental Halévy, composer of *La Juive*,
who had been Bizet's teacher. Perhaps because he was a member of

the family, it was Ludovic Halévy who broached the *Carmen* project to De Leuven, co-director of the Opéra-Comique. He explained first that the character of Carmen would be toned down; second, that "a pure Opéra-Comique character had been introduced, a very innocent, very chaste young girl"; third, that though the stage had to be peopled with gypsies and thieves, these were to be "comic gypsies." As for the death scene, it would come only at the end of a very lively act, "played in bright sunlight on a holiday." After considerable demurring, De Leuven capitulated. His final plea was, "Please try not to have her die. Death on the stage of the Opéra-Comique! Such a thing has never been seen! Never! Don't make her die, I beg of you, my dear child, don't!"[2] Six months after this conversation, De Leuven resigned, largely, it was rumored, because of his dislike of *Carmen.*

On the whole, the librettists served Bizet superbly, preserving much of the torrid atmosphere, the color, the restlessness of the story, and the psychology of Carmen herself. They fashioned a highly dramatic, compact libretto. Where they missed, Bizet missed as well.

To get the flaw out of the way, it is due to that newly introduced figure, Micaëla, of whom Halévy spoke to the director. We look in vain in the original story for "a very innocent, very chaste young girl."

This addition for decorum's sake turns out to be a simpering little country lass, "hair in plaits, with a blue apron," and her music is simpering. One feels Bizet's struggle to make her come alive, a struggle in which he did not succeed. Even her first-act duet with Don José is sentimentally blighted (*"Parle moi de ma mère"*), and at no time does Micaëla's music come up to the level of the rest of the work. Let her enter and down drops the opera into the vanilla soufflé of the French convention. That, at least, is my opinion; it is fair to add that not everybody agrees with me.

One of the most remarkable features of *Carmen*'s music lies in the absence of spectator-addressed arias, though the division into set numbers with spoken dialogue between the numbers, a tradition of the Opéra-Comique, is preserved. But all these set numbers are now so integrated into the drama that no aria-soliloquies remain;

---

2 Heroines did expire on that stage. De Leuven probably meant death by violence.

one protagonist is either singing with another or with the crowd, or
to another or to the crowd. The single exception is Micaëla's aria in
the third act. She sings it, under most unlikely circumstances, to
the audience. The tune could have been written by Gounod or
Thomas. In short, only when Bizet was being "practical" did he
slide back.

There are, to be sure, other differences between Merimée and
Bizet. In Merimée Carmen has a husband, a one-eyed horror named
García, whom Don José kills in a fight. Carmen has several more
casual affairs. She is, plainly, a thief, specializing in relieving strangers of their watches. She is more forthright in her amorality. The
band of smugglers is a ruthless organization, not at all "comic."

Merimée's story is told in the first person, the author traveling
in Spain for purposes of archaeological research. (Merimée was an
archaeologist and did travel extensively in Spain.) On a remote
plain he seeks shelter from the broiling sun, and in search of water
he discovers a cove. Another man has found shelter there before
him. The author strikes up an acquaintance with this man, who he
realizes almost immediately is a fugitive from justice. He is sympathetically drawn to the young man, and later he meets him again
at an inn, where he refuses to betray the stranger to a search party.
The stranger is, of course, Don José, who shortly after is arrested.
The author visits him in prison; there José reveals his story. Merimée
delineates the character of the young man, his early history and
gradual downfall, with greater clarity than it appears in the opera.
We feel more pity for the victim because we know him better.

These differences between narrative and drama are differences
in emphasis, not in substance. As such, they are perhaps well ad-
vised, considering that the theater is more physical than the printed
page.

Let us now turn to the opera itself and trace its story, helping
ourselves to portions of Merimée whenever such quotations aid us.

ACT I

The Prelude is a short and simple one. It gets things started, as a
prelude should, by plunging into the animated gaiety, the holiday
mood, the cheerful exuberance of the Spanish crowd, all of which
is musical material to be repeated in the last act with the entrance
of the bullfighter. The orchestra then presents the Toreador's Song,

repeats the arena music, and, changing abruptly after a dramatic pause, introduces the somber motive which in the opera represents Carmen, or rather the fate which is to overtake her.

We are on a square in Seville. On the right is the tobacco factory in which work the "cigarette girls"—so called by the young men of the town. Carmen is one of these girls. (We may wonder that a gypsy is thus gainfully and respectably employed; the explanation is furnished later.) On the left is a military guardroom, the headquarters of a regiment of dragoons. A bridge stretches across the back of the stage. A few of the dragoons are lounging about, smoking and talking. Among them is the brigadier Moralès. Other townspeople are coming and going. Moralès and the others join in the opening chorus: how pleasant it is to stroll and to regard the passing scene, they remark (*"Sur la place"*).

To the accompaniment of a charming little melody, Moralès calls the attention of his companions to a young girl who has just entered. She looks about her timidly—she is evidently a stranger from the country—while the young soldiers gallantly place themselves at her service. What is she looking for? The girl, Micaëla, replies that she is searching for a brigadier, a certain Don José. The soldiers know him, though he is not part of this particular company. Presently, at the changing of the guard, they expect him to arrive. Yes, he will be here, affirms Moralès in a rhythmic phrase which is supported by the other dragoons. Micaëla declines their flirtatious invitation to wait for Don José in their guardhouse, and with a quick *"au revoir"* takes her leave. She will return at the proper time. She sings these words to the same tune which the guards themselves have used for their invitation, a touch which helps to give a tone of banter to the entire opening scene.

A military march is heard in the distance; this is the signal for the change of the guard. The group relieved of duty line up before their officer while the new group enters, followed by a number of small boys.[3] While the guards execute the usual ritual of presenting arms and inspection, the ragamuffins line up in the same manner as do the guards, go through a hocus-pocus of their own, and sing their own military-sounding chorus. Then they strut out, still imitating the self-important air of the dragoons.

Captain Zuniga and Corporal Don José have entered, and Lieu-

---

[3] The librettists wanted them "as tiny as possible."

tenant Moralès tells José that a young girl has asked after him.
José guesses that it must be Micaëla. There follows a brief conversation between José and Zuniga, who, if we are to believe the text,
is a stranger in these parts. For he asks José if that big building opposite is not the factory where the cigarette girls are at work. Don
José replies that it is, and adds rather priggishly that the girls are
a flighty lot. "Are they pretty?" Zuniga wants to know. José says
that he has not noticed if they are; he is not interested in flirtation.
"Ah!" exclaims Zuniga, "I know what occupies you. A young girl
in a blue skirt and with her hair in plaits."

Here the omission of the dialogue is particularly to be regretted.[4]
The original libretto is much more reasonable. We learn there something of José's biography, as he tells it to his superior officer. José
was born in Navarre, was destined for a church career, but had
quarreled with a man over a game of *paume* (tennis) and had been
forced to flee the country. He enlisted in the army and hopes here
to advance successfully. In fact, José has just been assigned to new,
more important duty. Rumors have reached the authorities that
some of the girls in the cigarette factory are connected with certain smuggling activities. (We now understand why Carmen is
working in the factory.) He is to sift these rumors and ferret out
the smuggling. "That is all right," says Zuniga. "You take care of
the smuggling and I will take care of the women. Particularly one,
Carmen."

"As to the girls," José replies, "you can judge for yourself, for
here they come." The bell announcing the midday pause has rung;
it is the signal which attracts a crowd of young men. In a moment
the girls stream out of the factory, nonchalantly smoking cigarettes
—nonchalantly, that is, in present productions of the opera. In the
original production the chorus girls objected strenuously to this bit
of stage business. It made them dizzy, it made them ill; and they
threatened to strike.[5]

The young men comment on the girls and whisper to them "pro-

---

[4] The reader will remember that *Carmen* originally contained spoken dialogue. Guiraud,
a friend of Bizet's, later composed the sung recitatives which are universally used, now
that *Carmen* has become an international opera. In the conversion of spoken dialogue to
sung recitative a good deal of relevant information fell away.

[5] At one time the feeling against smoking by women was so strong that *Carmen* was
presented in Kansas City with scenery which showed the tobacco factory to be a dairy.
Carmen entered carrying a milk pail.

posals of love." This is obviously the expected ritual of flirtation. Then, in a languid chorus, its airy quality suggesting the floating upward of cigarette smoke, the feminine voices praise the pleasures of smoking. It is one of the most beautiful of the many beautiful choruses in the opera, delicately scored for muted strings, wood-winds, and harp (*"Dans l'air nous suivons des yeux la fumée"*— "We see the smoke curling in the air").

But where is Carmen? The young men have no sooner asked than she enters.

We have had all kinds of Carmens, French and German, Swedish and American; tall and short, lean and fat; behaving like obvious trollops or schoolteachers on a romp; blonde, redheaded, dark-haired; dressed in rags or in something approaching evening toi-lette; wrapped in an elaborate Spanish shawl or robed in Greek simplicity. They have entered running, gliding, undulating, charg-ing like a cavalry soldier, or slinking like a hyena. They have worn a rose in their hair or a cassia flower in their mouth or no flower at all. Yes, we've had all kinds. What then is the Carmen like whom Merimée created and whom Bizet set on the stage? This is she:

In her hair she wore a large bunch of jasmin, the petals of which ex-haled an intoxicating odour. She was simply, perhaps poorly clad, all in black, like most of the grisettes in the evening. Women of fashion wear black only in the morning; in the evening they dress *à la francesa*. When near me, my bather let slip to her shoulders the mantilla which covered her head, and by the faint light of the stars I saw that she was petite, well formed, and had very large eyes. . . . I doubt very much whether Made-moiselle Carmen was of pure blood; at least, she was infinitely prettier than any of her race that I have ever met. That a woman may be beauti-ful, say the Spaniards, she must unite thirty *sí*, or, if you please, she must merit description by the use of ten adjectives, each of them applicable to three parts of her person. For example, she should have three things black: eyes, lashes, and eyebrows; three things elegant: hands, lips, and tresses— etc. For the rest, see Brantôme.[6] My gypsy could not pretend to so many perfections. Her skin, though otherwise free from blemish, was nearly the colour of copper; her eyes oblique, but large and full; her lips a little thick, but admirably formed, and disclosing teeth whiter than blanched almonds. Her hair, perhaps a little too coarse, was black, with blue reflec-tions like a crow's wing, long and glossy. Not to tire you with a descrip-tion too minute, I will say, briefly, that to each defect she joined an

---

[6] A sixteenth-century French historian.

excellency enhanced by the contrast. It was a wild and savage beauty, a face which astonished you at first, and was never to be forgotten. Her eyes especially had an expression, at once voluptuous and fierce, that I have never met since in any other human glance. "Eye of a gipsy, eye of a wolf," is a Spanish saying which shows careful observation.

This, the author's description when he first sees Carmen, is definite enough. But we have additional instructions from Don José's lips, who tells us how Carmen looked when he first set eyes on her, the encounter corresponding exactly to her entrance in the opera:

She wore a red skirt, very short, which displayed her white silk stockings, with more than one hole in them, and tiny shoes of red morocco, tied with flame-coloured ribbon. She threw back her mantilla in order to show her shoulders and a great bunch of cassia-flowers that she wore in her chemise. She had also a cassia-flower in the corner of her mouth, and she came prancing along like a thoroughbred filly from the stud of Cordova.

Black hair, very dark eyes, copper-colored skin . . . short red skirt, white stockings, red morocco shoes—how many interpreters of Carmen make an attempt to suggest the creature envisaged by the author?

Immediately upon her entrance the tempo quickens and the young men eagerly inquire when they may expect Carmen's favors. When will she love them? Her reply—"I do not know. Perhaps never, perhaps tomorrow. But not today, that is certain"—forms the recitative which introduces the "Habanera," so called because its two-four rhythm and the melody itself are supposed to be of Cuban-Spanish origin. Whether Bizet actually used a Spanish melody—that question has been debated at length, but seems as unimportant as whether Dvořák did or did not use Negro melodies in the Symphony from the New World. For this "Habanera," as it emerged from Bizet's pen after many rewritings (thirteen, according to tradition), is entirely the composer's. Even the words are Bizet's, not Halévy's.[7]

The "Habanera" is Carmen's speculation on the nature of love; rather, on the nature of love as she knows it—"*L'amour est un oiseau rebelle.*" Love is a rebellious bird which none may tame, which follows no rule, observes no law. Her song is given an ad-

[7] See *Bizet and His World* by Mina Curtiss, for a comparison of Halévy's words and Bizet's version.

ditional amorous fillip by the whispering accompaniment of the chorus, which tends to lift the melody, and by the repeated excited interruptions to the words *"Prends garde à toi!"* Neither chorus nor orchestra can be separated from the voice—and there really ought to be a law forbidding mezzo-sopranos to sing the "Habanera" out of context in the concert hall.

At the end of the song the young men gather once more around Carmen. But she has lost interest in them as she glances at Don José. The Fate motive which we heard in the Prelude is once more brought into play by the orchestra. As Carmen retraces her steps to return to work, she takes a cassia flower from her corsage and throws it at José. A moment of silence—how well it conveys Carmen's decision!—a single dissonant chord by the orchestra, and Carmen runs off laughing, while the other girls mock José's bewilderment, to the melody of the "Habanera." The bell rings once more, the girls scamper away, and Don José is left standing alone, the flower at his feet. He picks it up. What effrontery this girl displays! Yet the perfume of the flower is strong, the flower itself is beautiful, and, if it is true that witches do exist, that gypsy assuredly is one of them.

José's musing is interrupted by the entrance of Micaëla, who bears with her a letter, a message, and a little gift of money, all from José's mother. What the message is is told in the ensuing duet by Micaëla (*"Parle moi de ma mère"*). His mother thinks of José night and day. She pardons him for leaving her and hopes that he will come back to her soon. She sends him through Micaëla a kiss, "a mother's kiss." This duet, as I have indicated, is astonishingly naïve both in words and music. Such words as "I remember my mother and I remember my little village. Oh, sweet memories of long ago!"—such words were written at a time when poets like Baudelaire and Mallarmé and Verlaine were giving a new direction to the French language. We may marvel how far French opera limped behind French letters.

After Micaëla's departure, Don José reads the letter and in another soliloquy vows, "Your son will obey you. . . . I love Micaëla and I will marry her." He dismisses from his mind "the witch and her flower."

Of a sudden there is an outcry inside the factory. The girls run out in great excitement, shouting for help. The noise brings Lieutenant Zuniga and some of the guards from the guardhouse. "It was Carmen!" scream the girls. In their effort to explain what has happened, they all speak at once, drawing Zuniga from this side to that. Bizet expresses this in a comic chorus in which the hen-cackles quite overwhelm Zuniga. José is sent into the factory to find out what caused the uproar. He returns with an angry and disheveled Carmen and the report that there had been a quarrel and that one of the girls had been injured by Carmen. (In the more explicit spoken version it appears that Carmen had slashed a girl's face, that the matter was more serious than a mere fracas, and this explanation motivates the need for stern measures against the gypsy.)

Carmen does not defend herself. All we hear from her is a "Tra-la-la-la" and a defiant "You can cut me, you can burn me, but I will say nothing." "Answer my questions!" Zuniga insists. Once again she merely replies that she will guard her secret. The melody to which Carmen offers her calm contempt is a Spanish tune and the words have a curious origin. They were taken from a poem by Pushkin, "The Gypsies," of which Merimée had made a prose translation.

Zuniga loses patience. If all she is going to do is to sing ditties, she might as well sing them in jail. The other girls are quite in accord: to jail she ought to be packed. Carmen lunges at a girl. Zuniga goes to fetch a rope. While Carmen reiterates her impudent song, with a solo violin imitating her, Zuniga tosses the rope to José. Regretfully—Zuniga is quite a ladies' man—he orders that "those pretty arms" be bound. Then he consigns Carmen to the custody of José. There follows the great scene which is to seal José's fate.

Carmen begins meekly, but from the beginning it is apparent that she feels herself the victor. "Where are you taking me?" "To prison—and there is nothing I can do about it." "I understand." "No, nothing—I obey my superiors." "Yes—but if you didn't, you would do my bidding. For you love me." José protests. But Carmen tells him that he has kept the flower which she gave him. Involuntarily his hand goes to his tunic. "The charm is working." José's answer forbidding her to speak is ineffectual. Very well, she will sing then. And sing she does, the "Seguidilla" ("Près des remparts de Séville"). Near the ramparts of Seville, on the outskirts of the town, there is a tavern run by her friend Lillas Pastia. There she dances the seguidilla and drinks Spanish wine. But it is no fun to be alone; she would like to have company. She has sent her old lover to the devil; she needs a new lover if she is to mend her heart. Don José once again and brusquely tells her to be silent. She protests that she is singing and thinking only to herself. Surely she cannot be forbidden to think; it is of a young officer who is not even a captain nor a lieutenant she is thinking. She is prepared to give her love to him. José stammers feebly. He is like a man possessed. He is drugged by the spell: if he yields to Carmen, will she keep her promise, will she love him? He unties the rope around her wrists. The melody of the "Seguidilla" is broken between the two voices, whispering in hurried conclave. Then Carmen finishes, her song emerging in triumphant confidence.

Zuniga returns, while Carmen *sotto voce* gives Don José his instructions: on their way to prison she will push him hard; he is to stumble; the rest will be up to her. To Zuniga she repeats a phrase of the "Habanera," now in slower tempo and a new tonality—another fine psychological stroke, indicating how sure of herself Carmen feels. As she and her escort reach the bridge, she pushes Don José and runs for dear life. The townspeople who have returned laugh at the bungling of the arrest, and the curtain falls.

This is the scene in Merimée:

I took Carmen by the arm. "Sister," said I politely, "you must come with me." She gave me a look as if she remembered me, but said resignedly, "Let us go, then. Where is my mantilla?"

She threw it over her head so as to show only one of her great eyes, and followed my two men as gently as a lamb. When we reached the guardhouse the quartermaster said it was a grave affair, and that she must be taken to prison. 'Twas I, too, who must conduct her there. I placed her between two dragoons, and I marched behind, as a corporal should in such a case. Thus we started for the city. At first the gypsy kept silence, but in the Street of the Serpent—you know the street, and how well it merits its name by all the windings it makes—in the Street of the Serpent she commenced by letting her mantilla drop upon her shoulders, so as to show me her pretty, wheedling face, and turning toward me as much as she could, she said:

"My officer, where are you taking me?"

"To prison, my poor child," I replied, as gently as I could, as a true soldier should speak to a prisoner, above all to a woman.

"Alas! what will become of me? Noble officer, have pity upon me! You are so young, so gentle." Then, in a lower tone, "Let me escape," she said;

"I will give you a piece of the *bar-lachi,* which will make you beloved of all women."

The *bar-lachi,* señor, is the loadstone, with which the gypsies pretend that one can work charms if one knows how to use it. Give a woman a pinch of it grated in a glass of white wine, and she cannot resist you.

I replied as seriously as I could, "We are not here to talk nonsense. You must go to prison; that's the order, and there is no help for it."

Now we Basque people have an accent by which the Spaniards can easily tell us; but in revenge there is scarcely one of them who can learn to say even *Bài, jaona* (Yes, sir). 'Twas not hard then for Carmen to know that I came from the Provinces. You know, señor, that the gypsies, having no country of their own, and always wandering from one place to another, speak all languages; and the most of them are equally at home in Portugal, in France, in the Provinces, in Catalonia—everywhere, in fact; even with the Moors and the English they can make themselves understood. Carmen knew the Basque dialect well enough. . . .

She lied, señor, she lied always. I do not know whether in all her life that girl ever spoke one word of truth; but when she spoke I believed her: she was too much for me. She spoke the Basque brokenly, yet I believed she came from Navarre; her eyes alone, her mouth, and her complexion stamped her a gypsy. I was bewitched and no longer paid attention to anything. I reflected that if the Spaniards had spoken aught against my country to me, I would have slashed them across the face as she had just treated her comrade. In brief, I was like a drunken man. I began to talk foolishly, and was ready to act likewise.

"If I were to push you, and you tumbled down, my countryman," she said in Basque, "it would not be these two Castilian conscripts who could hold me."

Faith! I forgot my orders, everything, and I replied:

"Well, my friend, my countrywoman, try it, and may Our Lady of the Mountain aid you!" At that moment we were passing before one of those narrow alleys of which there are so many in Seville. Suddenly Carmen turned about and struck me with her clenched fist in the chest. I fell backwards on purpose. With one bound she jumped over me and fled, showing us a pair of legs. . . . Well, they talk of "Basque legs," but hers surpassed them all, as fleet as they were shapely. I picked myself up quickly, but I managed to get my lance crosswise in the alley, and so well did it bar the passage that at the very start my comrades were hindered for the moment from the pursuit. Then I started off running myself, and they after me; but catch her!—there was no risk of it, with our spurs, our sabers, and our lances! In less time than I can tell you, the prisoner had disappeared. Besides, all the gossips of the neighborhood helped her flight, jeered at us, and put us on the wrong scent. After many marches and countermarches we were obliged to return to the guardhouse without a receipt from the governor of the prison.

ACT II

The analyst whose business it is to parse a work of music can and does find flaws which do not trouble the casual listener. Here and there, observes the analyst—who, of course, is stricter than he need be—the situation could have been better expressed, the musical writing could have been more apposite. But there are certain few acts in the operatic canon, egregious chapters, which seem beyond analysis and stand above caviling. The second act of *Carmen* is one of these. It is an example of great operatic creation. Not a bar of the music is superfluous, not a bar which does not serve, motivate, and promote the progress of the tragedy.

Its beginning is light, but it is this very lightness which renders more poignant Don José's anguish. In this act he becomes the leading protagonist—rather, the "led protagonist," led to his degradation.

The entr'acte before the rise of the curtain uses the theme of a military ditty that José sings on his way to Carmen. The scoring of it has something purposefully naïve about it, as if the ragamuffins of the first act could sing it. It mocks the military, who, indeed, don't come off so well in the ensuing action.

Lillas Pastia's inn is filled with gay company. Among them are smugglers and gypsy girls, including Carmen and her two friends, Frasquita and Mercédès. These are entertaining some of the officers. Moralès is one of them. Zuniga is present as well, sitting at a table with Carmen; but Carmen pays scant attention to him.

A few of the girls are dancing with the officers. Suddenly Carmen rises and, dispelling her own listless mood, breaks into a whirlwind song, a *chanson bohème*, in which she is joined by Frasquita and Mercédès. As she sings she dances—for "dancing and singing are married" (*"Les tringles des sistres tintaient"*—"The rhythm of timbrels sounds").

Frasquita now tells Zuniga that Pastia wants to close the inn for the night. Zuniga is perfectly willing to leave if Carmen will go with him. This she refuses to do. Zuniga guesses the reason and tells her that the soldier who had been imprisoned has just been set free again. (All this is casually handled in a short recitative. We had better consult Bizet's original version, where the discussion goes something like this: Pastia is anxious to close for the night because the authorities are watching him closely, though he hasn't of course the faintest idea why they are suspicious. Zuniga tells Pastia why. His place is known as the headquarters of the smugglers. No doubt he wants to close because he and his shady friends have some secret business on hand. However, this is no concern of Zuniga's, and so he suggests that he and the girls go off to the theater for an hour or so. At a sign from Pastia the girls politely decline. Zuniga then appeals to Carmen, whose refusal is sharp. He guesses why Carmen's mood is black: she is thinking of the soldier whom the authorities have sent to prison for a month and whose rank has been degraded. But he is now free again. If he is free, Carmen cries, all is well. She asks Zuniga and his friends to leave as soon as possible, and they accept this with good grace.)

Shouts are heard behind the scene, cries of *"Vivat!"* It is a welcome to the redoubtable toreador Escamillo, who bursts in, accompanied by a torchlight procession of his admirers. Zuniga and Moralès stay to drink a toast in his honor. Escamillo plunges into the Toreador Song, giving us a musical description of the thrills and dangers of bullfighting, but more particularly a musical expression of the insouciance and the swagger of the bullfighter (*"Votre toast, je peux vous le rendre"*—"I return your salute"). A persistent anecdote alleges that Bizet hated the Toreador Song, that he wrote it under duress, the baritone wanting something exciting to sing, and that he said, "They want garbage: here it is!" This merely proves that we must not take musical anecdotes too seriously. This one has no more validity than Beethoven's remark that his Eighth Symphony was much better than his Seventh. Casual words dropped under we know not what circumstances and prompted by we know not what passing irritation become imprisoned in the geological stratum of musical history, frozen in finality. The fact remains that the Toreador Song is excellent, that it offers a valuable contrast to Don José's Flower Aria, and that, by bringing Carmen's new lover into sharp relief, it helps to make the dramatic rivalry all the more vivid.[8] The uncertain and modest soldier versus the confident popular idol (introvert versus extro-

8 In Merimée's story, the most important figure opposing José, though only one of several, is García, her husband. The bullfighter, Lucas, plays an incidental role.

vert, we would say today), therein lies the rivalry. The Toreador Song is clearly an extrovert's theme song. If Bizet hated it, why did he use it in the Prelude? Why did he use it for dramatic emphasis at Escamillo's departure in the third act?

The others join in the Toreador Song. Carmen, looking at Escamillo, echoes the phrase, *"L'amour,"* just before the full chorus ends the number; it is a particularly expressive "cadenza," a promissory note for the future. Escamillo now asks Carmen her name. At his next fight he will pronounce it, as is the custom of the toreador. "My name is Carmen or Carmencita: it makes no difference." "And if," asks Escamillo, "someone were to tell you that he loved you?" "I would answer," says Carmen, "that it is useless." "That," Escamillo replies, "is not an agreeable response. But I am content to wait." "One is permitted to wait; it is sweet to hope."

Zuniga once more takes his leave. He will return later. "That would be wrong," says Carmen. "I will risk it," replies Zuniga drily. Escamillo and the crowd depart as well, leaving the stage to Carmen, Frasquita and Mercédès, and two of the leading smugglers, Dancaïre and Remendado.

Now that they are by themselves, professionally, they at once get down to business. A major expedition is planned, one which promises good rewards. To bring it off the men need the aid of the women. Why the women? Because when it comes to cheating, lying, and tricking, no one can surpass the female of the species. This admirable sentiment is expressed in a quintet of incomparable brilliance and wit, a quintet which reminds one of a symphonic scherzo, as fragments of the theme are distributed among the voices (*"de nous? . . . de vous!"*) in the manner in which the orchestral composer would distribute them among his instruments (*"Nous avons en tête une affaire"*—"We have a bit of business in mind").

There is perfect agreement among the five—until suddenly Carmen springs a surprise. Blandly but firmly she announces that they are welcome to set out on the expedition but she for one will not go with them. She is staying right here. Pressed for a reason, she confides that she is in love. This confidence provokes general incredulity, not to say hilarity. The two men answer it with a mocking little duet. It is impossible to take Carmen seriously. But it appears that she is serious, she means it.

Well, who is it this time? Whom has Carmen selected? Almost a nobody, she answers, a soldier who the other day helped her and for that was sent to prison. She is expecting him now. But is she sure that he will show up? No sooner does Dancaïre ask the question than we hear behind the scene the voice of José singing a gay ditty. The four friends open the shutters and spy on the approaching singer. He is very handsome—of that there is no question; and he might make a useful addition to the band of smugglers. Carmen really ought to try to enlist him. Carmen will try, she promises. She states her intention quite casually. She gives no indication either that she is aware of what she is about to do, that is, break a man's career, or indeed that she has given the matter any thought at all. At the moment she wants Don José, and that is all there is to it. Her evil is offhand, her immorality—or her amorality—unpremeditated.

"Halt! Who goes there?" "A dragoon from Alcalà," sings José. The use of "Alcalà" is a purposeful allusion. In Merimée's story Carmen sends to José in his prison cell a "bread of Alcalà." Alcalà is a little village near Seville known for the delicious taste of its rolls. In this bread Carmen has hidden a file; she has also sent a gold piece. José has refused to use that file. His code of honor does not permit him to attempt escape. Later—that is, when José is released from prison and comes to see Carmen—he returns the gold piece to her. Carmen, living by a code of her own, the gypsy code, uses this money to purchase an extravagant feast for the two of them. Thus José, by calling himself a dragoon from Alcalà, is expressing his gratitude to Carmen, but this implication remains obscure in the opera and has meaning only to readers of Merimée.

Don José has arrived. He is again in Carmen's presence. For that, he assures her, he would willingly undergo the prison sentence once again. Carmen tells him that his officers were at the inn just a short while ago and that she danced for them. José shows, to Carmen's delight, that he is jealous. But Carmen appeases him by promising to dance at once in his honor and for him alone. In Merimée Carmen, having no castanets handy, breaks a plate in two. This business has been retained by the librettists, but then Carmen finds the castanets (for musical reasons!) and accompanies herself with them, at the same time humming a wordless melody.

As she sings and dances, there are heard faintly in the distance the military cornets giving the signal for the retreat. Bizet combines Carmen's melody with that of the cornet call. At first the call is unheeded by her, but the soldier, his ears sensitive to the familiar sound, hears it at once. José stops her. He must return to the barracks. Carmen can hardly believe that she has heard right. At this moment, when she is doing her best to entertain him, when she is singing and dancing for him, when she is showing her love, he is thinking of returning? It is not to be believed! "Very well, Canary!"[9] she shouts in fury. "You take your shako and your saber and go, go, go!"

"You doubt then that I love you?" asks José in his misery. "Listen to me, Carmen! You must listen to me." The colloquy contrasts the ruthlessness of Carmen with the humility of José and serves as a prelude of ever-increasing urgency to Don José's aria. After his "You must listen to me," the voices are silent for a moment as we hear Carmen's Fate motive in the orchestra; then José begins his Flower Aria (*"La fleur que tu m'avais jetée"*—"I guarded the flower you gave me"). Famous though it is, it is in no sense a conventional operatic aria, but a psychological disclosure. It flows on in its lyric way without repetition and shows us a Don José more mature, more eloquent than the boyish soldier we have known in the first act.

The Flower Song is extremely difficult to sing, and few tenors can manage the final *pianissimo*, *"Carmen, je t'aime,"* with its strange cadence for the high woodwinds. What he says to her is simple enough. He has kept the flower which she threw at him, and through the long prison hours its perfume brought her back to his imagination. He railed against his fate, cursed the day he met her; yet he was filled with one desire only, to see her again.

Carmen is moved by his plea. She murmurs, "No, you do not love me, for if you loved me you would follow me." It is one of the quietest and yet one of the most curiously beautiful moments in the opera. Then she begins to describe to him the joy of living free and abandoned in the mountains without an officer one has to obey, without a call to retreat to which one has to listen. As she sings, José interpolates protestations which grow ever more feeble, until, with a last flare-up of resisting honor, he manages to break

[9] The dragoons wore a yellow uniform. An insult is intended. (See below the quotation from Merimée.)

away from an embrace. No, he cannot, he will not desert his flag
and plunge himself into shame and infamy. It is farewell forever.

At this moment a loud knock is heard. Zuniga has returned.
Since nobody bothers to open the door, the captain forces it, enters, and surveys the situation. He addresss an ironical reproach to
Carmen. What does she mean by taking up with a common soldier
when she could have had an officer? Peremptorily he orders José to
"decamp." When José refuses, Zuniga strikes him with a glove.
José draws his sword, but at a cry from Carmen the gypsies and
the smugglers rush to the scene, Dancaïre and Remendado seize
Zuniga and disarm him. What follows is an *allegretto* which almost
recalls a musical comedy turn but which in fact is a dose of stinging
sarcasm. The principals are being very polite as they threaten
Zuniga. Carmen regrets that "the fine officer has been played such
a nasty trick by his own infatuation and that he has arrived at an
inopportune moment." Remendado with a pistol in his hand and
Dancaïre with a knife invite him to leave the tavern at once for
"just a little promenade. War is war." Zuniga replies as he looks at
the knife and the gun that the logic of their argument is irresistible.

As he leaves, Carmen turns to José to ask him, "You will be one
of us from now on?" He answers, "I have no choice." His consent
might have been more gallantly couched, she observes, but it does
not matter. He will soon see how pleasant the wandering life can
be, with all the world as one's country and only your own inclina-
tion as law. This is liberty! Carmen's words are taken up by the
smugglers and the gypsies, and the curtain falls to the specious
tribute to liberty.

Here is Merimée:

"At the commencement of the Street of the Serpent she bought a dozen
oranges, which she made me put in my handkerchief. A little farther on
she bought, besides, a loaf of bread, a sausage, and a bottle of Manzanilla.
Finally she entered a confectioner's shop. There she threw on the counter
the gold-piece I had returned to her, with another which she had in her
pocket, and some silver. Then she asked me for all I had, too. I had only
a few small pieces, which I gave her, feeling much ashamed to have no
more. I thought she wanted to buy out the shop. She took all there was of
the finest and dearest *yemas* (yolks of eggs prepared with a crust of
sugar), *turon* (a kind of nougat), preserved fruits, as long as the money
lasted. All this I had to carry off in paper bags. Perhaps you know the

Street of the Candilejo, where is a bust of the King Don Pedro, the Guardian of Justice. That should have made me think what I was about. We stopped before an old house in this street. She entered the passage and rapped at the ground floor. A gypsy, true servant of Satan, came to open it. Carmen spoke some words in Romany to her. The old hag grumbled at first. To appease her Carmen gave her two oranges, a fistful of bonbons, and also a sip of wine. Then she put her cloak on her back and led her to the door, which she secured with a bar of wood. As soon as we were alone she commenced to dance and laugh like one possessed, singing, 'Thou art my *rom,* and I thy *romi* (husband, wife).'

"There I stood in the middle of the room, loaded with all our purchases, and not knowing where to put them. She dumped them all on the floor, and clasping me round the neck, cried out, 'I pay my debts; 'tis the law of the Calés (a name the gypsies give themselves in their own tongue).' Ah! señor, that day! that day! . . . When I think of it, I forget to-morrow!"

The bandit was silent a moment, then, after he had relighted his cigar, he continued:

"We remained together the whole day, eating, drinking—and the rest. When she had eaten bonbons like a six-year-old child, she stuffed handfuls into the old woman's water-jar—'to make her a sorbet,' she said. She smashed the *yemas* by throwing them against the wall—'so that the flies may leave us in peace,' she said. There was no trick or folly that she did not commit. I said I would like to see her dance, but what would we do for castanets? At once she took the old woman's only plate, broke it in pieces, and behold! there she was dancing the romalis, clacking the pieces of the plate together as well as if she had castanets of ebony or ivory. One would never be bored in that girl's company, I warrant you. Evening came, and I heard the drums beating the 'retreat.'

" 'I must return to my quarters for roll-call,' I said.

" 'To your quarters!' she cried with an air of contempt. 'Are you then a negro slave, to let yourself be driven about with a whip? You are a real canary, in character as well as clothes. Get out! You are chicken-hearted.'

"Well, I stayed, resigned beforehand to the guardroom."

ACT III

Bizet's orchestral entr'acte was originally intended for his *L'Arlésienne* score. It is a short pastoral, delicate and tender. What is it doing here, standing between the final loud chorus of the second act and the stealthy opening of the third? The question has puzzled many a commentator, some even suggesting that Bizet used it for convenience to save himself work. But Bizet was not Rossini. If he put it here he must have felt that an idyllic intermezzo was appropriate at the midway point of a tragic tale.

The scene is a wild rocky pass in the mountains. The time is night. A few of the smugglers are lying on the ground wrapped in their cloaks. Gradually others arrive at the trysting place; they are loaded down with bales of merchandise, obviously the fruits of the little affair of which Dancaïre spoke so highly in the preceding act. The gypsies companion the smugglers, partly because, as we have learned in Act II, they are indispensable to a shady business—and partly because Bizet needed feminine voices in the chorus.

The orchestra accompanies the action with the melody which has come to be known as the Smugglers' Chorus (*"Ecoute, écoute, compagnon"*—"Listen, my friend, a fortune lies below"). As always with Bizet at his best, the orchestra expresses the dramatic sense: the music moves with a slow, cautious rhythm, as if the smugglers were wary of every step they took. (As a matter of fact, they say so in the subsequent chorus.) The upward tread of the bass suggests climbing.

Neither mountain torrent nor thunderstorm can stay these good people from their appointed round, they sing—or words to that effect. Carmen and José, Dancaïre and Remendado, Frasquita and Mercédès, they are all here. Dancaïre counsels that they take an hour's rest, that they then reconnoiter the paths to ascertain if the contraband can be moved into town.

Evidently Carmen and José have quarreled and both are in a black mood. "Why are you staring?" she wants to know. He replies sadly that he is thinking of a village only a few miles away in which an old woman lives, his mother, who still believes him to be an honest man. How wrong she is! Carmen has no patience with such sentiment; why doesn't he go back to that mother of his if the smugglers' life does not suit him? This taunt but provokes another. Don José flares up: "If you once again speak of separation—" "Perhaps you will kill me," Carmen interrupts him. "I do not care. Fate is the master." For Carmen believes that her fate is foreordained. She sees no contradiction in this belief to her other creed: that she must be allowed unencumbered freedom to act as she pleases. Both motives permeate Merimée's story.

Carmen turns her back on José and seats herself near Frasquita and Mercédès, where she watches as the two girls spread cards before them. They are about to tell their fortunes from the cards. The predictions the two girls seek are the kind which young girls in the audience of the Opéra-Comique might have wished for themselves from a fortune teller. The dreams of these two gypsies are remarkably bourgeois. Frasquita sees a young lover who carries her off on his horse and becomes a famous chieftain; while Mercédès predicts for her own a rich old man who will install her in a castle. He will marry her and will then, most obligingly, die (*"Mêlons! Coupons!"*—"Let's shuffle and cut the cards!").

The duet ends with Frasquita pronouncing *"amour"* (what would French opera do without that word?) and the orchestra repeating the melody. "Now it is my turn," Carmen says, as the orchestra abruptly changes to the Carmen motive. She begins to consult the cards. For her the future holds nothing bourgeois, nothing comforting. "Diamonds, spades . . . Death! First I, then he: for both of us—death!"

Musing to herself—the interpreter of Carmen must here employ the darkest timbre of her voice—she observes that the cards never lie. You may shuffle them any way you wish. You may cut them as often as you want. The answer will always turn up true. If you are destined for happiness, the cards will say so. But if you are destined to die, if that is what fate has written, the cards will remain pitiless. For her, as often as she turns the pack, it is always death. *"Toujours la mort"* is the cadence of her tragic song. This is immediately contrasted with a repetition of the lighthearted prattle of the two girls, Carmen then adding her own somber repetition to form the trio. The scene, as a thousand audiences have acknowledged, is a masterpiece, and shows us in particular what is in general characteristic of the *Carmen* style: a chiaroscuro of the tragic and the gay.

Dancaïre has returned with the news that the pass is reasonably clear, though he has observed not one but three officials prowling about. They had all better act cautiously. The women assert that they are quite capable of dealing with all three. All that is needed is a little feminine smile, for what is an official but a man? They all leave, full of confidence, except José, who, according to Dancaïre's instruction, is to stay behind, posting himself as a lookout on a high rock. José trails off, leaving the stage empty for the entrance of Micaëla.

Why is she here and how did she find her way to this inaccessible spot? This is a little better explained in the spoken version, where Micaëla appears with a guide. The guide congratulates her on being so brave and thanks her for having paid him well. Micaëla is determined to make a last attempt to rescue her beloved. For such an enterprise she dares to confront the darkness and the lawless men. Though her motivation is, as I say, a little more convincing in the original scene, the suggestion remains inescapable that Micaëla is here simply to sing an aria (*"Je dis que rien ne m'épouvante"*—"I pretend that nothing frightens me").

This she does; it is a prayer to God to give her courage in her mission. The aria finished, Micaëla espies José on top of a rock. He is aiming his gun at somebody. He shoots. This proves too much for her courage, and the poor girl hides in terror.

The man José has aimed at is Escamillo, who now enters holding his hat, which has a bullet hole in it. He observes with a devil-may-care air, "An inch or two lower and everything would have been over."

José asks the stranger his name. Escamillo? Yes, José has heard of him and welcomes him. But why has he come from Granada? Escamillo explains that he is following the call of love. He loves a gypsy whom he hopes to find here. Her name is Carmen. She has a lover, a soldier who deserted for her sake and whom she used to adore. But now the affair seems to be finished. Carmen's loves last about six months.

José challenges his rival to a duel. They draw their knives, begin to fight, Escamillo slips and falls, and José is about to finish him off when Carmen and the others return, just in time to save Escamillo. All this is unconvincing dramatically and not particularly distinguished musically. But Bizet's lapse is a short one; in the next scene, the finale, we find him again master of the situation.

Gravely Escamillo thanks Carmen for having saved his life and invites the whole company to be his guests at the coming bullfight. "Anyone who loves me will be there," he says, with a meaningful glance at Carmen. Addressing the furious José, he politely—all these men are nothing if not polite—promises him a return match. For the moment he must take his leave. José, turning to Carmen, threatens her with a dark "Take care! I cannot bear to suffer much more." Dancaïre urges that they stop this nonsense: there is no time now for stupid quarrels; they must get on with their business.

But there is one further delay: Remendado discovers the hidden interloper, Micaëla. Once more, to the melody to which in the first act she had brought the dragoon his mother's message, she now implores the outlaw in his mother's name to return with her. Carmen peremptorily seconds the suggestion. "You want me to leave," José rejoinders, all the bitterness and humiliation welling up in him, "so that you may follow your new lover. No, I will stay, even if costs me my life." This is one of the opera's most poignant moments, Don José's grief, emphasized by the tremolo of the strings, seeming to stretch before us like an infinite road.

No, he will not cut the chain which binds them together forever, though the whole ensemble warns him of his peril. In vain! "I will force you to link your destiny with mine. I will not yield!"

But a further heavy blow is in store for José. Micaëla imparts the news which she has so far held back: his mother is dying. At this news José's defiance breaks. In a wild voice he cries, "Let us go!" then stops, faces Carmen, and hurls his parting words at her: "You have your way. I am leaving. But we shall meet again." Once more the Fate theme is intoned by the orchestra. As it dies away, we hear in the far distance the refrain of Escamillo's song. "On guard, Toreador! Remember in combat that two dark eyes are fixed on you, that love lies in wait."

ACT IV

Anyone familiar with Bizet's style will understand that it was not by accident that the composer set the darkest part of the tragedy in the brightest sunlight. The fourth act, the act of Carmen's death, the act of destruction foreseen and inevitable, opens in the lightest and gayest of spirits. The gaiety is never altogether erased; its sound reverberates in the final colloquy and is present to the very end of the opera. We have already observed the use of "light-dark" in the card scene. In the final scene the device of

darkening the dark through flecks of high color gains new expressiveness. As a device it seems simple enough; the way it is used
is the way of genius.

The customary orchestral entr'acte this time serves to announce
the noisy fiesta. As the curtain rises we are in the thick of it.

The setting of the last act has given stage designers no end of
trouble. According to the original directions, the stage is to represent an open place in Seville. At the back the walls of the amphi-
theater are to be seen. Its entrance is covered by a long awning.
Now, it is difficult to imagine Carmen's murder taking place in a
public square, nor does the open space seem to be the right setting
for the final duet. Various compromises have been tried, such as
constructing a small enclosed space within the general setting. In
the Metropolitan Opera production an extreme has been adopted:
the procession is dispensed with, the arena has disappeared, and the
chorus merely stands, sings, and looks expectantly (more or less),
leaving the pageantry to the spectator's imagination. The final duet
is then placed in a room which presumably serves as Escamillo's
dressing room. In the new production at the Paris Opéra, on the
other hand, a huge spectacle, employing some three hundred super-
numeraries, is offered to the audience. Escamillo's triumph over the
bull becomes equivalent to Radames' victory over the Ethiopians.
Neither solution is satisfactory.

The crowd has assembled. The usual souvenir vendors are at
hand, pressing their wares on the people; fans, oranges, programs,
fresh water, and cigarettes are for sale. Zuniga and two other
officers, one with Frasquita, the other with Mercédès on his arm,
mingle with the crowd. They are all expecting the appearance of
the company of bullfighters, the *"cuadrilla."* They do not have
long to wait, for presently they march in, dressed at their gaudiest,
their lances glittering in the sunlight, their hats held high. The procession follows the time-honored tradition, first the *toreros,* then
the policemen, then the *banderilleros,* then the *picadors.* All march
to the tune we have heard in the Prelude. The children, including
the boys of the first act, are present as well and in their high voices
they jeer the *"alguacil* [the chief constable] with the ugly face."
At last the star of the occasion, greeted *fortissimo* by the entire
ensemble, enters. After the uproar, the *"Vivat Escamillo!,"* dies
down, Escamillo quietly addresses Carmen: "If you love me, Car-

men, you will soon be proud of me." And Carmen replies, also quietly, "Yes, I love you, Escamillo. And I swear that I love no one else but you."

Escamillo goes to get ready. Now it is time for the *alcade*, the mayor, to make his appearance. Majestically he proceeds toward the arena and enters it, followed by the crowd. Frasquita and Mercédès seize the opportunity to impart a word of warning to Carmen. The two girls have espied Don José hiding in the crowd. Carmen had better be on her guard! But Carmen replies that she is not the woman to quake before such a man as José.

The crowd has now entirely disappeared, leaving Carmen behind. Suddenly Don José becomes visible. Carmen turns,[10] and the two protagonists now face each other (*"C'est toi!"*—"It is you!").

At once Carmen, with fatalistic calm, tells him that she had been warned of his being there, that she had been warned to fear for her life; but she had refused to run away. José assures her that he has come not to threaten but to supplicate. He implores her to forget all that has passed between them, as he is willing to forget. They can begin a new life together. "You demand the impossible," Carmen replies. "I have never lied to you. Now I tell you: between you and me all is finished." José pleads, at first humbly and quietly, to a melody which, heartbreaking in its tenderness, seems to me to bear a kinship to his Flower Song. "It is yet time," he begs, "it is yet time to save yourself and me." Carmen cannot be budged. She tells him that she knows that he will kill her, but whether she live or die, she will not yield. Their voices blend, each pursuing the thought, until the duet comes to a cadence, accentuated by drumbeats. In a whisper José asks the question to which he knows the answer: "You no longer love me?" He repeats the question in a voice of despair. Her answer is an inflexible no. But he, he still loves her. There is nothing he would not concede to regain her love. Does she want him to remain a bandit? Anything, anything that she asks he will do, if only—

It is useless. "Carmen will not yield. Free she was born and free she will die." At this point we hear the crowd in the arena hailing the approaching victory. Carmen tries to pass José and run toward the arena, but he stops her. As the tempo of the music quickens, he

[10] In some productions Carmen looks at herself in a mirror and sees Don José's reflection.

demands to know if the man whom they are acclaiming is her new lover. With the defiance characteristic of her nature, she spits out, "Yes, I love him." In the face of death itself she proclaims it. Once more the shouts of the crowd are heard. The tension mounting to its highest pitch, the orchestra repeatedly thunders out the Fate theme. And José, now half-crazed, cries that he will not suffer her to laugh at him in the arms of another. For the last time, will she change her mind? In answer, Carmen tears a ring from her finger, a ring which he had given her, and hurls it into a corner. The gesture proves the final whiplash. As the crowd begins to make its way out of the bull ring, Escamillo having triumphed, José seizes Carmen and stabs her. Without a word, without a murmur she falls and dies. For the last time we hear the Fate motive. José, turning to the onrushing spectators, sobs, "You may arrest me. It was I who killed her. Oh, Carmen, my adored Carmen."

The final scene, at once so simple and so expressive, is one of the great scenes in operatic literature. Neither Carmen nor José sings one phrase or speaks one word inconsistent with her character or his. José is driven to a despair which forces him to wipe out shame through crime. Carmen, facing that crime, cannot weaken, even for an instant, and meets the onslaught with the almost unthinking stubbornness which her fatalistic beliefs have instilled in her. Musically, the progression of the scene is not only gripping but so right as to seem inevitable. The economy of its musical means is admirable.

In that economy not only this scene, but most of the opera, mirrors Merimée's novelette. In the best operas, there does exist a relationship between the subject as treated in words and as treated in music. J. B. Priestley, discussing Merimée admiringly, speaks of his "restraint and detachment."[11] Yet he is a romantic, because "the overmastering passion, no matter how dryly he describes its effects, is to him its own justification, life as it must be lived however disastrous the consequences, and this is the pure essence of romanticism." The essence of romanticism in detached terms—Bizet brings it to us as does Merimée. As a final example of the author's style we may read *his* final scene, observing that the two treatments, though differing in locale, are much alike:

[11] In *Literature and Western Man.*

" 'So, my Carmen,' I said, after we had gone a little way, 'you really wish to follow me, don't you?'

" 'I will follow you to death, yes; but I will never live with you again.'

"We were in a solitary gorge. I pulled up my horse.

" 'Is it here?' she cried, and with one bound she sprang to the ground. She threw off her mantilla, cast it at her feet, and stood motionless, with one hand on her hip, looking me steadily in the eyes.

" 'You wish to kill me, I can well see,' she said. 'It is decreed; but you shall never make me yield.'

" 'I beseech you,' I said to her, 'be reasonable. Listen to me. All the past is forgotten. Nevertheless, you know well that it is you who have ruined me. 'Tis for you I have become a robber and a murderer. Carmen! my own Carmen! let me save you, and with you save myself.'

" 'José,' she replied, 'you ask the impossible. I love you no more; you, you love me still, and for this you wish to kill me. I might yet tell you some lie, but I do not care to take the trouble. All is over between us. As my *rom*, you have the right to kill your *romi*; but Carmen will be always free. Calli she was born and Calli she will die.'

" 'So, then, you love Lucas?' I demanded.

" 'Yes; I have loved him, like you, for a moment—less, perhaps, than you. Now I love nothing, and I hate myself for ever having loved you at all.'

"I threw myself at her feet, I took her hands in mine, I bedewed them with tears. I reminded her of all the happy times we had spent together. I offered to remain always a brigand to please her. Everything, señor, everything, if only she would love me again.

"She said, 'To love you, it is impossible. To live with you, I do not wish it.'

"Fury seized me. I drew my knife. I would have liked her to be afraid or to plead for mercy; but that woman was a demon.

" 'For the last time,' I cried—'will you stay with me?'

" 'No! no! no!' she cried, stamping her foot; and she drew from her finger a ring I had given her, and threw it among the bushes.

"I struck her twice. 'Twas Garcia's knife, which I had taken when I broke mine in his throat. She fell at the second thrust, without a cry. It seems to me that I can still see her great black eyes steadily fixed on me; then they became dimmed and closed. I remained completely prostrated for a good hour beside the body. Then I remembered that Carmen had often told me that she would like to be buried in a wood. I dug her a grave with my knife, and placed her in it. I searched a long time for her ring, and at last I found it. I placed it in the grave beside her, and also a small cross. Perhaps I did wrong. Then I mounted my horse, galloped straight to Cordova, and at the first guard-house I made myself known. I told them that I had killed Carmen, but I did not wish to tell them where her body lay. The hermit was a holy man. He prayed for her. He said a mass for her soul. . . . Poor girl! It is the gipsies who are to blame, for having reared her as they did."

LA TRAVIATA

COMPOSER: Giuseppe Verdi

LIBRETTIST: Francesco Maria Piave

FIRST PERFORMANCE: March 6, 1853
Teatro la Fenice, Venice

RECEPTION: Failure

CHARACTERS:

Violetta Valery	Soprano
Flora Bervoix	Mezzo-soprano
Annina, Violetta's maid	Soprano
Alfredo Germont	Tenor
Giorgio Germont, father of Alfredo	Baritone
Gastone, Visconte de Letorieres	Tenor
Baron Douphol	Baritone
Marquis d'Obigny	Bass
Dr. Grenvil	Bass
Giuseppe, servant to Violetta	Tenor
Servant to Flora	Bass
Commissioner	Bass

LA TRAVIATA
A "CHAMBER OPERA"

Traviata's color is that of ivory satin, *Trovatore*'s a slashing red, and *Rigoletto*'s a cloudy purple. If one remembers that Verdi created all three operas in the incredibly short period of three years, one may marvel at the versatility of the composer's palette. It was as if a painter were immediately to turn from two battle frescoes to a pastel portrait.

The timetable testifies to Verdi's creative energy. He composed *Rigoletto* late in 1850—he was then thirty-seven years old—in the space of forty days. He composed both *Il Trovatore* and *La Traviata* in 1852. *Il Trovatore* was produced in Rome in January, 1853. From Rome Verdi went to Venice. There, standing upright at a tall desk[1] and sipping many cups of coffee, he orchestrated *Traviata*. The opera was given at the Venice Theater on March 6. Total time for the three masterpieces—*less* than three years!

But chronology alone does not adequately document Verdi's achievement. We must note as well the difference in style, the newness of conception. *Traviata* is very different from the two operas which precede it. Those two, though new and in certain respects daring, still carry on not only the early nineteenth-century tradition of "blood-and-thunder" opera but Verdi's own early traditions, those of his previous works. *Traviata* is newer, more daring, more individual, because it abjures all big effects—it contains only one of the "big" numbers indigenous to the older operas, the finale

---

[1] Verdi had ordered this desk specially, to be ready when he reached Venice.

of Act II—because it concentrates almost entirely on a woman's fate, and because it achieves this concentration by the simplest means. In *Traviata* there is only one central protagonist, lovingly delineated; there is no hero and, strictly speaking, no villain.

Traviata has rightly been called a chamber opera. Not only is its drama chambered, but its melodic language is close and intimate, set in an orchestration which seems to have been written with one stroke of a pen, and in which delicate strings and woodwinds abound, the brass being almost wholly absent.

As nearly always in the world of opera, the inspirational drive was set going by the libretto, the music fructified by the drama. Verdi thought the subject "simple and tender." After *Il Trovatore* and *Rigoletto*, neither of which is simple or tender, *Traviata* must have filled a need, must have promised a change of pace to the restless worker.[2] But perhaps there was a more practical reason why Verdi chose Dumas' story and chose it with unusual alacrity. As a rule he was slow to make up his mind, at least after he had become successful and could afford to be choosy. But on *La Traviata* he settled immediately after the production of the play in Paris. We may assume that the success of the play, the stir, not to say the sensation, it caused in the intellectual world of Europe, had something to do with his decision.

Still, it was not a decision prompted by opportunity alone. Surely the figure of the lost woman—rather, the strayed woman (*traviata* is the past participle of the verb "*traviare*," "to stray")—touched the composer's heart. He responded to what was not a new story, the courtesan redeemed by love. Victor Hugo had treated it not so long ago in his successful play *Marion de Lormes*. Other authors had used the theme; still others were to use it later. What was new was its contemporaneousness, a certain immediacy which gave it freshness. Many men, aside from the chronicler, young Alexandre Dumas, remembered the woman who served as the model of this newest study of the oldest profession. Many readers knew of whom he was writing. If Dumas' novel was a *roman à clef*, the key was quite accessible.

The mutation of this real-life character to a novel, then to a play, then to an opera, and then to a legend presents a process of truth

---

[2] The subject which Verdi considered after *Traviata* was *King Lear*. Here would have been another change of pace, indeed! Unfortunately he did not proceed with *Lear*.

soaked in and finally absorbed by imagination. In the end, there is hardly a trace of truth left. Recollection plays a part in this process, the kind of recollection which tints *en rose*, remembers the romance and forgets the facts.

To none has this romanticizing process been applied with more favorable results than to the diamantine and short-lived courtesan of the middle of the nineteenth century, Alphonsine Plessis. Even before she passed from reality to fiction, the men who had known her heaped on her such an extravagant measure of enchantment that, reading these tributes, we must suspect invention rather than evaluation. Then—as Dumas got to work and the opera became popular and readers and operagoers shed tears over her fate—why, then she was glorified. More to be pitied than to be blamed? She was all pitied and not at all blamed. The miasma in which she must have lived became the exhalation of a flower garden. Her beauty, which indeed must have been great,[3] became legendary. "Her lips were red as cherries and her teeth the most beautiful in the world: she was like a Dresden figurine," wrote the younger Dumas of her. She might have been a duchess, claimed Jules Janin, a well-known journalist and observer of the social scene of Paris, who was the first to be responsible for the exuberant praise. She wore her laces and jewels as if she had been born "with a crown upon her head, and a crowd of flatterers at her feet," he said. "Her bearing tallied with her language; her thoughts with her smile; her dress with her person; and you would have looked in vain in the very highest circles for a woman who was more beautiful and in more complete harmony with her ornaments, her dress, and her conversation."

In her salon were to be found not only the members of the famous Jockey Club, but such lions of literature as Eugène Sue and Alfred de Musset. Liszt met her. She told him that his playing made her dream. Liszt was puzzled as to who this could be, this girl who addressed him without knowing him and yet treated him with condescension. It is probable that he enjoyed her favors, and this added a further glitter to her reputation. Liszt said, "I have, as a rule, no great liking for the Marion de Lormes or the Manon

---

[3] Her portrait (by Viénot) shows this. But how much idealization is there here?

Lescauts of the world, but she was an exception. She had a great deal of heart."[4]

So it was that *La Dame aux Camélias* became a *grande dame*. We forgot her origin, forgot her faults, and saw only the vision of the sick girl who gives up the man she loves so as not to bring disgrace on her lover's family, and for this sacrifice dies unforgiven.

Not a word of this story is true. If we trace the facts of her biography, we can observe once again how much power lies in fiction. Fiction is stronger than truth. (And music is stronger than fiction.)

Alphonsine Plessis came from a humble, poor home in Normandy. Her father, Marin Plessis, a mercer, was a brutal and depraved creature, from whom she fled. When she was fourteen she went to Paris and, thrown on her own resources, began to work in a millinery shop. She lived with a number of students in the Latin Quarter. At a public ball at which she appeared, she attracted the attention of a restaurant keeper who installed her in an apartment of her own, but was almost at once supplanted by a more desirable connection, the young Duc de Guiche. Her rise then began. She changed her name to the more euphonious Marie Duplessis and became ever more reckless, extravagant, and capricious. She flourished in a society which made important the perfume, the jewel, the champagne supper, and the candlelit salon. Between the *grand monde,* a world of elegance, haughty and conservative, and the *petit monde,* the region of the small citizen, frugal and prudish, there had arisen the new world of the *demimonde.* This was a society of intellectuals, writers and painters, and young as well as older men of wealth. In an almost frantic manner, they devoted themselves to the pursuit of the kind of pleasure frowned at by the bourgeois and not quite *recherché* enough for the highest rank of Parisian aristocracy. The women of this world, with all their garishness, often possessed a certain refinement, cultivated no doubt to please the men of breeding and of mind with whom they associated. Marie Duplessis was egregious among them. She was tall and very slender. Her face wore a melancholy and downcast expression, perhaps partly because of her disease but partly because

[4] From J. Wohl: *Franz Liszt, souvenirs d'une compatriote;* quoted by André Maurois in *The Titans.*

such an expression suited the ideal of beauty then fashionable. The successful woman looked virginal—but did not act it. She laughed little and spoke in a gentle voice. She dressed beautifully, of course, and carried herself in a way which made Théophile Gautier describe her as "a young woman of exquisite distinction." (But here we are guilty again of confusing hyperbole with facts!) Of the extent of her education we know little. The inventory of her possessions taken after her death listed a respectable library of books, including works by Byron, Chateaubriand, Molière, Goethe, etc. But whether these were read by her or were intended for her visitors we do not know.

It was only to be expected that Alexandre Dumas the younger, son of the celebrated author, should be introduced to Marie. Dumas *père*, rotund and joyous, amazing Paris with the plays, the romances, the novels, the descriptions of voyages, the *bons mots*, even the cookbooks which flowed unceasingly from his facile pen —that lusty *boulevardier* was known to everybody. His young son, dearly loved by his father, at least up to the time that he showed signs of becoming a rival, shared *père's* peregrinations and some of his father's fame. Until he became famous in his own right he was a celebrity by inheritance. As such it was foreordained that he should meet Marie Duplessis.

Alexandre *fils* had been told that this girl, whom he saw sitting in a box at the theater, was suffering from lung disease. They met, they laughed, they drank together. Marie was seized with a fit of coughing and fled into her dressing room. He followed her to see if he could help her. On a table beside her bed he saw a silver bowl; in it were some filaments of blood. He begged her to take care of herself. "If I do," she replied, "I shall die. Only a life of excitement can keep me alive." He fell in love with her and offered to devote his own life to her. She refused at first. She didn't want him to have a "sorry mistress who spits blood and spends a hundred thousand francs a year." Later she yielded, on the condition that Dumas was not to spy on her and to allow her complete freedom to do and live as she pleased. Dumas promised. What would he not have promised? He idolized her. He was twenty years old.

But the promise could not be kept. He not only wanted her all to himself, but he had the irresistible impulse to reform her. Perhaps as a conscious contrast to his father, Dumas *fils* was a moralizing young man. He thought Marie was a creature victimized by a ruthless society. In truth, she was anything but a repentant sinner. And he soon found out that she was constitutionally unable to tell the truth. "Lying keeps my teeth white," she replied to a reproach. In a short time Dumas was in debt to the tune of fifty thousand francs (some twelve thousand dollars). After a few weeks of happiness his life had become miserable. He was poor, and she was incapable of having mercy on her lover's purse, not so much because she desired money as money, but because luxury had become necessity to her. Dumas decided to break with her and wrote her a letter which in substance he later reproduced in the novel. "I am neither rich enough to love you as I would want, nor poor enough to have you love me as you would want. . . . It is unnecessary to tell you how miserable I am, since you know how I love you. . . . You are too tenderhearted not to understand the reason for this letter, too intelligent not to forgive me." We cannot tell what reply, if any, Marie made.

They parted. Alexandre soon left with his father on a voyage to Spain and North Africa. And she soon met another man, the scion of a rich family, a certain Count Edouard Perregaux, who married her the following year in London. The Count's parents were no longer living, so he had no one but himself to please. We do not know whether he loved her or, knowing that she was dying, married her out of pity. At any rate, one short year after, her life ended in respectability, as Countess Perregaux. When she died, her husband was with her, as well as the old Count de Stackelberg (who served as the model for the old duke in the novel). These two men were the only mourners at her grave. Dumas was still traveling with his father. But Marie did *not* die alone and penniless.

The news reached Dumas while he was still in Marseille. On the tenth of February, 1847, one week after Marie's death, he returned to Paris. He learned that an auction sale of Marie's possessions was being advertised. He went to visit her apartment, where her furniture, her dresses, and her jewels were on display.[5] There too he saw a copy of *Manon Lescaut*, a book of which the girl had been fond, and which also had made a deep impression on Alexandre. In his relation with Marie, he himself might have seen the

---

[5] The sale produced more than eighty thousand francs, more than enough to pay Marie's debts.

danger of becoming a second Des Grieux. It was probably after his
visit to the auction room that he decided to write the story of
Marie Duplessis. With it began Marguerite Gautier, the "Lady of
the Camellias."

With it began the work of imagination. In the beginning of the
novel Dumas states, "Not being old enough to invent, I content
myself with narrating." Fortunately this statement is merely a
literary device. Dumas did invent. He invented the camellias. The
real Duplessis was not known to have shown any preference for
that flower.[6] He invented the father and the family situation which
demands her sacrifice. His own father would certainly not have
disapproved of Marie Duplessis; on the contrary. Invented also
were the letters which Marguerite writes as she lies dying, letters
which summarize the story and intensify our sympathy, so that
we look back with fondness on the two lovers. Largely invented
—and aided by sentimental recollection—is the character of Marguerite herself, for Marie would have been unable to sell her jewels
and her horses for any unselfish cause, even the cause of love.

Invention turns a love affair into a work of art. That *La Dame
aux Camélias* is the work of a twenty-one-year-old author is an
astonishing fact; the book itself is both youthful and mature and
demonstrates an ability to tell a story which no doubt *fils* inherited from *père*. . . .

Verdi might never have chosen the theme had he known only
the novel. For the novel, which was published in 1848, created relatively little stir, though Verdi and Giuseppina Strepponi (later
to become Verdi's second wife), who both spent some time in
Paris during the year of its publication, may have read it. It was
the play, based on the novel, which aided Verdi to perceive the
theatrical potential of the story.

Dumas suddenly decided to turn his novel into a play; he had
worked three months on the novel, whereas the play was written
on an impulse within eight days. During the summer of 1849,
Dumas shut himself up in his little house in Neuilly and wrote
away, using whatever scraps of paper he could find. The second
act, he tells us, he finished between midnight and five o'clock in
the morning. There were fewer than twenty-five erasures in the

---

6 According to most testimony. However, Arsène Houssaye wrote that "she was imprisoned in a fortress of camellias."

whole manuscript. As soon as he had finished, he showed the work
to his father. The elder Dumas' comment was: "This is original, it
is touching, it is audacious, it is new. It will have an immense success, if the censor will permit the performance of the piece. But
the censor will never permit it." For three years Dumas *fils* attempted to obtain the consent of the censor. He carried his manuscript from one theater to another. The answer was always a firm
no. Then in 1851 Louis Napoleon became President of the Republic. His half-brother was a friend of the younger Dumas and it was
he who was instrumental in getting the censors to change their
mind. M. de Beaufort, chief judge of the censorship, felt that the
authorization would do no good. "Before the end of the second
act, the public will throw the seats on the stage."

The chief judge was mistaken. The success of the play was immediate. "A deluge of tears and a tempest of applause" greeted it.
Not that there were no voices raised in protest. Some spectators
saw in it an attack on marriage and family life. One critic declared
that it was a dangerous and cynical treatise. And one well-known
Parisian lady—according to Dumas—a habitual first-nighter, hid a
small whistle in the center of her bouquet and at periodic intervals
bent down and blew the whistle, while making believe that she
was smelling the flowers.

So great was the success of the play that the year after, it was
given its American premiere at the Broadway Theater in New York
with Miss Jean Davenport playing Marguerite; though it had to
wait nearly forty years before it was admitted to the stage in England. It has served as a vehicle for stellar actresses ever since, from
Sarah Bernhardt to Greta Garbo. When Sarah Bernhardt played
the part, Dumas sent her a special copy of the book, in which he
enclosed the original letter that he had written to Marie Duplessis,
which somehow or other he must have obtained after Marie's death.
Or had he, in typical author fashion, made an extra copy of this
heart-wrung missive?

The play is inferior to the novel. It has less power and less poetry.
Such a scene as the visit of the narrator and Armand to Marguerite's grave, one of the best in the novel, had to be omitted.
Dumas wrote a practical play which retains some of the novel's
charm but sacrifices much of its sweep.

Verdi saw the play in Paris in February, 1852, shortly after it had been produced. As soon as the play was published, he asked his French editor, Escudier, to send him a copy. Having read it, he commissioned Francesco Piave to fashion the libretto. Alphonsine Plessis, then Marie Duplessis, then Marguerite Gautier, now became Violetta Valery. On the whole, the libretto is a faithful adaptation of the play, allowing for the usual condensation required by music. Several characters are omitted, without much loss. The crucial interview between Violetta and the elder Germont follows almost word for word the text of the play.

Some of Verdi's sketches for *La Traviata* have survived, and they prove with what enthusiasm he worked on the theme, first outlining the general dramatic course of the opera before concentrating on the individual numbers. The wonderful orchestral prelude to the third act was set down in a single hour or two of inspiration. All in all the composition went smoothly and Verdi was satisfied.

Verdi's satisfaction was to suffer a severe jolt. From the beginning he had difficulties with the casting of the roles and would have preferred somebody else to the plump Salvini-Donatello[7] as his Violetta. When he arrived in Venice for the rehearsals, he jibbed at the appearance the lady presented. But it was too late to change. In addition he had to deal with a tenor whose voice was not in the best estate and a baritone who thought that the role of the elder Germont was not sufficiently important to suit him.

The first performance was a fiasco, the audience voicing its displeasure when the baritone sang *"Di Provenza"* badly, and breaking into hilarity at the beginning of the final scene when the doctor announced that Violetta had but a few hours to live. With his customary truthfulness, Verdi acknowledged the defeat to his publisher Ricordi the next morning, and to another friend, Emanuele Muzio, he wrote, "Is the fault mine or the singers'? Time will show."

Perhaps the performance was not altogether responsible for the audience's disappointment. Perhaps they felt let down because *La Traviata* was so simple and was given in contemporary dress. Opera audiences were used to rich spectacles, richly costumed. It is unlikely that they were shocked by the opera's theme. The initial

---

[7] She was the second wife of the famous Shakespearean actor Salvini.

shock had worn off by that time. That is evident from the enthusiasm with which the audience greeted the second production of *La Traviata*, which, with a better cast and in costumes which put the action back a century and a half, was a triumph. It too was given in Venice, though in a different theater.

La Traviata was quickly taken up by the other Italian theaters, and made its way abroad without any noticeable impairment to anyone's morals.

And now, more than a century later, how are we to regard this once pungent flower which has so long been pressed between the leaves of history that it is quite flat? Is the libretto hopelessly dated? Can we take it seriously? Can we even pretend to do so? Do we love the opera in spite of it? Not quite. We may smile at the naïveté of some of Piave's lines; we may find crude the black-and-whiteness of the contrast between the "fallen woman" and the "blameless virgin" in whom the dying Violetta predicts Alfredo will find his happiness; we may find incredible Papa Germont's righteousness and his conveniently belated remorse; and still we feel in the story elements of the sort of tender romance which we are unwilling to renounce entirely. Its soft charm still weaves a certain spell. Nor is the social problem with which it deals quite as passé as those would have us believe who think that Violetta would make a desirable addition to any family. Would a bourgeois father trying to marry off his daughter really welcome Violetta as the wife of his son? Is the problem altogether nonexistent today? No, there is something in the ill-fated love of Violetta and Alfredo which still can move us as a story. What Henry James said of the play is almost as pertinent to the libretto: *"Camille* remains in its combination of freshness and form and the feeling of the springtime of life, a singular, an astonishing piece of work. . . . Some tender young man and some coughing young woman have only to speak the lines to give it a great place among the love stories of the world."

But it is of course in the music of Verdi that the freshness blooms unabated. Here we have no flat flower, no faded souvenir. Here there is still the "springtime of life."

This music represents the last degree of the romanticizing process which was begun by recollection and continued by imagination. The girl who set the process in motion is buried in the Montmartre

Cemetery. Her tombstone is surmounted by a crown of artificial camellias, the predilection for which Dumas had invented. Reality and fiction are combined.

ACT I

The brief Prelude is based on two themes. Both of them are to be associated with Violetta; Verdi reveals at once where his interest lies. The first melody will not occur again until the third act, where it will be used to characterize the girl in her last mood of resignation. The second melody, a particularly important motive, we will meet in the second act at the crucial point at which Violetta bids Alfredo farewell.

The Prelude, which is an *adagio,* is succeeded by an orchestral and choral introduction marked *allegro brillantissimo e molto vivace.* The tempo is indicative of the hectic pace of Violetta's life. Indeed, much of the first-act music goes at a fast clip, with a considerable portion of it in three-quarter time. It is important that the conductor observe Verdi's intentions, which are to move the action along without letup. The pace of the usual performance of *Traviata* is too slow.[8]

The scene is Violetta's home. There is a party in progress. It is supposed to be a gay revelry, but as usual in opera, the chorus being required to look at the conductor, the revelry becomes a tame one. Among the guests are Dr. Grenvil, Baron Douphol, and the Marquis d'Obigny. The last enters escorting Flora Bervoix, who is Violetta's friend and confidante. Presently Viscount Gastone joins the party, bringing with him a young man whom he introduces to Violetta as Alfredo Germont. Gastone assures Violetta that she may count Alfredo among her most ardent admirers. Violetta greets the newcomers and invites her guests to be seated. Gastone, who manages to sit near the hostess, whispers to her that during her recent illness Alfredo called at the house every single day to in-

---

[8] When Toscanini conducted *La Traviata* with the NBC Symphony, the first act took 25:48 minutes. Compare this with the 31:09 minutes of another celebrated recording. Toscanini's tempo caused surprise and was censured by some critics. It was even claimed that he adapted his tempo to the exigencies of broadcast time. Only later, when there was opportunity to hear the recording, did the justice of the pace impress itself on the hearers.

quire after her. Violetta coquettishly says to the Baron, "That is more than you do," a remark which is not likely to endear the young man to Violetta's present lover. The company demands a toast, and since the Baron refuses to propose it, Alfredo is drafted to do the honors. All this scene is set to rapid, informal music.

"*Libiamo*"—"Let us drink"—a gracious and light melody, is the expected toast to feminine beauty, to youth's fire, and to Violetta's bright eyes. The melody is taken up first by the chorus and then by Violetta and then by Violetta and Alfredo singing to each other, the number ending in a thrilling crescendo.

A waltz is heard behind the stage, played by a small band. Verdi was fond of the device of a stage band, having used it in *Rigoletto* just previously. The guests are moving off to dance when suddenly Violetta turns pale and tries to suppress a cry of pain. It is nothing, she assures the company. They are to go on with the dancing; she will join them shortly. All but Alfredo obey her. Violetta, left for the moment alone, looks at herself in the mirror. "How pale I look!" she exclaims, the sad words forming a strange contrast to the continuing waltz music. She turns—and perceives Alfredo. He begs her to give up this febrile life which will surely kill her. If she were his, how he would watch over her and care for her!

"I have forgotten that there is such a thing as love," she laughs. But he assures her that, whether she believes him or not, it is true that he has loved her for a whole year and from afar. And he sings to her one of Verdi's famous melodies, which is to appear frequently throughout the opera, the "*Un dì felice*"—"On a blissful day." He sings to her of the mystery of love, which breathes through the universe, at once a sorrow and a delight. She answers him in character: her reply is couched in mocking coloratura. She has no heart to give, no emotion to bestow; he had better seek love elsewhere and forget her. Then the two voices are combined, Alfredo's sincerity being contrasted with further flighty coloratura. A beautiful and original conception![9]

[9] The reader may be interested in one critic's analysis of this celebrated duet: "Beneath its deceptive simplicity lies a depth of psychological understanding that gives us the measure of Verdi's ability as a dramatic composer. The contrast between the tender melody given to Alfredo and the cynical brilliance of Violetta's reply is obvious enough, but not on that account less admirable as a piece of character-drawing. But there is more to this passage than a contrast of character and temperament; it is a coherent musical

At the end of their duet, Gastone appears for a moment at the doorway. Seeing them together, he discreetly retires. Violetta once more admonishes Alfredo to speak no further of love and to leave her. He has no choice but to obey. Yet, at the last moment, quite unexpectedly, she takes a flower from her corsage and tells him that if he like he may bring it back. To Alfredo's joyous exclamation, "When?" she answers, "When it is faded." (The flower incident is adapted from the novel. During twenty-five days of the month, Dumas writes, Violetta wore white camellias, during the other five red.)

An ecstatic Alfredo takes his leave, as the dancers return and proclaim to the hostess—another *allegro vivo*—that it is time for them to depart, if only to seek a little rest so that they may enjoy another revelry the next night. The chorus is conventional, in Verdi's earlier manner, put here simply to serve as an ensemble number to separate the duet from the final scene.

Violetta, now left alone, expresses to herself her doubts, the stirring of the heart which she had denied possessing. "It is strange, it is strange," she muses, "that his words should so have affected me." She who has never known the joy of loving and being loved—is it possible that she can now change, or must she forever turn away from love? Her first aria, *"Ah, fors' è lui?"*—"Is it he?"—is a brooding questioning of herself. Was it perhaps this man whom she had seen in her imagination? Was it he who could wake her soul? Repeating Alfredo's melody in praise of love, she speculates on its mysterious power. Then, in a sudden change of mood, she recalls herself to reality. With a cry of "What folly! What vain delusion!" she ceases to dream or to hope. What can she hope for in this crowded desert that is Paris? What choice has she but to plunge herself deeper into the vortex of pleasure, pleasure, and more pleasure? The coloratura cadenza on the word "pleasure" prepares us

---

composition. Anybody might have devised the mere contrast between a gentle melody and a series of *fioriture*. Verdi did more than that. Alfredo's tune, so smooth at first, develops passion as he confesses his love, and its rhythm dissolves at the end into triplets without, however, losing its essential character of tender passion. It is those triplets that Violetta takes up, breaking up the *legato* line with hectic pauses and making an entirely different rhythmical use of them. So the one musical theme develops into the other with a complete naturalness and inevitability that is as convincing as the arrival of the second subject as the true complement to the first in a great classical symphony." Dyneley Hussey, *Verdi*.

for the second aria, the *"Sempre libera"*—"Free forever"—a complete contrast in its furious pace to the introspective soliloquy we have just heard. She is resolved to remain free, unencumbered, owing no responsibility; to live from day to day, to live only for passing enjoyment. But as the lady protests too much, she suddenly hears from beneath the balcony Alfredo singing once more the melody with which we are already familiar. The only effect of this is to make her shake off her doubts with ever greater determination. As the aria reaches its hectic climax, we are reminded that Marie said to the young Dumas, "Only a life of excitement can keep me alive."

ACT II

Scene One

The scene is a country house near Paris, where Violetta and Alfredo count the world well lost in their seclusion. Five months have passed. We have left Violetta asserting that she will never take love seriously. Just the opposite has happened. We are now to meet a new Violetta, one who, so to speak, has renounced coloratura, a woman tender and yielding. First, however, we learn of Alfredo's joy, as he enters to soliloquize, in the aria *"De' miei bollenti spiriti"* —"She is the cause of my happiness"—and he tells us that his beloved has banished everything and everybody for his sake, that the past no longer seems to exist, and that their life together, here in the country, has become a heaven to him.

Annina, Violetta's maid, runs in, much agitated. To Alfredo's questioning as to where she has been, she replies that she was sent to Paris by her mistress with the commission to sell all of Violetta's possessions, including her horses and her carriage. Learning that they are in debt to the amount of a thousand louis, Alfredo—who indeed seems not to have lived on this earth—realizes the precariousness of their finances and declares that he himself will go to Paris and somehow raise the required sum. Violetta is not to know of the reason for his absence. (This scene is followed by another tenor aria of poor quality which is invariably omitted.)

At last Violetta enters, immediately asks for Alfredo, and is told merely that he has left for Paris but that he will return shortly.

She wonders at his absence. A servant brings her a letter. Before
reading it, she tells the servant that she is expecting a businessman
to call and that he is to be admitted instantly. Then she opens the
letter, which turns out to be from Flora, who has discovered Violetta's hideaway and is inviting her to a party. They will expect
her in vain, says Violetta. Just then the servant returns, with the
news that the gentleman has arrived. It must be the man whom she
has been expecting. But it is not. Instead, a dignified and elderly
stranger enters, asks whether he is in the presence of Violetta
Valery, and introduces himself as Alfredo's father. Yes, the father
of that same Alfredo whom she is luring to his ruin.

The scene between the elder Germont and Violetta is pivotal.
Verdi planned and worked the scene through with loving care.
Much of it is carried forward in recitative, but it is a recitative of
great intensity, with expressive participation by the orchestra. The
recitative blooms into full-scale melodies—without any of the
stop-and-go traditional to the older operas—and these melodies are
all of the finest inspiration. There is Germont's aria (*"Pura siccome
un angelo"*—"Pure as an angel"), Violetta's agitated answer (*"Non
sapete quale affetto"*—"Do you not know what affection"), Germont's plea (*"Bella voi siete"*—"You are beautiful"), which leads
into an extended duet. After the duet, Violetta sings the melody of
"Dite alla giovine"—"Tell the young girl"—the notes of which
seem to be made of glistening tears. Germont's voice joins it. This
second duet is followed by another recitative, which culminates in
Violetta's agonized cry of *"Morrò!"*—"I shall die!" Once more the
two voices unite for the leavetaking and a closing cadenza. So rich,
so full is this music that the scene seems longer than it really is.
So much happens musically that we are unaware of the dramatic
fact that Violetta gives up the struggle rather too quickly.

Let us now follow this scene which, as I mentioned earlier, is a
condensation of the dialogue of the play:

Violetta reproves Germont with new-found dignity. "I am a
woman and you are in my house." Nor is his accusation just. Germont, glancing about, observes the splendor of the house. To
apprise him of the true state of affairs, she shows him a paper
which proves that, far from "ruining Alfredo," it is she who is
selling her possessions. Germont is instinctively drawn to this
woman, sweet and gentle, so different from the creature he had

expected to encounter. Why is it that the past rises up to accuse her? The past no longer exists, she assures him. God will erase it for the sake of her love for Alfredo.

Yet Germont must unburden himself of the task he has shouldered. He asks her as the father of a family for an enormous sacrifice (*"Pura siccome un angelo"*). He is concerned not with one child but with two. The happiness of both lies in her decision. Alfredo has a sister. The girl is about to be married. But the marriage can never take place unless the blot smeared on Alfredo's family can be wiped away. "I understand," replies Violetta. "You wish me to separate myself from Alfredo until after the wedding. It will be a grievous separation, but I am willing."

Germont asks for more. She must give Alfredo up, give him up forever. No! Violetta protests in horror. Never! Never! Can he not realize how deeply she loves his son (*"Non sapete"*)? Friends, family, the whole world, the very reason for her living on—she finds them all in her lover and only in her lover. Does Germont not know that she is prey to a deadly sickness? If she had to give up Alfredo, that would be tantamount to ending her life at once.

The father, though moved by deep sympathy, asks her to listen to him as calmly as she can (*"Bella voi siete"*). He points out to her that his son is young and changeable. The day may come when he will weary of her. Is it possible that a union such as theirs can endure? Violetta sorrowfully admits the justice of his doubts. "It is true," she whispers over and over again, as he pleads. There is time yet, Germont exhorts, to save the happiness of his children.

Weeping bitterly, she consents (*"Ah! Dite alla giovine"*). "Tell your young daughter that for the sake of her happiness a victim must be found, one ready to blot out the only ray of light she has ever known, one who is prepared even for death." Germont's reply, equally moving, is, "Weep, weep! I know how awful is the sacrifice which I am demanding."

"What is to be done?" Violetta asks humbly. "Tell Alfredo you no longer love him." "He will not believe me." "Then leave him." "He will follow me." "What then?" "Embrace me as your daughter and I shall be strong enough to know what to do." (These short questions-and-answers are superbly expressed in the music.) She asks him to go into the garden and wait for his son's return. And someday he must tell Alfredo the truth: that her action was born of her love. She will die, she exclaims in the final section of the scene, but he must look to it that Alfredo does not curse her memory. "You must live," replies Germont. He assures her that he can measure the enormity of the sacrifice she is making. And so they part.

Violetta sits down again to write a letter. She calls Annina, who starts in surprise when she sees the address.[10] Then, to the accompaniment of a melancholy clarinet, she writes another letter, which she conceals in confusion when Alfredo enters. "To whom have you been writing?" he asks. "To you." "Give me the letter." "Not now." Alfredo is ill at ease. He has had word from his father, a reproving letter. Still, when his father sees Violetta, he is bound to change his mind. She begs that she be excused from being present at the interview between son and father. Scarcely repressing her tears, she adds that later, when Alfredo has calmed his father, she will fall at Germont's feet. "All will be well, because you, Alfredo, love me. You love me. Is it not true?" And she ends with the great cry, the melody of which we have previously heard in the Prelude, "Love me, Alfredo! Love me as much as I love you!" All that is tender and compassionate in Verdi's nature seems to well up in this outburst of the forsaken girl. It is one of the high moments of the work, and it was not until Desdemona that Verdi was to achieve anything like it.

Alfredo, left alone, wonders whether it is not now too late in the day for his father's visit. The manservant enters hastily to tell him that his mistress has departed, taking the road to Paris. Annina too has disappeared. Alfredo is not disturbed, for he assumes that Violetta has gone to Paris to speed the sale of the property and that Annina will prevent her from doing so. A commissioner now enters (all this coming and going is awkwardly handled) to deliver a letter to Alfredo. He recognizes the handwriting. He is deeply troubled. He rips open the letter and gets no further than the opening words—"Alfredo, when this reaches you"—knows that Violetta has left him, turns with a wild cry, and finds himself facing his father, who has entered from the garden. In despair, Alfredo buries his face in his hands, while Germont embarks on an attempt

---

[10] It is quite unclear in the opera what this signifies. In the play, Marguerite writes to one of her former lovers, Arthur Varville, and it is obvious that she is forsaking Armand to take up her previous life.

to console his son. He finds nothing more convincing than to re-call to Alfredo his home, his happy childhood home, the beauty of Provence and its sparkling sea (*"Di Provenza il mar"*). This aria is hardly an adequate expression of the psychological situation. Musically, both its melody and its rocking accompaniment are old-fashioned, and one cannot free oneself from the suspicion that Verdi wrote it to give the baritone at least one aria: it is the only one he sings in the opera.

Germont's appeal fails, even in repetition (which is always cut in performance), and as Alfredo rushes off distracted, crying for vengeance, the curtain comes down. It is significant that the quality of the music declines the moment Violetta leaves the stage.

Scene Two

The scene is a richly furnished apartment in Flora's Parisian mansion. (Verdi's Flora seems to be a good deal more prosperous than her counterpart in the play.) There are gaming tables, re-freshments are being offered, and more or less the same crowd is assembled here that we met in Violetta's house in the first act. As the curtain rises, we see Flora, the Marquis d'Obigny, and Dr. Grenvil. (We wonder why the good doctor is to be found at every party. He really takes no part in the opera until the third act, when he makes the shortest medical call on record. Verdi must have felt that since he needed a bass voice in the final scene, he might as well employ him throughout the evening.) We learn at once from Flora that she has invited both Violetta and Alfredo to the party. The Marquis tells her that the two lovers have parted and that if Violetta does come it will be in company of another man, the Baron Douphol. The doctor confirms this. He saw Vio-letta with the Baron yesterday and they seemed happy.

The party appears to be a masquerade, for a bevy of female guests enter disguised as gypsies and ready to tell anybody's for-tune. After they sing their chorus, a new group of guests, includ-ing Gastone, appear; they are dressed as Spanish matadors and recommend themselves as doughty fighters. Once again all is gaiety and party spirit, and the two choral numbers are pleasant music. As the play at the gaming tables starts, Alfredo suddenly makes his entrance. Questioned by Flora, he peremptorily replies that he knows nothing of Violetta's whereabouts and sits down to play. He seems to give all his attention to the cards; yet he is quite aware that Violetta has appeared, that she is splendidly dressed, and that she leans on Baron Douphol's arm. The Baron informs her in a whisper that young Germont is here and warns her not to address a single word to him. All through this music, with its gaiety, there wanders a strange figure for the clarinets which seems to accent an underlying atmosphere of nervousness. Verdi makes us feel the tension underneath the levity. Violetta, at the sight of Alfredo, exclaims more to herself than to anybody in particular, "Why was I so rash as to come here?" This phrase, which seems to rise from a substratum of anxiety, is repeated twice later in the scene, with the same extraordinarily poignant effect.

Alfredo keeps winning. A slighting remark he makes about his former mistress angers the Baron, who suggests that he and Alfredo play against each other. The game begins while the other guests, including Violetta, gradually leave the room, only Alfredo and the Baron remaining behind. Alfredo's luck still holds, and the Baron asks that he be given his revenge on another occasion. "At any game you choose," replies Alfredo. They join the others. For a moment the stage is left empty.

But only for a moment. Then in great agitation Violetta re-enters. She has sent word to Alfredo to join her. So he does, in another minute. And the two young people hurl at each other the broken phrases of wounded love. Violetta begs him to quit the house. Alfredo refuses. If in the duel which is threatening he manages to kill the Baron, he will experience the satisfaction of depriving Violetta of her present lover and protector. "But it is for you that I fear," cries Violetta. "Very well, I will leave on one condition, that you accompany me." "This I cannot do, for I have sworn to another that I will forget you." "Is the other Baron Douphol?" With a painful effort she stammers out, "Yes." "Then you love him?" "Yes, I love him."

Goaded beyond sanity, Alfredo runs to the door and shouts to the company to return. Then, in the presence of everybody, he violently denounces Violetta. "This is the woman who, for the sake of our love, lavished her possessions on me. Blind and credulous, I accepted the sacrifice. Now it is time to repay my debt." With this, he flings a purse contemptuously at Violetta's feet. The guests, horror-struck by his brutal behavior, protest loudly. At this opportune moment Germont *père* enters—and do not ask how he happens to find himself in the house of a demimondaine! Only Piave and Verdi can answer the question.

Not only has he entered, but he has the presumption, after all the trouble he has caused, to censure his son for behavior unworthy of a Germont (*"Di sprezzo degno"*). This builds up to the big act-closing ensemble, the guests continuing to express their disapproval, Alfredo sobbing in torment, Germont being stern, Flora and her friends pitying Violetta, and Violetta's soprano voice floating above the concerted body of the music, in typical Verdian fashion. Violetta prays that time will bring the truth to light and that when it does, God will lighten Alfredo's remorse. At the end, Germont drags his son off, the Baron following them.

ACT III

With the last scene we return to the intimate atmosphere of *La Traviata*, to its chamber-music quality. In seemingly the most transparent of styles, by the ineluctable sweetness of his melodies, by the sincerity of his recitative, all the more heartbreaking because it is not grandiloquent, Verdi conveys the weariness and despair of the sick girl. The Prelude is one of the loveliest things he wrote. As in the first act, it is based on two themes, the first, played by divided violins, being the theme with which the first-act Prelude opens, the second a new theme which rises to great intensity only to sink down and die out in a series of gentle sobs.

The curtain rises on Violetta's bedroom. Violetta is asleep. Her maid, Annina, faithful to the last, sits by the fireplace. She is dozing. It is seven o'clock in the morning. Violetta awakes and asks for a sip of water. Annina gives it to her, opens the shutters, looks out, and observes with pleasure that Dr. Grenvil is even now coming to see them. This scene, as well as the one with the doctor, is set to musical material from the Prelude, the mood being continuous. Dr. Grenvil assists Violetta to seat herself. To his question she replies that her body suffers but that her soul is tranquil. She slept soundly the preceding night. "Take courage. You will soon be on the road to convalescence," the doctor assures her. With a smile Violetta calls this the white lie practiced by the medical profession. As Grenvil leaves, Annina whispers to him, "How is she really?" and receives the reply that she has but a few hours to live.

Again alone with Annina, Violetta recalls that this is a holiday. It is carnival time; all Paris is celebrating. How much money is there left for them? Twenty louis. Violetta bids her take half of the trifling sum and give it to the poor. She herself will not need money any more. Annina leaves the room to carry out her mistress' wish.

Now Violetta is quite alone. She takes a letter from her bosom. She reads it aloud—how many times has she read it already!—speaking the words to an accompaniment which cites Alfredo's declaration of love in the first act, the melody being played by a solo violin. This is the letter: "You have kept your promise. The duel has taken place. The Baron was wounded, but is now recovering. Alfredo has gone abroad. I myself have revealed your sacrifice to him. He will return to implore your pardon. So will I. Take care of your health and trust in a happier future. Giorgio Germont."

"It is late," she cries in a veiled voice. "I have waited, I have waited, but he does not come." She looks at herself in the mirror. Seeing her ravaged face—"Oh, how I have changed!"—her thoughts hark back to her former beauty. She sings a song of renunciation, a little aria of farewell ("*Addio del passato*"). She bids farewell to all her past, to her smiling dreams, to beauty, to flowers.[11] Nothing matters, for Alfredo no longer loves her. There is a curious touch at the end of the first strophe:[12] the aria ends with coloratura, on the words, "All is finished." It is as if the "*Sempre libera*" turned wan and pallid. As Violetta sinks back into silence, the strains of a bacchanalian chorus float up from the street, the echo of the carnival.

Scarcely have the sounds of distant revelry ceased when Annina returns, quite out of breath with excitement, to prepare Violetta for great news. Alfredo is coming! He himself follows hard on the heels of the joyous announcement, and the lovers rush into each other's arms. Never again will they be parted, they tell each other in rushed phrases that stumble over one another in excitement. They will turn their backs on Paris forever and breathe a happier air (the duet: "*Parigi, o cara*"). All will yet be well: her health

---

11 She calls herself in this song "*la traviata*," the only time the title is used in the text.
12 The second is usually omitted.

will bloom once more, sickness and misery will become but a memory.

But the shock of joy has been too much for her. She falters and turns deathly pale. It is nothing, she assures him, as she assured her guests in the first act. No, she is strong again, she wants to get up, get dressed, go out. But when she attempts it, she falls back with a gesture of defeat and the cry, "I cannot!" Alfredo begs Annina to summon the doctor again.

From the end of *"Parigi, o cara"* to the close of the opera we experience once again a sequence of melody and recitative so closely interlocked as to become one, and demonstrating, as it has been demonstrated in several scenes of the opera, Verdi's greatness as a musical dramatist. "If your return has not saved me, no one on earth can save me," sings Violetta softly. Immediately the strings rush in an upward scale to a great chord, which punctuates Violetta's exclamation of futile revolt: "Ah, great God! To die so young" (*"Ah! gran' Dio! Morir si giovine"*).

While Alfredo attempts to comfort her, Annina returns with the doctor as well as with Germont. The father has come to welcome Violetta as his daughter. But she has no illusions left. Nor has he. Seeing her state, the elder Germont is overcome by pangs of conscience. "I have been a foolish old man," he murmurs.

Violetta hardly hears him. She takes a miniature of herself from a casket and gives it to Alfredo (*"Prendi, quest' è immagine"*— "Take this, it is my image"). It will remind him of their happy days together, it will recall to him one who loved him beyond measure. Here, near the end of the opera, Verdi uses the massed chord effect with which we are familiar from the *"Miserere"* of *Il Trovatore;* these chords sound like heralds of death. If one day he should meet another girl with whom he could fall in love, he is to give her the portrait and tell her that it is a gift from one who is praying for them both. The other voices join Violetta's voice in a brief quintet.

Then suddenly we hear once more, for the last time, the melody of Alfredo's song. A trembling of strings begins. "How strange!" Violetta whispers. "How strange! The pains have ceased. . . . I feel awakening in myself the strength I used to possess. I am returning to life. . . . Oh, joy!" she cries, and with that cry falls back lifeless.

"She has perished," announces the doctor.

We wonder why Verdi ended the opera with the doctor's matter-of-fact statement. Dumas' play ends with this line: "Sleep in peace, Marguerite! Much shall be forgiven you, because you have loved so much."

OTELLO

COMPOSER:	Giuseppe Verdi
LIBRETTIST:	Arrigo Boito
FIRST PERFORMANCE:	February 5, 1887 Teatro della Scala, Milan
RECEPTION:	Success

CHARACTERS:

Otello, Moor of Venice	Tenor
Iago, Otello's ensign	Baritone
Cassio, Otello's lieutenant	Tenor
Roderigo, a Venetian gentleman	Tenor
Lodovico, ambassador of Venice	Bass
Montano, former governor of Cyprus	Bass
A herald	Bass
Desdemona, bride of Otello	Soprano
Emilia, Desdemona's companion	Mezzo-soprano

OTHELLO
AND OTELLO

". . . the climax of tragic opera."

DONALD JAY GROUT

Less than *Hamlet* but more than *Macbeth* and much more than *Julius Caesar* does *Othello* invite personal interpretation. Those of us who have got beyond accepting the play simply as the story of a husband who raises an unholy fuss about a lost handkerchief are provoked into cogitating on the meaning of the tragedy as a whole and the nature of the noble Moor specifically. We plunge into the sea of its poetry to chart the topography of its hero's traits. What reefs, what rocks lie in Othello's soul? "Both the best and the worst of men," Mark Van Doren called Othello; we may add that he is both the simplest and the most complex of men.

The play itself is both simple and complex. It is a domestic tragedy, played on a something less than regal level. It is earthbound, no ghost appearing from the grave, no weird sisters pointing the protagonist to a course which he himself wants to pursue. Moon and stars, wind and tempest, earthquake and portents, these are absent or assume but a slight role in the upheaval which takes place in the house and the bedchamber. The coincidences which make the trickery succeed, Iago enjoying exceptional luck, are simple. The innocent bystanders, Cassio and Emilia, as well as the not-so-innocent bystander, Roderigo, all of whom serve destruction's progress, are simple people. The direct instrument is not a scarf of knightly purple but a handkerchief spotted with strawberries, a "trifle light as air."

Yet *Othello* is a mystic play, and its last meaning is as undecipherable as mystery itself. No amount of reasoning will exhaust Othello's character, no analysis will satisfactorily dissect Iago's apparently unmotivated malevolence. As we watch this play, we are borne along on two swift currents, the icy current of evil which "ne'er feels retiring ebb" and the warm current of love which makes us cry, "The pity of it!" The sources of these currents are undiscoverable; both empty into the infinite.

No wonder, then, that the play has challenged many to ponder, to interpret, to pass it through the "quick forge and working-house of thought," to react strongly for or against it.

I once heard an American psychoanalyst trace Othello's jealousy not to a feeling of inferiority because he was older than Desdemona, not to his "sooty" complexion—though both entered into his motivation—but to the traumatic blow dealt him long ago, when (as he tells us in the autobiographical speech before the Senate) he was in his "boyish days . . . taken by the insolent foe; And sold to slavery."

I once heard Thomas Mann assert that Othello was a man obsessed by the wish for death. Mann himself felt a deep affinity to the play. He knew it in German translation and he believed that this translation, by Schlegel and Tieck, had brought the play closer to German-speaking people than it is to English-speaking audiences. For the German version is written in modern poetry, or at least modern enough for practical purposes, having been completed in the early nineteenth century, and thus avoids the difficulties and obscurities of Elizabethan language, with its "an' if you list" and "gennets for germans."[1] To show what he meant, he read in translation, aloud in his mellifluous voice, the speech of the dying Othello. And it did sound beautiful when he read it.

I once heard an Italian critic proclaim that Othello's motivation was so unconvincing that the play cried out for the "unreasonableness of musical treatment." Is it not too much to ask us to believe that Othello, in one single scene, without hearing anything from

---

[1] "Spanish horses for relatives," the result of Othello's marrying Desdemona. Iago to Brabantio (Act I, Scene 1).

Desdemona or allowing Cassio to tell his side of the story, is stretched on the rack? Such sudden tempest in a man's soul can only be accepted in the world of opera.

Not at all, say others. There is nothing improbable in this play. Othello's credulity is plausible in terms of his character, his trust in "honest Iago" has logic, a suffering soul's logic to be sure, but logic all the same. His seeming gullibility was, at any rate, quite acceptable to Elizabethan audiences—who looked for other qualities than verisimilitude in their plays—and is acceptable to modern audiences, as well. Only German professors who turn the pages back and forth cannot accept it.[2]

What kind of a man is Othello? To A. C. Bradley, whose *Shakespearean Tragedy,* published in 1904, is still one of the most stimulating books on the subject, Othello is the victim of "the shock of a terrible disillusionment." To Coleridge, Othello was a trusting soul felled "by the superhuman art of Iago." To Schlegel, Othello was a barbaric nature covered over by the mask of military discipline and a superficial refinement which Venetian sophistication had taught him. To other German critics Othello is a puppet of Fate, Iago being aided by "a perverted world order."

These few examples may suffice to document the point that diverse minds find diverse interpretations of the play. And the creative mind takes from Othello what suits him best, what is of use to his imagination and the bent of his thinking.

This brings us to Verdi and the tremendous music drama which he began to compose at the age of seventy-two and which, in many aspects, represents the crowning glory of his achievement. This is tantamount to saying that *Otello* is the crowning glory of Italian opera. And this may be tantamount to saying that *Otello* is the crowning glory of *all* opera.

Before discussing the work itself, let us note that Verdi made a wise choice. Of all the tragedies of Shakespeare, none lends itself better to operatic treatment than *Othello.* Not only is the plot direct and clear, but the play is free of side issues, such subsidiary themes as the Polish war in *Hamlet* or the Gloucester-Edgar relationship in *King Lear. Othello*'s stageworthiness has been com-

---

[2] These points have been treated in a highly regarded essay by Elmer Edgar Stoll: *Othello: An Historical and Comparative Study* (University of Minnesota, 1915).

mented upon by (among other scholars) M. R. Ridley, the editor
of the *New Temple Shakespeare:*

> It is superb theatre, with the severest economy and concentration, and
> it is by far the most intense of all. There is no relief, none of that alter-
> nating increase and decrease of strain that is so clearly marked in the
> others, none of those periods in which, even though there is no comic
> relief, the action seems for a few moments to stand still while we recover
> ourselves. From the moment of the landing in Cyprus Shakespeare has the
> fingers of one hand on our pulses and the fingers of the other on the levers
> of the rack. It is the most cruel play he wrote, and the most pitiful.

Concentrated, economical, cruel, pitiful—these are characteristics of good music drama. (Boito did begin the libretto with the
landing in Cyprus.) Incidentally, *Othello* has always enjoyed special popularity in Italy, the intensity of its emotion making an appeal to the Mediterranean mind. In Italy too Othello found what
many believe to be his greatest interpreter, Tommaso Salvini.[3]

In a way all of Verdi's adult life served to ready him for the task
of setting *Othello* to music. All of his life he was fascinated by
Shakespeare, and references to the poet are numerous in Verdi's
letters. *Macbeth,* which he composed forty years before *Othello,*
served, so to speak, as a trial run. *Macbeth* contains scenes which
come close to the play, the sleepwalking scene notably. Yet it is not
Shakespearean; Verdi was not at home in the witches' foul and
filthy air. Nor was he as a young man up to a Shakespearean task.
But when a French critic pointed this out and wrote that "Verdi
did not know Shakespeare," the composer, who usually shrugged
off critical remarks with indifference, was stung to a rejoinder: "I
may not have rendered *Macbeth* well, but that I do not know, do
not understand and feel Shakespeare, no, by heavens, no! He is one
of my very special poets, and I have had him in my hands from
my earliest youth, and I read and reread him continually." Verdi
called Shakespeare "the great searcher of the human heart." Two
years after he completed *Otello,* we find him quoting *Hamlet.* It
was proposed that Verdi be honored in a special commemorative
festival to celebrate the fiftieth anniversary of the premiere of
his first opera. He rejected the idea firmly. If a commemoration be

[3] He visited the United States five times, on one occasion playing Othello to the Iago
of Edwin Booth.

necessary, let it take place "fifty days after my death. . . . Does not
the grand poet say, 'O heavens! die two months ago, and not forgotten yet?' "

In the summer of 1879 Verdi, the conductor Franco Faccio,[4]
and the publisher Giulio Ricordi were having dinner at Verdi's
apartment in Milan. The conversation turned, perhaps not accidentally, to Shakespeare, to *Othello*, and to Boito, the intellectual
and fine-grained young man, himself a composer as well as a
librettist, who, they said, profoundly loved the play. Verdi
knew Boito: nearly two decades before, the poet had written the
words to "The Hymn of the Nations," an inconsequential work
which Verdi had produced for the London International Exhibition in 1862. After that the two men had drifted apart. Verdi did
not particularly like Boito, remembering certain unflattering remarks the poet had made about the older man's music. But during
the seventies Boito's opinion of Verdi underwent a change; he became enthusiastic about *Aïda* and the *Requiem*. Verdi, who was not
the man to carry a grudge, was ready to ascribe Boito's offending
opinions to the sins of youth. Ricordi, too, had set Verdi straight.
He took care to keep Verdi informed of Boito's change of heart,
and he hinted that the composer and librettist of *Mefistofele*, then
a successful opera, though unwilling to write a libretto for just
anyone, would deem it an honor to write one for Verdi. The world
of opera owes Giulio Ricordi more than one debt of gratitude, for
without his tact and foresight we might not have had an *Otello*
(or a Puccini, whom Ricordi encouraged and supported).

At any rate, Faccio brought Boito to see Verdi a day or so after
the dinner, and three days later Boito sent Verdi an outline of a
libretto on the subject. (This suggests that the plot to interest
Verdi had been hatched previous to the dinner. It is hardly possible for Boito to have sketched a libretto in three days.) Verdi
thanked him and kept the manuscript for further consideration.

The year after, Boito revised the libretto of *Simone Boccanegra*
for Verdi, and thus the composer had a further opportunity to
work with the younger man and to take the measure of his quality.

For the moment, however, no progress was made. Verdi may
have felt that his career was behind him; *Aïda* was to have been

---

[4] He was a composer of operas as well, one of his works being nothing less than
Amleto, to a libretto by Boito.

his last opera. It was another five years before Verdi actually began
the composition of what he then called *Iago*. The whole project
nearly had come to grief the year before; at a banquet to Boito in
Naples, Boito was reported to have said that he was sorry not to be
composing *Iago* himself. Verdi offered to return the manuscript of
the libretto "without the slightest resentment." But Boito refused
to accept such an offer and had little difficulty in proving that he
had been misquoted.

What it was that terminated Verdi's reluctance, other than the
natural self-renewing power of genius, we do not know. It is a
safe guess, though, that his interest in Shakespeare as well as his
satisfaction with the libretto submitted were contributing causes.
The composition proceeded in great secrecy, Verdi still declaring
that he would not write another work for the stage. He didn't fool
many. The rumor factory kept busy, and the singer Maurel prog-
nosticated in an interview that Verdi was preparing a surprise for
the musical world; in his *Iago* he would give "the young musicians
of the future a severe lesson." Verdi was not at all pleased. "Heaven
forbid!" he wrote to Ricordi. "It never has been and never will be
my intention to give lessons to anybody."

As the work proceeded, Verdi was besieged by singers in the
hope of procuring parts, as well as by opera houses vying for the
honor to be first to produce the new opera. It was a foregone conclusion that this privilege would be awarded to La Scala and that
the conductor chosen by Verdi should be his friend Franco Faccio.
Up to the last the work was kept secret; when the principal artists
were engaged for it, they were made to promise to divulge no details of it or of its production. Verdi reserved the right to withdraw
the opera during the rehearsals or even after the dress rehearsal.

We have several contemporary accounts of the premiere (February 5, 1887). One such is a book written by a British writer,
Blanche Roosevelt, entitled *Verdi, Milan, and Othello*. The enthusiasm was unprecedented, even for a work by Verdi. The square in
front of La Scala was black with people from early morning on.
In the dead of winter—"an Italian does not feel cold on an occasion
like this!" The audience, convened from all of musical Europe, was
seated fully an hour before the performance was to begin.

When, at the end of the first act, the public having tried in vain
to coax Verdi to show himself during the act, the composer took a

curtain call, an immense and simultaneous shout made the theater rock. At the end of the opera Verdi was called out twenty times. The audience rose in a body. Many wept. When the composer left the theater, his admirers unharnessed the horses from his carriage and drew the carriage to his hotel. Back in his apartment and listening to the shouts of the people outside, Verdi was plunged into a melancholy mood. He felt as if he had "fired off my last cartridge." But then that mood passed, and with a smile on his face he said, "If I were thirty years younger, I should like to begin another opera tomorrow, provided only that Boito write the libretto."

That Boito may claim a considerable share of the success of the work is apparent from a comparison of play and libretto. The more we study the libretto, the higher becomes our admiration. *Otello* is *Othello,* though with important differences of which more needs to be said in a moment. Boito labored not only to shorten the play but further to simplify and "concentrate" it. He cut away the entire first act, the expository act in Venice, using elements of Othello's speech before the Senate as a reminiscence within the love duet which closes the first act of the opera. He suppressed one or two telling passages, such as Iago's suspicion (or pretended suspicion) of an unlawful relationship between Emilia and Othello. Because Desdemona's father does not appear, the words which may drop the first drop of poison on Othello, and which Iago cunningly uses later, remain unspoken:

> BRABANTIO: Look to her, Moor, if thou hast eyes to see.
> She has deceiv'd her father, and may thee.

Bianca, Cassio's mistress, is eliminated, with no great loss. So is the Fool, who as a matter of fact hardly ever appears in productions of the play. Roderigo plays a less important part and the nocturnal scene in which he is stabbed by Iago (Act V, Scene 1) is excised, so that we get the news of his death merely in one line by Emilia. The end of the tragedy is shortened, Emilia is not killed, and no mention is made of the punishment which is to overtake Iago. Boito added choruses which launch the first act in warlike tension and in the third act provide the great finale. (It is interesting, however, to learn that Verdi planned at the beginning to compose *Iago* without any choruses.)

What Boito did accomplish is to preserve the essential characteristics of the three principal protagonists, Othello's immense capacity to love and loathe, Iago's fanatic drive, Desdemona's obtuse unawareness. The cruelty of the conflict, the deep damnation of Othello's downfall, the relentlessness of the destruction, the simple nobility of the retribution—all these remain in the opera as they are in the play. Boito's language, though not of course Shakespearean, is vivid and of very high quality.

This language served Verdi's music as well as if the composer himself had written the words. But it would have been unsuitable to the young Verdi; a new musical flexibility was needed to do it justice.

Verdi's climb was a constant one. Beginning with genius—the raw material must be present—but a blatant genius, often naïve, occasionally vulgar, he refined, deepened, and subtilized himself in the alembic of his self-criticism. Constantly higher, that movement upward is characteristic of certain artists, though others do not show it. Mendelssohn, Schumann, Botticelli—the distance between their early works and their late works is relatively inconsiderable. Beethoven, Michelangelo, and Verdi traveled a far journey. Far, indeed, from *Oberto*, his first opera, to the *Requiem*. Even measured against *Aïda*, Verdi's previous operatic stop, the distance is amazing. In *Otello* he has abjured all rough magic, has banished all easy effects, and has done away with all set "numbers" which announce themselves as such. *Otello*, though theatrically effective, is not theatrical in the derogatory sense in which we use the word. Yet—here is not a new composer speaking, but the same Verdi, the same Verdi who could and did and still would invent beautiful melodies which issue gratefully from human throats and fall gratefully on human ears. These melodies are now amalgamated into a musical structure so homogeneous, so continuous, so expressive in the service of character and situation, that we are no longer conscious of them as separate numbers. Indeed, it is difficult to excerpt from *Otello*—with one or two exceptions such as Iago's *"Credo"* or Desdemona's Willow Song—any "arias."

If we were to listen to Verdi's opinions rather than his music, *Otello* would be a most un-Verdian work. Several times Verdi warned against making opera symphonic. He pleaded that symphony and opera were two separate arts, the first the natural tradition of the North, the second the natural tradition of the descendants of Palestrina. Yet *Otello* is nothing if not symphonic. Not only does the orchestra play a major role (perhaps *the* major role), but many of the themes are short and so pliable as to be able to be manipulated and developed symphonically. From the "oom-pah" of his orchestra's early accompaniments Verdi arrives at an orchestral expression as sonorous as the Greek chorus—and as profound.

To the inspiration of Shakespeare and the inspiration of Boito (who himself shows astonishing growth if we consider that twelve years before *Otello* he penned the vulgar libretto of *La Gioconda*) Verdi matched the mastery that he had gained by a lifetime of musical experience and by a lifetime of introspective thought. His musical character delineation is especially remarkable. It is a characteristic of the play that each of the three major protagonists expresses himself in language which has individual tone and cadence; Stoll calls this the "poetic identity" of the characters. In *Otello* this becomes "musical identity."

In the play we see Othello first as the assured and mature man in all his dignity, then as the trusting lover, then as a somewhat impulsive but just commander. Throughout all the early scenes, in whatever aspect he is shown, he is a poet. Then, when the rope tightens around his heart, we see him fall into a raving, ranting, shaking invalid, stripped of self-control and shrouded in a black night through which glimmer only occasionally some pale lights of his great love. We see him capable of base cruelty and blood-lust. At the end, after the tragedy has been consummated, we see him rise once more to being the noble Moor he once was, to being the poet. All this is paralleled in the opera, the music at every stage filling the character. So we hear Otello as the general in the beginning of the first act, as the lover in the scene which closes the first act, as the tormented human being in the second act, as the tormentor in the third, and finally, in his ineffably beautiful farewell, as the soul, steeped in guilt, which acknowledges the necessity for atonement. Every facet Verdi illumines in music—now harsh, now pitiful—music which we understand and feel.

We have noted that the character of Iago held a special fascination for Verdi, that most un-Iagoesque of men. Even before he began the composition of the opera, he described to one of his friends, the painter Domenico Morelli, how he, Verdi, would play Iago if he were an actor.

. . . I would have a long thin face, thin lips, small eyes close to the nose, as monkeys have, a high receding forehead, with the back of the head well developed. His manner would be absent-minded, *nonchalant,* indifferent about everything, skeptical, bantering, and he would say both good and evil things lightly, as if he were thinking about something completely different from what he is saying, so that if anyone were to reprove him and say: "What you're saying or what you're doing is monstrous," he could perfectly well answer: "Really. I didn't see it that way; let's say no more of it then!" A fellow like that might deceive everybody, even his own wife, up to a certain point. But a malicious looking little fellow makes everybody suspicious and deceives no one!

We may compare this to the opinion of a stage producer, Margaret Webster:

The universal acceptance of Iago as "honest," another postulate which has been widely questioned, has been often belied in the theatre. Iagos have adopted the sinister mien of a typical Italianate villain to an extent which would cause any sensible housewife to hide the silver spoons the moment he crossed the threshold. . . . Iago is very fully revealed in the text, without the aid of sidelong glances, evil chuckles, and a waxed moustache. The brilliant speed of his small, unscrupulous thinking, the dash of recklessness, the complete worldly armory of his mind, the plenitude of will and the absolute lack of imagination are all full and clear and contrasted unerringly with Othello's utterly alien make-up. A theatrical cast of villainy will ruin both of them.[5]

How alike these two observations are!

Verdi's musical characterization of Iago is as precise as that of Otello. Iago sings a language quite his own. One of the characteristics of that language is the employment of the shake or trill. It occurs again and again, usually in a low register, and blackens the music with skepticism. We hear that trill in the vocal line early in the first act, when Iago, complaining that the Moor has passed him by in preferment, says:

> He (in good time) must his lieutenant be,
> And I (God bless the mark!) his Moorship's ancient.[6]

[5] *Shakespeare Without Tears.*

[6] "Ancient" is equivalent to our "ensign," and denotes the lowest commissioned rank in the army.

"Alfiere"—"ancient"—Iago sings and with the word shakes out "evil things lightly." We hear it again in the *"Credo,"* again in the speech about jealousy in Act II, and again at the close of the third act, when Iago, standing erect and pointing to the inert body of the fallen Otello, exclaims, *"Ecco il leone!"*—"Behold the lion!"

The nonchalant, bantering tone of which Verdi spoke is present as well. It pervades the music of the first act, where Iago is the hail-fellow-well-met, everybody's friend and comrade in arms, bluff, plain, straightforward, "honest" Iago. It is the dominant motive of the third-act scene in which he draws the unsuspecting Cassio into speaking of and laughing over Bianca, with Otello listening. This scene is set to light, almost jocular music, as if it were the scherzo of a symphony. A grim scherzo, indeed!

As for Desdemona's musical characterization, it is here that we see most clearly the old Verdi at work. He endows her with the same sort of fluid melody that he has given to Violetta and Leonora and Elisabetta. Her lyric sweetness comes to the fore immediately in the first act when she addresses Otello as *"Mio superbo guerrier!"* —"My proud warrior!"—a phrase which would have fallen well from the lips of Violetta. Her melodiousness remains present through all of her pleading with Otello, her bewilderment, her disillusionment, her anxiety, and finally her fright, her voice becoming small and pitiful in the Willow Song of the final act.

DIFFERENCES BETWEEN PLAY AND OPERA

We have spoken of the remarkable similarities between play and opera, of the sensitive justice and the responsive understanding with which two men born to a different culture and a different language, removed in time from the original author by three centuries, treated Shakespeare's drama. But there are dissimilarities between play and opera, and these are no less interesting. We may assume, knowing that Verdi offered a number of suggestions to which the younger man acceded, that the changes made were made by Verdi and Boito together, working in full cooperation.

The first of these changes concerns those lines in which Shakespeare has expressed philosophical thoughts, those in which the poet observes the world around him. There is not much room for philosophical animadversion in an opera. Apothegms are unmusical. So we do not hear the Duke of Venice say:

When remedies are past, the griefs are ended
By seeing the worst, which late on hopes depended.
To mourn a mischief that is past and gone
Is the next way to draw new mischief on.

Nor do we hear Cassio muse in his grief:

O, I have lost my reputation! I have lost the immortal part of myself,
and what remains is bestial.

Nor Iago answer:

As I am an honest man, I thought you had received some bodily wound;
there is more offence in that than in reputation. Reputation is an idle and
most false imposition, oft got without merit and lost without deserving.

(On the other hand, Falstaff's similar reflections on honor were
used by Verdi—with delectable results!)

In the process of concentrating, some of the most famous lines of
the play—some popular quotations—fell by the wayside. Such as
Iago's "Put money in thy purse!" or his "Who steals my purse
steals trash," or the lines beginning "Not poppy, nor mandragora,"
or Othello's tragically simple, "But yet the pity of it, Iago! O Iago,
the pity of it, Iago."

Finally, Othello's soliloquy in the last act, the most introspective
of his utterances, in which he is torn between the love which suffuses him anew and the necessity of meting out punishment as if
he were the instrument of Fate—that speech, which softens anguish
by reflection, and is the very essence of poetry, is entirely omitted.
It is replaced—and perhaps this had to be so—by the orchestra, in
a famous recitative passage for bass cellos, beginning with the
lowest note of that instrument:

It is the cause, it is the cause, my soul.
Let me not name it to you, you chaste stars!
It is the cause. Yet I'll not shed her blood,
Nor scar that whiter skin of hers than snow,
And smooth as monumental alabaster.
Yet she must die, else she'll betray more men.
Put out the light, and then put out the light.
If I quench thee, thou flaming minister,
I can again thy former light restore,
Should I repent me; but once put out thy light,
Thou cunning'st pattern of excelling nature,

I know not where is that Promethean heat
That can thy light relume.

We can observe a difference more fundamental than omission. It
is a difference which sheds a light on Verdi's mind. *Othello* is a play
of sexual passion; it is erotically oriented. That eroticism is expressed in language rather than situation, because such was a necessity of the Elizabethan theater, with its employment of boys for
female parts.[7] That language, particularly when Othello himself
speaks it (and we must repeat that he is one of the greatest poets
among Shakespeare's characters) is of almost Oriental richness and
suggestiveness. The sexual note of the play is sounded at the outset
when Iago, rousing Brabantio, tells him: "I am one, sir, that come
to tell you your daughter and the Moor are now making the beast
with two backs." A little later (Scene 3), when Iago analyzes virtue ("Virtue? A fig!"), he speaks of "carnal stings, our unbitted
lusts." When Desdemona arrives at Cyprus (Act II, Scene 1),
some typical Elizabethan bantering goes on between Emilia and
Iago, with Desdemona listening. In spite of Desdemona's innocence,
one feels the sexually flirtatious tone of the scene. Iago scolds
women for being "players in your housewifery, and housewives in
your beds." Much later in the play, that scene is echoed (Act IV,
Scene 3) when Emilia and Desdemona discuss adultery; here
Emilia's earthy remarks serve as light relief against Desdemona's
sad Willow Song:

DESDEMONA: Wouldst thou do such a deed [commit adultery] for all the
world?
EMILIA: The world's a huge thing. It is a great price for a small vice.
DESDEMONA: Good troth, I think thou wouldst not.
EMILIA: By my troth, I think I should; and undo't when I had done it.
Marry, I would not do such a thing for a joint-ring, nor for measures
of lawn, nor for gowns, petticoats, nor caps, nor any petty exhibition;
but, for the whole world—'uds pity! who would not make her husband
a cuckold to make him a monarch? I should venture purgatory for't.

Othello's sexuality breaks through time and time again. In his
trance, Othello speaks of "noses, ears, and lips." "Lie with her! lie

[7] Physical contact is rare and restrained in Shakespeare's love scenes, even in *Romeo
and Juliet* or *Anthony and Cleopatra*, presumably because it would have struck Elizabethan audiences as ridiculous.

on her!" He babbles of goats and monkeys, which, to the Eliza-
bethans, were the most procreative of the animals. In the great
speech which ends with "Farewell! Othello's occupation's gone!"
he cries out:

> I had been happy, if the general camp,
> Pioners,[8] and all, had tasted her sweet body,
> So I had nothing known.

Verdi sets the "Farewell" speech to music; Boito translates the
words faithfully, but he eliminates the reference to "pioners" and
softens the erotic bitterness.

In short, all the examples I have given of the sexual imagery
which pulses through the play—and Shakespeare was nothing if
not consistent in his imagery—are either toned down or eliminated
altogether. A few remain, for Verdi and Boito were too faithful to
the play to distort it. But the evidence suggests that Verdi felt the
play more in terms of searching "the human heart" than in terms
of its occupation with physical attraction.

So it is that the music is noble, heartbreaking, soliciting tenderness and shaking us to the very core, of enormous stature and wild-
est power, bringing to the fore all the intensity of the tragedy, all
its ingredients—except one. It is not erotic music.

Verdi's musical mind was not erotically inclined and his music is
not sexually slanted, as Wagner's is or Puccini's is. Verdi treats of
love, of course. His women and men can be loving, tender, self-
sacrificing, melting, passionate even—as Aïda is—but passionate in
an unbodily sense, without reference to "carnal stings."

Perhaps the difference can be further illustrated by two small
quotations: "Villain, be sure thou prove my love a whore," says
Othello. "Villain, be sure you prove that Desdemona is impure
(*è impura*)," sings Otello in the opera. When Othello lashes out at
Desdemona, in that horrible moment of vilification, he says:

> I cry you mercy then:
> I took you for that cunning whore of Venice
> That married with Othello.

Verdi recognizes that here stands the apex of Othello's verbal
cruelty. He forms the lines into the apex of the music; he ends with

---

[8] Pioners were sappers, the lowest rank of soldiers.

them the third-act scene between Otello and Desdemona, to be
followed by a scarifying orchestral postlude. Even at this moment
he can not bring himself to use the word "whore," a word for
which there is of course an exact equivalent in Italian.[9] He or
Boito substitutes the words *"vil cortigiana,"* "vile courtesan." Perhaps this is no more than a little bowdlerizing, such as was to be
expected from men working in the nineteenth century. But I
think it is more, if we set the fact alongside the omission of Shakespeare's most daring poetic images, such as (in addition to the ones
already quoted) Othello's "naked abed" or his "summer flies . . .
that quicken even with blowing," or "the bawdy wind, that kisses
all it meets."

Both play and opera are tragedies of love turned awry by evil.
Both measure up to the demand made on greatest tragedy that
destruction cannot be senseless but must be based on a tragic flaw
in the hero's character. Yet play and opera differ in at least one
characteristic. The reason for the difference can be found in Verdi's
mind; he interpreted the play in a manner which was natural to
him. It is fortunate that an artistic creation can be differently interpreted: even so is our artistic wealth augmented.

In relating the sequence of the opera, I shall quote here and
there such lines from the play as are directly reflected in the opera.

ACT I

There is no overture, merely a lightning flash by the orchestra
to set the scene. The lightning seems inverted: it jags upward from
earth to heaven, as the curtain opens on a dark and stormy scene.
The scene is laid in Cyprus, outside the castle. At the left there is a
tavern with an arbor; in the background the quays of the port and
the sea. Iago and Roderigo and some of the townspeople, as well as
Venetian soldiers, are eagerly scanning the horizon and trying to
make their voices heard through the tumult of sea and sky and
the "wind-shaked surge." They descry a vessel, though at first it
is impossible to make out what flag it flies. A new flash of lightning
reveals that its sail carries the emblem of Venice, the winged lion.
It is Otello's ship, it is the vessel of the General.

9 In the final scene Boito does use the word "prostitute," but it is hidden in a passage
where two voices sing together.

Now the people, fully aware of the danger which threatens the ship, describe in powerful chorus the ferocity of the tempest, the force of the skyward gushing waves. They pray that the ship which carries so noble a load be saved. Suddenly Iago observes that the main sail has burst. "To the rescue!" cries the chorus, only to discover to their joy that the ship has rounded the cliff and has glided into the harbor. It is safe, the danger is over. Voices behind the scene cry, "Welcome! Welcome!" Proud and with military bearing Otello enters, followed by Cassio, Montano, and his guard. In triumphant accents he sings the *"Esultate."*[10] "Rejoice!" he announces. "The proud Musselman is buried beneath the ocean! Ours is the victory." He is answered by the jubilant townspeople. Long live Otello! The war is over! He enters the castle, while the chorus in a magnificently rhythmic *allegro vivace* celebrates *"Vittoria,"* the victory.

The storm having spent itself and the people having retired to the background, Iago and Roderigo are able to converse in comparative calm. Roderigo, that lovesick puppy, threatens to drown himself. He is in love with Desdemona but sees no prospect of having his desire gratified. Iago advises him not to be a "silly gentleman." He may look on Iago as a true friend who will help him. Desdemona shall be his. It is impossible for this girl long to continue to be faithful to the Moor.

IAGO: If sanctimony and a frail vow betwixt an erring barbarian and a supersubtle Venetian be not too hard for my wits and all the tribe of hell, thou shalt enjoy her.

He, Iago, would welcome nothing more than to revenge himself upon Otello. Surely he has no cause to love the Moor, for, says Iago, pointing to Cassio, who has just re-entered from the castle, Otello has promoted Cassio to the rank of captain (Boito specifies "captain," "his lieutenant" in the original), a rank which by the rights of war and seniority should have belonged to himself.

The conversation is carried in a sardonic recitative, ending with the line, "Were I the Moor, I would not be Iago." While Iago pumps hope and expectations into Roderigo, the townspeople have gathered a large pile of wood. Now they light a comforting fire. Clouds of smoke begin to rise from the pile. There follows a

10 Probably the most difficult entrance for a tenor in all opera!

choral passage, the lighthearted *"Fuoco di gioia!"*—"Flame of joy!"
—its orchestration suggesting the sparks of the flame, dancing in
the night. While the people sing, some make the scene festive by
hanging Venetian lanterns from the branches of the arbor, while
others begin to do justice to the Cyprian wine.

When the fire dies down, we find that Iago and Roderigo have
joined Cassio and a few of the soldiers who are grouped around a
table; Iago now proposes a toast and invites Cassio particularly to
join him. Cassio refuses. "Come now," presses Iago. "This is a night
of revel, a celebration." "No," answers Cassio, "I have drunk one
cup already and my brain is confused." "You must drink one
toast at least, a toast to the marriage of Otello and Desdemona."
This Cassio does not dare to refuse. "You, Iago," asks Cassio, "shall
chant her praises." Drawing Roderigo aside, Iago quickly informs
him that this handsome young knave may very well turn out to be
his rival. He has already observed Desdemona looking at Cassio
with unfeigned interest. But there is an easy way to get rid of this
nuisance: if one can contrive to make Cassio drunk, one can pick
a quarrel with him and provoke him to combat. An uproar would
ensue which would disturb Otello's wedding night and disgrace
Cassio. "Trust in me," replies the determined Roderigo.

Even before these detailed instructions, Iago has set the intrigue
in motion by intoning the first strophe of his Drinking Song: *"Chi
all'esca ha morso"*—"He who has ever experienced the sting of
temptation . . . let him drink with me." It is a *brindisi*, of which
Verdi had composed many, but which here differs from anything
he had previously attempted in the subtlety of its orchestration and
the appositeness of its melodic line. In this soldierly song Iago's
gruff voice slides on the word *"beva"*—"drink"—while the orchestra uses a trill, indicating who is the instigator of the revel. The
song is only superficially rollicking; a threat lurks underneath.[11]

The ensemble joins the song. And Cassio gets himself thoroughly
drunk. Montano returns to remind Cassio that it is his turn to take
over the watch; he is shocked by the condition the young man is
in. Iago quickly informs Montano that Cassio is to be found in

[11] Boito paraphrases the first of the two songs Shakespeare uses. He naturally eliminates all reference to one of Shakespeare's favorite satirical themes, one which must have
been sure-fire with Elizabethan audiences, the drinking prowess of the English: "I learned
it in England, where indeed they are most potent in potting."

like condition every night before he goes to sleep. Seeing Cassio stagger, first Roderigo and then the others burst into laughter. Cassio naturally takes a dim view of this derisive laughter. He threatens Roderigo. Roderigo in turn calls Cassio a ribald drunk-ard, at which moment Montano intervenes in an attempt to sepa-rate the two. Cassio's inebriated fury now turns on Montano. The two men draw and begin to duel, as Iago whispers to Roderigo, "Quick, quick! Arouse the town. Spread the alarm. Let them ring the bell of the fortress."

How extraordinarily "graphic" is the music of this turmoil! What Verdi does is to break up the musical material of the drinking song to form fragments which, always increasing in speed and dynamics, first express the laughter of the townspeople, then Iago's hurried stage managing, then the clash of Roderigo, Cassio, and Montano, then the fright of the people, who call for help—until, as the quarrel rises to the highest pitch, with the orchestra ham-mering out the rhythm, Otello appears on the fortress. His voice cuts through the tumult. "Put up your swords!"[12] The command is instantly obeyed.

What have we here? Otello asks. Have we turned Turks? Are we ourselves guilty of the kind of behavior for which we have cen-sured them? Who began the quarrel? He turns to Iago, who an-swers simply, "I know not.[13] Friends but a moment ago, some mad-ness seems to have smitten both of them; like wild beasts they turned on each other. I would rather have lost a leg in action than to have witnessed this." Otello demands an explanation from Cas-sio. But neither he nor Montano can account for the cause of the quarrel. Montano is wounded. Confronted with so inexplicable a breach of discipline, Otello's anger mounts; his blood begins to rule his judgment. At this moment Desdemona appears; her gentle sleep, too, has been disturbed. With a curt command, Cassio is told that he is no longer Otello's captain. Iago is to take over the watch and to quiet the citizens. Montano is to be given surgical aid, and

12 The command seems to me a translation in music of Othello's line in the first act of the play:
> "Keep up your bright swords, for the dew
> will rust them." (Scene 2)

13 "*Non so.*" Toscanini rehearsed with the interpreter of Iago (Valdengo) for the better part of an hour to have him express these two monosyllables in just the right tone of ingenuous honesty. The result can be heard in the recording.

all are to return to their homes. Otello will remain on the fortress
until his commands have been carried out.

And so he remains with Desdemona. Within a few bars and by
simple means Verdi works the transition from storm and war and
intrigue to the starlit night, to peace, trust, and to love. What follows is the last moment in which Otello and Desdemona can experience the benison of serenity. We may call it a love scene, but it
is of mature love, a partnership in tenderness, of which the music
speaks.

In the deep night the blatant clamor ceases (*"Gia nella notte
densa"*). Even so does the anger in his soul give way to content-
ment. Let wars rage, let the world sink, if after every tempest such
felicity can be born. Desdemona calls him her proud warrior and
recalls what bitter sorrow, what long sighs, what hope deferred
they had to overcome before they could reach each other. They
both reminisce. They recall how he would beguile her ear with
the story of his youth, speak of his adventures, of sieges and of
battles, of hairbreadth escapes, of burning desert and vast deserted
fields, of the chains which he bore as a slave. As they tell each other
twice-told tales, Otello sums up the story of their first meetings
with a phrase into which Verdi has poured the essence of beauty:
"You loved me for the dangers I had passed, and I loved you that
you did pity them."

The words Boito uses are a condensation of Othello's speech before the Senate in the play. Asked what magic he employed to
seduce Desdemona, Othello replies to the Senators and to his infuriated father-in-law with one of Shakespeare's most eloquent
justifications:

> Her father lov'd me, oft invited me,
> Still questioned me the story of my life
> From year to year,—the battles, sieges, fortunes,
> That I have pass'd.
> I ran it through, even from my boyish days
> To th' very moment that he bade me tell it.
> Wherein I spake of most disastrous chances,
> Of moving accidents by flood and field,
> Of hairbreadth scapes i' th' imminent deadly breach,
> Of being taken by the insolent foe

And sold to slavery. . . .
This to hear
Would Desdemona seriously incline:
But still the house affairs would draw her thence;
Which ever as she could with haste dispatch,
She'ld come again, and with a greedy ear
Devour up my discourse. . . .
My story being done,
She gave me for my pains a world of sighs.
She swore, in faith, 'twas strange, 'twas passing strange;
'Twas pitiful, 'twas wondrous pitiful. . . .
She thank'd me;
And bade me, if I had a friend that lov'd her,
I should but teach him how to tell my story,
And that would woo her. Upon this hint I spake.
She lov'd me for the dangers I had pass'd,
And I loved her that she did pity them.

Is it not curious that, using a formal plea as his material, Boito was able to furnish Verdi the right poetry from which the composer could draw an intimate and inward love scene? Here again much of the beauty of the poetry is transplanted into the music, the culminating two lines ("She loved me," etc.) seized for the culmination of the melody, the whole forming a scene of love, if not a conventional love duet. What a distance separates this ineffably beautiful music from, let us say, the second-act Duke-Gilda duet of *Rigoletto!*

The scene ends with Otello's cry: "Let death come now." No moment can surpass this in ecstasy. Joy overwhelms him. A kiss, he asks of Desdemona, a kiss and yet another. (Much later we shall hear how this theme is used as tragic reminiscence.)

The stars of the Pleiades are descending into the sea, the night is far advanced. "Come," concludes Otello, "Venus stands on high."

ACT II

The brief Prelude hints at evil forces at work.

A hall in the castle. In the center there is a door which opens onto a terraced garden. Iago and Cassio are on the stage. Iago is giving him "sound" advice: he is to enlist Desdemona's intercession

with Otello. For is she not now the General's general? A word from
her, a word from that kind soul, will restore Cassio to grace. It is
not difficult to contrive a meeting with her: she will shortly appear
in the garden, as is her habit, and Cassio is to wait for her there.
Let him repair there at once.

Iago remains alone. No counterpart exists in the play to the ensuing great *"Credo,"* though Shakespeare allows Iago several short
soliloquies. The *"Credo"* is pure Boito-Verdi, and, regarded solely
as an operatic soliloquy, it is highly effective. It does not, however,
in my opinion, quite fit into the style of the music drama, being a
little too much of a set piece and too frankly self-revelatory to be
consistent with Iago's mental habits. He tells us that the God who
has created him in his image is a cruel God. He himself was born of
a "vile germ of nature"; being a human being, what else can he be
but villainous? This, then, is a villain's creed: that the honest man is
a wretched fool, that every word he utters is a lie, every tear, every
kiss, every smile a farce. Man is a plaything of fortune, from the
first breath he draws to the last, when he feeds the worms. Struggle
and squirm though he might, death is the outcome. And after
death? After death there is nothing. Heaven is an ancient lie.

This contradictory speculation—at its beginning Iago admits a
cruel God and at its end he denies an afterlife—is quite un-Eliza-
bethan. None of Shakespeare's villains is an atheist.

No sooner has Iago concluded the *"Credo"* than Desdemona and
Emilia appear in the arbor. Cassio approaches and Iago exhorts him
to hasten toward Desdemona. Iago calls upon Satan to aid him, to
fetch Otello, so that he may chance upon his wife and Cassio together. Satan (or the playwright) fulfills Iago's wish: Otello enters
at this very moment. Iago, pretending not to see Otello, murmurs
to himself quite audibly, "I like not that." "What are you saying?" asks Otello. And from here on Iago's technique, Otello seemingly having to drag his thoughts from him, follows the play virtually word for word, and we cannot describe the scene in the
opera better than by quoting the pertinent lines of the play:

OTHELLO: Was not that Cassio parted from my wife?
IAGO: Cassio, my lord? No, sure, I cannot think it,
             That he would steal away so guilty-like,
             Seeing you coming.
OTHELLO: I do believe 'twas he. . . .

IAGO: My noble lord—

OTHELLO: What dost thou say, Iago?

IAGO: Did Michael Cassio, when you woo'd my lady,
    Know of your love?

OTHELLO: He did, from first to last. Why dost thou ask?

IAGO: But for a satisfaction of my thought;
    No further harm.

OTHELLO: Why of thy thought, Iago?

IAGO: I did not think he had been acquainted with her.

OTHELLO: O, yes, and went between us very oft.

IAGO: Indeed?

OTHELLO: Indeed? Ay, indeed! Discern'st thou aught in that?
    Is he not honest?

IAGO: Honest, my lord?

OTHELLO: Honest? Ay, honest.

IAGO: My lord, for aught I know.

OTHELLO: What dost thou think?

IAGO: Think, my lord?

OTHELLO: Think, my lord?
    By heaven, he echoes me,
    As if there were some monster in his thought
    Too hideous to be shown. Thou dost mean something:
    I heard thee say but now, thou lik'st not that,
    When Cassio left my wife. What didst not like?
    And when I told thee he was of my counsel
    In my whole course of wooing, thou cried'st "Indeed?"
    And didst contract and purse thy brow together,
    As if thou then hadst shut up in thy brain
    Some horrible conceit. If thou dost love me,
    Show me thy thought.

IAGO: My lord, you know I love you. . . .

OTHELLO: Nay, yet there's more in this.
    I prithee speak to me as to thy thinkings,
    As thou dost ruminate, and give thy worst of thoughts
    The worst of words. . . .
    By heaven, I'll know thy thoughts!

IAGO: You cannot, if my heart were in your hand;
    Nor shall not whilst 'tis in my custody.

OTHELLO: Ha!

IAGO: O, beware, my lord, of jealousy!
    It is the green-eyed monster, which doth mock
    The meat it feeds on. . . .

OTHELLO:	O misery! . . . Why, why is this?
	Think'st thou I'ld make a life of jealousy,
	To follow still the changes of the moon
	With fresh suspicions? No! To be once in doubt
	Is once to be resolv'd. . . .
	Nor from mine own weak merits will I draw
	The smallest fear or doubt of her revolt,
	For she had eyes, and chose me. No, Iago;
	I'll see before I doubt; when I doubt, prove;
	And on the proof there is no more but this—
	Away at once with love or jealousy!
IAGO:	I am glad of it; for now I shall have reason
	To show the love and duty that I bear you
	With franker spirit. Therefore, as I am bound,
	Receive it from me. I speak not yet of proof.
	Look to your wife; observe her well with Cassio;
	Wear your eye thus, not jealous nor secure:
	I would not have your free and noble nature,
	Out of self-bounty, be abus'd. Look to't.

Iago's summing up—"Look to your wife"—is set to a smooth melody, the very smoothness of which renders the suggestion the more vicious. After the final *"Vigilate"*—"Look to't"—Iago stops, to observe, with Otello, the scene in the garden. Desdemona is surrounded by women and children, sailors of Cyprus and of Albania, who pay tribute to her, offering her flowers and other gifts. They sing a pleasant little hymn,[14] accompanying themselves. For this accompaniment Verdi specified small harps and a special mandolin-like instrument, the gusla. Otello joins the music to exclaim, "This song has wrung my heart. No, no! If she be false, then heaven mocks itself."

The choral interlude (which of course does not occur in the play) serves not only to relieve the tension of an act otherwise unmitigated in cruelty, but also to slow Otello's fall from trust to deep doubt, a peregrination into Hell for which Shakespeare used several scenes. As it is, Boito does not entirely succeed in conveying the required passage of time.

Desdemona appears, followed by Emilia. At once she begins to plead for Cassio. Otello puts her off. He has "a pain upon my fore-

14 Toscanini thought that this was the weakest music in the opera and he considered abbreviating it. But then he changed his mind: "Verdi may be allowed a little weakness."

head, here." Desdemona tries to bind his forehead with her handkerchief. Otello lets it fall. Emilia picks it up. Once more Desdemona pleads. Beginning with her melody, Verdi now builds a quartet. We *expect* Verdi to give us a quartet; yet how unexpected and new does this music sound! *"Se inconscia, contro te, sposo, ho peccato,"* Desdemona sings. "If, unknowingly, I have offended you, my husband, say that you forgive me."

The words are Boito's, who simplifies as well the incident of the handkerchief. In the play Iago had been demanding that Emilia steal it. When she finds it, she first intends to have it copied and then returned to Desdemona. Instead she gives it to her husband to ingratiate herself with him, and earns from Iago the approbation of being "a good wench." In the opera Iago threatens Emilia and, commanding her to hand over the handkerchief, he snatches it from her.

Desdemona ends the quartet with a repetition of the melody with which she began. Then Otello asks to be left alone. The women leave, while Iago pretends to go, but remains standing near the door. There is a tormenting transition in the orchestra, leading into Otello's "Desdemona false!" mumbled to himself. Iago, standing by the door, conceives the idea of hiding the handkerchief in Cassio's lodging. Then he turns to face his victim. For Iago is already certain of victory.

Once again Boito transcribes the play: the colloquy between the two men follows in detail Shakespeare's dialogue of Act III, Scene 3. Otello turns upon Iago with all the fury that the informed feels toward the informer. And Shakespeare's lines, which tumble from Otello's mouth in breathless phrases—"Avaunt! be gone! Thou has set me on the rack"—are exactly mirrored in the music.

> OTHELLO: Ha! ha! false to me?
> IAGO: Why, how now, general? No more of that!
> OTHELLO: Avaunt! be gone! Thou has set me on the rack:
>   I swear 'tis better to be much abus'd
>   Than but to know't a little.
> IAGO: How now, my lord?
> OTHELLO: What sense had I of her stol'n hours of lust?
>   I saw't not, thought it not, it harm'd not me.
>   I slept the next night well, was free and merry;
>   I found not Cassio's kisses on her lips.

Otello gropes for the world that was his before he found "Cassio's kisses on her lips." Now blessed ignorance has slid from him. The orchestra, with the tremolos of the strings, seems to rend the veil. No mercy here, no comfort, as Otello launches into his "O, now for ever farewell the tranquil mind"—*"Ora e per sempre addio."*

> O, now for ever
> Farewell the tranquil mind! farewell content! . . .
> Farewell the neighing steed and the shrill trump,
> The spirit-stirring drum, th' ear-piercing fife,
> The royal banner, and all quality,
> Pride, pomp, and circumstance of glorious war! . . .
> Farewell! Othello's occupation's gone!

This superb apostrophe—with its renunciation of all the spirit-stirring appurtenances of Otello's profession—takes its musical inspiration from the military imagery of the speech.

Wilder and wilder does the music become, Otello demanding proof, demanding certainty, demanding an end to writhing doubt —until Iago offers to furnish such proof. An expectant calm ensues. Slowly Iago begins his narrative. Now he assumes the fascination of a hypnotist as he leans over Otello and quietly unfolds Cassio's putative dream.

> In sleep I heard him say, "Sweet Desdemona,
> Let us be wary, let us hide our loves!"
> And then, sir, would he gripe and wring my hand,
> Cry "O sweet creature!" and then kiss me hard,
> As if he pluck'd up kisses by the roots
> That grew upon my lips; then laid his leg
> Over my thigh, and sigh'd, and kiss'd, and then
> Cried "Cursed fate that gave thee to the Moor!"

It is the dream of a dream, false and yet incapable of being controverted. Horrible as this, Iago's latest lie, is in the play, it becomes even more horrible in the opera, because it is set to a gentle, somnolent melody which seems to make the dream an honest one. Music is capable of such irony. (*"Era la notte"*—"It was night, Cassio was sleeping.")

To name but one example of the skill with which Verdi treated the words, we may take the line "Cursed fate that gave thee to the

Moor!" which Cassio is supposed to have spoken in his sleep. The
line is so accompanied by the orchestra that the word "Moor"—
"*Moro*"—is sung *a cappella*, thus making the one word which is
likely to hurt Otello most keenly stand out by itself. "Such was
the dream," Iago concludes, his voice dying away on a high note.
Then Iago adduces the proof of the handkerchief.

> IAGO: Tell me but this—
>   Have you not sometimes seen a handkerchief
>   Spotted with strawberries in your wife's hand?
> OTHELLO: I gave her such a one; 'twas my first gift.
> IAGO: I know not that; but such a handkerchief—
>   I am sure it was your wife's—did I to-day
>   See Cassio wipe his beard with.

Otello cries for "Blood! Blood! Blood!" and, kneeling, utters the
vow for vengeance which Verdi fashions into the famous duet:
"*Sì pel ciel*"—"Now, by yond marble heaven." Boito omitted the
beginning of Otello's vow, one of the most famous passages of the
play. In the music, however, this passage can be felt and we can
indicate the *spirit* of the duet by remembering the lines which precede "Now, by yond marble heaven":

> IAGO: Patience, I say. Your mind perhaps may change.
> OTHELLO: Never, Iago. Like to the Pontic sea,
>   Whose icy current and compulsive course
>   Ne'er feels retiring ebb, but keeps due on
>   To the Propontic and the Hellespont;
>   Even so my bloody thoughts, with violent pace,
>   Shall ne'er look back, ne'er ebb to humble love,
>   Till that a capable and wide revenge
>   Swallow them up.

Iago, kneeling with him, joins the oath. The two voices unite and
the duet closes with the cry, uttered by both in unison, "*Dio
vendicator!*"—"God be the avenger."

ACT III

In this act Boito departs from the play, rearranging some of the
scenes and adding material of his own required for the finale. Yet
by and large he remains faithful to Shakespeare.

We are in the great hall of the castle. To the left there is a large portico which leads to another hall. At the back there is a colonnade through which we glimpse a vista of the outdoors. Otello and Iago are on the scene. A herald enters to announce that the arrival of the ship which is to bring the Venetian ambassadors to Cyprus has just been signaled. He is dismissed by Otello, who turns to Iago. "Continue!" he demands. Iago continues. He reports that he has bid Cassio to meet him here. He suggests that Otello hide himself to overhear Iago's conversation with Cassio. Iago will attempt to draw him out; Otello is to be careful not to betray his presence. He will have the opportunity not only to hear Cassio's words but also to observe Cassio's looks, his smiles, his gestures. Turning to go, Iago suddenly arrests himself and whispers, "The handkerchief." Otello replies, "By heaven, I would most gladly have forgot it." It is one of Shakespeare's extraordinary psychological touches which Boito and Verdi retained: Otello wanting to dismiss from his mind that one concrete bit of proof and Iago, the virtuoso of cruelty, reminding him of it.

Iago leaves. The mood of the music softens as Desdemona appears. She asks how fares her husband. He answers, "Well, my lady . . . Give me your hand. It seems a hand hot and moist. That denotes a liberal heart." Desdemona replies that her hand has not yet known sorrow nor age.

The moment Desdemona mentions that she has sent for Cassio to speak with Otello, Otello complains of a pain in his head and asks Desdemona to lend him her handkerchief. She does so. But it is not the handkerchief Otello wants. Where is the handkerchief which he gave her? "I have it not about me," replies the unsuspecting girl. "That is a fault," reproves Otello. And over a mysterious accompaniment of the orchestra he tells her that it is a charmed handkerchief, a talisman of love. To lose it or to give it away were to bring misfortune.

Desdemona is not to be put off: the story of the handkerchief is but a trick to postpone giving audience to Cassio. Her advocacy of Cassio soars in long lyric phrases. Otello is unable to check her, until he breaks out with a terrible cry: "The handkerchief!" For the first time Desdemona perceives the extent of her husband's perturbation. What does his wrath import? she asks as she bursts into tears.

Not even her tears can arrest Otello's madness. "In what am I at fault?" Desdemona begs, looking at this man who now appears strange and frightful to her. "What," he cries, "are you not a vile courtesan?" "No, as I am a Christian," she protests, shocked to the core of her being. And then, the irony made bitter by the fact that once more we hear the sweet melody which introduced the scene, Otello seems to calm himself, as with elaborate courtesy he asks her: "Give me once more your white hand." Then the momentary deception falls from him; he can no longer contain his wrath. "I cry you mercy, then, I took you—pardon me if I wrong you—for the vile courtesan who married Otello." At this the strings shake, the orchestra cries out, Otello pushes Desdemona from the room, and then, spent and exhausted, sinks into a chair.

The "symphonic" development by which the scene is constantly intensified and built toward the final expletive is so compellingly coherent that the listener is, as it were against his will, dragged into the whirlpool, that he suffers Desdemona's shame, that he feels both anger against Otello and pity for him—and for all blind fools. Equally wonderful is the musical transition, but a few bars long, from Desdemona's exit to Otello's soliloquy, the orchestra leading from paroxysm to introspection. Otello's soliloquy, one of the high points of the score, is preceded by a brooding scale which reminds one of Beethoven. This is followed by a four-note phrase, which acts as the seminal motive of the monologue. Otello begins: *"Dio! mi potevi scagliar"*—"Had it pleased heaven to try me with affliction." Verdi over and over again repeats the four-note phrase, as insistent as a throbbing pain, until he reaches the words, "But there where I have garnered up my heart," at which the strings change to a tremolo of grief, almost unbearable in its sadness. Otello's voice rises, expands, flies upward, into a recollection of his love, and a pale sun shines through the murk. Only for a moment or two! Soon enough he reverts to the reality of disillusionment. From nobility he sinks to bestiality, crying, "Damnation! Confession! The proof!" And at this moment Iago enters: Cassio has arrived, he announces. This is Othello's monologue, as Boito uses it:

> Had it pleas'd heaven
> To try me with affliction, had they rain'd
> All kinds of sores and shames on my bare head,

Steep'd me in poverty to the very lips,
Given to captivity me and my utmost hopes,
I should have found in some place of my soul
A drop of patience. . . .
But there where I have garner'd up my heart,
Where either I must live or bear no life,
The fountain from the which my current runs
Or else dries up—to be discarded thence . . . turn thy
   complexion there,
Patience, thou young and rose-lipp'd cherubin!
Ay, there look grim as hell!

I have said that the Cassio-Iago scene serves as the scherzo of
Verdi's symphony, that it trips along in the lightest of staccato
music, broken into by expressions of anguish from the hidden
Otello. Iago cooly and nonchalantly decoys Cassio into speaking of
Bianca, Cassio's devoted mistress. "I can't help laughing when I
think of her," confesses the young man. "Her kisses pall on me."
Otello believes that they are discussing Desdemona. Presently Cassio
relates the curious incident of the handkerchief, found in his
lodging, left there by he knows not whom. Drawing the handkerchief from his doublet, he shows it to Iago, who waves it in the
air to let Otello see it.

The scene is terminated by trumpet signals and the sound of the
welcoming cannon being fired. Cassio departs, Otello bursts from
his hiding place with the hoarse question, "How shall I murder
her,[15] Iago?" while shouts of *"Evviva!"*—"Hail to the lion of San
Marco!"—are heard behind the scene.

Iago suggests that Desdemona's fate be settled not by poison but
that she be strangled in her bed, the very bed which she has con-
taminated. Otello answers, "The justice of it pleases." As for Cassio,
Iago assures Otello, he himself will provide. With this Otello ap-
points Iago as his captain.

Now the ambassadors must be received. Iago exits. Lodovico, as
well as Roderigo, the herald, dignitaries of the Venetian Republic,
soldiers, and people of Cyprus enter. Iago reappears escorting Desdemona and Emilia to the state occasion. Lodovico extends the
greetings of the Doge and the Senate of Venice and delivers into

15 Is this intentional or a mistake by Boito? It is "her" in Boito, "him" in Shakespeare.

Otello's hands their message, a roll of parchment which Otello opens and reads. As he reads, Lodovico observes that Cassio is missing. Why? Iago answers that a cleft has opened up between Cassio and Otello. "He will soon be restored to grace," interposes Desdemona. Otello, who has overheard the exchange, mutters to himself, "Are you sure of it?" and then continues to read. "I hope so," Desdemona continues. "I feel a real affection for Cassio."[16] These last words break Otello's restraint altogether. Throwing the parchment aside, he cries, "Devil! Hold your tongue." General horror is the reaction to this outburst. Otello summons Cassio. Lodovico, who cannot believe his eyes and ears, asks, "Is this the noble Moor?" Cassio enters, and Otello proceeds to the official announcement: "Good Sirs! The Doge" (here he whispers to Desdemona, "How well you pretend!") "has recalled me to Venice. My successor in Cyprus is to be he who was my aide, Cassio. The mandate of the doge is our law. The garrison and guard as well as the ships and the fortress" (once more Otello turns to Desdemona, *sotto voce:* "Continue your weeping") "I leave in charge of my successor." Lodovico turns to Otello: "For pity's sake, comfort her." Instead, Otello strikes the supplicating Desdemona furiously and in a voice from which all humanity has been emptied he exclaims, "*A terra!—e piangi!*"—"To the ground, and weep!"

Here begins the finale, a form with which all who have heard Verdi's previous operas, or indeed any nineteenth-century opera, are familiar. Principals and chorus, with the orchestra, combine to form a climax which soars to the full capacity of voice and instruments. As before in Verdi, the ensemble is led by the highest voice, here Desdemona's. We have then the kind of act close Verdi constructed in the second act of *La Traviata* or in the Council Scene in *Simone Boccanegra*. Yet, once again, what a difference is here! Not only does this finale outweigh previous Verdian ensembles in true power,[17] but it outranks them in cohesion and psychological truthfulness.

[16] Here Boito's rearrangement of the scenes works to the opera's disadvantage. For Desdemona to espouse Cassio's cause once more, after experiencing Othello's reaction in the scene where he vilifies her, is demonstrating a naïveté which transgresses what is allowable even to an Elizabethan heroine. In Shakespeare the Lodovico scene *precedes* (Act IV, Scene 1) the scene in which Othello calls her "that cunning whore" (Act IV, Scene 2).

[17] I don't mean in decibels. *Aïda's* second act finale is louder.

Iago's part in the ensemble is particularly active. First he exhorts Otello to be quick in his revenge—time is against them. He repeats, he himself will "see to Cassio." Then, turning to Roderigo, he suggests that his hope of possessing Desdemona will be foiled by her departure on the morrow, unless—unless some accident should befall Cassio. In that case, Otello would be forced to remain in Cyprus. Roderigo, who is quite under Iago's thrall, understands. Iago assures him that he will be nearby; the hunt will be nocturnal and cannot fail. He need but unsheathe his weapon and thrust home.

Higher and higher the finale mounts until, at the last, Otello, rousing himself, exclaims, "Away . . . away with all of you!" Lodovico attempts to lead Desdemona from the hall, but she turns from him and, running toward Otello, exclaims, "My husband!" He looks at her: "Light of my soul, I curse you!"

The massive and marvelous tonal structure is ended, the crowd disperses, and once more Otello is left alone. In broken music and to broken phrases he cries for blood; convulsively he recalls, "The handkerchief, the handkerchief!" Then he faints. Iago, re-entering, observes his supine commander and listens to the cries of the people outside who, unaware of the true state of affairs, still hail "The lion of Venice." Standing erect and pointing with his foot to the inert body of the Moor, Iago exults: "Behold the lion!"

ACT IV

The Prelude is a small tone poem for the woodwinds, the musical material consisting of four themes. First the English horn chants the melody which anticipates the Willow Song; three flutes respond with sounds like the fall of hidden tears, to be followed by two clarinets playing empty chords which seem to express the numbness of the heart. Before the curtain rises, the woodwinds unite in a passage which, later, introduces each verse of the Willow Song.

We can never cease to marvel that Verdi, the composer of nineteenth-century "grand" opera, was able to preserve all the simplicity and all the poignancy of what is one of the simplest and most poignant scenes in all of Shakespeare's plays. Indeed, because he had music at his command and because Shakespeare himself conceived the scene with music as his aid, Verdi is able to bring home to us this touching idyl in a way that words cannot.

The scene is Desdemona's chamber, furnished with a bed, a *prie-dieu*, a table, a mirror, and several chairs. In front of the image of the Madonna above the *prie-dieu* a lamp is burning. It is night. On the table a single candle is lighted. Desdemona tells Emilia that Otello, seemingly more calm, has commanded her to retire and wait for him. She asks Emilia to lay on her bed the white sheets of her wedding night. Then, seating herself before the mirror as Emilia combs her hair, her mind roams in reminiscence. Present sadness begets recollective sadness. She recalls a song which she had heard her mother's maid sing. The poor girl's name was Barbara; she was in love, and he whom she loved forsook her. She died singing the song, the song of the willow tree. Desdemona sings it now, each strophe dying away in the echo of one word, *"Salce"*— "Willow."

Suddenly Desdemona starts. She seems to hear a knocking at the door. No, it is nothing, merely the wind. Once more she takes up her song.

Her eyes itch. Does that bode weeping? She bids Emilia good-night. But then, as she sees Emilia turn to go, all her fears well up within her, and she cries out, "Ah! Emilia, farewell."[18]

Desdemona turns for comfort to the picture of the Madonna. Her prayer, the *"Ave Maria,"* could well have become a mawkish operatic number, were it not that Verdi held it in bonds of simplicity. Its beginning, forty-four syllables on one note, is almost like the recital of a litany; then it floats up to ethereal heights. To be sure, the prayer must be sung by the interpreter of Desdemona as simply as the Willow Song and not as a vocal showpiece.[19]

Desdemona retires. Immediately afterward a small door opens, and Otello appears in silence. The orchestra is heard alone, beginning with the passage for the bass cellos to which we have referred. As Otello approaches the table and places his scimitar there, we

[18] The effect here is one which can only be managed in music. Desdemona says *"Buona notte"* on a low F-sharp. Then, as Emilia starts to go, Desdemona's voice rises to the "Ah!" on a high A-sharp with the orchestra, to sink back on the last syllable of *"Addio"* to the same low F-sharp with which she began.

[19] It is one of Renata Tebaldi's achievements that she sings both the *"Salce"* and the *"Ave Maria"* with utmost simplicity.

hear an agitated phrase for the violas, repeated as if waves of pain were sweeping over him. At first Otello is uncertain whether to snuff the candle or not. Then he does so. The only light in the room now is that of the lamp above the *prie-dieu*. A spasm of fury seizes him. He approaches the bed, stops, raises the curtain, and contemplates the sleeping Desdemona for a long time. At this moment there rises from the orchestra a new motive, one which bears a strange similarity to the opening melody of *Parsifal*. Otello, the orchestra seems to say, believes that he is acting as a ministrant of justice who is about to perform an appalling duty. But as he looks at Desdemona, his love returns.[20] Again it is the orchestra which tells us this, as it intones the motive of their love which we heard at the end of the first act. Otello kisses Desdemona three times. At the third kiss she awakens.

"Have you prayed tonight, Desdemona?" he asks. It is not his purpose to kill her soul. "Talk you of killing?" she asks in fright. She pleads first for her life, then begs for but a night, an hour, a moment of life. She denies that she loves Cassio, a denial which only serves to whip Otello's mania. And in a final paroxysm, with the orchestra indicating the ebbing of life's spark, he smothers her.

Otello looks at Desdemona's lifeless body. "Calm as the grave," he murmurs. (It is curious that Boito did not use one of the most heartbreaking lines of the tragedy, heartbreaking because it is so plain, so monosyllabic: "My wife, my wife, my wife? I have no wife.")

He is roused by a furious knocking at the door. It is Emilia. Otello admits her. She runs in with the news that Cassio has slain Roderigo. "And Cassio?" asks Otello. "He lives." A moan is heard from the bed. "I am slain unjustly," gasps Desdemona.

"Who dared this crime?" Emilia cries. Desdemona's answer is, "No one. I myself." With a final sigh she dies. "She is a liar," replies Otello. "It was I who slew her. She was Cassio's woman.[21] Iago can tell you so." Emilia screams for help. Summoned by her cries, Lodovico, Cassio, and Iago (later Montano, with soldiers) enter. In a few words Emilia apprises them of the tragedy. She

---

20 "When he comes in to kill Desdemona he is painfully aware that his love for her is as deep as ever, that he destroys what he loves best." Gerald Evans Bentley (Introduction to *Othello*).

21 Thus in Boito. In Shakespeare: "Cassio did top her."

confronts Iago. "Is it true that you thought Desdemona guilty?"
The intrigue of the handkerchief is exposed, and Cassio corrobo-
rates the fact that he found it in his lodging. Montano, entering,
reports that the dying Roderigo had revealed all of Iago's schemes.
He orders Iago's arrest. At last Otello, the blind man, perceives the
truth; and running toward the scimitar on the table he cries out,
"Has heaven no lightning left?" "Give me your sword," demands
Lodovico.

Here Otello begins his final speech, the summing up of his
crime, the assertion of his atonement. All fury spent, he speaks
calmly. Once a commander of men, now he is once more in command of himself. Verdi, attaining the height of his powers, forms
the speech into one of the greatest threnodies of music drama,
"Niun mi tema"—"Let no one fear me, though I am armed . . .
Here is my journey's end. . . . Oh, glory! Otello is no more."[22]
He lets fall his sword and turns toward the bed, contemplating
Desdemona. How pale she looks, how tired, how mute—and how
beautiful. She who was born under an evil star is now cold, as
cold as she was chaste. (These words correspond to Shakespeare's
"Cold, cold, my girl?") A cry of engulfing grief escapes him: "O
Desdemona! Desdemona! dead, dead, dead!"

Suddenly Otello draws a dagger from his doublet and stabs himself. The orchestra flashes as if it had glimpsed the glint of steel and
then sinks down into a mysterious hush, from which rises once
more the theme we first heard when Otello looked at the sleeping
Desdemona, death being related to sleep. Otello's final words, sung
to the motive of his love, are Shakespeare's:

> I kiss'd thee ere I kill'd thee. No way but this—
> Killing myself, to die upon a kiss.

---

[22] Particularly effective in Italian: *"Otello fu."*

TOSCA

COMPOSER:	Giacomo Puccini
LIBRETTISTS:	Giuseppe Giacosa Luigi Illica
FIRST PERFORMANCE:	January 14, 1900 Teatro Costanzi, Rome
RECEPTION:	Success

CHARACTERS:

Floria Tosca, a singer	Soprano
Mario Cavaradossi, a painter	Tenor
Baron Scarpia, Chief of Police in Rome	Baritone
Cesare Angelotti, former Consul of the Roman Republic	Bass
Spoletta, an agent of the police	Tenor
A Sacristan of the Church of St. Andrea della Valle	Baritone
Sciarrone, a police officer	Bass
A Jailer	Bass
A Shepherd Boy	Contralto

A Cardinal, Officers of Justice, an Executioner, a Scribe, an Official, a Sergeant

TOSCA, PLAY
AND OPERA

"For years, I've had one great ambition. You'll laugh at me. Everybody does. They say I'm crazy. But I don't care." He paused. Then announced solemnly, "Tosca. With Garbo."

Bergmann turned, and gave me a rapid, enigmatic glance. Then he exhaled, with such force that Chatsworth's cigar smoke was blown back around his head. Chatsworth looked pleased. Evidently this was the right kind of reaction.

"Without music, of course. I'd do it absolutely straight." He paused again, apparently waiting for our protest. There was none.

"It's one of the greatest stories in the world. People don't realize that. Christ, it's magnificent."

CHRISTOPHER ISHERWOOD, *Prater Violet*

That overfleshed melodrama with its booming villain and its unstable heroine, dank with its threat of a fate worse than death, "one of the greatest stories in the world"? That central scene in which, as one cynic observed, a man chases something which he is as obviously unable to take advantage of as the woman is to give it to him, a scene to be seriously appraised? One can hardly believe that even a German movie director, to whom Isherwood assigns the opinion, would judge so. We have come to regard *Tosca* as spongy dramatic substance, over which Puccini poured the sauce of his sumptuous melodies.

Speaking from the point of view of the theatergoer and for the moment considering *Tosca* as a play "without music," "absolutely straight," let us inquire whether the work is really quite so bad as its present reputation. Has it no dramatic strength of its own? If it is, and if it hasn't, how is it possible that *Tosca* the opera lives when most operas with out-and-out asthmatic stories die of plot strangulation?

If at this late date we are able to examine the venerable drama (venerable only because it is more than a half-century old) without prejudice, it may appear that Puccini—as shrewd a judge of theatrical values as ever entered the opera house by the stage door —did not lapse into error when he diligently, earnestly, and perhaps not even entirely honestly, took steps to acquire this property from Sardou, and that generations of audiences are not altogether bereft of taste when they respond. We need not call it a dramatic masterpiece or ascribe subtle psychological values to it. But we must not denigrate it altogether. There is something in this play! The truth lies somewhere between Isherwood-Bergmann and Bernard Shaw, who particularly disliked the author of *Tosca* and coined for him the word "Sardoodledom." Perhaps Henry James was nearest the mark when he called Sardou "that supremely clever contriver."

A contriver—yes. And supremely clever, surely. The contrivance Sardou had inherited. It is one which still serves the novel, the play, and the film. Interweave fact and fiction, paste them into a handsome frame as is done in those *collages* which combine a real leaf or a butterfly with an artist's crayon drawing, mix research and invention, and you get the historical novel or the historical drama. Both have been especially successful in France and have there been brought to a high state of craftsmanship. In the background of *Tosca* hovers the shade of the inimitable Dumas *père*. It was he who knew better than anybody how to cook a tale of equal parts of history and of fable and to spice it with the seasoning of sex. D'Artagnan, Richelieu, and Milady—what could be better than these three ingredients, bravery, craftiness, beauty? This is Sardou's formula as he worked it in *La Tosca*, in *Madame Sans-Gêne*, in *Robespierre*, in *Fedora*.

The action of *Tosca* is played at a moment in history which was of particular significance to France. An understanding of the his-

torical background may give us a little more respect for Sardou's
work and may elucidate certain points of the libretto. The libretto
needs such commentary—except of course for the fate-worse-than-
death scene, which is quite self-explanatory—if only to tell us what
are the causes of the political skulduggery. Why does Cavaradossi,
who is quite as much of a Roman as Scarpia, shout "Victory! Victory!" in the second act? Whose victory over whom?

The pivotal historical person, around whom swirl the political
tides, has been eliminated in the opera, though she plays a considerable part in Sardou's play. This person is the Queen of Naples,
Maria Carolina, wife of Ferdinand IV. It was she who ruled the
Kingdom of Naples, her husband being little more than a slothful
puppet, a king in name only. Maria Carolina was a remarkable
woman, ugly yet licentious, pedantic yet ignorant, ruthless beyond
all semblance. She ruled from 1792 to 1805, thirteen fateful years.
Her political allegiance was strongly anti-French and pro-Austrian,
naturally so since she was the daughter of Maria Theresa; and,
being pro-Austrian, she took part in the combined efforts of Austria, Britain, and Russia to oust Napoleon from what threatened to
become a dominating position in Europe. Her court advisers were
foreigners and included the British Ambassador, Lord Hamilton,
and his beautiful and notorious wife, Lady Hamilton, who was
united to the Queen by bonds of closest friendship (and more than
friendship).

Against this foreign queen and her ineffectual king the young
Neopolitans grumbled, sighed, fretted, and eventually combined in
secret resistance. In the last decade of the eighteenth century two
movements arose in Naples. The first was "intellectual" and expressed itself in a reawakened interest in indigenous Neapolitan
culture, its theater, and its music. Floria Tosca—she, too, is a historical figure—benefited by this new enthusiasm.

The second of the Neapolitan movements, more consequential,
was a pro-French movement. Its leaders sought in an alliance with
France the freedom and human dignity which the French Revolution had promised. They studied Voltaire and revered Napoleon. In
the Queen's view they were traitors. For she was about to declare
war on France.

This she did—though the proclamation was signed by Ferdinand
—in 1796. Immediately, to stamp out the pro-French element in

Naples, a campaign of terror was inaugurated. Innocent and guilty were arrested, given short trials, and summarily executed. At the beginning of the war the French invaded Italy, occupied it as far as Rome, repulsed a strong Italian counterattack, and in December, 1798, under General Championnet, marched on Naples itself. Ferdinand and Maria Carolina fled to Palermo. The French took Naples. General Championnet proclaimed a republic for Naples (in January, 1799), the "Parthenopian Republic." To administer this new republic, an assembly of twenty-five men was chosen. Angelotti was one of these; later he became a consul of the allied "Roman Republic." Neither republic lasted more than six months. The French were soon defeated by the combined armies of the British, Austrians, Russians, and one recruited by Maria Carolina. Once more she was in power; she re-entered Naples. Hundreds of citizens were killed and thousands more were arrested, among them Angelotti.

Many of these arrests were carried out by a special secret police organized by Maria Carolina. "Besides the visible police, there sprang up at the same time, organized and paid for by the queen, an immense secret force—increasing from year to year as the system developed—of spies, who infested and disturbed every rank of society. . . . The most harmless speeches were construed into treason; the innocent extravagances and enthusiastic chatter of boys and students reached the royal ear as evidences of Jacobinism—indications of conspiracy, terrible signs of coming revolution."

Two months after Maria Carolina's reconquest of Naples, Pope Pius VI died in Rome (August 29). Immediately, on the Queen's orders, a band of Neapolitans invaded Rome and captured it on the twenty-seventh of September. Ferdinand, relinquishing all pretense of power, remained in Palermo, and the Queen, her ministers, and her police force now took over the governing of Rome as well as of Naples. The secret police of Rome, with its spies and informers, was headed by Baron Scarpia.

By the end of 1799 Napoleon had lost all of Italy except Genoa. General Melas—an Austrian commanding the allied troops—proposed now to retake Genoa as well. But here Napoleon made one of his surprise moves, executing it with required boldness. He reinvaded Italy, and instead of concentrating on Genoa he by-passed the city. His "Army of Reserve" swept down to a point below the city. On June 9, 1800, a preliminary battle was fought at Monte-bello and won by the French; but this was only a prelude to what was to be the decisive battle, the Battle of Marengo, on June 14, 1800. This battle remains celebrated as an example of snatching victory from the jaws of defeat. For the better part of the day the French seemed badly beaten, and it was only the arrival of General Desaix and his nine thousand men which turned the tide to French victory. But that victory was decisive and complete.

These facts of a complicated, seesaw history are punctiliously observed by Sardou. His historical writing could serve as a textbook. The only liberty that he allowed himself was this: he put Maria Carolina in Rome three days after the Battle of Marengo.[1] In point of fact she was on a voyage to Vienna, possibly to solicit further aid from the Austrians. Her ship had just put in at the harbor of Livorno, having encountered bad weather on its way north. There two reports reached the Queen: first, one of Italian victory at Marengo, and later one describing the true state of things, the defeat. This incident is cleverly put to use by Sardou. In the play a great festival celebrating the supposed Neapolitan victory is planned in the Queen's honor. Tosca is to sing (second act: the great hall of the Palazzo Farnese). Scarpia is there, and the Queen charges him in menacing terms to deliver the head of Angelotti, who has escaped. Tosca, the feted star, enters and is about to sing to the accompaniment of an orchestra led by the composer Paisiello. (Sardou was a historical name-dropper.) Just as Tosca is ready to sing, a dispatch is brought to the Queen. She opens it, reads the news of the defeat, and faints dead away. The festivities are immediately halted. Dramatically this was a convenient device, since Tosca was a part written for Sarah Bernhardt and the Divine Sarah could not sing. She didn't have to.

In the opera all this is changed: The festival scene is eliminated, Tosca does sing but one hears her song merely through an open window—which puzzles most of the spectators and angers the sopranos, who'd rather sing *on* stage—and, as I have said, the figure of Queen Carolina is altogether excised. Perhaps it would not do to have another female detract attention from Tosca herself (though this does not seem to have worried Sarah Bernhardt). Whatever the reason, Puccini let history go by the boards.

[1] Sardou specifies that the action of *Tosca* takes place on June 17, 1800.

One further point: In the play it is made clear that Scarpia himself is frightened. The Queen hints that he had better produce his prisoner—or else. This threat tends to make Scarpia's actions a little more believable.

To summarize, let us restate that Sardou can be awarded an A-plus for the accuracy of his history. He uses events leading up to the Battle of Marengo correctly, as he adroitly makes use of the panicky atmosphere of the war between France and Italy. It is not his fault that his details become clouded in the condensation by Illica and Giacosa. The result is a diminution of quality, though enough of Sardou's dramatic workmanship remains to allow us to guess—rather than to know—that the simple melodrama derives added interest and perhaps added stature from history. We will enjoy *Tosca* more if we keep history in mind.

Let us remember, then, that Scarpia is the Police Commissioner of a conquered Rome, that he acts on behalf of the Queen of Naples, that he is a diplomat and a baron, thoroughly depraved and devoted to his cruel work. Cavaradossi in the play describes him thus: "Under the guise of perfect politeness and fervent religion, now smiling, now making the sign of the cross, this scoundrel . . . is an artist in evil, refined in his villainies,[2] cruel for the love of cruelty, bloody even in his pleasures."

Angelotti has been convicted of the crime of treason against Naples because he was a member of the pro-French Republic only recently extinct. But if that were not enough, he has further and special cause to fear persecution. He tells Cavaradossi (again in the play) when they meet in the church the story of his misfortune. Once when he was in London he was accosted by "one of those creatures who during the night infest the public gardens." This girl was particularly beautiful and so tempting that he spent the night with her. A few years later in Rome he met her again. To his horror he recognized her: she was now Lady Hamilton, the confidante of the Queen, the mistress of Lord Nelson, and "the true sovereign of Naples." She knows that he has recognized her. Two days after, Angelotti's house is searched, his papers seized. Nothing incriminating is found. But shortly after, somebody introduces two volumes by Voltaire into his library. The books are

[2] The usual operatic Scarpias are anything but "refined." Barking and lunging like Desperate Desmond, they add to our impression that *Tosca* is a crude melodrama.

found, and he is condemned to three years of imprisonment. Once again Sardou uses historical material. The story of Lady Hamilton is true.[3]

Cavaradossi is a member of the intellectual reform movement to which we have referred. Like Angelotti, he comes from a well-known family. He is wealthy, an aristocrat, and a dilettante painter. Scarpia in the play sneeringly calls him "a liberal like his father," and in the opera, "a Voltairean." Cavaradossi is obviously in sympathy with the French. Tosca, at the advice of her father confessor, begs him to shave off his "French mustaches," which advertise his sentiments to every beholder. But then she changes her mind: the mustache becomes him.

The sympathy which at once unites Angelotti and Cavaradossi is based on a political bond, a way of thinking and feeling.

Only Tosca lives above the realm of politics. She is equally admired by the Liberals as she is by the Queen. She does live for art and love.

ACT I

The action takes place in the interior of the Church of St. Andrea della Valle. A curious change of churches has here taken place. In Sardou's play the church is a different St. Andrea, the small and exquisite St. Andrea al Quirinale, one of the finest creations of Bernini. We can only guess at the reason why Puccini changed locales. He may have wanted for his stage setting the more spacious and imposing interior of the larger church. Or he may have preferred a church where official celebrations were more likely to be held. At any rate, in transferring the locale, he chose one to which it is extremely improbable that a prisoner from the Castel Sant'Angelo would have fled, its site being at the very center of eighteenth-century Rome.

There is no prelude. Three crashing chords only are heard—the ominous motive of Scarpia—and the curtain rises. On the extreme right of the church a chapel is to be seen; it is separated from the main interior by an iron gate. This is the Attavanti Chapel. An easel has been placed on the left of the stage; on the easel there is

[3] See a recent biography of the lady, *Emma in Blue*, by Gerald Herman and Desmond Stewart.

a large canvas, but we cannot see the painting itself, as it is cov-ered with a cloth. Various appurtenances of the painter's craft are lying around, as well as a basket containing food and wine. In the center of the stage stands a holy font, surmounted by a statue of the Madonna. It is midday. The time is important, though it is not mentioned in the libretto. Since it is midday, the church is officially closed and therefore presumably open only to people who work there or are specially admitted. Up to the end of the act the persons of the play are free from casual interruptions. We must keep this in mind if we are to understand how a public church is used like a private house.

A man dressed in prison garb staggers in.[4] He is trembling with fear and looks about him anxiously. He is searching for something. He searches at the basin, at the column, at the foot of the statue of the Madonna. His sister has told him the object's hiding place. He finds it: it is the key to the private chapel of the Attavanti family. Angelotti cautiously unlocks the door and disappears into the chapel, there to find a temporary refuge.

The music, which expresses Angelotti's fear with stumbling, nervous chords, now changes to a tripping motive which charac-terizes the Sacristan. This weak relative of Verdi's Friar Melitone is one of Puccini's least successful comic characters. He acts as servant to the painter Cavaradossi; he disapproves of his employer, taking good care, however, to hide his feelings. He is gluttonous, cowardly, and reactionary. His dramatic purpose is to show that in the fetid political atmosphere danger lurks everywhere; even a man not to be taken seriously could seriously compromise you. But the irony remains undeveloped, the character unimportant.

How dirty those paint brushes are, the Sacristan complains to somebody behind the scenes; he is always busy washing them. But where is the painter? The Sacristan had expected him to be at work. He peeps into the basket, with a little too much enthusiasm, and as its contents are untouched he is convinced that Cavaradossi has not yet arrived. Just then the Angelus sounds and the Sacristan says his prayer in Latin.

Presently Cavaradossi does enter, ready to get to work. He climbs to the scaffold and uncovers the painting on which he is working.

[4] At the Metropolitan Opera Angelotti enters through an open window, a good piece of staging.

It is a painting of Mary Magdalene, with blue eyes and flowing gold hair. The Sacristan, turning to speak to Cavaradossi, sees the painting—obviously for the first time though we do not know why —and exclaims in surprise, "By all the Saints, it is her portrait!" Whose? An unknown lady's who in the last few days has been coming to the church to pray[5] and, as Cavaradossi smilingly assures the Sacristan, has been so rapt in her devotion that he has painted her without her noticing it.

Cavaradossi begins his work. But, as is the way with painters on the operatic stage, he stops his work after a few daubs and falls into a reverie. He contemplates the painting on the easel; then, taking out a locket containing a miniature of Tosca, he looks upon this picture and on this. He compares diverse forms of beauty: his own dark-haired Tosca (which explicit direction did not prevent Maria Jeritza from donning a blond wig) and the fair unknown, the dark eyes of his beloved and the blue eyes of his model. Yet all forms melt to one, in the pure, harmonious concept of Beauty which he as a painter is attempting to fix on canvas. Unexceptional philosophy and, of course, a very good aria, the *"Recondita armonia."* Its effect is heightened by the censorious grumblings of the Sacristan, which in their monotony serve to set off the richness of the melody. But what the Sacristan mutters—imprecations against all free thinkers such as this painter and all enemies of the "holy government"—that gets lost.

The Sacristan takes leave of the painter, first hinting that if Cavaradossi is not hungry he himself could have use for the contents of the basket. The church is now silent. Cavaradossi is at work. Angelotti, thinking that the church is empty, reappears, ready for flight. Cavaradossi turns at the sound of the scraping of the key in the lock. Angelotti, at first terrified, sees him and suddenly, with a cry of joy, identifies Cavaradossi as a friend. But it takes a moment before the painter recognizes this emaciated, ragged prisoner who stands before him and claims his acquaintance. Immediately after, there is satisfaction on his side as well. Cavaradossi recalls "the Consul of the extinct Roman Republic." Generously he offers help. At this moment the voice of Tosca is heard calling

[5] It is quite unbelievable that the Sacristan should not recognize the lady as the Marchesa Attavanti; the chapel in his church belongs to her family.

"Mario!" Cavaradossi gives Angelotti the basket of food and hurries him once more into his hiding place in the chapel. He will get rid of Tosca in a "brief instant" and then they can plan what next to do. At once Cavaradossi decides not to take Tosca into his confidence, whether out of doubt of Tosca's ability to keep a secret or out of a wish to keep Tosca away from political trouble we do not know. . . .

The compression of the whole exposition is extreme. It is no wonder that the audience is bewildered, having little idea of what the scurrying and the secrecy are about. In the play we first get an explanatory scene in which the Sacristan talks to Cavaradossi's servant. The two discuss war—General Melas is winning every victory over that French upstart, Napoleon, and Genoa has been captured—and the Sacristan produces a newspaper from which he reads the announcement of a forthcoming celebration in honor of the Queen. There follows some conversation as to "Can one take this General Bonaparte seriously?" to which the servant answers, "I don't but my master does." We gather that both the Sacristan and the servant disapprove of Cavaradossi's views on politics, views which he undoubtedly inherited from his father, who had lived in Paris and had associated with "the abominable Voltaire."

Later, after Angelotti emerges from his hiding place, he tells the whole story of his life to Cavaradossi (including the episode of Lady Hamilton), as I have indicated. The painter in turn confides to Angelotti his love for Tosca, relates the story of her life, her great triumph as a diva, and speaks of the discord within the harmony of their love. For Tosca is not only madly jealous but also excessively devout. She is forever afraid of her lover's liberal and secular views, which he has made no attempt to hide. But both of them hope soon to escape the oppressive atmosphere of Rome. Tosca is engaged for Venice the next season, and Cavaradossi's own offer to paint a fresco in the church without remuneration may protect him from being molested by the police, until they can both find refuge in Venice.

Sardou not only takes the opportunity to acquaint us fully and vividly with the man who is Tosca's lover, but he shows us what a careful craftsman he is by detailing the measures taken to effect Angelotti's escape. The omission of this plan is one of the weaknesses of Puccini's first act. What sense does it make in the opera for Angelotti first to hide in the chapel and then for no good reason to bob out of his concealment?

In the play the plan is this: Angelotti's sister, the Marchesa Attavanti, has bribed one of the jailers to take advantage of the confusion caused by the French war to effect her brother's escape. She has concealed a woman's costume, a veil and a fan, as well as scissors and a razor, in the family chapel, the key to which she has smuggled to her brother through the accomplice. It appears, then, that the attractive stranger who seemed so devout that she did not even notice Cavaradossi's presence, spent her time in the church not for purposes of prayer alone. Angelotti is to go to the chapel at nightfall before the church is closed, spend the night there, and disguise himself as a woman. The accomplice is then to come for him and to conduct him to a meeting place where a carriage is to be waiting to transport Angelotti outside of Roman territory. In short, Angelotti's escape is well planned and his presence in the church logically explained.

What has gone wrong with the plan? Simply this: that the accomplice has not appeared. Cavaradossi tries to soothe Angelotti's anguish, saying that the helper may have been unavoidably detained. There is nothing to do but wait. At any rate, there is no immediate danger until the sound of the cannon from Castel Sant'Angelo spreads abroad the news of the escape of the prisoner. It is curious that Puccini did not take advantage of one incident in this scene. At one moment the two men do hear a fearful knock at the church door. Both men are struck dumb with terror. But the noise proves to be only that of a ball thrown by some players in the street against the door. Thus reassured, they continue their conversation.

I believe it is psychologically significant that Puccini used virtually nothing of this colloquy. To be sure, he would have had to condense it in any case, sung speech requiring a slower measure than spoken words. But the fact that he cut the scene to a mere stump indicates, as is indeed indicated by his other operas, that he was less interested in the men than he was in the women. His orientation was fixed toward the eternal feminine. With the exception of Gianni Schicchi, it was the female characters of his operas with whom he dealt lovingly, short-changing the men. So he hurries on toward Tosca's entrance. . . .

We ourselves have been guilty of keeping Tosca waiting outside much too long. *"Perchè chiuso?"*—"Why is the door closed?"— she asks with immediate suspicion as she sweeps into our presence. And then: "To whom were you talking?" She heard, she says, the rustle of a garment. Cavaradossi tries to reassure her and takes her in his arms. "No," she says, "not before I have paid my respects to the Madonna." She distributes the flowers she has brought at the font. Almost immediately we get a picture of Tosca: a jealous woman, a charming one, temperamental, religious at least in the observance of form. She is portrayed in the music, which, from the moment of her entrance, has a sweeter, richer sound.

Now the music returns to a recitative style, and Tosca tells Cavaradossi the news of the day. Tonight she is to sing, but her appearance need only be brief and afterward she and her lover can go off to his villa together. Cavaradossi replies hesitantly: "Tonight?" and the fleeting appearance of Angelotti's music suggests to us the reason for his hesitancy. "It is the night of the full moon, the moon which gladdens the heart." There is no response. Tosca is perturbed; she asks what every woman under the circumstances asks: "You are not happy?"—meaning, "You no longer love me." Cavaradossi's reply sounds tame to her and Tosca, her irritation now pushing to the fore, responds with one of those little phrases— "You say it badly"—in which we recognize the stroke of Puccini's workmanship, its quick-falling cadence conveying to us an impression of her nervous mood as effectively as would long and elaborate musical passages.

Tosca recalls to him the rapture of their being together, just the two, silent in the starry night and the perfumed air. The appeal is enchanting enough to convince any man. Cavaradossi yields, but briefly, to the siren song, and then, Angelotti's problem still uppermost in his mind, asks her to leave and let him get on with his work.

As she turns to go, she sees the portrait of the blonde woman, the Mary Magdalene. She starts. The model is much too beautiful to please her and the portrait reminds her of somebody. But of whom? Yes, she has it: it is the portrait of the Marchesa Attavanti. From this recognition it is but the briefest jump to the conclusions of

jealousy. "You see her. You love her. She loves you. Those foot-
steps that I heard . . ." Cavaradossi tries to calm her and she makes
him swear that the two are strangers. Still, the eyes of the portrait
trouble her. Cavaradossi—it is his turn now to be seductive—
assures her, in music which is the counterpart of Tosca's plea but
has a more masculine texture, that no eyes on earth could equal
Tosca's eyes. If not altogether set at ease, Tosca is at least mollified.
"How well you know the art of making love. . . . But . . . you
must paint her with dark eyes."

In the short duet that follows, Tosca asks Cavaradossi to remain
at his work in the church until nightfall and to promise her that
he will admit no woman, be she fair or dark-haired. Once more
Cavaradossi has to reproach her gently; she now asks his pardon
and embraces him. When her lover remonstrates, "Before the
Madonna?" Tosca replies that the Madonna is kind and will understand. Then, with a final admonition, "Make her eyes dark!" she is
gone. A beautiful scene, as animated musically as is its heroine!

Cavaradossi turns and immediately addresses himself to Angelotti. What is to be done now? Angelotti says that his sister has
hidden woman's clothing beneath the altar. He will stay in the
church until darkness falls and then disguise himself. His sister has
dared much to save him from Scarpia. At the first mention of the
dreaded name, we hear the chords which characterize the Baron and
which are heard at the very beginning of the opera as a warning
superscription. It is at this point that Cavaradossi comes to a brave
resolve. He will save Angelotti even at the risk of his own life. He
has a better plan, he tells the fugitive: The chapel opens onto a
garden from which a path leads through the fields to his villa. Let
Angelotti take the key to his house and repair thither immediately,
carrying the woman's clothes with him; there is no need to put
them on now: the path is sure to be deserted. As Angelotti is about
to act on this instruction, Cavaradossi gives him a final comfort. If
there should be danger, if Scarpia's minions should track him to the
villa, let him hide himself in the well in the garden. At the bottom
of the well there is water, but halfway down he will discover a
narrow passage which leads to a cave. No one can find him there.

At this moment the cannon of the Castello is heard. Angelotti's
escape has been discovered. Once more Cavaradossi comes to a sudden decision, one which makes no sense (he does not act quite so

foolishly in the play) and the purpose of which seems to be chiefly to get him offstage: he himself will accompany Angelotti.

No sooner have both men quit the church when the Sacristan runs in shaking with good news. He is dumfounded to find the place empty. He is disappointed as well, for he would have relished the pleasure of irking the painter with his news: it is nothing less than that Bonaparte has been routed and crushed. He now has to content himself to retail the message to the choirboys. There will be a torchlight procession, a victory celebration will take place in the Farnese Palace that evening, and Tosca will sing a cantata. It means double pay for the boys, which fact provokes them to genuine enthusiasm, to which they give vent in a waltzlike chorus. The music suggests that Puccini was not unfamiliar with *Die Meistersinger* and the chorus of apprentices in the first act. As there, so here, the chorus is interrupted by a sudden entrance: Scarpia and his minions appear, with the orchestra once again crashingly proclaiming the Scarpia motive. Such unseemly behavior in church— what is the meaning of it? the Baron asks. The Sacristan, who is nothing if not a coward, is about to slink away without offering an explanation, but Scarpia sharply bids him stay.

How does Scarpia choose this very church in his search for the escaped prisoner? We are not given even the barest hint of the means by which so soon and so surely he has traced the beast to its lair. Once again we must turn to the source, for Sardou leaves no such loophole. In the play we learn that the accessory to the escape, the man for whom Angelotti had been waiting, has been found and has, under duress, given the entire plan away. Scarpia, then, is not guessing; he knows the fugitive's hiding place. It is his task merely to track him down.

"Where is the Attavanti chapel?" asks Scarpia. The Sacristan goes to point it out to him—and discovers to his surprise that the door of the chapel is open. He is now utterly confused.

"A great mistake, that cannon shot!" muses Scarpia to himself in a passage which bristles with subdued menace. The prisoner now has been warned. The search of the chapel provides one clue, a fan marked with the crest of the Attavanti family. It is no doubt part of the costume with which the prisoner had been supplied. Turning from the chapel, Scarpia's glance lights on the portrait on the easel. "Who is the painter?" he asks the Sacristan. Scarpia is obviously pleased with the answer; he is beginning to put the pieces of the puzzle together. Cavaradossi makes a desirable suspect, being known to Scarpia as a Freethinker and a Voltairean.

One of Scarpia's agents emerges from the chapel with Cavaradossi's basket. It is empty. No great acumen on Scarpia's part is needed for him to guess who consumed the provisions. At this moment, most opportunely for Scarpia, Tosca reappears in the church. (She does not do so in the play, where the scene in which Scarpia provokes Tosca is placed in the second act.)

But here she is, to her own ill luck. Scarpia, seeing her, at once decides to use "Attavanti's fan as Iago uses Desdemona's handkerchief." If he can sufficiently incite her jealousy, he may catch her off her guard. Tosca appears to be extremely nervous. Mario is no longer here. Why not? Where is he? It cannot be, she murmurs half to herself, that he is deceiving me. No, it cannot be!

Scarpia approaches her with seeming courtesy and suavity. He compliments her on her piety. She, the pride of the stage, coming to church to pray! This is so unlike certain impudent creatures who impersonate the Magdalene but really come to church to meet a lover. Upon this hint she reacts violently. What proof has he? He shows her the fan, which she too recognizes as Attavanti's.

She very nearly bursts into tears. Pressing his advantage, Scarpia sympathizes with her and asks her in what way he can comfort her grief. He would give his life to dry those tears. Tosca hardly listens. She must catch those "two traitors." She will trap them together at the villa. With this she leaves impetuously.

As soon as her back is turned, Scarpia commands three agents to follow her; they are to shadow her wherever she goes.

While this cat-and-mouse business is being enacted in the foreground, the church bells begin to sound. They summon the congregation to a festive service, the *Te Deum* which is to express thanks for the victory. Now the organ joins the bells, as the people begin to assemble. Scarpia, foreseeing triumph, holds an impious soliliquy during these pious preparations. "Go, Tosca! Scarpia nests in your heart. It is I who have unfettered the falcon of your jealousy!"

The finale of this act, the great choral *Te Deum* juxtaposed against Scarpia's comments, is one of the most effective large scenes to be found in Puccini's work. It is not usual for him—up to

Turandot—to compose mass effects; even the close of the second act of *Bohème* is a crowd scene in miniature. But here he paints with broad strokes; here he combines the orchestra, the baritone voice, the chorus, the organ, the bells, and bursts of cannon to pile up excitement in a continuous crescendo, the very weight of the sound being overwhelming. At the very last, Scarpia joins the service—Tosca has made him forget his God, he exclaims sanctimoniously—and adds his prayer to the sacred anthem.

ACT II

What happens in Puccini's operas in the interval between acts one and two? That depends on which opera we are considering. Nothing in *Bohème* or *Turandot*, the action being continuous, and quite a lot in *Butterfly*, several years elapsing—time enough for "Trouble" to be born and grow to an uncertain age.[6] But it is *Manon Lescaut* which may well hold the record for the operatic between-curtains broad jump, since at the close of the first act Manon and Des Grieux elope to Paris not yet lovers, and at the beginning of the second act Manon has not only terminated her idyl with Des Grieux and taken a second lover, but has already tired of that second lover.

The interval between Acts I and II of *Tosca* is a short one in time, from the afternoon to the evening of the same day, but the jump is nonetheless troublesome, as, once more, several incidents germane to the dramatic development have been suppressed. Puccini used virtually nothing of Sardou's cogent second act. This act not only sketches the mordant and morbid society gathered around the Queen but it also applies the pressure on Scarpia, who knows that he had better deliver the prisoner but hasn't the vaguest notion of how to go about his task. What he fears is not only the Queen's command but the revenge of Lady Hamilton, who will not spare him if Angelotti manages to save himself. It is only gradually, as he watches Tosca's agitation, that he arrives at a possible solution of the difficulty. The fan he found in the church, Attavanti's fan, provides the means of making Tosca lose her balance. Skillfully, slyly, and slowly he convinces Tosca that her lover is unfaithful. "A jealous woman can be more helpful than a police agent," he

[6] Judging by the variously aged children to be seen in various opera houses.

observes. Circumstantial evidence and Cavaradossi's peculiar behavior in the church aid Scarpia; with the result that Tosca quite
loses her head and, determined to get at the truth, rushes out to
Cavaradossi's villa. She is closely shadowed by Scarpia, his aides, and
the Marquis Attavanti, who as a putative cuckold husband provides
some comic relief and whom Scarpia drags along as a possible witness to his wife's treachery. It is Tosca, then, who guides, "falcon-
like," the hunters onto the right scent; it is Tosca who discloses the
location of a hideaway which is unknown to Scarpia. Such is the
progress of the play.

The torture scene, the second act of the opera, has its counterpart in the play, where it takes place in the third act, in Cavaradossi's villa. Once having found the villa, Scarpia and his men in-
vade it in force. Again the dramatic circumstances are tauter and
more exciting. For while the torturers pursue their grim task in the
room, we the audience know that Angelotti is hiding in the well
outside; at the end of the act the searchers return with the news
that he has been found—dead by poison.

Yet enough of Sardou's torture scene is preserved by Puccini
to provide strong stuff for music. Let us detail the progression of
the libretto:

We are in Scarpia's apartment in the Palazzo Farnese. He is
seated at a table laid for his supper, waiting for the return of
Spoletta, his aide. He betrays, says the stage direction, "a feverish
anxiety," which is interpreted by the average Scarpia by sitting
still and looking at the conductor. Tosca is a good hawk, he muses,
and he assures himself that his minions must by this time have
both men in their clutches. He hopes that by dawn both of them
will be swinging from the gibbet. He summons Sciarrone, a gen-
darme, and asks him whether Tosca has arrived at the palace. Re-
ceiving an affirmative answer, Scarpia bids Sciarrone open the great
window; as he does so, we hear the strains of a stately gavotte. The
dancing, then, is still progressing. Tosca has not as yet sung. Scarpia
tells Sciarrone to wait for Tosca until she finishes her cantata, and
then—better still—he writes a note to her summoning her. She
will come, he says to himself, for love of her Mario. For that same
love she will give herself to him. The composer here permits him to
come as near to an aria as Scarpia ever does, the music and words
expressing the mixture of cruelty and eroticism inherent in the

character. Scarpia's imagination dwells on the pleasures to be derived from Tosca's surrender. "There lies a richer savor in a conquest by violence than in soft consent."

Sciarrone, re-entering, announces that Spoletta has returned from his mission. Scarpia welcomes him. "Well, my brave friend, how was the hunt?" Spoletta, trembling with fear, makes his report: They had pursued Tosca to a villa hidden by foliage. She had entered but very soon she had reappeared and departed alone. He, Spoletta, had scaled the garden wall and searched the house. He found nothing, not a sign of Angelotti. Scarpia springs up pale with fury, his brow contracted, and curses Spoletta. The terrified man stammers that he did come upon the painter and that Cavaradossi behaved in so scoffing and supercilious a manner that it was clear that he knew where the fugitive was hidden. In any case, Spoletta thought it best to arrest him; he was even now waiting in the antechamber. "That is not so bad," says Scarpia, and we hear in the orchestra the theme which is to be associated from now on with the tortures inflicted on Mario, a snakelike theme winding around one note.

The choral cantata in honor of the victory is heard through the window. The strains of the cantata, above which Tosca's voice later soars, contrast effectively with the violent action which begins as Spoletta introduces Cavaradossi into Scarpia's presence.

Scarpia orders Spoletta to bring in, along with the captive, the executioner and the judge of the Fisc. (It was the business of this judge to determine the right of the Crown to the estates of traitors.) Mario faces Scarpia defiantly. Why has he been brought here? Scarpia replies with studied courtesy. "You are aware, no doubt, that a prisoner escaped today from the Castel Sant'Angelo?" Cavaradossi denies such knowledge. "Yet it is rumoured that you aided him in the church, providing him with food and clothes." "A lie," replies Mario. "And that," continues Scarpia, in his seeming calm voice, "you guided him to your house in the suburbs." "Where are the proofs of these accusations? Your henchmen searched the place and found nothing." "That only shows how well he was concealed." Spoletta, furious, recalls that Cavaradossi openly laughed at him. "I am still laughing," replies Cavaradossi. "Take care," Scarpia warns him. "This is the place for tears."

While this interrogation proceeds, we continue to hear the voice of the chorus with Tosca's voice floating above it. But now Scarpia, irritated, bangs the window closed and thunders at Cavaradossi, "Where is Angelotti? Do you deny having succored him? And given him clothes? And offered him an asylum in your house?" To all of which Cavaradossi replies: "I deny it." Then, changing his tone to one of paternal calm, Scarpia urges Cavaradossi to make a clean confession; it will save him much anguish. But the plea is no more effective than the threat.

The scene is sparsely accompanied by the orchestra, for Puccini knows that the terse interrogation must move along without much adumbration. But what there is of orchestral underscoring, nervous tremolos, scarifying drumbeats, is extremely effective in heightening the tension, and the whole scene proves how superb a musical dramatist Puccini could be—*without* a set aria.

Suddenly Tosca enters breathlessly. She has come in response to Scarpia's note. "Say nothing of what you saw or you will kill me," whispers Cavaradossi to her. Scarpia decides that the time has come for Cavaradossi's "formal" arraignment before the judge. The orchestra rises to great force, the tragic theme which has been indicated previously is now presented in full, and the henchmen lead Mario into the torture chamber. "Just the ordinary procedure at first," Scarpia instructs them. "Then do as I direct."

The stage is now set for the climactic and central duel between the Baron and the actress, the great scene which, in the play as well as in the opera, gives *Tosca* its *raison d'être*.

It begins, as such scenes do, quietly and suavely. "Let us talk as friends," Scarpia tells Tosca, while she simulates an ease which she is far from feeling. "What about the fan?" Tosca shrugs it off. "It was just foolish jealousy." "Then the lady was not in the villa?" "No, he was alone." "Alone? Are you sure?" "Nothing escapes a jealous woman. I am sure." "How you protest! It would seem as if you feared to betray yourself."

Scarpia turns toward the door and asks Sciarrone how things are progressing in the chamber. "He keeps denying," reports Sciarrone. "Then let us insist a little more." Tosca demands, "To satisfy you, then, one must lie?" But it is a lame piece of irony, and Scarpia answers it easily. Slowly—and to a new theme, the effect of which as usual Puccini hammers home by constant repetition—Scarpia breaks down her defenses and describes to her, with evident relish, how her lover lies bound, an iron bar pressing against his temples; at each denial the bar is tightened, blood gushing from his head. It is up to her to save him. Tosca groans, "Cease—cease!" But when she still refuses to divulge the secret, Scarpia, enraged, tells his men to proceed to the limit.

Tosca, approaching the closed door, calls out to Mario and hears his suffocated reply: He despises the pain; she must remain silent. Scarpia laughs at Tosca's anguish, laughs at her calling him a monster. To him she is merely the actress being more superbly tragical in real life than she has ever been on the stage. The door is to be opened so that Tosca cannot avoid hearing her lover's groans. The iron band is to be applied more tightly.

As the previous musical material is summoned to a great crescendo, Scarpia keeps hammering at Tosca, "Where is Angelotti?" As she sobs, "It is too much to bear," we hear for the first time the melody of the *"Vissi d'arte,"* the aria which is to come. She begs Mario's consent to speak. He forbids it. This exasperates Scarpia, who, fearing that Mario may once again instill new courage in Tosca, screams to Spoletta, "Silence him!" Tosca falls prostrate on the sofa, and Spoletta, showing some vestige of humanity, murmurs a prayer of the *"Dies Irae."* A final and terrible cry from Mario is followed by dead silence. Then the silence is broken as Tosca, in a choked voice, blurts out, "In the well . . . in the garden."

Scarpia orders the torture to cease. Mario has fainted and is brought back. Tosca rushes over to him, covering his face with tears and kisses, while we hear a now tragic reminder of the gentle phrase from their duet in the first act. In a voice made weak by pain, he asks her, "Did you speak?" "No," she says, "no, love." At this moment Scarpia loudly and triumphantly instructs Spoletta, "In the well in the garden." Hearing this, Mario turns on Tosca: she has betrayed him.

And now, the conscientious commentator is obliged to say, Puccini, as well as Illica and Giacosa, thoroughly fall from grace. It is the point at which they most depart from the original and at which they become most inept. Curiously, the music diminishes in quality in proportion to the libretto's awkwardness. We know that Puccini needed, perhaps more than other composers, the right words and situations for the development of his music. We know that the labor of the libretto was with him more time-consuming than the composing of the music. It is therefore significant that because somehow or other the librettists could not get the dramatic situation right, Puccini could not get the music right.

Sciarrone rushes in with bad news: Melas, contrary to previous report, has been vanquished; Napoleon is the victor of the Battle of Marengo! It is of course straining the credulity even of a melodrama to assume that a subordinate would interrupt Scarpia unannounced to blurt out news which could just as well have waited for another moment or two. But worse is to follow: at the news the orchestra bursts into old-fashioned *fortissimo* blares, and Cavaradossi, losing the last remnants of whatever sense he may have possessed, screams out, "Victory! Victory!" Would any man, even a tenor, indulge himself in so gross a piece of exhibitionism, making sure thereby that he prove himself guilty and sign his own death warrant? From the cry of "Victory!" Cavaradossi proceeds to a short aria—he has recovered his full voice in a remarkably short time—"The dawn of revenge is here,"—"*L'alba vindice appar*'"— set to a martial strain, as poor an aria as Puccini committed in any of his major works.

We have only to recall how the news of the Battle of Marengo is conveyed by Sardou, once more to regret the fact that this dramatic opportunity was not properly evaluated by the composer.

Scarpia, exasperated by Mario's defiance, orders the agents to remove him. They drag him off while Scarpia forcibly restrains Tosca from leaving and closes the door.

Now, as Scarpia and Tosca are once more alone, the cries of torture echoing in her thoughts while certain triumph prevails in his—now, as their struggle must rise to its climax—Puccini's genius takes renewed fire; out of the two motives so congenial to him, eroticism and menace, he fashions one of his most exciting melodramatic scenes.

Scarpia seats himself once again at the table, smiling and sure, and invites Tosca to join him in his interrupted supper, to taste a sip of the wine of Spain, and together with him to calculate some means of saving her lover.

To this Tosca responds with one bitter word: "*Quanto?*"—"How much?" She spits it out—and he laughs at the question. "I know," he says, "that I have the reputation of being venal. But to beautiful women I do not sell myself for money." Another prize tempts him more. He has long admired Tosca, and now her tears and misery have but incited his fervor, her look of hatred but stimulated his desire. When he saw her clinging to her lover, as a savage beast protects her young, that was the moment he swore to himself that she would be his.

An idea strikes Tosca. She will go to the Queen. Certainly, replies Scarpia. The way is free. She may speak to the Queen; but the best that the Queen could do would be to pardon a corpse. Looking at her, he exclaims, "How you hate me!" But her hate is impotent. As he pursues her, we hear distant drumbeats. It is the escort of condemned men, Scarpia explains. They are setting up new gallows now. Mario has an hour to live; whether more depends on her.

The exhausted Tosca sinks onto the sofa, and while Scarpia keeps his mocking gaze fixed on her, she breaks out into the famous lament of *"Vissi d'arte."* She has lived for art and for love. She has never harmed a living soul. She has been devout, she has adorned the Virgin's mantle with gems. Why is it that the Lord has deserted her now? Why has she deserved such punishment?

Puccini was supposed not to have been overly fond of this aria, for he felt that it slowed the progress of the action. And it is true that dramatically it creates an awkward moment, because Scarpia, all during the aria, has to remain mute and listen. Yet one is not so sure that Puccini's afterthought was right; for aside from making us grateful for the beauty of the aria, a beauty which a thousand repetitions cannot extinguish, it serves as an eddy in the turbulence of the entire act; this very resting point helps to give greater movement to the scenes before and after.

Scarpia's only reply to Tosca is, "Decide!" She throws herself at his feet, wringing her hands for mercy. Scarpia pretends to relent; she is too beautiful for him not to give in. He will grant her a life if she will grant him a moment. There is a knock at the door, and Spoletta enters to tell Scarpia that Angelotti killed himself when they came to arrest him. What shall be done with Cavaradossi? What are His Excellency's instructions? Scarpia turns to Tosca with a laconic "Well?" There is another one of those silences which Puccini manages so effectively. Then Tosca, covering her face and weeping, nods.

She insists that Mario be set free at once. Scarpia, however, explains to her that the forms will have to be observed and he will

have to have recourse to a ruse. Everyone must believe Mario dead.
To assure her that he is to be trusted, she may overhear the orders
he will give to Spoletta. He tells Spoletta that he has changed his
mind, that Cavaradossi is to be shot—but, "just as with Count
Palmieri," this is to be a simulated execution. "Just as with Count
Palmieri—!" Does he, Spoletta, understand exactly? He does.

"I want to tell him myself," interposes Tosca. Scarpia accedes.
At four in the morning Spoletta is to let Tosca pass to Mario's
presence.

Spoletta disappears and Scarpia turns to her with a passionate,
"I have kept my promise." Not quite yet: Tosca demands a safe-
conduct so that she and Mario can flee from the Roman state, flee
forever.

As Scarpia goes to his desk to write the safe-conduct, the orchestra asseverates the reptilian motive which has woven itself
through the act. While he is engaged, Tosca wanders about the
room distractedly; almost without knowing it, she finds herself
near the supper table and with a trembling hand she takes up a
glass of wine. As she does so, her eye alights on a sharp knife. A
startling surge in the orchestra tells us what plan has occurred to
her. She conceals the knife, waiting for Scarpia to sign and seal
the paper. He brings it to her with the ardent exclamation, "Tosca,
mine at last!" With all her force she plunges the knife into his
heart. "This," she cries rather than sings, "is Tosca's kiss!" Scarpia
falls. In the agony of death he calls for help. In vain! It is Tosca
now, the sluice gates of her hate fully open, who taunts and jeers
him.

It is instructive to contrast the scene in Sardou with the scene
in the opera, instructive because either scene in its field could
hardly have been bettered and the comparison may help us to perceive the nature of the tools available to the artist who uses words
and pantomime, and the artist who uses words and music.

Let us recall that Tosca was written to give scope to the skill of
an illimitable actress. Bernhardt's exit in the second act was described by one of her biographers, Reynaldo Hahn:

What a feeling for effect and what technique in the way in which, after
the murder of Scarpia, she wets the napkin to wash away the blood she
has on her hands, in which she examines her dress to make sure that she
had not stained it, with which she looks out of the window by raising

herself lightly on tiptoe! . . . The exit is a miracle of execution. Sarah half opens the door, puts her head out to peer into the corridor, then her shoulders, then her whole body, with the undulating movement of a reptile; the door closes softly, very softly, while the train of her dress disappears. . . . And while the curtains are lowered, we imagine that Tosca, furtive, palpitating, slinks off against the walls, silent as a shadow.

Effective as this pantomime undoubtedly was, I believe that the end of the act of the opera—without a Bernhardt or her equivalent —is even more effective, and it is so for the obvious reason that Puccini had the orchestra at his command.

As Tosca cleanses her hands and goes about her search for the safe-conduct, this orchestra takes over; it sings a dirge which is almost heroic in its slow dozen measures, as if death had freed the sordid scene, surpassing its blood and noise. After the famous last line "And before him all Rome trembled!"[7] the orchestra breaks up the Scarpia motive into weak fragments. The music diminishes almost to a silence, until after a final drum roll, very far away, the curtain falls.

Here then are the two versions of the scene:

(The Play)

TOSCA: I want a safe-conduct which will protect us until we have left Roman territory.

SCARPIA: That is reasonable. (*He walks to his* secrétaire, *where he stands and writes. Slowly Tosca wanders to the supper table. With a trembling hand she takes up a glass of Spanish wine which had been poured by Scarpia. As she does so, as she lifts the glass to her lips, she notices lying on the table a carving knife with a sharp blade. She pauses, steals a glance at Scarpia, who with his back to her is still writing, slowly replaces the glass on the table, and draws the knife nearer.*)

SCARPIA: (*Reading aloud what he has written*) "The lady Tosca and the cavalier who is accompanying her are to be allowed to pass freely from the city of Rome and through Roman territory—Vitellio Scarpia, Regent of the Roman Police." (*He turns to her. Once more she has taken up the glass, which she now empties at a gulp.*) Are you satisfied now? (*He shows her the document. Now he is standing quite close to her.*)

TOSCA: (*While she pretends to read the paper, her hand gropes for the knife.*) Yes. This is in order.

---

[7] In the first draft of the libretto this line had been eliminated, and it is a tribute to Puccini's usual dramatic acumen that he insisted on restoring it.

SCARPIA: Then I demand what is due me. (*He embraces her and ardently kisses her nude shoulder.*)

TOSCA: (*Stabs Scarpia in the chest.*) Here it is!

SCARPIA: Ah! You cursed creature! (*He falls.*)

TOSCA: (*With a cry of joy and a ferocious laugh*) At last! . . . It is done! . . . At last! . . . At last! . . . It is done!

SCARPIA: (*Clinging to the arm of the couch*) Help! . . . I die!

TOSCA: I hope you will! . . . Butcher! You who tortured me a whole night long. . . . Is it not my turn now? (*She leans over him and looks at him closely.*) Look at me! Say to yourself in your agony that you died at the hands of a woman. . . . Die, you ferocious beast! Die, in your rage, die without hope! . . . Die! . . . Die! . . . Die!

SCARPIA: (*Trying to raise himself*) Help! . . . Come here! . . .

TOSCA: (*Runs to the door, where she listens, then turns to Scarpia*) Scream all you like. Your blood is choking you. No one hears you. . . . (*Once more she goes to the door to listen, without taking her eyes off Scarpia. She drops the knife on a little side table. Scarpia, with a last effort, manages to rise. He stumbles a few paces forward, his back to the audience. He stands before Tosca. She quickly snatches up the knife; raising her arm, she is ready to strike again. Thus they regard each other for one second, he suffocating, she menacing. Finally, after a futile effort, he recoils and collapses on the couch, uttering a deep groan. From the couch he falls to the floor. She puts back the knife and exclaims coldly*) It is finished. (*She takes the candelabrum and by its light watches Scarpia die.*) Now we are quits! (*Calmly, without ceasing to look at him, she takes a carafe of water and moistens a napkin. She cleans her hands and tries to erase a spot of blood from her dress. She crumples the napkin and throws it into a corner of the alcove. She walks to the mirror and readjusts her coiffure. Then she turns once more toward the body of Scarpia.*) And it was before this that a whole city trembled! (*A roll of drums far off. Trumpets announce the dawn. She shudders.*) The dawn! . . . The day! . . . Already? (*She snuffs out the candles of the candelabrum.*) But the safe-conduct! . . . What have I done with the safe-conduct? (*She looks for it on the table, searches the room, and at last notices it in the clenched hand of Scarpia. She bends over him to force it out of his hand, lets his lifeless arm fall to the floor, and hides the safe-conduct in her bosom. Another drum roll, closer. She is about to go but notices that the flambeaux are still lighted. She starts to extinguish them but changes her mind, takes one in each hand, and places the one she is holding in her left hand to the left of Scarpia. Then, passing before the body with her back to the audience, she places the other to the right of the dead man. She looks around her and sees the crucifix above the* prie-dieu, *lifts it off the wall, carries it carefully by its handle, the head of Christ facing the audience, kneels before Scarpia, and places the crucifix on his chest. At this moment the third drum roll from the citadel is heard. Tosca rises and makes for the door, draws the bolt, and opens one wing. The antechamber is in darkness. She listens intently. Then, stealing cautiously away, she disappears.*)

CURTAIN

(The Opera)

SCARPIA: I have kept my promise. . . .

TOSCA: Not yet. I want a safe-conduct, so that he and I can flee the country.

SCARPIA: You really mean to leave?

TOSCA: Yes, forever!

SCARPIA: As you wish. (*Goes to his desk to write; he breaks off to ask Tosca:*) Which road will you choose?

TOSCA: (*While Scarpia is writing she has come to the table and, with a trembling hand, takes up the glass of wine which Scarpia poured for her. As she raises it to her lips she sees a sharp-pointed fruit knife on the table. Scarpia is still writing. With infinite caution she tries to get hold of the knife while answering his questions.*) The shortest.

SCARPIA: Civitavecchia?

TOSCA: Yes. (*At last she has the knife hidden behind her back.*)

SCARPIA: (*Has signed and sealed the safe-conduct; he folds it up and advances on Tosca with open arms.*) Tosca, at last you're mine! . . . (*But his lecherous tones turn into a terrible cry: Tosca has stabbed him to the heart.*) Ah, cursed creature!

TOSCA: This is Tosca's kiss!

SCARPIA: (*He staggers toward Tosca. She shudders and pushes him away from her. He falls, shouting, his voice suffocating with blood.*) Help! I'm dying! Ah! Help! I'm dying!

TOSCA: (*Watches Scarpia as he struggles in vain to get up.*) Does your own blood choke you?

SCARPIA: Help! I die!

TOSCA: Killed by a woman! You have tortured me enough! Can you still hear? Look at me! Scarpia, it is I, Tosca! Die and be forever damned!

SCARPIA: Ah . . .

TOSCA: He is dead! . . . Now I forgive him! . . . And it was before him that all Rome trembled! (*Without taking her eyes off the body she returns to the table, puts down the knife, dips a napkin in water and wipes her fingers. Then she straightens her hair at the mirror. She cannot find the safe-conduct on the desk; it is still clenched in Scarpia's fingers. She forces it out of his hand and lets his lifeless arm fall to the floor. She bestows the paper in her bosom and blows out the candles. Then she feels a pang of remorse. A candle is still burning; she takes it to light another, setting one to the right of the body, the other to the left. There is a crucifix on the wall; she kneels down beside Scarpia and places it on his chest. Then she rises and leaves the room very cautiously, closing the door behind her.*)

CURTAIN

With all the parallels we observe the differences. First, not only does the play use more words than the libretto, but the action itself is more detailed. Note that in Sardou one blow does not fell Scarpia, that Tosca is ready to deliver a second blow, thus giving Bernhardt the opportunity to assume, her arm raised, another effective pose. More significant than these details is our impression that the Tosca of the play is a more revengeful, more bloodthirsty, more inexorable creature than the Tosca of the opera. The libretto softens the character, the music softens her even more. This is epitomized by the words Tosca utters after Scarpia expires: "Now we are quits" in the play, "Now I forgive him" in the opera.

Puccini makes his Tosca say, as she stabs Scarpia, "This is Tosca's kiss!" He invented the line. Once more this gives us a hint of the orientation of the composer's mind.

ACT III

The scene represents a parapet on top of the Castel Sant'Angelo.[8] In the background the outlines of the Vatican and St. Peter's can be descried. The night is serene, the sky studded with stars.

The entire first scene serves as an orchestral prelude. The stage is empty. A series of descending chords conveys a sense of open-air freshness, of untroubled air—a strange contrast to the febrile indoor scene we have just witnessed. In the distance, very faintly,

8 Sardou's fifth act, which is so short that it fills but a dozen pages, is divided in two parts, the first taking place in "the death cell" of the Castel, the second on the parapet. Puccini's version is an improvement, as the action proceeds without a halt.

we hear the tinkling of cowbells. A shepherd boy sings his simple little song in dialect. Presently the church bells begin to proclaim the break of morning. (Puccini took a great deal of trouble over those bells. There is extant a letter from him in which he inquires of competent authority the actual notes which are sounded in St. Peter's belltower.)

A jailer with a lantern emerges. He is presently joined by a detail commanded by the sergeant of the guard. They are the condemned man's escort. As Cavaradossi is ushered in, the orchestra sounds the main phrase of the aria he will sing in a moment, *"Lucevan' le stelle"*—"The stars were shining." The sergeant hands over the warrant to the jailer. Cavaradossi signs the piece of paper. He is informed that the execution will take place in an hour. A priest is at his service. Cavaradossi refuses but begs the jailer for one final favor. He has only one possession left, a ring. This he would be glad to give to the jailer if he would allow him to write a letter. He must write to the one person dear to him—would the jailer deliver this last farewell? After a momentary hesitation the jailer accepts the bribe, and Cavaradossi begins to write his letter while the solo cello recalls the love music to us. He begins his famous aria as if he were musing to himself, quietly. But then, as memories of his happiness crowd in on him, as he thinks of the rapturous kisses and languid caresses of his Floria, both the voice and the orchestra mount in a unison of grief. "I die despairing," Cavaradossi cries out, "and yet never before have I loved life so much."

Cavaradossi's farewell to the world having been expressed and the orchestra having echoed it in a postlude (let us say nothing of the boors in the audience who spoil the effect by bursting into applause, genuine or purchased, as soon as the tenor stops sobbing), Spoletta now appears, accompanied by the sergeant and closely followed by Tosca. She runs to Cavaradossi, who, his head buried in his hands, at first does not see her. He jumps to his feet, and Tosca silently shows him the paper, Scarpia's safe-conduct. They read it together. Looking at Tosca, Mario says questioningly, "This is Scarpia's first act of grace." "And his last," she replies, and tells him what she has done. Now her hands are stained with blood. Overcome with love and gratitude, Mario takes her hands in his, those hands made for caressing children, for plucking roses, for praying. This melody, *"O dolci mani"*—"Oh, sweet hands"—is one of the tenderest strains in the opera, a mixture of love and sadness.

Tosca informs her lover that everything has been prepared for their flight. A carriage, money, and jewels are ready. The only task remaining is for Mario to go through with the simulated execution. Then all will be well. For a while they dare to anticipate in a hopeful duet the raptures of their future life together. But then, realizing their present situation, Tosca looks around uneasily. "They are not coming. Why not? . . . Be sure to fall quickly, as though you were dead." "Do not worry," replies Cavaradossi. "I shall fall naturally." The duet closes with an *a cappella* passage for the two voices and a final gentle promise that she, Tosca, will close his eyes with a thousand kisses.[9]

A prison bell tolls the hour of four. It is the appointed hour. The sergeant, the jailer, and Spoletta appear with the firing squad. In a whisper Tosca reminds Mario once again to fall at the first volley, and he, smiling, promises to act as convincingly as Tosca does in the theater.

While Cavaradossi is guided to the place against the wall where he is to stand, Tosca watches the proceedings in anxiety. The orchestra intones the dirge which we have already heard in the second

[9] Ricordi greatly disliked most of this scene. He felt that Puccini had written "fragmentary music . . . which makes pygmies out of the characters." He liked neither the *"O dolci mani"* phrase, for which Puccini had used a melody from one of his early operas, *Edgar*, nor the following music. If his objections were centered on the *a cappella* passage, he may have had a point, for this passage has always struck me as being singularly maladroit.

Puccini, who was usually sensitive to criticism and easily wounded, here defended himself. He wrote Ricordi a calm answer: "Your letter gave me an extraordinary surprise. I am still under its spell. Nevertheless, I am positive that if you reread this third act, you will change your opinion. This is not pride on my part. No. It is the conviction of having illuminated to the best of my ability the drama which was before me. You know how scrupulous I am in interpreting a situation or words. . . . As for the fragmentary quality, I did this purposely. The situation cannot be expressed in uniform and calm music as in other love duets. Tosca's thoughts are continually preoccupied with how well Mario will simulate his fall, and how he will bear himself in front of the shooting soldiers. . . . I really cannot understand your own unfavorable impression. Before I set to work again—and even if I wanted to would there be time?—I shall run over to Milan and we'll discuss it, we two alone, with a piano and with the music in front of us. If your impression persists, we'll search for some method of coming to an understanding 'as good friends,' as Scarpia says. It is not, I repeat, pride on my part. It is my defense of a work which is the fruit of my labor—and how much labor!"

Not a note of the scene was changed. Ricordi accepted it.

act, warning us of what is to happen. The slowness of the ceremony drives Tosca frantic. Why do they delay, why do they delay? She knows it is a comedy, but why must it take so long? Once again Puccini draws the cord of suspense to the breaking point.

The sergeant offers to bind Mario's eyes; he waves him away. The officer gives the sign to fire. He lowers his sword. Tosca, putting her hands over her ears, murmurs, "How splendid Mario is!" and, as the shots ring out, she adds, "How well he dies! He is a true artist."

The sergeant inspects the body; Spoletta joins him and, preventing the sergeant from giving the *coup de grâce,* covers Cavaradossi with a cloak. Tosca, fearing that Mario might move too soon—that is, before the soldiers have all gone—calls to him in a repressed voice, "Don't move! Don't speak! Now they are going. Now they are descending. Now! Up, Mario, quick! Let us flee!"

There is no answer. She bends down to help Mario up—and touches blood. With a cry of terror she perceives the horrible truth. He is dead. She throws herself sobbing on his body. From below there are heard the cries of Spoletta, Sciarrone, and the soldiers. They have discovered Scarpia's murder. Spoletta, running in, cries out, "You shall pay dearly for his life." "With mine," replies Tosca; and with a final defiance, "Scarpia, oh, Scarpia, before God!" she hurls herself over the parapet into the void.

In the course of our comparison of play and opera, it will have become apparent to the reader that the play, whatever its one-dimensionality and black-and-whiteness, is yet a tight and careful construction and that, if nothing more, we may give Sardou a full meed of approbation as a theatrical craftsman. The opera, on the other hand, shows cracks in the jointure; several loose threads hang from the libretto.

But in the end—that is, in the opera house—all this is not too important. Perhaps the reader will feel that we have pecked at the libretto too insistently. The purpose was not to cavil, but to show that a strong original drama serves well, even when its strength has become more than a little vitiated. *Tosca* the play is such good theater that *Tosca* the opera remains good theater.

It remains so if the performance is tempered with restraint, if the singers feel something of the genuine emotion which the composer felt. Puccini may have written faultily here or there, but he never wrote insincerely. The fact that *Tosca* does frequently strike us as insincere and occasionally as vulgar is to a large extent attributable to the insincere and vulgar performances to which it is subjected. A blasting Tosca and a bleating Cavaradossi—these were not foreseen either by Sardou or by Puccini.

TURANDOT

COMPOSER: Giacomo Puccini

LIBRETTISTS: Giuseppe Adami
Renato Simoni

FIRST PERFORMANCE: April 25, 1926
Teatro della Scala, Milan

RECEPTION: Success

CHARACTERS:

Princess Turandot	Soprano
The Emperor Altoum, her father	Tenor
Prince Timur, dethroned Tatar King	Bass
Calaf, the Unknown Prince, Timur's son	Tenor
Liù, a young slave girl	Soprano
Ping, the Grand Chancellor	Baritone
Pang, the General Purveyor	Tenor
Pong, the Chief Cook	Tenor
A Mandarin	Baritone
The Prince of Persia	Baritone
The Executioner	Baritone

THE RIDDLE
OF *TURANDOT*

Turandot is the quiz opera par excellence.

The asking of riddles, the test by questioning, the challenge by conundrum—these are devices used in the arts from time immemorial. Almost always the game is played for high stakes. It was fortunate for Oedipus that he knew the answer to the Sphinx's riddle—"What is it that walks on four legs in the morning, two at noon, and three in the evening?"—for had he not replied "Man" the Sphinx would have devoured him alive. In mythology and legend, in drama and novel, the hero is confronted with some sort of quiz: he must know a recondite fact, interpret an arcane meaning, or choose the right casket. (One suspects, however, that Portia led Bassanio to the lead casket by winks and hints and sighs.)

Nor is the quiz unknown in the operatic field. Mime is allowed to ask Wotan three questions. Wotan retaliates by asking three, knowing perfectly well that the dwarf cannot answer the last question. Here is a fixed quiz if ever there was one.

At least the quiz in *Turandot* is an honest one. The prize is the Princess and the stake is the stake on which is impaled the head of the unfortunate suitor who cannot solve the riddles. The results are frightful. Not only does the Prince of Persia lose his head (at the beginning of the opera), but later, as the courtiers Ping, Pang, and Pong reminisce, they draw up a list of no fewer than twenty-six previous victims, all princes, all unable to answer the questions, all dead.

Three enigmas are propounded. "The riddles are three—death is one." But outside of the opera itself, in the history of its creation, there lies a further enigma, the solution to which we can only guess at. The question is, why did Puccini take so unconscionably long a period to compose this work? What was it that held him back? Why did he, a careful but certainly not a dilatory craftsman, require more than three years to create three-quarters of an opera, in total length a little shorter than *La Bohème*, which he completed in about two and a half years? What were the difficulties which so protracted the task that death intervened?

The question is not an idle one. For had the work not progressed at a snail's pace, had he taken no more time with *Turandot* than with the preceding work, the "Triptych," Puccini might have lived not only to finish the opera but, what is equally important, to make the corrections, the shaping and smoothing and cutting, the adjustments in balance, the clarification of the character of the Princess, in short the creative improvement of detail which a masterpiece requires to make it a masterpiece.[1] *Turandot* could have been, as Puccini intended it to be, the capstone of his edifice. As it is, it is an opera containing astonishing greatness. But it is a capstone with rough edges.

The answer that while Puccini worked on *Turandot* he was a sick man, that the labor proceeded under the shadow of death, is not satisfactory. Health is not a requisite for the completion of great works, as innumerable examples—Watteau and Renoir, Robert Louis Stevenson and Friedrich Schiller—can testify. On the contrary, ill health often acts as a spur. What, then, is the answer?

We must examine the many letters which Puccini wrote to his two librettists, Giuseppe Adami, a successful playwright, and Renato Simoni, another playwright and something of an authority on China; we must read carefully Puccini's other statements about his final aims and ambitions. He wanted to go beyond the "slight" music (the word is his own, spoken in one of his frequent self-deprecating moods) he had composed and produce a work of grand proportions, a new kind of opera, one of epic breadth and seriousness. That seriousness was to be leavened, contrasted with and relieved by comic elements taken from the *commedia dell'arte*.

---

[1] Puccini kept revising *La Bohème* up to and even after its premiere. Consequential revisions were made in *Madama Butterfly* after its initial failure.

Both elements, the heroic and the comic, were present in the original play of *Turandotte*, written by the eighteenth-century playwright Carlo Gozzi. There the comic figures are four, because the company of actors for which Gozzi wrote included four actors who specialized in comic parts and were masters at improvisation. Puccini reduced the four figures to three and instilled in those three traits of modern nervousness and melancholy, traits which characterized the composer himself.

Ping, Pang, and Pong, the three ministers who take so lively a part in *Turandot*'s action, emerge as ambivalent characters. Some hint of this development is to be found in a later play, based on Gozzi, by Schiller. The German poet added philosophic seriousness to the comic figures. Puccini knew Schiller's play. But the composer goes further: his three courtiers are mercurial fellows, now sentimental and gentle, now harsh and cynical. They berate Turandot, yet do her bidding; they try to save the Prince, yet do their best to make him betray his secret. They are mystics—and contradictory. Not an easy challenge to meet for a man who had never before created contradictory characters, nor composed music in divided styles, nor attempted to juggle the comic and the tragic masks (which Strauss and Hofmannsthal had done in *Ariadne auf Naxos*).

But there is more: Puccini required a third element. Neither the heroic nor the comic sufficed. He could not altogether abjure the theme which in his previous operas had served as the mainspring of his inspiration. Call her Manon or Mimi or Cio-Cio-San, it was always the same character who accelerated his romantic pen. Without her he could not compose, the charming fragrant little creature who meets love, is destroyed by it, suffers melodiously, and expires not with a shout but with a sigh. So he added to the old fable of the man-hating goddess the character of Liù, the faithful and loving slave girl with her full heart and blind adoration. Liù is his invention: you will not find her in Gozzi.

When we have said all that, we still have not catalogued the task. For the first time in any of his operas, Puccini made the crowd, the chorus, a protagonist. It is possible that he was inspired to do so by Moussorgsky's *Boris Godunov*, with which he had become acquainted late in life. Puccini had previously used choruses for musical effects: he had used them well in the third act of *Manon Lescaut*, the second act of *Bohème*, and in the scene which closes the first act of *Tosca*. But up to *Turandot* they had always been incidental or atmospheric additions. For the first time the chorus takes part in the action itself, and indeed in the first act of the opera it has the leading role.

Four themes there are: the legendary-icy, the cynical-comic, the softly romantic, and the theme of the people, exotic and barbarous. Two of the themes were new to him, one was familiar, one only half-familiar. We can understand why he proceeded so hesitatingly. He may have known that it was the last composition he was to undertake; even before he began it he told his wife that he was suffering strange pains in his chest and had lost his voice. If then it was to be his swan song, Puccini, always exigent with his librettists, turned into a despot who demanded the impossible, scowled at every word and regarded every line of the text with hypercritical eye, changed his mind, fumed, fretted, complained, stopped the work, put it aside, could not rest, started over again. He begged Simoni and Adami: "Put all your strength into it, all the resources of your hearts and heads, and create for me something that will make the world weep." He asked Simoni to drink coffee at night. "You won't be able to sleep and you'll think of *Turandot*." To quote but one letter out of many:

> If I touch the piano my hands get covered with dust. My desk is piled up with letters—there isn't a trace of music. Music? Useless if I have no libretto. I have the great weakness of being able to write only when my puppet executioners are moving on the scene. If only I could be a purely symphonic writer! I should then at least cheat time . . . and my public. But that was not for *me*. I was born so many years ago—oh, so many, too many, almost a century . . . and Almighty God touched me with His little finger and said: "Write for the theater." And I have obeyed the supreme command. Had He marked me out for some other task perhaps I should not be, as now, without material. . . . I get such nice encouraging letters, but if, instead of these, one act of our glittering Princess were to arrive, don't you think it would be better? You would give me back my calm and my confidence, and the dust would not settle on my piano any more, so much banging would I do, and my desk would have its brave array of scoring sheets again. O you of the city, think to more purpose of one who is waiting in the country![2]

Though Puccini took an active part in the shaping of all his

[2] Undated letter to Adami, 1920.

librettos, it is truer of this one than of any other that he virtually
wrote it himself, and it might have been a lot easier had he in fact
written it himself. As it was, he used to send Adami detailed prose
versions, and when the poets returned the verses he was not satisfied or wanted to alter a particular dramatic situation. Ping, Pang,
and Pong gave him especial trouble. He instructed Adami: "Do a
little of what Shakespeare often does, when he brings in three or
four extraneous types who drink, use bad language, and speak ill
of the King. I have seen this done in *The Tempest,* among the Elves
and Ariel and Caliban." It is significant that for the first time in
his life Puccini mentions Shakespeare in connection with one of his
own operas.

The dramatic plan pivoted on Turandot's conversion into a
human being. This was to be accomplished in a final duet, to which
the composer attached the utmost importance. "It must be a great
duet. These two almost superhuman beings descend through love
to the level of mankind, and this love must at the end take possession of the whole stage in a great orchestral peroration." This he
did not live to accomplish.

What a pity! What cause for regret that libretto and music were
so long in the making! For had the opera—begun in the summer of
1920 and left unfinished by the winter of 1924—been truly
finished and revised by this genius of the theater, we might now be
in possession of one of the greatest of the music dramas of the
twentieth century. Francis Toye says that *Turandot* "brings a particularly vivid realization of what the world lost by Puccini's pre-
mature death."

Even as it is, *Turandot* is a wonderfully fascinating work and
contains some of Puccini's finest music. Ernest Newman thought
that it was the composer's masterpiece. Similarly, Mosco Carner,
who recently published a critical biography of the composer, believes that Turandot "represents the consummation of his whole
creative career."

The consummation, yes; but to repeat, not a "finished opera,"
neither in the actual nor the psychological sense. Because the conversion of the Princess from an iciness which is so inhuman as to
be symbolic to a humanity which Puccini no doubt intended to be
as warm and loving as are the hearts of his other heroines—because
that conversion is insufficiently motivated and occurs too suddenly,

it leaves us but half-convinced. Because that all-important last scene, which must "take possession of the whole stage," was never finished, we leave the performance with a sense of frustration. Yet *Turandot* is an opera we would not willingly do without. The unfinished can offer artistic satisfaction, as works by Dickens or Schubert, Leonardo or Michelangelo prove.

ACT I

We are in Peking,[3] in fabled times. Before the wall which surrounds the city stands a vast crowd, silent and sullen. The rays of the setting sun illumine the stage. On the right we see a big bronze gong suspended; its purpose is to signal the arrival of any suitor who demands access to Turandot's palace. Here and there on the wall we see long poles from which are suspended the heads of some of Turandot's unsuccessful suitors, gruesome mementos of the Princess' cruelty. Puccini establishes the mood of horror in an orchestral announcement—it is too short to be called a prelude—of eleven bars, adding to his usual orchestra exotic instruments such as the gong and the xylophone.

A herald appears who, in hieratic tones, recites a formula with which the crowd must be all too familiar: Turandot will be the bride of a prince of royal blood, provided he shall solve three riddles she poses. If he fails, he must lose his life. The last who has attempted it was the Prince of Persia. He has failed and he will die this day at the rising of the moon.

Whipped to a frenzy by this announcement, the crowd surges forward and cries for the executioner. More blood is what they want, blood what they crave. They make as if to storm the palace. The guards hold them back with their whips. All is turmoil, evil, tyranny. Puccini gives us the scene with mastery: he plunges us into an atmosphere fetid and feverish.

Out of the confusion of the crowd a young girl's voice is heard. Her companion, an old man, has been pushed down by the mob. She calls for help. A youth hurries to her aid, bends over the old

---

[3] Ever since the travels of Marco Polo, China has held a special fascination to Italians. At about the time that Gozzi wrote his play, Tiepolo painted in Vicenza a series of frescoes on Chinese themes. These extraordinarily beautiful pictures could serve as costume and scenic sketches for a performanc of *Turandot*.

man, and recognizes him as his father. He shouts with joy: he has found him after so long a separation, after so much suffering. Blessed be that suffering, since it led to their meeting once more. Both father and son are fugitives from their country, vanquished by a usurper to their throne, driven out. Their whereabouts must remain unknown, their identities a secret. The Unknown Prince entreats his father Timur not to call him "Son" when anybody may overhear them. There is danger everywhere. But how did Timur reach Peking? The old king relates that he would have perished had not little Liù fled with him, dried his tears, begged bread for him, looked after his needs, and been his constant companion. "Who are you, Liù?" asks the astonished Prince. "I am nothing," she answers, "a slave." "Why then have you shouldered so great a burden?" "Because," she replies—in a phrase which in its melodic sweetness betrays the composer's love for the character—"one day in the palace you smiled at me."

The crowd has regathered. As the sky darkens and night draws near, their fury increases. The women murmur, "Sharpen the knife!" Then the cry is taken up by the rest of the chorus. A dozen assistants of the executioner chant a wild rhythmic phrase, which is one of the pivotal motives of the opera, to the words of "In the reign of Turandot." The entire chorus is worked up to a tremendous climax with the full orchestra being supplemented by Chinese gongs, trumpets, and trombones on stage, and culminating in a unison outcry. Then suddenly the mood changes. A silence falls on the people. The moon appears. The people apostrophize its pale visage, this head without members, this silent planet, this mistress of the dead. The strings shimmer like moonlight on a tombstone, while the woodwinds glide evilly across the musical texture. One is reminded of certain moments in *Salome*, where too the moon appears as a symbol. But even Strauss offers us no stranger fantasy than this superbly conceived chorus.

From afar we hear a melancholy chant. It is sung by a procession of boys and accompanied by—curiously!—two saxophones behind the scene. The melody is one of genuine Chinese origin, one of several Chinese melodies which Puccini used. Now the stage is bathed in silver. By this light the funeral cortege begins its procession, led by the executioner's assistants, with the priests and mandarins following. Last of all appears the Prince of Persia, young and handsome, lost in his dream, unheedful of the crowd around him. At the sight of the victim, the blood-lust of the people dissolves into pity. In as prompt a turnabout of sentiment as only a crowd in the theater exhibits, it now asks for mercy for the young man doomed to death, the people addressing themselves to the unseen Turandot. The Unknown Prince—he, too, is suffused by pity— exclaims, "Oh! That I might see her so that I could curse her!"

Once again the scene, which belongs almost entirely to the chorus, rises to a climax, the demand for mercy increasing in force, when suddenly Turandot herself appears on the imperial balcony. The cold moonlight plays upon her face. The crowd prostrates itself. Only the Prince of Persia, the Unknown Prince, and the executioner remain standing. At the sight of Turandot's beauty, the Unknown Prince has covered his dazzled eyes.

Silently Turandot raises her hand in an imperious gesture. It is a gesture all understand: the final condemnation. The cortege moves on. And the Unknown Prince, quite beside himself, sings (in a strange, almost atonal phrase) of the divine beauty, the miracle of the apparition he has just beheld. Even in an instant has horror turned into love!

The sight alone of Turandot has bewitched the Prince. As yet he has but looked at her, he has not heard her voice. (With the exception of *La Muette de Portici* by Auber, I cannot think of one example in which the heroine of an opera is introduced mutely, though Marguerite appears to Faust as a silent vision.) Turandot's fascination has engulfed him. He hardly hears his father's urgent plea to fly at once. The Prince cries out for Turandot three times at the very instant that behind the scene the Prince of Persia echoes the cries and dies. This *memento mori* passes unheeded. The new suitor has made up his mind; at once he hurries toward the great gong.

At this moment three figures jump in and bar his way. They are the three masques, Ping, Pang, and Pong. With their entrance the music changes its character and becomes rhythmic and jocular, as befits the three. They advise the Prince to go back whence he came, wherever that may be, and if he wishes to play the lovesick fool to do so in his own domain; there he may lose his head if he like. But not here, not here in Peking, where there are enough fools already. "Let me pass!" the Prince urges. Pass? For what? A Princess? What

after all is she? Merely a woman with a crown on her head. Undress
her, she appears as a thing of flesh and blood, as do all the others.
He can find for himself a hundred candidates for his love, quite
equivalent to Turandot who, when all is said and done, has but one
face, two arms, and two legs.

Their sardonic eloquence is stemmed by voices floating down
from the balustrade of the palace. Turandot's maids bid them all
be silent, for it is the hour when Turandot seeks repose. But it
makes no difference either to the three courtiers or to the Prince,
still wrapped in his ecstasy. (This little scene is expressed in an
andante lento for which Puccini writes "advanced" harmonies of
great beauty.) The three renew their noisy reasoning: He cannot
win, they say; Turandot's riddles are insoluble, quite insoluble.

As a countermeasure to such warning, the Prince hears, out of
the darkness and far in the distance, the voices of the dead suitors,
who plead with the living suitor to attempt the trial. We still love
her, sing the ghostly voices.[4] The Prince protests that it is he alone
who truly loves her. The indefatigable three try one more rebuttal:
There is no such thing as Turandot. She, God, man, the people, and
their rulers, they are all illusion. Who would want to gamble
reality for an illusion? This bit of philosophy failing too, they point
to the bastion where the executioner appears to show the severed
head of the Prince of Persia. Even so will the white moonlight kiss
the face of the Unknown Prince.

Ping, Pang, and Pong having made no impression, it is now the
father's turn to recall his son to reality. Liù adds her plea, in the
aria *"Signore, ascolta!"*—"Listen, my lord!" Timidly she approaches the Prince and through tears she tells him that everywhere
she wandered his image was before her, encouraging her, hearten-
ing her to "the shadow of a smile." If he now is to perish, both she
and Timur will die on the road of exile. It is a moving aria and
Liù alone comes near to being heard by the Prince. He replies to
her in gentle accents. "Do not weep, Liù! For the sake of that smile
which you offered me I beg of you not to abandon my father."

All individual entreaties having proved futile, the pleaders now
unite their voices in concerted dissuasion. This is the finale of the

---

[4] Except for his first opera, *Le Villi*, Puccini did not introduce supernatural motives
into any of his works. Is it significant that he did so in his last opera or is it a mere
coincidence?

act, a movement of large design, a musical crescendo of great intensity. The finale, as indeed the plan of the entire first act, proves how seriously Puccini accepted his own challenge of composing more than "little" music. It "testifies to the consummate power of organization, which Puccini achieved in his last period" (Mosco Carner). Once more the gong gleams in the moonlight and exerts its pull on the Prince. Nothing can stop him. He tears himself loose from the three masques who hold him. Thrice he pronounces the name of Turandot and, seizing the hammer, thrice he strikes the gong. Ping, Pang, and Pong exit, laughing sardonically. The curtain falls.

ACT II

Scene One

Nothing whatever happens in the first scene of the second act. Our three friends from the *commedia dell'arte* sit around; they ruminate, speculate, and equivocate. Because the stage is not the lecture room, extended reflections are unwelcome to audiences. This long scene, therefore, tends to drag in the theater, particularly when heard by audiences who do not understand the language. Yet it contains music of remarkable beauty. Heard on records in the living room, the scene makes its full effect. For it is then the music can be best appreciated; with its two contrasting parts, one mocking, the other sentimental, it serves as a scherzo in a symphony, the trio being the slower section, the scherzo proper the rhythmic section.

The scene plays in a pavilion formed by a great curtain which is curiously decorated with Chinese symbols and fantastic figures. There are three doors, one in the middle and one at each side. Ping pops his head through the center door and calls for his two companions. They enter. Three servants follow them, each carrying a different colored lantern, red, green, and yellow. They place the lanterns ceremoniously on the table and retire.

The three masques are left alone to converse about the latest suitor. The suit will end either in a funeral or in a wedding, and they are quite prepared to assist at either. They have ready the red lanterns used at a feast, or the white ones which form the traditional funeral decoration. With equal ease they can provide the palanquin of scarlet red for the bridal couple or the stately coffin. Incense or sweet tea—they have prepared both. All this they express in a rhythmic singsong, as if they had no feelings at all one way or the other and were merely appurtenances of tradition.

But then they fall to musing on China, the land they love, old China, which had slept tranquilly for seventy thousand centuries. Until—until Turandot was born. Then the tumbling of heads began, then tragedy struck. Consulting some papyrus scrolls which are lying on the table, they read aloud the catalogue of death. In the year of the Mouse six suitors died. In the year of the Dog eight were executed. In the terrible year of the Tiger thirteen perished. And so on and so on[5] until now the three are weary of all the work involved, of all the horror, until now they have become nothing but the "ministers of the executioner."

Ping's glance looks into the distance. A nostalgic smile plays on his lips as he recalls the little house which he owns on the Lake of Honan. The lake is blue, the house is surrounded by bamboo, and inside there is a collection of sacred books. How he longs to return there! How he longs to recapture lost tranquillity! The others dream of the faraway as well. Pong owns forests near Tsiang, Pang thinks of his garden at Kiù. Will they ever see this beauty again? It does not seem likely, for here they are in Peking in the midst of a world populated by fools in love. This whole section, an *andantino mosso*, is exquisite and is brought to a close by a typically Puccinian postlude in the orchestra, as the three return to a further enumeration of Turandot's crimes. Nothing but blood and frenzy remains in the world. Love must end, they sing in unison; mankind must vanish. Even China will disappear. Would that the day arrive when they could be given the task of preparing the nuptial couch for Turandot, to accompany bride and groom with lanterns and to sing in the garden until morning! All three proceed to sing the little ditty which befits the imagined wedding feast.

From these idle speculations, from this dream of a better world, they are awakened by the sound of trumpets, trombones, and drums from within the palace. They hear as well the sound of the people, who are even now assembling for the latest contest. Ping jumps up and recalls them to their duty. The servants remove the

[5] In Gozzi's play there were ninety-nine victims.

lanterns, and the three masques, with heavy hearts, go out to join
the others at the palace.

Scene Two

The second scene takes place in the huge square in front of the
palace. In the center, an enormous marble staircase stretches to the
very top of the stage. Eight tall scholars, old and impressive, mount
to the top of the stairs, carrying sealed scrolls which contain the
solutions to Turandot's latest riddles. Various ministers and officials
hurry by. The crowd gathers quickly, among them Ping, Pong,
and Pang, now wearing the yellow robes of a state occasion. Amidst
the clouds of incense one discerns the white and yellow standards
of the Emperor. The Unknown Prince stands off the staircase on
one side. On the other side Timur and Liù seem almost lost in the
mass of people. All this while the orchestra plays a ceremonial
march, which comes to a climax as the clouds of incense roll away
and the Emperor Altoum becomes visible, seated on an ivory throne
at the highest point of the staircase. He is all white, very ancient,
and seems a fragile god descending from the clouds. The crowd
prostrates itself and greets him with a hymn: "May you live ten
thousand years!" Then all is silence. In the high, almost toneless
voice of extreme old age, the Emperor addresses the stranger. His
words are almost unaccompanied by the orchestra, yet we have to
strain to hear them. An atrocious oath binds him to Turandot's
will. His scepter is dripping with blood. Enough of blood! Young
hero, desist!

The Prince in a firm voice demands to be put to the task. Three
times the Emperor tries to dissuade him, and three times the Prince
insists. So be it, then! This stranger who seems so determined to die
must fulfill his destiny.

At this the people rise. Turandot's women enter to strew flowers
on the staircase. The hymn continues. The herald repeats the formula we have heard at the beginning of the first act. The chorus
of children in the distance intone once more the song in praise of
Turandot. And finally Turandot appears, dressed entirely in gold.
She advances to the foot of the throne. With an ice cold glance
she scans the figure of her latest suitor and then begins her address
to him. It is the first time that we hear her voice, and the apostrophe

is some sort of justification of her edict (*"In questa Reggia"*—"In this kingdom").

In this very palace a thousand times a thousand years ago there lived the Princess Lo-u-Ling. The gentle princess lived in joy and serenity until one night the barbarians entered China and conquered it. A man, "a man just like you, stranger," seized Lo-u-Ling and carried her away. In vain did the princess cry out in that terrible night of atrocity. In vain! Her cry and her death resound forever in Turandot's mind. That cry has planted there—she says, to the accompaniment of one of the great themes of the work—the undying determination for revenge. No man shall ever possess Turandot. The horror of which her ancestor died lives on. Her hatred seems to become intensified by her own words. Her song rises menacingly. Once more she turns to the Prince and ends her song with the already familiar phrase, "Stranger, do not tempt fate. The enigmas are three, death is one." To which the Prince answers, "No! The enigmas are three, life is one," repeating her own melody higher in the scale. Still higher, they repeat the phrase together.

The trumpets impose silence and Turandot begins the asking of the riddles.[6]

What is it which appears as a phantom at night, which floats over humanity in the darkness, which the whole world invokes, but which disappears with the dawn, only to be born again in the heart? Each night it is born and each day it dies. Immediately the Prince replies, "Yes, it is born again, it is born exultantly and bears life with it. It is hope!" The eight wise men break open their scrolls and confirm the correctness of the solution. Turandot too, shaking with suppressed fury, must acknowledge: "It is hope; yet hope deceives."

Nervously she descends to the midway landing of the staircase. From there she propounds the second enigma.

What is it that flickers like a flame yet is not fire? Now it burns like a fever, now it subsides into languid repose. It grows cold when life is lost and burns when victory is won. It is silent yet has a voice which you can hear. . . . The answer does not immediately occur to the Prince. The Emperor and the crowd encourage him. Out of the crowd the voice of Liù cries, "Answer, for the sake of love!"

---

[6] The riddles are given here in free translation.

He does answer, for the sake of love. The mysterious substance of which Turandot speaks—it is blood.

"Blood" it is, crow the wise men. The people express their pleasure—but Turandot at once suppresses such manifestations. She descends the stairs and takes up her position at the bottom directly in front of the Prince who, overcome by the sight, sinks to his knees. (Thus the stage direction, one which it is reasonably certain Puccini would have changed, for it is hardly practical for the average Italian tenor to jump from a kneeling position and sing the last answer, as the stage directions later specify.)

Bending over him, Turandot flings her last riddle at him. "What is like ice—yet burns? What is it that in setting you free enslaves you, and in enslaving you turns you into a king?" The Prince stops breathing, as a little moan of uncertainty is heard in the orchestra. Turandot smiles triumphantly. "Fear has unsaddled you. You are lost!" As the strings of the orchestra rush upward, she repeats, "What is the ice which creates fire?"

Dead silence ensues, one of those typical Puccinian silences made more dramatic by the repetition of sound, the moans of the orchestra. Then suddenly—suddenly the Prince jumps to his feet. The solution has come to him. He is now sure of his victory. The ice which burns—it is Turandot. For the third time the old men break their scrolls and assent, while all the people burst into an immense jubilation.

We may halt our story just long enough to list the riddles' answers in the three treatments of the subject; each set is indicative of the artist's interests.

Gozzi: 1. The Sun. 2. The Year. 3. The Lion of the
      Adriatic (Venice).
Schiller: 1. The Ear. 2. The Eye. 3. The Plow.
Puccini: 1. Hope. 2. Blood. 3. Turandot.

Turandot refuses to accept defeat. She appeals to her father not to throw his daughter into the arms of a stranger. But the Emperor upholds the oath. Still Turandot remains defiant: neither he nor any other man shall ever possess her. Is it possible that he would want her against her will, that he would take her by force, a reluctant trembling woman? No—he wants her only as a willing, as a loving woman.

It is the Prince himself who gives her a second chance. She had proposed three riddles. Three times he had found the answer. Now it is he who will propose an enigma, just one. If before dawn she can tell him what his name is, she is released from the bargain and he will accept defeat and death.

Turandot acquiesces, the Emperor and the crowd unite in singing the praises of this generous victor, and the curtain falls.

A superb scene, superb not only for its pageantry, color, movement, and dramatic suspense, but also for its use of music, a sparing use, new with Puccini, which eschews obvious tone painting of the riddles and contents itself with underscoring and tightening of tension while yet preserving the ceremonial nature of the scene.

ACT III

Scene One

We are in the great garden of the palace. It is still night. The scene begins in a nocturnal mood. The harmonies of the orchestra sound melancholy, and as the curtain rises we hear the voices of eight heralds proclaiming the latest sad command: No one is to sleep this night. The name of the stranger is to be discovered; else all are to die. *"Nessun dorma!"*—"No one is to sleep in Peking this night."

This phrase, *"Nessun dorma,"* is taken up by the Prince, alone on the stage, musing to himself. He then repeats it.[7] Turandot, like the others, will not sleep tonight; alone and sleepless in her room she will look at the stars. No one will reveal his name; from his lips alone will she learn it at dawn. His kiss will melt her silence. At dawn he will become victorious. . . . This is perhaps the most beautiful aria in the score and one of the most beautiful which Puccini allotted to the tenor voice.

The orchestral postlude serves as the bridge to the next scene. In the darkness we perceive the dim outlines of several figures. They turn out to be a number of townspeople led by the three courtiers. As in the first act, the three try to swerve the Prince from his intention, and as in the first act they attempt various devices. Again

[7] The two phrases, *"Nessun dorma,"* are sung an octave apart, *pianissimo!* This causes much discomfiture among Italian tenors, though a Swedish tenor could sing it. Jussi Bjoerling's first recording of the aria (recorded in 1944) is a record collector's treasure.

the music begins in a scherzo vein and carries us through several episodes.

Ping, Pang, and Pong tempt the Prince. Death threatens everyone in Peking. Every house is in danger. What is it he would take as recompense for relinquishing Turandot? Is it woman's caresses? At this Ping surrounds him with seductive girls. Like Parsifal, the Prince repulses them. (The short scene is an ineffective piece of stage business, musically undistinguished.) Perhaps he prefers riches. Chests of gold and jewels are brought in, but riches make no more of an impression on the Prince than did the temptation of love. So the three sing of fame and glory, which could be his; indeed, they will help him to conquer empires if only he will leave Peking.

This prospect fails as well. Changing their attack, the trio now attempt threats. Did the Prince know the full extent of Turandot's cruelty, of the horror she is capable of inflicting? They assure him that he does not, that the Princess is infinitely resourceful, and that China is expert in fantastic tortures unknown to the rest of the world. The crowd, maddened with fear, take up the threats. But the Prince replies: "Threats are as useless as temptation. Let the world perish! I want Turandot."

There is a sudden commotion, and shouts of "We have found the name!" are heard behind the scene. The guards drag in Timur and Liù. Ignoring the Prince's protests that "they know nothing," the three courtiers and the guards call for the Princess. Introduced by her motive, proclaimed by trombones and trumpets, Turandot appears on the threshold of the pavilion.

Bowing before her, the crafty Ping informs her that if anybody knows the secret, these two do. Turandot turns with cold disdain to the Prince. "You are pale, stranger." No, replies the Prince; it is her own fear she sees reflected on his face in the light of the breaking dawn. Turandot orders Timur to speak. But the old man, frightened and bleeding, remains mute. The ministers are about to seize him to torture him when Liù steps forward and declares that she alone knows the name of the stranger. "Yes," asserts Liù, "I alone possess the key to the secret." The crowd demands that she be put to the rack. The Prince throws himself in front of Liù to protect her. Turandot commands that he be bound hand and foot. Now Liù's torture begins, and is expressed musically in an orchestral language reminiscent of the second act of *Tosca*. At last, like Tosca, Liù can resist no longer. "Let her be!" Turandot commands. "She will talk." "I would rather choose death," replies the fainting girl. And suddenly something in Turandot's heart seems to melt. For the first time she asks a human question in human accents. "What is it," she demands of Liù, "that has given you the strength to suffer like this?" "Love, Princess." "Love?" repeats Turandot in a tone of wonder. A love, Liù confesses, which is secret, unspoken, offered without recompense. She bids the guards to bind and torture her. However dreaded be the pain, it is only a last tribute to the love she feels.

Only for the moment has Turandot weakened. She is her old self again as she demands that the guards tear the secret from the girl, while the crowd calls for the executioner. When the figures of the executioner and his assistants loom up, Liù turns once more to Turandot and begs to be heard. This, then, is her greatest aria (*"Tu che di gel sei cinta"*—"You who are bound by ice").

"You who are bound by ice," Liù prophesies, "will be overcome by flame.[8] You will love him as I did. Before the sun rises, I will have closed my eyes, so that he may remain victorious." Saying so, she snatches a dagger from the belt of one of the guards and plunges it into her heart. There is a general shock and vain cries of "Speak, speak! The name! The name!" But Liù is forever silent.

The old man bends down and weeps for his "little dove," while Ping—again showing a different side of his character—tries to comfort him. Liù's body is carried away, the old man walking beside it, while chorus and orchestra intone an awe-stricken and beautiful funeral dirge. "Sleep well, Liù," they sing, as the strains of the march die out.

Turandot's attendants have covered her face with a white veil; through the last fearsome scene she has remained standing, rigid, statuesque, without a gesture, without a word. Now she and the Prince are left alone on the stage.

"It is at this point that Puccini laid down his pen."[9] Sketches for

[8] Note the similarity to the imagery of the third riddle, "ice" and "flame."

[9] These words were spoken by Arturo Toscanini at the first performance of *Turandot* at La Scala, April 25, 1926. He stopped conducting and left the performance unfinished. It was probably the only time that Toscanini spoke publicly in a theater and the only time *Turandot* was performed without Alfano's ending.

the beginning of the duet remain, but the bulk of the duet and the final scene were composed by Franco Alfano, one of Puccini's contemporaries. No new musical material is used. Alfano looked at his task as a labor of love, but it is impossible for another author, no matter how sympathetic, to finish the unfinished. The rest of the opera therefore need not detain us long.

The Prince tears the veil from Turandot's face and exhorts her to be a woman. Still she repulses him. She is the daughter of the heavens, free, untouched, and he must not profane her soul. In answer he takes her in his arms and kisses her. The kiss seals her fate. She who is "bound by ice" melts into the warmth of womanhood. She weeps, "Dawn is here and Turandot's sun is setting."

She confesses that at first sight of him she loved him; her hate was only the memory of all those she had sacrificed. But she has hated him too for his pride: she foresaw that he was destined to conquer. Now that he has conquered, she begs him to leave her, taking his secret with him. No, replies the Prince gently, it is no longer an enigma, no longer a mystery. He will give her his name and with it his life: he will entrust his life into her keeping. He is Calaf, son of Timur. Involuntarily Turandot proclaims, "I know your name! I know your name!" At this moment the trumpets sound to signal that the appointed hour has come.

Scene Two

After a brief orchestral interlude, the curtain rises on the exterior of the palace.[10] The stage is bathed in the rosy light of sunrise. The Emperor, the court, and the people are assembled. The Prince and Turandot enter. She ascends to the top of the stairs and in a strange new voice she speaks to her father. "I know the stranger's name," she says. "It is—Love." Calaf rushes to her, and with a final chorus of joy the opera ends.

If we were to judge Puccini's last work by the tenets suggested by his popular operas, by *Bohème, Tosca,* or *Butterfly,* we might be disappointed. There is only one living, sympathetic character in

---

[10] In many productions the same set is used as that for Act II, Scene Two. In the original production at La Scala, the second act was played in the interior, the final scene outside the palace.

Turandot. Nor does this opera, with all its melodiousness, contain such an abundance of fresh tunes as we find in *Manon Lescaut.* This is not what the opera offers. Yet it offers much that is treasurable. On the stage it is exciting, not only for its music but for its drama and pageantry as well. The exotic colors which we see in setting and costume we hear in the music. Puccini has been successful in creating a Chinese aura, the China not as it is (his use of genuine Chinese themes is unimportant), but the China as he imagined it. The exotic becomes more interesting when it is imagined than when it is literally presented. As Puccini grew older, he learned to use the orchestra with ever surer mastery, so that even his failures, such as *La Fanciulla del West* and *Suor Angelica,* are worth noting from the orchestral point of view. *Turandot* is no exception. Its rich orchestral palette combines with original harmonies to delight the ear, stimulate the mind, and convey to us a sense of high drama.

Whether Puccini would finally have succeeded in convincing us of the conversion of the Princess, whether he would have made believable the catharsis for which he strove, whether he could have accomplished the mutation of grandeur into humanity—that we cannot know. Perhaps he would not have succeeded, and it might have been a subconscious realization of an inadequacy that troubled and retarded his work. The empyrean was not Puccini's natural habitat.

But all that is theory, a gray theory which need not becloud our appreciation of the work. We turn away from the opera with a feeling of sadness, knowing that whatever there is here is all we have from the pen of a composer who, had he lived longer—ah, well, who knows what he might have accomplished?

DIE MEISTERSINGER VON NÜRNBERG

COMPOSER: Richard Wagner

LIBRETTIST: Richard Wagner

FIRST PERFORMANCE: June 21, 1868
Hof-und-National Theater, Munich

RECEPTION: Success with the public, not
with the critics

CHARACTERS:

Hans Sachs, shoemaker		Bass
Veit Pogner, goldsmith		Bass
Kunz Vogelgesang, furrier		Tenor
Konrad Nachtigall, tinsmith		Bass
Sixtus Beckmesser, town clerk		Bass
Fritz Kothner, baker	All	Bass
Balthasar Zorn, pewterer	Mastersingers	Tenor
Ulrich Eisslinger, grocer		Tenor
Augustin Moser, tailor		Tenor
Hermann Ortel, soapmaker		Bass
Hans Schwarz, stocking weaver		Bass
Hans Foltz, coppersmith		Bass

Walther von Stolzing, a young knight from Franconia — Tenor

David, apprentice to Hans Sachs — Tenor

Eva, Pogner's daughter — Soprano

Magdalena, Eva's attendant — Soprano

A Night Watchman — Bass

THE MORAL OF
DIE MEISTERSINGER

A long, exact, and serious comedy;
In ev'ry scene some moral let it teach,
And, if it can, at once both please and preach.
                                    ALEXANDER POPE

Will Durant in *The Life of Greece* says that we are as unable to judge Pindar's *Odes* from the words alone as we would be unable to judge Wagner solely from the text of his music dramas, supposing that by some catastrophe the music were lost.

Let us indulge in a variation of this supposition: What would we think of Wagner if both music and words of *one* work alone, that being *Die Meistersinger*, were no longer in existence, if we had no knowledge of his ever having composed something smiling? What would we think of Wagner? We would think of him as a mighty but as the most humorless of composers. Other predominantly serious composers—Bach, Beethoven, Brahms, Verdi (he even without *Falstaff*), Tchaikovsky—temper tragedy with humor and tint the edge of seriousness with wit. Not Wagner. He shows no humor, permits no levity,[1] with the possible exception of the Siegfried-Fafner scene in Act II of *Siegfried*, in which, to be sure, the humor is pachydermatous. Search the ten dramas and leave the eleventh aside: nowhere will you find a sign of the comic spirit, a gay flag

---

1 We are speaking of Wagner's mature works, not the early *Das Liebesverbot*.

among the somber standards. He never comes off his high purpose. If not he himself, then Cosima was fond of comparing him to Shakespeare. But of Shakespeare's way of varying king and clown he would have none. No, this modern interpreter of ancient tales was at all times deadly serious. And yet!

And yet he created *Die Meistersinger*.

More remarkable than the mere existence of the unique product is the success of the venture, the perfection of the result. How was it possible, one asks, that without any previous essay in the comic form, without undergoing the required training which David the apprentice recommends to Walther the novice, without testing the difference between "pitch and wax," Wagner accomplished, in the form seemingly most alien to his bent of mind, a comedy which meets all of our demands on comedy, including that it be funny?

Success in an unfamiliar form through one work and one alone seems to be a prerogative of musical talent. I know of no painter who painted but one still life and that a good one, no writer of novels who wrote but one play and that a good one; while, as we know, Beethoven made only one attempt at a violin concerto and succeeded in producing what we regard as the peer of violin concertos.

THE CREATION OF THE PLAY

We have long accepted biographical proof that the circumstances of a man's career need not reflect themselves in the work at hand. It is possible to write a *Don Quixote* in jail, provided you are a Cervantes. Still, one cannot help being astonished that Wagner managed his broad and relaxed smile at the very moment when every muscle of his being must have been tautened almost beyond the endurance of one who could endure much. He wrote the text when his fortunes were at their nadir, when his financial troubles, ubiquitous in his life before King Ludwig rescued him, were becoming well-nigh catastrophic, when he had suffered the humiliation of the Paris failure of *Tannhäuser*, when he had a right to despair that *Tristan* would ever be put on the stage, when he was still under at least partial interdict[2] for his role in the revolution of 1849, and when, separated from his wife, he was suffering the

[2] He was finally allowed to return to Germany, but not to Saxony.

aftertremors of his love affair with Mathilde Wesendonck. It is
difficult to imagine conditions less favorable to the creation of a
comedy. He was homeless and alone. He wrote to his wife Minna
(December 28, 1861):

> How I'm racking my brains every day to find a speedy mode of reset-
> tlement! If you only knew (unfortunately, you don't) how things stand
> in my innermost depths. I want rest, nothing but rest; equilibrium, full,
> undisturbed home security. . . . I absolutely need domestic order and
> convenience.

This letter was written in a shabby hotel room in Paris. There
he worked, confident and hopeful, in spite of all recent failures,
keeping before his mind's eye the streets of old Nuremberg while
he looked out on the Quai Voltaire.

Confidence in himself? Wagner was filled with it to the roots of
his hair. At about the same time that he wrote to Minna, and when
he had been engaged in working out the text for less than a month,
he wrote to Mathilde Wesendonck: "How you will open your eyes
at my *Meistersinger!* Keep your heart secure against old Sachs, or
you will fall in love with him!" And to his friend Peter Cornelius
he wrote: "You can have no conception of my poem: I can't work
at it without becoming shamefully arrogant." Later, when he had
finished the libretto, he summoned Peter and other friends to
Mainz (the headquarters of his publisher, Schott) because, as was
his wont, he wished to read the poem aloud. "Don't be put off by
any hardship," he wrote; "it will be a sacred evening."[3] It was this
very "shameful arrogance," which declared as "sacred" an evening
devoted to a lecture of his work, that kept Wagner going. The
fanatic force within him, at once admired by and frightening to
his contemporaries, was so strong that a doubt could not reach even
the moat of his consciousness. He was sure that *Die Meistersinger*
was destined to become a masterpiece, when only the text lay on

---

[3] Wagner tells us in *Mein Leben* that Peter Cornelius showed up a day ahead of
schedule, "despite floods, washed-out railways, and other travel adventures." Wendelin
Weissheimer, a man who saw a great deal of Wagner in this period, has left us a description of the evening. Everybody who had any sort of connection with the Schotts
tried to wangle an invitation to meet the celebrity. Those fortunate enough to be invited sat around the walls of the room in comfortable armchairs while Wagner read
from a reading desk which Schott's wife had placed in the center. The company enjoyed
the reading and laughed over David and Beckmesser. Wagner was a superb actor.

his desk with the ink hardly dry, and before he had written a note of the music.

In preparing himself for *Die Meistersinger,* Wagner, whose intellectual curiosity was as keen as his artistic conscience was scrupulous, delved into the history of the Reformation as well as the manners and customs of sixteenth-century Nuremberg. He consulted several reference books, copied out and studied the poetry, rules, regulations, procedures, names, and biographies of the historic Mastersingers.[4] Almost every character in the opera is a historic character (though some in name only), and the description of the trial in the Mastersinger School (Act I) is historically authentic. But of study, of parading erudition, of preening literary allusions, *Die Meistersinger* exhibits hardly a trace. It does not smell of the lamp. It smells of fresh lilacs.

Let me now return to Durant's supposition. If the music of all of Wagner's operas were indeed lost and only the texts remained, some scholar could well conclude that here was a man born to write comic, not tragic, operas. Is it not obvious that the *Ring* has a dull, repetitive text, and *Tristan and Isolde* a well-nigh incomprehensible one? But *Die Meistersinger*—that's a different story! It shows Wagner's real flair, a flair for bourgeois comedy. (So much for archaeological conjectures!)

So leisurely and expansive a work could hardly have been created at a headling pace. Many years elapsed between the first glimmer of the idea and the completion of the text. And only after its completion did Wagner, the composer, begin.

Wagner's musical thoughts needed to be set in motion and to be kept in motion by his literary imagination. He had first to conceive a theme, then to outline the action, then to put flesh and bones on the skeleton of the outline, and finally to write the verses, before he could compose the music. He thought of music, and specifically his orchestra, as a means to an end, a servant of the needs of drama, a guide, an illustrator, a commentator who could illumine legend, clarify relationships, bring hidden thoughts to the surface, and stir dramatic turbulence. (It goes without saying that

---

[4] Most helpful proved a rare book by one Johann Christopher Wagenseil about Nuremberg and its guilds, published in 1697. He managed to borrow a copy from the Imperial Library in Vienna and was allowed to keep it for twenty-four hours, during which he made copious notes.

he verbalized this function of his own music into a general theory
which was to be applied to all opera.)

THE FIRST SKETCH

He pondered long, sometimes for years, on each project. He
would store it away in his mind to let his dramatic ideas mature.
So with *Die Meistersinger*. He sketched a tentative draft of the
comedy in 1845, when he was thirty-two years old, sixteen years
before he was to finish the text. This first sketch was written under peculiar circumstances. Exhausted by the task of the composition of *Tannhäuser*, Wagner had been sent by his physician to
take the cure in Marienbad. He carried with him the first ideas
for a Lohengrin drama, and while, according to the prescribed
regimen, he was promenading in the pine woods, his thoughts concentrated on the plan for an opera on the Lohengrin subject. And
indeed he foresaw, though as yet dimly, a sequel to the legend, in-
volving Parsifal. Stimulated by one subject, his brain responded
by searching for others. But was he not to take a rest? Could he
altogether ignore his doctor's command to relax? The way toward
relaxation was for him not idleness but a change of domain. To
smooth out his coruscated fatigue he would swerve from lofty
legend and try his hand at comedy. He had read something of the
history of the sixteenth-century German Mastersingers, the craftsmen and tradesmen who practiced poetry and singing as a hobby
and codified the art into rules. Wagner had been captivated by the
figure of the Marker, the watchdog appointed by the Masters'
Guild, who acted as a guardian of the versifying and singing rules
and marked down all refractions of the sacrosanct regulations. On
his walks there came to him the idea of a conflict between Hans
Sachs, the famous cobbler-poet who is considered something of a
classic in German literature, and the Marker. In a humorous scene
a sarcastic Hans Sachs was to take revenge on the pedantic Marker
"by giving him a practical lesson in singing." Hans Sachs was to
represent the popular artisan-poet, the Marker the hidebound tradi-
tionalist. Wagner tells us that he saw in his mind's eye a scene in
which the Marker exhibited his slate covered with censoring chalk
marks while Hans Sachs triumphantly displayed a pair of finished
shoes. This was the beginning.

He then imagined another incident, to be played nocturnally in the narrow streets of medieval Nuremberg: a crowd of citizens, convoked by nobody knows what, break into sudden clamor, to be followed by fisticuffs and fighting, neighbor thrashing neighbor, until as inexplicably and quickly as the disturbance began the crowd disappears and the tumult dies. This was a recollection of an experience Wagner had had many years before when he and his brother-in-law had visited Nuremberg and had called on a local carpenter who fancied himself as a singer. Wagner pretended that he was the famous basso Lablache and that he had come to hear his unknown Nuremberg colleague sing. The samples which the carpenter thereupon exhibited in the stillness of the night summoned the irate neighbors, and for a little while it looked as if Wagner and his companion were to be embroiled in a free-for-all. A man got knocked down; then suddenly the people took fright, they fled, the next moment the streets were deserted, peace and quiet reigned once more, and Wagner and his brother-in-law strolled home arm in arm.

So the first sketch of *Die Meistersinger* took shape and served to calm Wagner's nerves as he carried out what he interpreted to be his doctor's orders. Yet he was far from ready to proceed with the subject, and once having committed the sketch to paper, he turned with renewed energy to *Lohengrin*.

Sixteen years went by. During these years Wagner had traversed more outward and inward experiences than fall to the lot of most human beings in a lifetime. Though he had accomplished prodigious labors—he had completed *Lohengrin;* had written the book of the *Ring;* his theories of opera and drama had become crystallized; he had composed part of the Tetralogy, having led Siegfried to Fafner's cave; and he had created *Tristan and Isolde*—he seemed now farther removed from security and public approbation than in the days of *Lohengrin.* Even now Wagner was in Vienna hoping for the "ideal production" of *Tristan* which was so vital to him. The hope proved vain. Difficulties arose in the preparation of the work in Vienna; from Karlsruhe as well, where *Tristan* was to be produced, the news reached Wagner that the opera had been withdrawn. It was at this moment, perhaps stimulated by another visit to Nuremberg in September, 1861, that the old project rose once again in his thoughts with an insistence that would not be denied.

Did he once again, this time without benefit of medical advice, seek for the one palliative which could assuage his wounds?

The Wesendoncks, who were staying in Venice, invited him to join them there for a change of scenery. While he was with them he mentioned to Mathilde that he was thinking of *Die Meistersinger* and asked if she still had the draft which he had written down at Marienbad and which he had given her. Yes, she had it, but it was of course among her papers at home and she could not return it until her own return. He left Venice and, his further presence in Vienna being useless, *Tristan* having been abandoned, he proceeded to Paris with the definite intention of writing *Die Meistersinger*. Having come to that decision, his mood changed to renewed confidence and exuberant strength. At once he plunged into work, certain that the new project was to make his fortune. He did not even wait for the old sketch. What he needed he carried with him in his mind. He had already broached the plan to his publisher, telling him that he was breaking off his work on the *Ring*, to take up a new music drama, quite different from anything he had so far brought off. The style of this new work was to be, both in the poem and the music, "easy and popular." It was to be small in scale, melodious, a thoroughly "practical" opera. He was sure that all the theaters would take to this work without difficulties, the more so as it required neither a so-called first tenor nor a great prima donna. It was to be completed quickly. And it would be highly remunerative! Yes, it was sure to be a box-office attraction. In the meantime, would Schott let him have an advance sufficient to maintain himself? Schott at first had given an evasive answer to this proposal, but later furnished the needed advance. The final form of the poem was written down in a bare month. Wagner finished the text on January 25, 1862.

THE QUALITY OF THE COMEDY

Let us pose another question we cannot answer. How did it happen that the man who baked such prose biscuits—jawbreakers every one of them—as *Art and Revolution, The Art Work of the Future, On the Drama and the Nature of Dramatic Poetry*, essays which deal turgidly, obtusely, and self-consciously with questions of philosophy, sociology, and aesthetics—that this man could sit down and conceive a libretto which is clear and savory. The philosophy of *Die Meistersinger*—for of course anything by Wagner must contain philosophy—is expressed in terms which even a non-German can understand. It is homespun, but international. It is gracious and kindly, and, barring a bit of flag-waving at the end of the play, anything but arrogant. The same pen which wrote the "*Wahn*" Monologue wrote *German Art and German Politics* (and one shortly after the other). How is one to account for it?

We have called the comedy bourgeois, but this term must be applied in the best sense of the word. The action being set in the center of a comfortable society—no kings, no gods, no heroes—such a setting helped to curb Wagner's grandiloquent tendencies, and by keeping Valhalla away and Schopenhauer at bay, his genius roamed the streets of an actual town, re-created or invented ancient tranquillity, gave gentle expression to gentle wisdom, and presented us with a protagonist who, enlightened and sane yet *not* too-good-to-be-true, wins our liveliest affection. It is of course Hans Sachs who is the master of the Mastersingers.

One need not claim that the comedy bubbles over with the wit of *The School for Scandal,* nor that its satire is as incisive as that of *Le Bourgeois Gentilhomme.* But the least one can claim is that as a play, without the music, it can be perused with pleasure. Though the plot is ingenuous enough, one hardly notices it, because it is swept away by the general bustle and drowned in a flood of friendliness (in which even Beckmesser participates).

THE CHARACTERS OF THE COMEDY

That is not to say that the entire population of his Nuremberg is equally interesting. Of the principals Eva is the least original. Though she has charm and feminine grace and quite a bit of spunk, she is too much of the German Fräulein, she is a little too apple-cheeked and naïve. She is the counterpart of the pure miss who inhabits the Victorian novels. Like her Victorian cousins, she is capable of getting around her father, at least sufficiently to keep a tryst with the man she loves. But if she had told old Pogner straight out that there was no satisfactory husband to be found among the members of the Guild, no dire punishment would have overtaken her. (But then there wouldn't have been any play.) Yet even Eva is touched with poetry. When in the third act she understands, in a flash of comprehension, all that Hans Sachs has done for her, she expresses her gratitude in terms of most sensitive poetry. It is one of the best moments of the play.

Though the composer at all times saw himself as the hero, Wagner twice made the hero a composer. Once in *Tannhäuser,* once in *Die Meistersinger.* Walther von Stolzing is the artist, a poet-composer. So much of him is autobiographical. He stands for the art which is new, fresh, daring, heedless of whom it offends, yet art which (as it turns out) has roots in tradition. So much of him is autobiographical and symbolic. But Walther is a young man as well and a likable one. Born as a knight, a member of the nobility, he is frank, high-minded, idealistic, and proud, though his fortunes have fallen upon sparse days. (*"Stolz"* is the German word for pride.) He is inexperienced in the ways of the world. He acts on impulse. He falls in love with Eva at first sight and decides on an impulse to win her by seeking admission to the Guild. At the end he impulsively rejects the triumph that he has won, though fortunately Hans Sachs persuades him to reconsider. That he is willing to be led by Sachs and follow the older man's counsel makes us respect Walther all the more. What saves Walther from being just a hero, or a symbol, or "the Lover," is the humor with which he is endowed. That humor comes to the fore in his colloquy with David when the apprentice confuses rather than instructs him; in the allusion to the Marker in his Trial Song; in his discussion in the third act with Hans Sachs during which he shows excellent sense. (It is perhaps unnecessary to add that not a trace of this humor transpires in ninety-nine out of a hundred performances. Ah, those German tenors!) Wagner manages even to make gentle fun of him. In the second act Walther recounts to Eva the humiliating experience he has undergone during the trial. In his wounded pride, he bursts into a lengthy harangue in which he berates all that the Guild stands for, and in his mind sees himself surrounded by jeering, leering Mastersingers. At the very height of his anger he is suddenly interrupted by a menacing sound. What is it? Walther takes it as a signal for knightly action; his hand is on the hilt of his sword. Eva has to deflate him by telling him that it was just the signal of the night watchman making his rounds.

The other tenor, young David, is a successful comic character.

His love of mischief, his self-importance, his bustling about and mixing into other people's business, his overbearing manner with the other apprentices, his real affection for Hans Sachs, and his un-digested pedantry add up to a delightful figure. Puzzling, however, is his romance with Magdalena, who, being Eva's nurse, must be twice his age. David is young, and Magdalena's age, as indeed her whole personality, is indeterminate.

Veit Pogner, the rich goldsmith, represents the attractive aspects of the bourgeois. He wants to use his wealth constructively in the cause of art. By offering his dearest possession, his own daughter, as prize, he hopes to demonstrate to the world that the burgher is capable of as grand a gesture as the king. Pogner is solid and has both feet on the ground. Yet his plan is impractical and, if we were to take it seriously, heartless. But we needn't take it seriously; we have been well trained in accepting the fictional convention that fathers offer their daughters' hands to men who perform one serv-ice or another. The plan contains a kernel of vanity, as Pogner him-self recognizes. Still, it is a magnanimous gesture. (No burgher in Wagner's Germany was willing to do half so much for art.) Being a kind man and loving his daughter, he has cause to regret the whole thing when he finds that it may lead to Eva's unhappiness. The preparations have progressed too far for him to turn back; yet he is assailed by doubt. That doubt wins our sympathy.

Sixtus Beckmesser—an appropriate name: its very sound is sharp[5] —is the snake in the Nuremberg grass. Vain, narrow-minded, ego-tistical, and crafty, he represents the unattractive aspects of the Guild. He is the product of years of inbreeding, an example of what is likely to happen when a closed little artistic society shuts the door to new ideas. Even sensible people are capable of electing to an important post so rigid a fool as Beckmesser is. This comes about, Wagner seems to say, when one grows deaf to the music of the future. We know that in Beckmesser Wagner caricatured the critic Hanslick, whom he detested—and with reason—to the point of insulting him in public. The caricature of Hanslick was a first idea. Wagner was persuaded to change the original name of the Marker, Hanslich, to one less directly allusory.[6] As he worked on

---

[5] Wagner found the name in Wagenseil's book. "*Messer*" is German for "knife"; "*messen*" means to measure, to judge.

[6] The change was made while he was writing the poem.

the text, the figure of the critic-by-rules not only changed its name but took on a little of the good humor which pervades the work. In the end Beckmesser became less malevolent than was first intended. Wagner was too good an artist to spoil the comic mixture by an overdose of venom. So Sixtus is more ludicrous than he is obnoxious; he is more to be laughed at than to be hated. As a matter of fact, when he finally is held up to the scorn of the whole festive assembly, when he slinks away, bride and reputation gone, we begin to feel a little sorry for him.

Hans Sachs fulfills the demand that good comedy contain elements of tragedy. The humorous is the serious halted just in time and set on a bright road. Hans Sachs' serious outlook on life, his resignation which derives from seeing and understanding the world all too clearly, his acceptance of a society where much is illusion, much frustration, much vanity—these are or could be traits of a tragic character. But he is not a tragic character; he is not a Lutheran Wotan. For the resignation in his soul is amended by humor, and his knowledge of the catalogue of humanity's foibles leaves place for affection, affection even for the foibles. Hans Sachs is an optimist. He thinks all will end well, provided one does not expect the resolution to be perfect. He carries hope with him; he has it with him even when the rules and regulations are recited. Because he hopes, he is receptive to new ideas. He is able to listen to a new voice; he judges this voice to be strange but secure. Though it frightens the other Masters, Walther's song pleases him. Sachs is the artist with the tolerant though critical view. He is the intellectual artist, Wagner seems to tell us, comparing him to Walther, the purely intuitive artist who sings "as he must" without much ratiocination.

Hans Sachs might have become, in Wagner's occasionally heavy-handed drawing, an all-wise philosopher, and as such he would have been insupportable, a philosopher *ex machina,* whose function would have been to come down from the clouds of pure reason and resolve the plot, bringing the boy and the girl together. That he did not become such a creature, that we like him instead of being awed by him, that we believe in him, that he is convincingly human—that is a tribute to Wagner's skill. How deeply does Wagner feel this creation! How admirably does he know to blend Hans Sachs' wisdom with genial shrewdness, his nobility with common sense, his cosmic view with his concern with the next-door neighbor! Both the shoemaker and the poet are present.

In creating Hans Sachs Wagner had before him the record of a historical personality which seemed to have been an attractive one. The sixteenth-century Sachs was a prolific poet[7] and some of his output is of remarkable quality. His contemporaries testified to his kindness; he was a beloved popular figure. After the death of his first wife he married a young girl; the marriage proved to be a happy one. All this is unimportant, though; Wagner's Sachs is more real to us than the real Sachs.

That reality he assumed slowly. The reader will remember that in the first draft sketched in Marienbad, Sachs was, though a principal protagonist, more schematic and less kindly. He represented, as Wagner wrote in *A Communication to My Friends* (1851), "the art-producing folk spirit." The development of the part into something greater, at once more significant and more corporeal, occurred in the long interval which ensued between the first sketch and the final text, an interval during which Wagner became older and a better artist. Could it have been that the deep despond which Wagner felt when he contemplated his outward circumstances in that hotel room in Paris helped to soften his pen and, as compensation, prompted him to limn a figure of peace? This we do not know, in spite of Wagner's multitudinous letters and the explanations which the composer was so fond of vouchsafing us. He promised Mathilde she would fall in love with Hans Sachs. He promised it early but in the end he delivered.

One aspect of Sachs' character needs yet to be discussed. The belief has long been current that Hans Sachs is in love with Eva and that he renounces her nobly and unselfishly. Nine years after Wagner's death this theory was advanced by the "official" spokesman of Bayreuth, Houston Stewart Chamberlain (*Richard Wagner's Drama*, 1892). Two years later a Frenchman, de Brinn Gabast, wrote (in *Les Maîtres Chanteurs*) that while the struggle of genius versus pedant is one feature of the conflict, the center of the drama lies in Hans Sachs' "renunciation of Eva." There may be something in this—but not much! The theory draws its justification from certain indications in the text, as well as from some explanatory com-

[7] It is estimated that he wrote 4,275 Master Songs, some 2,000 poems, some 200 dramatic works. Goethe called him "a true talent."

ments which Wagner offered to the meaning of the Prelude to the
third act. Perhaps the theory was given further plausibility by our
knowledge of Wagner's behavior and attitude toward the eternal
feminine. The older Wagner (he occasionally signed his letters
"Sachs") could easily have been attracted to a young Eva—if she
admired him! But this is external biography—not what is written
in the book or the score.

There is clear evidence that Sachs loves Eva as an older man
might love a young girl, daughter of an intimate friend, whom he
has known since she was a baby. There is clear evidence that Sachs
is pleased by Eva's affection for him. By stretching a point we
could admit that Sachs' pleasure in the relationship is enhanced by
the youth and beauty which Eva's person represents. But there is
no evidence whatever of Hans Sachs' seriously considering competing for the prize or carrying off the goldsmith's daughter. On
the contrary: in the first act, when the competition is announced,
he jocularly replies to Beckmesser's insinuation that he himself has
an eye on the daughter, "The wooer will have to be of a younger
generation than you and I." He then urges an amendment to Pogner's proposal: Eva is not only not to be forced to accept the winner of the competition against her will but "the plain people" are
to have a voice in judging the contest. Obviously if Hans Sachs
had wanted to enter the competition, he would have won it. Yet
he goes out of his way to propose that Eva be left free. In neither
of his two self-revealing monologues is there the slightest indication
of such a love. His thoughts are occupied with art, with illusion,
with human vanity. He treats Eva always with avuncular affection,
the older person to the younger, never on an equal plane. In the
third act, when he brings Eva and Walther together and Eva impulsively throws herself on his neck and declares that if she still had
command of her own heart she would give it to Hans Sachs and no
one else, Sachs replies that he knows a sad tale of Tristan and Isolde
and he wants no part of King Mark's fate.[8] Surely this is not the reply of a man in love. In the quintet which follows, Sachs does say
something vague about renunciation: "I should have liked to sing
my song before this enchanting child, yet I knew that my heart's

---

[8] As he does so, four bars from the music of *Tristan* are heard in the orchestra. Such
innocent self-advertisement has been indulged in by several composers, Mozart quoting
Figaro in *Don Giovanni*, Puccini quoting *La Bohème* in *Il Tabarro*.

sweet disturbance must be set at naught. It was but a morning-dream. . . . The song I heard [Walther's Prize Song] tells me that the poet's prize belongs to youth." One may interpret this as one wills.[9] The significant fact remains that he calls Eva "the child" and that his thoughts gravitate once again toward art, poetry, song, "the poet's prize." No, Sachs is deeply fond of Eva, he is concerned with her happiness, he is touched by her trust in him, he may even be a little flattered by her innocent teasing of him; but to impugn to him a wintry desire is to belittle him. To ascribe to him a personal renunciation is to blur the clarity of Wagner's intent. The renunciation and the resignation which lie in Sachs' soul are of philosophic, not of amorous, cause.[10]

The characters of the comedy possess the privilege of expressing themselves through music. Would we know them half as well if they used only words? Wagner need not, of course, be judged as a self-sufficient poet, however much he desired such judgment. Still, here his language is remarkably fresh and apt, even considered solely as poetry. As we have indicated, the fustian and the bombast are absent in most of the text, the rhyming scheme is less forced, the imagery fresh. He was particularly happy in giving his language slight archaic touches which, without becoming "quaint," enhance the authenticity. The language sounds as if it could have been spoken in old Nuremberg. Only the scholar knows when he uses the verse form which the historic Hans Sachs employed. Only the scholar cares.[11]

It is not surprising that Wagner's richest poetic efforts are devoted to Hans Sachs, though, as we have remarked, Eva is not left penniless. To Walther von Stolzing he has given some fine and quite a few priggish lines. It is curious that the song Walther sings at his

---

[9] One must be cautious in interpreting words which the composer relegates to a concerted number, where they cannot be understood by the audience, and are known only to those who read the score.

[10] For details of the renunciation theory see *Wagner and Die Meistersinger* by Robert M. Rayner (Oxford), an excellent monograph which unfortunately is out of print. It ought to be reprinted.

[11] For example, the historic Sachs ended many of his poems with his own name, forming a signature in the last line. Wagner used the convention in the second-act soliloquy:

> *"Dem Vogel der heut sang*
> *Dem war der Schnabel wohl gewachsen;*
> *Macht er den Meistern bang,*
> *Gar wohl gefiel er doch Hans Sachsen."*

trial ("*Fanget an!*"), and which he needs must improvise hurriedly, is first-rate poetry. So is the preceding address to the Guild in which Walther tells them how "he learned to sing" ("*Am stillen Herd*"). How well the knight describes his life in the castle, shut up the long winter evenings, during which he consults an old book; how well he praises the coming of spring, when in the fresh open air he gives voice to his song! On the other hand, the Prize Song, which he works at more carefully, is—considered as poetry—pompous. If the Marker had been intelligent, "his judgment unclouded by love and hate," he should have given Walther a passing mark for the Trial Song but might have flunked him in the contest.

What kind of contest is this, anyway? Who aside from Beckmesser are the competitors? In the first act Kothner says, "Get ready, all you bachelors!" Who are the bachelors in the Masters' Guild? We don't know, and there is no indication whatever that anybody but Beckmesser proposes to woo the goldsmith's daughter. On the contrary, we have the impression that most of the Masters are either safely married or too doddering to contemplate matrimony.

Well, finally the competition does take place. When Beckmesser is laughed off the stage and Hans Sachs, quite against all rules, calls an expert witness to testify that the song which Beckmesser attempted to sing is indeed a work of art, and then when Walther appears to sing that song, it is immediately understood that he has won. If there were any other contestants, did they remain unheard? The prize contest is spurious, more so than the contest in the Wartburg, where there are at least three troubadours who have a try at it.

Not one spectator in a thousand gives this a thought. What's a little lack of logic in a plot which serves such music as Wagner here unfolded?

THE MUSIC OF DIE MEISTERSINGER

He was going to finish composing the music in less than a year. Instead, it took him six years. Not in October, 1862, as he had planned, but in October of 1867 did he write *Finis* to the great work. Early in 1862 he moved to Biebrich, a little town near Mainz, and plunged into the composition. There he received an unexpected visit from Minna and for a time they lived together in pleasant domesticity. Then an unfortunate incident destroyed it all: a parcel came from Mathilde Wesendonck. It was merely a Christmas present which had been making the rounds of various post offices, owing to Wagner's frequent changes of address, but it sufficed to inflame anew Minna's wound. She packed up and returned to Dresden.

Once more Wagner was alone. At the beginning of June a new small disturbance arose. A family which included several children and a piano moved into a part of the house. At once Wagner began house hunting, but could find nothing suitable and finally had to make up his mind to share the house with the children and the piano.

Two love affairs, neither of long duration nor of great import, hardly hemmed the progress of the work. Of greater moment was his drawing closer to the Bülows. Hans and Cosima came to stay with him toward the end of July. Bülow played through the first act of *Siegfried* and copied out the one hundred and forty-five pages of the music of *Die Meistersinger* which had by then been completed. Immersed in this music, Bülow, never the most confident of men, renounced all ambition to compose music himself. His absorption in Wagner only added to Cosima's disillusionment in her husband. She saw that she could never succeed in her ambition to make a great composer of Bülow, and by contrast, she formed an estimate of the extent of the genius in the man who had now become her friend.

A ridiculous little accident during the summer delayed the composition for over a month. Wagner, who was very fond of animals, found that his landlord's bulldog had fleas. He offered to hold the dog while a servant applied disinfectant. The animal snapped and bit Wagner's right thumb.

The matter of money became pressing before long, most of the original advance which Schott had given him having been spent in his removal to Biebrich and in supporting Minna in Dresden. After a further appeal to Schott, which proved negative, he applied to the Wesendoncks. This money, too, did not last long, and there were ominous signs that even the generous Wesendoncks had had enough of being mulcted for the privilege of being Wagner's friends. Once more he returned to the fray with his publisher. Schott replied irritably that "a mere music publisher cannot supply

your needs; this could only be done by an enormously rich banker
or by a prince who has millions." Wagner then decided that he
simply had to earn some money, even if it meant doing what he
most disliked to do, giving concerts. He set out for Leipzig, the
city of his birth. Then he went to Dresden to visit Minna. He was
deeply touched to find that Minna had prepared a comfortable
home for him with his old curtains and carpets in place. Curtains
and carpets always meant a great deal to him. The interlude lasted
but a day or so. Before the week was over Minna and he had quarreled once more. Minna saw him off to Vienna. She was crying in
the cab, for she felt that she would never again see her husband.
Her premonition proved to be right.

In Vienna he took the occasion to read the text of *Die Meistersinger* aloud in the presence of Dr. Hanslick, who became pale and
left before it was over. Three orchestral concerts were given—all
a great success with the public but a financial failure, the expenses
outrunning the receipts. Concert tour or no tour, by the end of
the year he was once more heavily in debt. This, according to his
young friend Wendelin Weissheimer, whom we have already
quoted, is how Wagner acted when, as the Italians say, he was "on
the green":

He had given splendid dinners after each of the concerts, and his hotel-
keeper had a two months' bill against him for food and lodging. One
evening when Tausig and I were with him, he bemoaned his wretched position. We listened to him sympathetically, sitting miserably on the sofa,
while he paced up and down in nervous haste. Suddenly he stopped and
exclaimed, "Here, I know what I need," ran to the bell and rang it
vigorously. Tausig whispered to me, "What's he up to? He looks just like
Wotan when he has come to some great resolution!" The waiter came in
slowly and hesitatingly—these people soon see how the wind is blowing—
and was no less astonished than we when Wagner said, "Bring me at
once two bottles of champagne on ice!" "Heavens above! In this state of
things?" we said when the waiter had gone out. But Wagner gave us a
fervid dissertation on the indispensability of champagne precisely when a
situation was desperate: only *this* could help us over the painfulness of it.[12]

In March, 1863, he set off for a concert tour in Russia. There he
had better luck: the Russian public paid handsomely. (In most of

[12] From *"Erlebnisse mit Richard Wagner und Franz Liszt."* The quotation has been
translated by Robert M. Rayner.

these concerts he played the *Meistersinger* Overture and almost invariably it was received with great enthusiasm.) He returned to Vienna with a large sum of money in his pocket, the equivalent of some five thousand dollars. He needed now only to be a little prudent in order to be able to finish *Die Meistersinger* in comfort. (He had, be it understood, no intention of settling past obligations.) But prudent he could not be. He took a house near Vienna and furnished it with great extravagance. To this episode belong the *Briefe an eine Putzmacherin*, the *Letters to a Milliner*, which were later published and which furnished good material for making Wagner appear ludicrous to those who wanted to make him appear ludicrous. He ordered satin dressing gowns and velvet hats, silk underwear, armchairs covered in damask, easy chairs of violet silk, and sundry other sybaritic appurtenances. Living alone, he engaged for his personal needs not fewer than three servants: a valet, whose wife did the cooking, and a chambermaid.

In November Bülow arranged a concert in Berlin. It was on that occasion that Cosima and Wagner became deeply conscious of their love for each other. The confession of that love followed.

Further search for money and attempts at borrowing followed. At length his creditors became so insistent that he had to flee once more. Friends scraped together the fare necessary to remove him to Switzerland, where he invited himself to the home of old acquaintances, the Willes, who lived in a pleasant house near Zurich. Herr Wille was away on business but Frau Wille received him and cared for him. When Herr Wille returned, he let Wagner know that he resented a prolonged invasion of his privacy. What was even more troublesome, it soon became evident that Wagner's whereabouts were known to his creditors, who had seized his possessions in Vienna and sold them off. They were now about to descend on him in Zurich.

Again he changed locale. He hid away in Stuttgart. There was no hope of finishing *Die Meistersinger* in peace, no prospect of quickly raising funds, no additional appeal possible to his friends. Everywhere—in Vienna, in Paris, in Mainz, in Dresden—creditors were waiting to seize him. A few days after his arrival in Stuttgart, as he was beginning to worry how he was going to pay his hotel bill, he was informed that a gentleman from Munich was downstairs to call on him. Who could this man be? Surely a creditor!

His whereabouts then had been discovered: he was caught. While he was wondering what to do, the visitor sent up word that he had come as a delegate from the King of Bavaria. The day was May 3, 1864. It was the day of rescue.

This is not the place to detail once more Wagner's relationship with King Ludwig, a chapter in biography which has been dealt with by many, best of all by Ernest Newman, in his biography, *The Life of Richard Wagner*. That the relationship on Wagner's part was a flagrantly exploiting friendship, that on the King's part it was shot through with puerile and pullulating infatuation, that the King's letters furnish more evidence for a case history than of magnanimous zeal, that Cosima and Wagner shamelessly deceived the half-mad ruler—all this makes no difference to the outcome, the outcome being *Die Meistersinger* and the continuance of Wagner's work. It is difficult to see how Wagner could have carried on had not a sickly royal angel stepped down to lift him up.

Yet even with Ludwig's intervention, it took another three years to complete the music. During that time *Tristan and Isolde* was produced in the Munich theater, with Bülow conducting. Cosima openly joined Wagner. And after severe vicissitudes, social scandals, political scandals, a temporary eclipse and quick renewal of the King's favor, Cosima and Richard finally found refuge in Triebschen. There Wagner obtained what he needed, the security and the peace, the luxury, the beautiful surroundings, and the woman he could truly love and who was singularly devoted to him. There at last the music flowed from his pen without interruption.

What can be said about this music? Not very much that is meaningful—or, in technical terms, a great deal! We who have come merely to enjoy it know that of all of Wagner's major works it is the easiest to enjoy. It is the most accessible throughout, being freer than his other dramas of prolonged stretches during which somebody barks philosophy or tells a twice-told saga in a sandy recitative voice. Certainly we get a bit of lecturing. But these dry spots, what do they signify, compared to the fullness of music that reaches our ravished ears? *Die Meistersinger* sings with glorious melodies, one after another after another. The tunes soar aloft. Melody—it is the salient characteristic of this work. What various and beautiful tunes they are, and how great is their range! There are dance tunes and folk tunes and conventional songs ending in conventional cadences; there are hymns and marches; there are melodies that sound softly in the night and there are others that exult in the sunlight; there are ceremonial ditties; there are grave melodies and tunes that children could sing; and in the quintet there is a melody treated in a style as "modern" as anything Wagner wrote, with the possible exception of the *Siegfried Idyl.*

It seems as if, when he came finally to compose *Die Meistersinger,* Wagner had no further need to follow his own precepts too didactically. He ignored his assertion that only alliterative rhyme could fulfill the requirement of music drama. He ignored his own invective against arias. Nor was he entirely faithful to his system of using symphonic themes; at least they are not as fragmentized as they are in the *Ring.* The themes are still here but they approach vocal expression. One could no doubt prove that they have become longer, moving closer to song melodies. They resemble buds more nearly than seeds, ready to burst into flower. With all that, *Die Meistersinger* abounds in polyphony, polyphony shared both by the voices and the supremely eloquent orchestra. The composer's skill is equal vertically and horizontally. In such a scene as the end of the first act, the polyphony becomes as complex as the exterior of the Milan cathedral; yet, like the cathedral, it is not fussy, but fused to make one overwhelming impression.

It has often been remarked that a great work develops its own style, a style consistent with yet differing from the general style of its creator. This is of course true of *Die Meistersinger,* with its unique combination of melody and polyphony. The melody helps to make it a romantic, youthful comedy; the polyphony helps to give it the archaic charm which is suggested by setting and words.

In short, though Wagner remained Wagner, though in *Die Meistersinger* he remained true to himself—true occasionally even to his faults—he was never less theoretical. What about those set numbers which he scorned? Here we find such set numbers as David's Chaplet Song, the call of the night watchman, the Dance of the Apprentices, Walther's Trial Song, the Prize Song of course, the choruses of the tradesmen, the quintet, etc. That quintet so obviously runs counter to Wagner's proclamations that he felt some pangs of conscience about it, and at one point he was ready to delete it, just to save his principles. Fortunately Cosima persuaded him to think better of it. It remains in the score, one of its musical

high points, though no different dramatically from the sextet of
Lucia di Lammermoor, the action of the drama being suspended
while the characters line up and sing their hearts out.

In still another aspect did Wagner ignore his own instructions.
He had much to say against the lavish use of the chorus. The audience, he claimed, was interested in protagonists, not in an anonymous crowd. There is no chorus in *Das Rheingold* or *Die Walküre*
or *Siegfried* or *Tristan und Isolde,* barring a few measures chanted
by the sailors. Yet here—and of course very rightly from the dramatic point of view—he gave the chorus a leading role.

One final point may be mentioned: the remarkable economy of
the orchestration of *Die Meistersinger.* No fatty brass choir is at
work; there are no tenor tubas or bass trumpets or contra trombones, such as you find in the *Ring.* Not even an English horn is
used. The orchestration of *Die Meistersinger* is more or less that of
Beethoven's Ninth. Perhaps Wagner kept the size of the orchestra
down because he kept in mind his wish that *Die Meistersinger* be an
easy opera to produce. Those brass and percussion instruments
which are employed are used sparingly. During the scene of the
brawl, with all the excitement, when one would expect the drum-
mer to be mighty busy, the tympani is silent until the climax, the
moment when water is doused on the quarrelers and the riot is
quelled.

Can this music be analyzed? It can, score in hand. Yet even for
the student it is unnecessary to memorize the names of the *Leit-
motive* and then to hunt for them in the music. Unnecessary and
unprofitable. What good is it to be able to name by name such
themes as "Community of Art" or "Spring's Behest" or "Jealousy"
or "Eva's Anxiety"? Musical meaning and mood are lucid without
nomenclature.

As music, then, and in a totality crowned by melody, not as a
detective game, is the work to be loved and resung in our hearts.
How astonishing that at the beginning not everybody could hear
its melodiousness! More than one "Beckmesser" heard in the work
"of melody not a trace." Let's not be too condescending about this,
almost a century after. Now it *is* difficult to understand that John
Ruskin, who surely had a sense for beauty (an eye, if not an ear),
could write to the wife of the painter Burne-Jones:

. . . of all the affected, sapless, soulless, beginningless, endless, topless, bottomless, topsy-turviest, tongs- and boniest doggerel of sounds I ever endured the deadliness of, that eternity of nothing was deadliest—as far as the sound went.

Commitments in condemnation are more troublesome than commitments in praise.

THE OVERTURE

Wagner called it a prelude. The distinction between prelude and overture is somewhat inexact though ordinarily an overture is defined as a musical composition which comes to a close, while a prelude leads into the act without pause. The introduction to Act I of *Die Meistersinger* does lead directly into the opening chorale; on the other hand, it is of such proportions as to merit the title of Overture, and for concert use Wagner furnished it with a formal ending.

This miraculous composition, a fanfare to the festival of life, opens with the simplest chord there is, the C major chord. Knowing Wagner's bent of mind, one is sure that he meant the tonality to be symbolic. The rhythm as well is elementary, the four-square common time.

The Mastersingers march past us. Let us note that while their theme glows with pride and they march with a stately tread, these part-time poets are by no means presented in caricature. The music is gay and friendly and devoid of ridicule, though much later in the Overture we do hear a facetious theme which is associated with Beckmesser. Wagner, having presented the collective titular protagonists, then turns to the two young people, to Walther's wooing. At once, all is sweetness and lyricism. Other themes are introduced, such as the music associated with the banner which the Mastersingers carry in their procession, a hint of the Prize Song, then a diminutive and perky melody which is a foreshortened mirror image of the Masters and which denotes the apprentices, then more romantic discourse, and so on in rich unfolding, until the Overture develops into the polyphonic style which is characteristic of the whole work. At the apogee of the composition, after we have sampled the joyful, romantic, and comic elements, Wagner builds be-

fore our astonished ears a section in which three themes are heard
simultaneously and a fourth makes a passing appearance, the whole
being a feat of legerdemain of which there is hardly an equal in
symphonic music. The Overture ends in a glorious burst of sound.

It has been remarked that though the Overture contains a
number of the themes used in the work—Wagner himself wrote
that it presented "the main motives of the whole drama"—there
is no reference to be found to its principal character, Hans Sachs.
The explanation usually adduced is that Wagner composed the
Overture long before he tackled the rest of the music,[13] and that
"the profounder depths of the character did not reveal themselves
to Wagner until he had begun to create him musically" (Ernest
Newman, *The Wagner Operas*). In other words, Hans Sachs had
not grown to the stature which he was eventually to achieve, and
therefore Wagner omitted him.

I am not so sure that this explanation will serve. Was not the
text finished and in it was not Sachs realized in all his wisdom?
Was not the character precisely presented by its poet, much as the
musician was later to enhance it? Is it not likely that Wagner, being
by that time quite aware of Sachs' importance, was in point of fact
so fully aware of it that—whether by conscious or subconscious
process, who is to tell?—he felt that the shoemaker poet ought to
have a piece of music all to himself? This the composer gave him
in the third-act Prelude.

ACT I

The time is the middle of the sixteenth century, on the afternoon
before St. John's Day, which falls in June. The place is St. Cath-
erine's Church in Nuremberg. The curtain rises at the moment
when the service is about to end with a chorale sung by the congregation[14] (*"Da zu dir der Heiland kam"*—"As the Saint appeared to thee." The Saint is St. John the Precursor.)

At the left of the church we see part of the congregation seated
on benches. Eva, daughter of the goldsmith Pogner, and her nurse

---

[13] It was completed in April, 1862, and first performed in Leipzig on the thirty-first of
October of that year, under Wagner's direction.
[14] The chorale is an excellent re-creation of the genuine Lutheran style. Wagner had
studied Lutheran chorales before composing this one.

Magdalena are seated on the last bench. Leaning against a pillar is the young knight, Walther von Stolzing. By look and gesture he is conveying to Eva his ardent admiration, and Eva indicates that she is not exactly averse to the knight's sentiments. During the pauses between the strophes of the chorale,[15] the orchestra lets us know that the two young people have fallen in love.

The service ended, the congregation gets up and disperses. As Eva and Magdalena prepare to leave the church, Walther approaches Eva and in great agitation begs her to stay but a moment. Approaching a lady in church constitutes a considerable breach of etiquette, but Walther would have dared an even more grievous breach to learn but one fact, the fact that spells life or death for him. What is it he wants to ask her? To gain a moment alone with him Eva gets rid of Magdalena by sending her back to look for the shawl she has "forgotten" on the bench. When Magdalena returns with the shawl, before Walther can blurt out the question, Eva repeats the ruse: now it appears that it is her brooch which she has left behind. "Is it light or dark that I face?" demands Walther. "Tell me—" And once again Magdalena returns, with the brooch. But quickly perceiving the situation and being a woman herself, Magdalena now finds that she too has "forgotten" something, her prayer book.[16] At last Walther manages to put the all important question: Is Eva betrothed?

As Magdalena returns, she acknowledges the presence of the young knight, curtsies, and asks whether she may announce his visit to Master Pogner. "If only I had never entered his house!" exclaims Walther impulsively. Magdalena fails to understand. Had Sir Stolzing not been received with all due courtesy? "That is not what he means," says Eva. "He wants to know if I am betrothed." Magdalena is shocked. Surely this is not the place to talk of betrothals!

At this moment David, Hans Sachs' apprentice, enters, and without paying attention to the three people busies himself about the church. Magdalena is in love with him, and seeing him she softens

---

[15] Here again Wagner is correct historically. Such pauses were customary, to enable the minister to read out the next line for the benefit of the members of the congregation who could not read.

[16] That, at least, is the way I interpret the little episode, though the text does not explicitly say so. Otherwise it would be just another coincidence.

sufficiently toward Walther to formulate a reply. The question, it appears, cannot be answered simply. Eva is indeed a promised bride. "But the bridegroom is not yet chosen," interrupts Eva. "That is true. No one knows as yet who he is to be. On the morrow she is to wed the winner of a competition in mastersinging." "But I myself will award the prize," protests Eva. "A Mastersinger? What is that? A competition? How is it to be judged? The bride awarded to whom?" Walther is thoroughly puzzled, when Eva, in an upwelling of feeling, breaks in with the confession "You and none other." Then she turns to the scandalized Magdalena and begs her to help her "obtain this knight." It is true that she made his acquaintance only yesterday but she fell in love with him because he looked so much like David. "Like David?" Not like the apprentice, of course, nor the king with the long beard who played the harp, but like the young hero who conquered Goliath, as he is portrayed in the picture by Dürer.[17]

The mention of David brings an audible sigh from Magdalena's lips. Promptly young David reappears with a self-important air. "Who is calling? Here I am." "What mischief is he perpetrating here in church?" "Mischief!" he replies solemnly to Magdalena's question. God forbid! He is preparing the room for a meeting of the Mastersingers, a song trial.

What a stroke of luck! The knight is in just the right place at the right time. Let him submit to the trial, win admission to the Guild. Then he may compete for Eva's hand tomorrow.

David is exhorted to do everything possible to help Walther; he is to instruct him in the forms and rules of the Masters. In the meantime, Magdalena urges, it is high time that they return home. When shall they see each other again? Walther proclaims, "This evening surely. Whatever is to be done here, however new and strange everything seems to me, of one purpose I am sure: I will do all in my power to win you. If not with my sword, then with my song."

This expository scene is set to charming and easy music in which the motives of the young people's love are contrasted with the humorous staccato melody associated with David. The scene ends in a little old-fashioned trio (which includes a bit of coloratura for the soprano).

---

[17] Wagner invented this. No such picture is listed in Wilhelm Waetzoldt's *Dürer and His Time*.

Now David and Walther are left alone. David is unable at once
to get down to business, for a number of the apprentices have
come in to prepare the place. They urge David to help along with
the work. But he informs them disdainfully that he has more
important things to think about than manual labor. Their reply
is a chaffing chorus, at the end of which David, turning to Walther, exclaims, *"Fanget an!"*—"Now begin!" It is the traditional
formula uttered by the Marker for the song to begin. Walther
does not even know who the Marker is. Nor had he ever been present at a trial of mastersinging. Nor is he aware that to become a
Mastersinger one needs to graduate through various ranks, the
lowest being Pupil, the next Friend of the School, the third Singer,
and the last Poet. To none of these distinctions can Walther lay
claim. David, in a mock-tragic plaint, calls out Magdalena's name.
What an impossible task she has given him! How is he to instruct
one so ignorant?

The instructions begin (*"Mein Herr! Der Singer Meister-Schlag"*
—"Dear Sir! The master diploma cannot be won in a day"). It is
a long litany, primarily of autobiographical content, detailing how
difficult the road to mastery is and how long he, David, has pursued it. He has the best of teachers, the famous Sachs, who is
teaching him both how to make shoes and how to write poetry.
The moment he has polished the raw leather properly, he is set
to work to analyze the difference between vowels and consonants,
short and long syllables. As soon as he has made the thread properly
taut, he must grasp the proper construction of a rhyme, hard and
soft. And so on and so on, at great length, David continually mixing up the art of poetry with the art of producing a serviceable
pair of shoes. "God help me!" exclaims Walther. "I don't want to
learn to be a cobbler. Instruct me rather in the art of singing!"

How much there is to know! David tells Walther a few of the
melodies which need to be recognized, categorized, memorized,
and named by name. These codifications Wagner found in Wagenseil's book, and he sets them before us here with appropriately
humorous music. Out of David's lips tumble all sorts of pedantic
information: he speaks of the "Writing-Paper and Black Ink"
melody, of the "Red, Blue, and Green" tone, of the "Straw" theme
and the "Parsley" tone, the "British Tin," the "Fresh Pomegranate"
theme, the "Snail" and the "Pelican" tones, the "Lonely Gour-
mandizer" mode, and heaven knows how many others. He reels

them off while the orchestra comments, as if his own set of instructions were a manufactured prize song, composed by rote. The long scene, of which I have here given only the briefest synopsis, is delightful musical spoofing. But in the theater it is static and tries the patience particularly of a non-German audience. (It is usually shortened.)

The apprentices themselves grow impatient with David's talking. When is he going to get to work? But Walther has one final question. What is a Mastersinger? The answer: the poet who, observing the rules as they have been laid down by the Masters, finds original words and rhymes and then clothes them in a strain of his own invention, it is he who shall be called Master. Walther replies, "I shall have to try as best I can."

Now David turns to the apprentices and observes that they have arranged the room all wrong. It is plain to see that he alone knows the proper procedure. Since this is not a full-scale meeting but a trial singing, the benches must be arranged in a semicircle, and the small-size, not the big, tent for the Marker is to be used. This is to be provided with a table, a chair, and a slate. Ah, yes, the slate! It is to be kept handy for the Marker. Ah, yes, the Marker! Does Walther quake before him? The candidate is allowed to make seven mistakes. If he blunders more than seven times—then, well, then he fails miserably! Let him beware, the Marker has sharp ears. And suddenly David bursts forth with a simple tune, one which undoubtedly runs counter to all the rules he has learned, but which sounds fresh and spontaneous: *"Glück auf zum Meistersingen!"* He wishes Walther luck. Let him win the trial, let the chaplet be awarded to him, let them bestow on him the sign of success, a flower wreath made of silk.[18]

This melody is taken up by the other apprentices, who gleefully dance around Walther, until suddenly they break off, having perceived that two of the august members of the Masters' Guild have arrived for the meeting. These are Veit Pogner, goldsmith, senior member of the Guild and father of Eva, and Sixtus Beckmesser, town clerk and Marker.

---

18 The first syllable of the word *Blumen* (flower), and *Seide* (silk), and the third syllable of the word *beschieden* (awarded) are set to two notes each, a practice of which Wagner disapproved in theory. When the apprentices take up the song the coloratura is expanded, all of course for humorous effect.

They are deep in conversation, while the orchestra accompanies them with a theme which Wagner is to build into a long crescendo during the gradual assembling of all the Mastersingers. Beckmesser argues against what seems to him a dangerous clause in the coming contest: if Eva is empowered to refuse the winner of the contest, of what use are his skill and art? But Pogner proves adamant: would he want to win the maid against her will? Very well, but will Pogner put in a good word for Beckmesser with his daughter? This Pogner promises to do.

Now Walther steps forward. Pogner is astonished to see him here in the school. Walther has a ready explanation: he forgot to mention to Pogner yesterday that the real reason he came to Nuremberg was his love of art. The purpose of his visit lies in his hope of becoming a Mastersinger. This obvious fib is accepted by Pogner at face value; overjoyed, he turns to Vogelgesang and Nachtigall, two of the Mastersingers who have just entered, to tell them that here is a young aristocrat, a knight, who wishes to become one of them and devote himself to art.

Standing off to one side and cogitating sourly on the best way of winning the goldsmith's rich daughter, Beckmesser suddenly becomes conscious of the presence of a stranger. He instantly senses danger. "Who is this fellow?" Pogner assures Walther that though the rules have to be punctiliously observed and no favoritism can be shown, he shall do what he can and propose him for today's trial.

Twelve of the Mastersingers are now assembled. It is time for Fritz Kothner, the official spokesman of the Guild, to proceed to the roll call ("*Zu einer Freiung und Zunftberatung*,"—"The Masters were summoned to a trial and council session"). Each Mastersinger, name by name, responds and takes his place on the bench. Only one does not answer, Niklaus Vogel. He is sick, reports one of the apprentices. (We may conjecture that Vogel fell sick for stylistic reasons. The episode serves to vary Kothner's song with the alto voice of an apprentice.)

What is the order of business? Is it time to choose a new Marker? No, that can wait until after the holiday, the more so as Pogner now asks permission to speak. He has an important proposal to submit.

During his travels throughout the length and breadth of Germany, he tells his audience, he has observed that the burgher, the plain citizen, is held is small esteem. He is considered mercenary, caring for nothing except money and possession. Art is supposed to mean little in his life. The devotion which men like themselves, the members of this Guild, have shown to poetry and singing is not generally acknowledged. In order then to give some tangible proof of such devotion, Pogner has decided to offer his dearest possession to the Mastersinger who in public contest is to come forth with the most original and most beautiful Prize Song. His dearest possession? It is the hand of his daughter. The contest is to be held on the morrow, during the festival of St. John, when the entire population of Nuremberg is to assemble on the green (*"Das schöne Fest, Johannistag"*—"The feast of St. John, as you know, we celebrate tomorrow").

The proposal is received with great excitement and lively acclamation by the other Masters. (It can hardly be news to them. We have already heard it discussed twice.)

"Understand me right," continues Pogner. "I do not offer an inanimate gift. Though the Masters are to choose the winner, when it comes to marrying the winner, Eva must be left free to accept him or to refuse him." This restriction puts a decided damper on the general enthusiasm. "Why not let her marry whom she wants and forget about the contest?" asks Beckmesser. Pogner answers that though Eva can reject the winner, she may not take another lover. He *must* be a Mastersinger.

At this moment Sachs rises and suggests a way out of the difficulty. The mind of a woman, he says, is not dissimilar to the mind of the simple people, the folk, whose judgment, though unschooled in the intricacies of the Mastersinger rules, is sound and unspoilt. Therefore, since they are so desirous of showing the people how highly the Mastersingers value art, why not leave the decision to the people? Surely they will agree with Eva. Surely they will choose the man the maiden wants.[19]

The Mastersingers protest vehemently. The proposal is dangerous and senseless. What will become of "Art" if the folk are to be

---

[19] It must be admitted that the part of Sachs' proposal which supposedly is to aid Eva in choosing a mate is not very intelligent. Does Sachs really think that a lover can be chosen by the democratic process, by votes? What Sachs has to say about art, on the other hand, is true and sensible. Do we have here an intentional touch of irony on Wagner's part implying that the philosopher knows little about women, much about art?

given a general vote? Sachs rejoinders that surely no one could accuse him of being negligent in his observance of the rules of the Guild. Yet once a year, it seems to him, these rules ought to be put to the test, lest the Masters become so obsessed in the observance of the letter of the law that they forget its spirit. Art needs to be refreshed by contact with "those who know nothing of the *Tabulatur*" (the set of rules of the Guild—see below). Only the apprentices applaud the novel suggestion. One of the Master-singers expresses the general sentiment: "If the mob speaks, I shut up." It is voted then that Pogner's proposal be accepted in its original form. Better so—than having the people butt into their prerogatives.

The meeting now returns to the order of the day. They have come to hold a trial and Pogner has a candidate, a young man who is seeking admission to the Guild. Walther steps forward and bows to the company. Beckmesser at once raises objections. It is too late in the day to hold a trial. The other Masters view the young knight with suspicion. An aristocrat presenting himself? One had better be cautious. The music depicts the atmosphere of hostility and puzzlement in an expressive passage in which Wagner com-bines the voices of the Mastersingers with sarcastic jumpy phrases in the orchestra.

Pogner wants it understood that though he recommends the young Stolzing, the young man is to be examined in due form. Kothner therefore puts the traditional questions. First, is he of legitimate birth? Pogner vouches for this, while Sachs observes that birth makes no difference, only ability counts. To the next question: Where did he learn to sing? Walther replies with the aria (and it is an aria) *"Am stillen Herd"*—"At the silent hearth." He describes how, snowed in during the winter, he had been thrilled by the reading of an ancient book. It inspired him, and it is the book's author, Walther von der Vogelweide, whom he calls his teacher.[20]

"A good teacher!" Sachs acknowledges. "Yet dead for ever so long," Beckmesser objects. "What school did you attend?" is Kothner's next question. Walther replies (second stanza), "When

---

[20] Walther von der Vogelweide, literally Walther of the Bird Meadow, was the most important thirteenth-century German poet, one of the school of troubadours (*Minne-singer*).

the frost had passed and summer had come again, then all I read
in the old book I heard in the forest. I learned my singing by
listening to the forest sounds." "Uh-huh!" taunts Beckmesser.
"He learned his art from finches and tomtits!" Kothner begins to
have his doubts, but Sachs wishes to proceed. "What difference
does it make where he learned his art, as long as he has art?"

To Kothner's final question, whether the aspirant is ready to
give a demonstration of his ability, Walther answers enthusiastically
(third stanza): All that he has gleaned from book and dale, everything that he has seen and observed and felt, he is ready to express
in song.

Beckmesser inquires, "Does anybody know what he is driving
at?" Nobody does, but they decide to let him try, anyhow. It is
all very strange.

"Does the gentleman choose a sacred subject?" Kothner wants
to know. "What is holy to me, the subject of love," replies Walther. "That we consider secular," observes Kothner drily. Therefore the Marker may listen alone, without any ecclesiastic expert.
He is to lock himself up within the curtained booth.

Beckmesser bows sarcastically to Walther and tells him that he
is allowed seven mistakes. Kothner next motions to the apprentices
to bring him the "Leges Tabulaturae," the Laws of the Tabulatur,
which are engraved on a board. These he proceeds to read aloud.
A song must follow a certain plan; each stanza must contain two
strophes sung to the same melody, to be followed by the "after-
song," and so forth, and so forth, in wearisome detail (there is no
point in following the instructions in detail, historically accurate
though they are), until Kothner ends on an elaborate coloratura
flourish, which is imitated with glee by the orchestra. (This speech
is boring; when pedantry is parodied, the parody itself is likely to
become pedantic.)

Walther is to sit in the "Trial Chair." He shudders. How is he
to summon inspiration sitting stiffly in a chair? But he yields. "The
singer sits!" Kothner calls out, and Beckmesser, from within the
curtains, replies, "Now begin!"

Walther's song fastens on these words: "Now begin!"—"Fanget an!" Thus proclaims the spring through the woods. "All life
obeys that command. All creatures respond, lifting their voices in
a paean to spring's liberation." At this moment a chalk scratch on

the board is heard from within the booth. "Envious winter,"
Walther continues, "hides in a thorn hedge and schemes how best
to spoil the gladness of the season." We have here another aria, of
great beauty and dramatic conviction, a young man's song. Now
fully in the swing of his inspiration, Walther springs from the
chair and continues with his rhapsodic singing, frequently interrupted by the sound of the chalk marks, until the curtains of the
booth are flung peremptorily aside and Beckmesser emerges spit-
ting the question, "Have you finished? For if you haven't, *I* have!
I have filled up my slate." The Marker holds up his slate. Every
inch of it is covered with chalk marks.

Never, says Beckmesser to the Guild, never in his whole professional career has he come across so flagrant a case of incompetence. He proceeds to detail some of the mistakes, which range
from "faulty rhymes" to "mixing various modes," going directly
from the "blue-knight's-spur mode" to the "high fir-tree mode";
not to mention incorrect numbers of syllables and wrong accents,
all resulting in a totally incomprehensible conglomeration, "without a trace of melody." The others agree, Kothner summarizing
the case by saying, "I did not understand a blessed word." What
seems especially unforgivable to his judges is that the young knight
jumped from the chair.

They are about to proceed to the formal declaration of Walther's
failure when Sachs rises in disagreement. The song, he says, is undoubtedly novel in substance and strange in form. If it travels new
paths, he, for one, does not find these paths confused but straight
and sure. How are they to judge something which cannot fit their
rules but which seems to obey rules of its own? Beckmesser is in-
censed: Sachs is opening the door to bunglers. "Why such burning zeal?" Sachs wants to know. "Your judgment would perhaps
become more discerning were you to listen more calmly. We must
hear this knight to the end. I ask only what is permissible under
our laws. Is it not written that 'the Marker's judgment is not to be
influenced by love or by hate'?" Since Beckmesser is himself a
wooer, how could he resist the pleasure of branding his rival? The
argument threatens to deteriorate into a personal duel between
Beckmesser and Sachs. "Let the cobbler stick to his last!" Beckmesser sputters at Sachs, his ire getting the better of his prudence.
"Since the shoemaker considers himself a great poet, the quality of

his shoes has deteriorated. Just see how badly this pair fits. . . . I'd give all of Sachs' rhymes if tomorrow he would deliver my new pair of shoes!"

The Masters press to make an end of it. Pogner tries to restore peace, Sachs tells Walther to keep on singing, if only to annoy the Marker. Out of this chatter of the Masters, the acidulous protests of Beckmesser, Pogner's evident discomfiture, Sachs' calm appraisal, the delight in the row which all the apprentices exhibit, and, hovering above all, Walther's song, which now continues as it were by its own momentum, Wagner forms his great finale, a gigantic choral-orchestral structure, a crescendo of brave proportion, which builds and builds until at last the Mastersingers raise their hands and pronounce that the knight has *"versungen und verthan"*—"sung falsely and failed." At the height of the tumult we hear the Chaplet Song, now sung by the boys in ironic comment. Walther, with a proud, contemptuous gesture, leaves the chair and departs. The Masters make for the door, the apprentices begin to dismantle the scene. Only Sachs remains behind. He glances thoughtfully at the empty chair, as we hear a reminiscence of Walther's song in the orchestra. Then that chair too is removed by the apprentices, and Sachs turns away with a humorously resigned gesture of "Ah, well!" as the curtain falls.

ACT II

We are about to hear one of the most exquisitely wrought acts of the operatic repertoire, an act in which the dramatic interest hardly ever flags and the musical inspiration is of the purest vein. This, Wagner's "Nocturne," is an unparalleled achievement.

After a brief prelude, the curtain rises. The scene is a corner of old Nuremberg. The front of the stage represents a street; it is intersected by a small narrow way which winds toward the back in a crooked path. Following this path one sees the vista of the town. In the foreground there are two houses, an opulent one on our right, which belongs to Pogner, and a humbler one on our left, which is Sachs'. Close to Pogner's house stands a lime tree. In front of the tree there is a stone bench. The door to Sachs' house is overhung by a lilac bush; the door, divided into a separate lower and upper wing, leads into his workshop.

The beautiful June evening is far advanced; night is closing in. The apprentices are about to fasten the shutters of the houses; they sing happily of the coming holiday, while David hopes that the silken chaplet will one day be awarded to him. Magdalena arrives, bringing a basket of goodies. She has come to ask David how their protégé has fared in the afternoon's trial. When she learns the bad news, she snatches the basket away from David and hurries into the house, shaking her head in disappointment.

The apprentices, who have observed this scene, gather round to polish off a few supercilious remarks about David's incompetence as a charmer. David replies as a boy would: he clenches his fists and is about to get into a fight, when Hans Sachs strides down the path. The boys scurry away and David is summarily collared by Sachs and ordered to return home, to lock up, bring a light, and put the new shoes on a last.

As Sachs and David enter the workshop, Pogner and Eva stroll down the street. Pogner wonders if Sachs is at home. He would like to talk to his old friend. Something is evidently troubling him. But he changes his mind. Of what use is talk, of what use advice just now? The plan must be carried forward. Was his plan idealistic or did it contain a drop of vanity? So he muses, then turns to Eva and asks why she is so silent. To a new motive in the orchestra which henceforth is to be associated with the city of Nuremberg, he drinks in the mild evening air and observes that tomorrow promises to be a fine day. Will it not be a fine day for her? Is she not proud of the honor which is to be accorded her before all the people of the town, rich and poor? "Must it be a Mastersinger?" Eva asks timidly.

Magdalena appears on the stoop and beckons Eva. Supper is waiting. "I hope there are no guests," Pogner remarks with a touch of irritation in his voice, and Eva exclaims, "Perhaps the knight?" He looks at his daughter wonderingly. "I didn't get much pleasure from him today," says Pogner absent-mindedly. It begins to dawn on him why his daughter is showing so lively an interest in this stranger. Has he been stupid all along?

Eva edges her father into the house; then in hurried whispers she learns from Magdalena of Walther's failure. What is she to do now? Her first impulse is to ask her friend, Hans Sachs, for counsel. But she can hardly make herself scarce before supper;

perhaps afterward she will attempt it. At any rate, Magdalena has a message for her which cannot wait much longer. From Walther? No, from Beckmesser. With a contemptuous shrug, Eva goes into the house followed by Magdalena.

The stage is now empty. Sachs, dressed comfortably in his work clothes, emerges from the shop and asks David to place table, stool, and workbench at the door of the shop so that he may work in the fresh air. David wonders what in the world could have troubled Lena and why Master is working tonight. Getting no answer, he retires and Sachs is left alone with his work and his thoughts.

The orchestra leads from David's motive into a reminiscence of Walther's song before the Guild. We know very well what is occupying Sachs' thoughts, even before he begins his monologue *"Was duftet doch der Flieder"*—"How sweetly does the scent of lilac float in the air." The perfume of the night invites him to give voice to his thoughts. What has he got to say? So little, and what he can say is so simple. It would be better if he bid the poet in him be silent and got to work on the shoes.

So he does, to a sharp, rhythmic, "cobbling" motive of the orchestra. Yet not for long, for the motive weakens, and again there drift out of the orchestra the lyric strains of youth and love. What is he to think of this curious song of the young knight? He feels it and cannot understand it. He cannot quite remember it nor yet forget it. He cannot gauge its worth nor measure it by rule. None of the rules he knows could be applied to it, yet there were no mistakes. The song sounded old and at the same time new, as if it had been commanded by spring, in obeyance to an eternal necessity.[21] Yes, surely, it frightened the Masters! No matter, it pleased Hans Sachs.

As he concludes, Eva emerges from the house and makes her way toward Sachs' shop. "Good evening, Master. Why are you working so late?" He is delighted to see her and invites her to chat with him.

Now follows the charming scene between the older man and the young girl, set to delicate and ironic music. The irony results

21 At these words the orchestra plays the melody to which Walther in Act I had told of his learning to sing from Walther von der Vogelweide. The composer underscores the "eternal" continuity of art.

from a double play: Eva tries to pump her friend about the afternoon's happenings while Sachs, refusing to be pumped, in turn attempts to sound the extent and fervor of Eva's love for the knight. He tells her that he is working late in order to finish the shoes of the proud man who hopes to win her tomorrow. Eva turns up her nose at the mention of Beckmesser. Yet, says Sachs, he is one of the few available bachelors. "Why couldn't a widower succeed?" asks Eva coquettishly. "He would be too old for you." "Too old? Age is not the question here. Only art is important." She suggests that now she could become both wife and child to him, whose wife and children had died long ago. But Sachs only laughs. He knows quite well what is troubling Eva, why she has braved the night to come to tease him. Is there nothing then that can be done to prevent Beckmesser's victory? she asks despairingly.

Sachs cannot think of what to do but he admits that his head is not quite clear. He cannot marshal his thoughts as clearly as he might, for he has had a hard day, full of annoyance and grief. "Ah!" exclaims Eva eagerly. "Perhaps in school? Didn't a trial take place today?" Finally Eva has brought the conversation around to the subject which alone interests her. Indeed, parries Sachs, there was a trial at which a most ignorant young man sought to gain admission. He failed, failed hopelessly. Did he then sing so badly? Was his art so worthless? "Nothing can help him," replies Sachs. "He can never become a Master. For he who is born a Master must expect the cruelest treatment at the hands of other Masters." Was there then no one to befriend him? "Befriend him? Him, before whom all felt small, this Sir High-and-Mighty, so sure of himself? Let him depart, let him not rumple those comfortable rules which we have designed by the sweat of our brow. We want no changes around here!"

Eva is near to tears. No one is going to help her plight. No one feels kindly toward her lover. She alone must fight for him. She *will* fight—and defy the whole congregation of Mastersingers.

Magdalena has appeared and urges Eva to return to the house. Her father is noticing her absence. What's more, Magdalena must unburden herself of her message. What is it? Simply that Beckmesser wants to try his Prize Song on her; he is about to appear to serenade her. Eva's solution is: "You go to the window dressed

in my clothes." The ruse delights Magdalena. Perhaps David will
see her and become jealous.

Suddenly Eva hears a footstep. It must be he, it must be Walther! He is coming! Pogner's voice is heard from within the house,
but Eva no longer heeds it. She tears herself away and runs toward
Walther.

The lovers embrace and pour out their ecstasy in a duet (*"Ja,
ihr seid es"*—"Ah, it is you!"). But their joy cannot last long, for
Walther confesses that, though he sang with all his heart, he was
deemed unworthy. Try as he did, the Masters condemned him. "Ah,
those Masters!" He launches into a diatribe against the whole
school. His place is not in a school, his place is in the open, in
freedom. They must flee, he must take her away at once, for how
can they now remain here? Here he can see only the mocking faces
of the Masters, grinning at him, begrudging their love, snuffling
and screeching in derogation. As his anger mounts to a climax, he
is interrupted by a strange sound, the call of a horn. What is it?
His hand is on the hilt of his sword. And suddenly the orchestra
melts into a phrase which suggests both the love of these young
people and the enchantment of the summer night. Despair and
bitterness are wafted away, as Eva soothingly tells him, "Beloved,
curb your anger. It is nothing more than the signal of the night
watchman. Hide here, under the lime tree. The watchman will
pass." The faithful Magdalena, who has once more appeared at
the doorway of the house, calls softly, "Eva, it is high time." Eva
turns to go into her house, as Walther asks, "You are fleeing from
me?" She answers, "I am fleeing from the decree of the Masters."
No matter how often one hears this question-and-answer, one
cannot fail to fall under its spell. Even in high art perfection is a
rarity; here is a moment of perfect beauty.

The night watchman appears on his round and sings his traditional chant: "Attend, ye good people, and let me tell you: the
clock has struck ten. Guard well your fire and your light, so that
none shall suffer harm. Praise God, who is our Lord."

Hans Sachs, who had disappeared into the shop at the end of
his scene with Eva, now opens the door a little and observes, "This
sounds serious. An elopement is being planned? Careful! That
must not be." Evidently he has overheard everything the lovers
have plotted.

Walther, underneath the lime tree, worries why Eva is tarrying. The figure emerging from the house seems to be Magdalena. But no, it is Eva in Magdalena's clothes, Eva, who throws herself into his arms and urges him to flee at once in utmost haste.

As they turn to run away, Sachs opens the shutters. A bright beam of light falls across the street, so that Eva and Walther suddenly find themselves clearly illuminated. They draw back hastily. They cannot pass through the light. What are they to do? There is another way through the city, but Eva is not familiar with it and they are likely to chance on the night watchman. They must wait until the cobbler has quit his post. "I shall force him to do so," says Walther. "Do not show yourself to him," Eva cautions. "He knows you. It is Sachs." "Hans Sachs, my friend?" "No, not even he is your friend."

As they hold this whispered conversation, they suddenly hear the sound of a lute. It is of course Beckmesser, who has come up the street and now scans the windows of Pogner's house. He tunes his lute, ready to begin the serenade. Sachs, perceiving this, withdraws his light and opens the lower part of his door.

"Do you observe what is happening?" Eva asks. "Somebody else has come to bar our way. It is Beckmesser." His arch-enemy? Walther is all for killing him but Eva counsels against such sanguinary action. It might waken her father. Better to let him sing his song. They can wait out the serenade, hidden there near the tree. She draws Walther onto the seat under the lime tree, sighing. "What trouble men are!"

Beckmesser, not seeing his expected audience of one at the window, makes his presence known; he begins to strum his lute. At this very moment, a blow from Sachs' hammer on the last shatters the calm of the night. Sachs, having once more moved his work-bench into the open, gets to work on the shoes with a will. He hammers. He sings. He sings on top of his voice. The song he invents to lighten his nocturnal labors is a shoemaker's song. At the sound of the "Oh's!" and "Tra-la's," Beckmesser starts in annoyance. "What is the meaning of this vulgar shouting?" The meaning will appear presently to Eva, to Walther, to the audience, but not to Beckmesser. Sachs has seized upon the circumstance of Beckmesser's serenade to even the score with the learned Marker and at the same time to prevent the elopement of Walther and

Eva. An ingenious scheme, but it is to have consequences he could not foresee.

Sachs sings about Eve, the original Eve. Yet the tale contains allusions to the present Eva (*"Als Eva aus dem Paradies"*). When the Lord drove Adam and Eve out of Paradise, the hard stones of the road hurt Eve's poor naked feet. The Lord took pity on her and sent an angel after her with instructions to make her a pair of shoes. "As for poor misguided Adam," said the Lord, "thou might as well provide relief for him, too, and measure him for a pair of boots." The musical style of Hans Sachs' song is decorated with furbelows and flourishes, quite in the tradition laid down in the Masters' *Tabulatur,* while the words are an adroit imitation of one of the historic Sachs' Biblical poems.

Beckmesser approaches Sachs. "Why are you awake so late at night?" "Because I'm trying to finish your shoes. But what brings *you* here at this hour? You must be worried about those shoes. Don't worry—you see I am at work." Saying thus, he hammers lustily and sails into another stanza. "Oh, Eva! Hear my plea! Have pity on the cobbler's fate and on his handiwork. Is not the work of art which a shoemaker creates trodden upon? And thoroughly despised? If an angel did not from time to time offer me consolation and call me into Paradise, I'd send the whole shoemaking business to the devil! As it is, I am content to remain both a shoemaker and a poet." As a countermelody to this stanza, we hear a theme which expresses the resignation that the poet feels and which is to assume great significance in the next act. Here, then, the ditty becomes both a cobbler's song and a poet's. Eva feels this instinctively. "The song troubles me," she whispers to Walther. "I know not why."

Beckmesser is in despair. How is he to serenade with all that hullaballoo going on? Magdalena has just appeared at the window in Eva's clothes. It is now or never. So he sidles up to Sachs in an attempt to win him by flattery. "Why do you insist," asks Beckmesser, "on finishing the shoes? I had almost forgotten about them. I wish to consult you not as a shoemaker but as a critic. I value your judgment and therefore I want to sing for you the song with which I hope to win tomorrow's competition." "Don't try to flatter me," Sachs replies. "Didn't you tell me this afternoon that the quality of my shoes has deteriorated since I fancied myself a poet? I took this very much to heart. I no longer bother about verse and rhyme. You see I am busy with your new shoes." So they spar, until Beckmesser loses his temper altogether and bursts out in a torrent of vituperation against Sachs, one to which Sachs listens silently and with great attention. After Beckmesser runs out of breath, Sachs inquiries, "Was this the song you meant? It sounded somewhat irregular but it sounded quite brave."

At last they reach an agreement. Sachs is to stop singing and to assume the function of the Marker in judging Beckmesser's song. If Beckmesser makes any mistakes, these are to be marked not with a piece of chalk on a slate but with a hammer blow on the shoes. What can Beckmesser do but accept the situation? Anything is better than having Sachs continue to bawl. The hour is advancing; there is danger that the girl might withdraw from the window.

So the Marker marked, the judge judged takes his stance and begins his serenade. His song is obviously a spoofing of the aria to be found in the old operas, a composition which pays no attention to the sense of the words, making the accents fall wherever the melody forces them to fall, though the words are turned into a farrago (*"Den Tag seh' ich erscheinen"*—"To me the day appeareth"). Beckmesser does not get very far. Three times Sachs records what to him seems a mistake. After the third hammer blow Beckmesser protests savagely. There is a bit of technical discussion, after which Sixtus begins again. As the song proceeds, the hammer blows rain down more and more frequently. The comedy is enriched by Beckmesser's frantic attempts to sing the love song in an ingratiating voice to the girl at the window while mounting fury engulfs him.

"Have you finished?" interrupts Sachs. "No. Why do you ask?" "Because I have finished the shoes." The parallel with the afternoon is now complete: like Walther at the trial, Beckmesser in the street has failed. Just the same, he plows doggedly on with the tune. All this while—and to tell the truth Beckmesser's serenade is a bit longer than the fun warrants—Eva and Walther have been watching, listening, half-amused and half-bemused, half-comprehending and half-puzzled by Sachs' strategy.

By now Beckmesser's singing has deteriorated into howls and bays. The noise has wakened David, who perceives that his Magdalena is leaning out of the window listening to the serenade of some stranger.[22] This, coming on top of Magdalena's recent rebuke, is too much for David. He arms himself with a cudgel, springs out, and begins enthusiastically to belabor poor Beckmesser. By this time the neighbors have been aroused, and now, in various stages of deshabille, they gather in the street. Seeing one man thrashing another, they take sides without having the faintest idea what the quarrel is about. Old rivalries and jealousies are awakened. Old scores are rereckoned. The cobblers are sure it is the fault of the tailors, the tailors the cobblers, the locksmiths the butchers! Bakers, grocers, flax weavers, pewterers, tradesmen, journeymen, apprentices—they all join the melee, flaying about, hitting violently, shouting on the top of their voices. The music of the scene is dominated by one melody descriptive of blows raining down on somebody's back. With this motive Wagner builds the fugal tonal structure which ends the act. This scene—called the "Brawl Scene," the *"Prügel Szene"*—gave the anti-Wagnerites a particular opportunity to assert that Wagner's music was not music at all but a "doggerel of sounds." Of sound and fury we get plenty, yet it is apparent that the musical structure is held within as sure a design as a populous canvas by Brueghel.

The women of the town open their windows, and seeing that their menfolk are in danger of killing one another, let out anxious screams. Then, rallying to action, they fill vessels and buckets with water.

What has happened to our principals during all this? Pogner, in his nightgown, has come to the window. He has mistaken Magdalena for Eva, has drawn the nurse into the room and firmly fastened the window. Sachs has extinguished his light so that, unseen, he can continue to keep the two lovers under his surveillance. They remain hidden under the tree, until Walther, believing the opportunity for flight has come, draws his sword and, clasping Eva in his arm, decides to make his way by force through the crowd.

---

[22] The device of mistaken identity is no more successfully used by Wagner than it is in the old comedies, no more convincing here than in the last scene of Beaumarchais' *Figaro.* How is it possible that Beckmesser mistakes Magdalena for Eva while David does not? How is it possible that David does not recognize Beckmesser? How is it possible that later Pogner mistakes Magdalena for Eva and Eva for Magdalena? Myopia is very serviceable in comedy.

Walther and Eva are about halfway up the little street when of
a sudden the horn of the night watchman is sounded. It is at this
moment, too, that the women manage to douse copious streams
of water on the fighters. The effect is instantaneous. Neighbors,
apprentices, journeymen, the Mastersingers fly in all directions.
Sachs springs from his shop, reaches Walther, and takes him by
the arm while he pushes the half-fainting Eva back to her house to
be received by Pogner, who has appeared on the stoop. Sachs' next
concern is for David. Seeing him still thumping Beckmesser, he
administers a mighty wallop and sends the boy flying into the shop.
All this while he has a firm grip on Walther, whom he now forces
to enter the shop with him. Then he closes the door behind him.
Beckmesser, at last freed from his incubus, hobbles away as fast
as his battered legs will carry him.

In less time than it takes to tell it, the stage has emptied. Of the
madding crowd not a soul remains. Now when the night watchman
enters once more, he can scarcely believe his eyes. All is peace, all
is quiet. He sings his song again, this time in a quavering voice,
exhorting the people to "beware of ghosts and specters." It is now
eleven o'clock. Once more he blows the signal on his horn as he
walks slowly down the empty little street. The moon has risen and
Nuremberg is bathed in its soft light. Midsummer magic, in-
violate and tranquil, has been restored. The magic spreads into
the orchestra with a silver sound, though we are still able to hear
a small echo of the brawl. At the very last, as the night watchman
disappears around the corner, the bassoon reminds us of Beckmesser's attempt at serenading: it sounds limp now and ineffectual.
Suddenly, to a loud chord, the curtain falls.

The charm of this act close—the slumbering streets, the silent
stage, the only voice that of the orchestra—is ineluctable. We find,
curiously enough, a similar mood in another opera, a comedy of a
very different nature: the close of the first scene of the third act
of Verdi's *Falstaff*.

ACT III

The Prelude to the third act opens with the theme which previously served as counterpoint to the Cobbler's Song and which
denotes Sachs in his mood of philosophic resignation. The theme

is now presented with grave clarity, until from the horns and the bassoons there rises a new melody, the tune of the hymn which the people of Nuremberg are later to send up to the blue sky. The musical material is then developed, first to increasing perturbation and intensity, in the end to be allayed by "benign and blissful resignation" (Wagner's own explanation). "Benign" this music is, a wonderful pendant to the Overture.

Scene One

The curtain rises to show the interior of Sachs' workshop. The door in the background is the one which leads to the street and of which so frequent use has been made in the preceding act. At the right there is a short set of steps, which lead into another room. (In some productions, the steps are omitted.) On the left a large window overlooks the town. Sachs is sitting by that window, absorbed in reading a big folio volume that rests on his knee. The sun shines brightly. It is morning.

Preceded by his breezy motive, David comes up the street and peeps in at the door. He becomes more than a trifle nervous when he perceives that his master is sitting there. Surely he is going to be punished for last night's fracas! But since Sachs takes no notice of him, David decides to chance the encounter and enters. He has a basket on his arm, the contents of which he proceeds to investigate. He finds flowers, ribbons, and at the bottom both a cake and a sausage. He is about to devour these delicacies when Sachs, still unaware of the apprentice's presence, turns over a leaf with a loud rustle. David starts, hides the edibles, and stammers out that, as ordered, the shoes have been delivered to Herr Beckmesser. No sign of recognition from Sachs. "That bodes ill," murmurs David. He had better say something in his defense. Is it possible for an apprentice to be faultless? Can his master not understand what got into him when late at night he saw a stranger serenading his own Lena? Just a misunderstanding, that was all. Now everything is explained, and Lena has sent him this basket. "Oh, please, Master!" he pleads, "say but one word."

Sachs closes his book, his gaze still far away. Then he perceives his apprentice kneeling before him and the basket of flowers and ribbons there on the table. How festive it looks! David reminds Sachs that today is a festive day: it is the feast of St. John. Indeed?

If it is, asks Sachs, do you remember the verse which celebrates St. John's Day? Recite it for me. David takes heart. Yes, he knows the verse well. And promptly he begins: "On the shores of Jordan stood St. John, baptizing all who sought him"—"*Am Jordan Sankt Johannes stand.*" But in his anxiety David sings the song to the melody of Beckmesser's serenade. When Sachs calls him to order, David corrects himself and begins the song anew in its proper melody. St. John baptized all comers, among them the child of a German woman who then wended her way toward Nuremberg. When she arrived there, it turned out that he who was called John near Jordan's strand was called Hans at the shore of the Pegnitz (the river which flows through Nuremberg). "Hans!" Suddenly David realizes that it is his master's name day.[23] Ashamed of his own forgetfulness, David offers flowers, ribbons, cake, and even the sausage to the illustrious bearer of the name Hans. He suggests that Sachs might well compete for the hand of the bride this afternoon. Surely in his present condition Beckmesser would not stand a chance. It would be much gayer if once again a woman reigned in the house. Sachs smilingly sends him away, bidding him to dress up in his best clothes for the coming festival. Overjoyed at having escaped punishment, David gathers up his basket and disappears.

Preceded by a reiteration of the renunciation theme, Sachs begins the second of his famous monologues, the "*Wahn*" Monologue. Though the monologue speculates on human nature and is a general plaint, it serves, as much as anything in the opera does, to illuminate the specific nature of Hans Sachs, its combination of idealism and world-wisdom. In thus revealing himself, he enriches us.

How shall we translate the word "*Wahn*"? It is not "vanity," though something of this meaning sticks to the word, particularly as Thackeray used it, both in his title and in the summation of "*Vanitas vanitatum.*" It is not out-and-out "madness," though madness is implied. The dictionary gives such meanings as "erroneous opinion," "hallucination," "craze," "delusion." Perhaps "illusion" comes nearer the mark, the illusion which men fabricate for

[23] The name day in Reformation Germany and indeed well into the present century was considered a more important occasion for celebration than the birthday.

themselves to permit them to believe what they want to believe. It is this murky illusion which envelops society in a cocoon of folly. It is ubiquitous folly which Sachs marvels at and grieves over and which he tries to define. The *"Wahn"* Monologue is akin to Macbeth's bitter definition of life as a tale told by an idiot; but the definition is transposed into the sweeter language of comedy.

"Wahn! Wahn! Überall Wahn!" Wherever Sachs searches, be it in the chronicle of cities or the history of nations, he finds proof of idiotic illusion. Men will not live together but will plague one another in useless cruelty, hurting not only one another, but each himself. The hunted imagines himself to be the hunter. The man who is wounded is deaf to his own cry of pain. This irrational round dance encircles all; this ancient sickness has always permeated the world and always will. If there is surcease, it is but of momentary duration. The snake has been scotched, not killed. Of a sudden folly rears its head anew.

Then Sachs looks around him, his thoughts turning to a sunnier view. Around him he sees old Nuremberg, one of the most peaceful and even-tempered of the world's cities. As he turns toward the window through which the morning light floods the room, the full orchestra pays a tribute to Nuremberg. Then, using the same motive, the composer hurries the tempo and weakens its stateliness; the music, becoming out of breath, presages the course of Sachs' next thoughts. Even here madness can awaken. One fine evening a simple shoemaker wanted to prevent a folly that two young people were about to commit. What was the result? The old madness is set going, streets and alleys are soon filled with a raging rabble, with man, woman, youth, and child, who fall to blindly, slamming and whacking one another they know not why. God knows how it all came about!

At that moment the orchestra, which has been cudgeling us with the music of the brawl, comes to a stop and, descending as it were from unknown regions, the strains of the midsummer-magic music reach us. What caused the outbreak? It must have been a goblin, Sachs continues. Or was it a glowworm unable to find its mate? Or was it the scent of the lilac? St. John's Eve? "But now," proclaims Hans Sachs, as the mood of the music once more changes, this time from night to day, "St. John's Day has arrived. And now let us consider how Hans Sachs can turn 'Wahn' to a nobler end.

If none of us is safe from folly, not even in Nuremberg, let us at least use folly for a purpose."

It has been objected that neither a fight in the street nor a plan for an elopement by two lovers furnishes a sufficient reason for the seriousness of Sachs' reflections. It seems to me, on the contrary, that the very triviality of these incidents lends additional poignancy to Sachs' conclusions. At any rate, the music of the monologue is beautiful beyond description.

The door to the chamber opens and Walther von Stolzing appears. Sachs welcomes him. Did he finally manage to get some sleep? Sachs inquires. Walther replies that he did sleep a little. He feels refreshed because toward morning he dreamt a beautiful dream. Sachs, wasting no time, asks, "Did your dream give you a hint how you might win the prize today?"

The Walther-Sachs Discussion

There follows now a remarkable scene in which Wagner presents us with an aesthetic discussion. Here are two men standing on the stage, the younger poet asking questions, the older poet instructing him. It is a Platonic dialogue set to music. Isn't any such discussion out of place in the theater (except in rare instances, such as Hamlet's advice to the players), and doubly out of place in the less intellectual world of opera? It is. Yet Wagner manages to set the discussion to music which continuously holds our interest, filling artistic advice with a rich fluid of melody. Once we understand in some detail what Walther and Sachs are talking about, we will find that this scene, though "long, exact, and serious," is one which is able to "at once both please and preach."

Walther at first does not dare to retell his dream; it might vanish in the attempt to hold it fast. But, instructs Sachs, that is the very task of the poet, to fix a dream through words.

When Sachs urges that Walther use the dream as the material for a Master Song, Walther objects smilingly that it had nothing to do with the Guild or its rules or the Masters. Sachs reproves him gently. The Masters are not as intractable as they appeared yesterday. If they were, he not only would not have prevented Walther's flight but would have flown with him. The Mastersingers may err, they may be overly fond of their comfort; yet perhaps there was some justification for the fright which they felt as they heard the song. "Your song, with its passion, was to them something which could be used to seduce their daughters; for the state of matrimony a different tune and different words are required." "I heard that different tune," says Walther laughing, "last night. The street resounded with its noise." "Never mind. Follow my counsel. In short, create a Master Song."

"A beautiful song, a Master Song? How shall I distinguish between them?" To a new motive in the orchestra Sachs details his definition of a Master Song (*"Mein Freund, in holder Jugendzeit"*). In youth, when our heart swells with first love, every man is something of a poet. Then it is easy to compose a beautiful song. Youth itself, the springtide of life, sings for us. Summer, autumn, and winter follow. Life rolls on. Worry and pain, along with a little joy, strife and quarrels, business and childbirth, we live through all of them. The man who after such experience can still sing a beautiful song—it is he who is a Master, his song a Master Song. The test of the artist is that he remain a poet in spite of life.

What is all this to Walther? He is in love.

"It won't do you any harm to learn the Masters' rules. You may well want to use them as companions on your way. They may help you to preserve what now lies in your heart."

Who made these rules?

Men who had undergone much, who had suffered the world's distress, who knew the anguish of living. Out of that anguish, out of that wilderness, they designed a plan to help them recapture the memory of youth.

How is it possible that in age one can feel again the raptures of spring?

It is possible through the art of poetry. Poetry can work this miracle. This art cannot do without rules, though to be sure they must be forever refreshed. "I shall teach you the rules—but you must give them new meaning."

"How shall I begin under the rules?"

Sachs replies, "Pose your own rules, then follow them."

Taking up a pen and spreading a sheet of paper before him, Sachs writes down what Walther dictates, the Prize Song.

The Prize Song cost Wagner no end of trouble; he recast it several times, both in words and melody, before he was satisfied.

Indeed, one can understand his wish for perfection. The plot depended on the composition of a Master Song which is not only to win a competition but to win it against expressed hostility. The song must be heard in full; it must be convincing. The Prize Song *is* convincing. Wagner uses for it themes which throughout the two previous acts have been associated with love and its idealism and which have been taking more definite shape as the opera progresses. As we hear them now in the confines of a set piece we enjoy them all the more. The Prize Song, as a song, sounds unforced, flowing, natural; one expects this from its "author," who learned his art in glade and forest.

As I have indicated in my essay, a smaller praise must be handed to the poetry. Walther sings of a vision he had at dawn (*"Morgendlich leuchtend"*—"Bathed in the sunlight of a rosy dawn"). He came upon a beautiful garden. As he tarried there, a fair maiden embraced him and pointed to the tree of life. Morning gave place to evening. The stars broke into a dance. He saw the laurel tree bedecked not with fruit but with stars, etc. All this is symbolism of the foggiest sort.

While Walther sings, Sachs helps along by practical and friendly comments. He points out, for example, that the second stanza does not end with the same tone as the first. That's not quite as it should be; but he accepts the unconventionality as a "law of springtime." When, after two stanzas, Sachs suggests a third, Walther declines. Moved by the ardor and sincerity of the young poet, Sachs decides not to press Walther further; he urges Walther, however, to remember the melody, for he may be called upon to sing it to a larger audience.

The conversation then descends from Parnassus to Nuremberg, where, Sachs tells Walther, the Stolzing servant has arrived, carrying bag and baggage. No doubt he was directed to the right house by a "dove" whom they both know. It is time now for Walther and himself to put on their best array.

The stage is left empty. Not for long; presently Beckmesser appears outside the shop window. He peers in and, seeing the place empty, he enters. He is all dressed up, but it is evident that he is miserable. There follows a scene in pantomime, with the orchestra expressing quite clearly and unmercifully what is troubling Beckmesser. Painful memories crowd in upon him. Every bone in his body is aching. He looks through the window at Pogner's house opposite. Has he still got a chance? His self-confidence returns, but presently, as he thinks of his rival, it ebbs away. He fancies he hears—and he does if he is listening to the orchestra—the noise of the mocking women and boys of yesternight. He slams the window closed and idly turns toward the table. Idly he observes a sheet of paper lying there. He glances at it, he takes it up, he reads it with growing indignation, and at length he ends his silence by breaking out furiously with "A song for the competition! And by Sachs! Now I understand everything." Then, hearing the door open behind him, he hastily conceals the paper in his pocket. Sachs, dressed for the festival, comes forward and sees Beckmesser.

Sachs greets him somewhat ironically by asking whether he is still worried about the new shoes. This is the last straw. Beckmesser breaks out into the Nuremberg equivalent of Billingsgate. Sachs is a low-down humbug, the instigator of all the mischief. Because Sachs has his eye on the rich heiress of the goldsmith, he first suggested some absurd clause for the contest. It was he who tried to drown out the serenade, it was he who put on his apprentice to belabor Sixtus black and blue. But however wily Sachs' schemes, he, Beckmesser, is going to cross them.

"You are badly mistaken," replies Sachs. "Whatever my plans may be, I assure you I am not a wooer." A dialogue of particularly neat give-and-take follows:

BECKMESSER: You are not singing today?
SACHS: Not in the competition.
BECKMESSER: No Prize Song?
SACHS: Surely not.
BECKMESSER: What if I had proof to the contrary?
SACHS: (*Glancing at the table*) Ah, the song! I left it here. Did you filch it?
BECKMESSER: Isn't this your handwriting?
SACHS: Ah, is that it?
BECKMESSER: The writing quite fresh.
SACHS: And the ink not yet dry.

Etc., etc. To the accusation that he is the worst of all rogues, Sachs replies composedly, "Perhaps. Yet I have never absconded with anything found on a stranger's desk. Therefore, to save your good name, I will give you the paper. It is yours if you want it."

The offer acts like a shock on Beckmesser. Knowing that his own poor Prize Song is done for, and unable to think of a better one, he now finds this gift, like a shower of gold from heaven, nothing less than a poem by Sachs. At once he becomes mistrustful again. Has Sachs learned the poem by heart? Sachs assures him that he need not worry. "May I make use of it as I see fit?" "As you wish." "May I sing this song?" "If you do not find it too difficult." "And if I succeed with it?" "I would be indeed surprised."

Beckmesser is overwhelmed. The poem is sure to be excellent. But Sachs is to swear that never, no matter where he may hear the song again, and under what circumstances, will he claim that it is his. Sachs swears it. Beckmesser jumps for joy. With trembling protestations of friendship and gratitude—Beckmesser promises that he will do his best to have Sachs elected Marker, though to be sure a Marker who uses chalk, not a hammer—he limps away.

The scene is a delightful piece of comedy, both dramatically and musically. Yet one cannot altogether suppress a little twinge of doubt as to the propriety of Sachs' behavior. Though Beckmesser lays his own trap and undoubtedly deserves to be caught in it, Sachs edges him into it. He is not giving altogether straight answers. He does not lie, but he does not tell the whole truth either: that the poem is by Walther. Perhaps this is what he meant when he said that *"Wahn"* can be used to a good end. Yet Sachs playing a trick is not what we expect from our beloved philosopher. No matter; in the next scene he rises again in our esteem.

A minute or two after Beckmesser has rushed away, frantically to study the new poem, another visitor comes into view. Sachs is expecting this caller. It is Eva, dressed resplendently in her bridal gown, but pale and wan of visage. She calls ostensibly to complain that the new shoes do not fit properly. It is of course a pretext which Sachs pretends to take seriously. What's wrong with the shoes? Are they too large? Too tight? Where? At the arch? The heel? Oh, Sachs ought to know where the shoe really pinches her! So she tells him at the very moment when the door of the chamber opens and Walther appears. She utters a cry of joy and remains motionless, her foot on the shoemaker's stool, her gaze intent on her beloved. Sachs is working away at the shoe, or pretending to. Grumbling about the hardness of a shoemaker's life, always at work day in, day out, he tells Eva that he has thought of a solution for himself: he is going to get away from such toil by wooing her this very day. Eva does not hear a word he says. "Well," he remarks, "I had better stick to my cobbling. But I wish that somebody would sing me a song while I work. I heard a good one today. Is there a third verse to it?"

Walther, contemplating Eva with a rapture equal to hers, sings the third stanza of the Prize Song, while Sachs admonishes, "Listen, my child, this is a Master Song." When it is over, he returns with the shoe, fits it on her foot, and asks, "Does it still pinch —or have I succeeded?" Eva bursts into tears, falls on Sachs' breast, and clings to him, sobbing uncontrollably. The orchestra, in a passionate sweep, tells us of the emotion that suffuses the young girl. Sachs tears himself away from her as if displeased and takes Eva over to where Walther is standing. While the lovers find each other, he continues to make light of the moment. The shoemaker's lot is twice as bad when he is a widower. He is called upon to mend all that is broken, patch what is torn. But the girls want him only when there are no younger men conveniently at hand.

Eva is not misled by this wry chaffing. "Sachs, my friend, how infinitely much I owe you!" she cries out. With his help she has grown up to be a woman; it was he who taught her how to feel, it was he who made her recognize what was noble, brave, and free. If she had her choice, she would choose him, him alone. His would be the prize. But the choice is no longer hers, for the force of love has engulfed her, the force which exhilarates and frightens. Even he, she knows, stands in awe of that force. Eva's speech is one of the most intense moments of the opera, its music curiously reminiscent of *Tristan* even before Hans Sachs replies softly that he knows a sad tale of Tristan and Isolde and has no wish to share King Mark's fate.

Magdalena appears at the door. Sachs, making an end to the display of serious emotion, calls David out. He demands that the assembled company pay strict attention: an important ceremony is to take place. To the strains of the chorale tune at the beginning of the first act, he announces that he has summoned them to a christening. It is the custom of the Mastersingers, when a new successful song is born, to give that tune a name by which it shall be known to posterity. Such a child has been created here by Sir Walther. Hans Sachs and Eva Pogner are to act as godfather and godmother, while David and Magdalena have been called as witnesses. As the laws of Nuremberg do not recognize a mere apprentice as a legitimate witness, and since David has sung his verse well today, he has decided to promote the boy to *"Gesell"* (journeyman). The overjoyed David kneels and receives the traditional box on the ear.

Sachs names the new song: it is to be called "The Interpretation of the Morning Dream." Eva, the youngest relative, is to pronounce the blessing.

Sach's half-humorous speech is cast in an archaic style, appropriate to a ritual. The similarity of the music to Kothner's reading of the laws of the Mastersingers is striking, yet the same style takes on a warmth and friendliness here which were absent from the previous caricature. Of such subtlety is music capable.

Eva, invited to speak the appropriate words, begins the great quintet (*"Selig, wie die Sonne"*—"The sun of my happiness smiles"). She sings of the joy that this sunny day has brought her, the day when her lover has invented a gentle and lofty song. David and Magdalena dream of the time when they too will be united; while Walther sings of his own good fortune. As for Sachs, his thoughts turn to the realization that the poet's prize belongs to youth.

The quintet ends in a blaze of voices. At once Sachs bids them all make haste and meet at the festival. The curtain falls, but the orchestra continues.

Scene Two

The final scene need not be discussed in as great detail as the preceding ones. Introspection now gives way to resolution, discussion to pageantry, all of it being self-explanatory and the outcome easily foreseen. Fanfares for horns and trumpets along with the march of the Mastersingers anticipate the approaching festivity. When the curtain rises again, we are in an open meadow just outside the town. Flags, flowers, and gay ribbons bestrew the stage. In the background we see the Pegnitz River; boatloads of men, women, and children are arriving. At the left a platform has been raised; there the various guilds are to assemble. The apprentices escort the incoming members of the guilds to their places.

Right now the shoemakers are arriving; they line up and, freely drawing on the familiar cobbler's theme, they extol the importance of their craft. After a moment the tailors appear; they relate a self-glorifying anecdote, how a sly tailor saved a beleaguered city.[24] After that it is the turn of the bakers.

Now things really get started: a bevy of girls arrives. The apprentices call for a dance, the town band obliges. This Dance of the Apprentices is an ingenuous tune—very un-Wagnerian!—in three-quarter rhythm of a type known as the *Ländler*, a country dance. David invites one of the prettiest of the girls to dance. The apprentices warn him that Magdalena is watching. He hastily breaks away, but realizing a trick has been played on him once again, he resumes dancing with even more enthusiasm. The dance comes to a sudden end when a cry of "The Mastersingers!" goes up.

In solemn procession they march in, Kothner carrying the banner, with Pogner leading Eva by the hand. When they are all assembled, the apprentices call for silence, and Sachs comes forward to make the welcoming address. At the sight of Sachs, the whole assembly breaks forth in a heaven-storming hymn: "*Wacht auf!*" —"Awake! The day draws near. . . . I hear a nightingale's song." The words were written by the historic Hans Sachs as a greeting to Luther—it is he who is hailed as "the nightingale"—but the melody is Wagner's. The effect of the hymn is joyous on all, except on Hans Sachs. He is sunk in thought. And just as he rises to speak, we hear in the orchestra the theme of resignation, the "*Wahn*" motive. Beginning in a veiled voice, he first thanks the people for their affection; then he pays tribute to Pogner and the generosity he has shown in offering, for art's sake, so rich a prize in the coming contest.

It is Beckmesser's turn to begin. He has been madly busy trying to master the song, but the devilishly difficult words will not stick in his memory. Well, there is nothing to be done now. He is committed to it.

The apprentices lead Beckmesser to a small mound of turf which they have firmly rammed down and which they have decorated with flowers. Beckmesser stumbles onto it and stands there very ill at ease,

[24] In the course of their song Wagner used a short quotation from what was in his time one of the most popular Italian operatic arias: "*Di tanti palpiti*," from Rossini's *Tancredi*. The joke is lost on the audiences of today. Rossini would have enjoyed it. He died the year *Die Meistersinger* had its premiere.

while the populace wonders what kind of wooer this might be. To them he doesn't appear to be the right one, not at all. The apprentices stop this prejudicial whisper by calling for *"Silentium."* Kothner utters the signal, *"Fanget an!"* Beckmesser preludes on his lute and then lets us hear the latest product of his skill. What he has done is to take the words of Walther's Prize Song and fit them to the same old melody which he had composed previously. In the course of this Procrustean procedure the words have become twisted in his mind, and what emerges is nothing but rhymes of fruity nonsense. The Mastersingers look at one another. They cannot believe their ears. The nervous Marker gets himself more and more embroiled, until the crowd, unable to restrain its mirth, breaks into loud guffaws. At this Beckmesser rushes up to the Mastersingers and screams that it was not he who wrote this mishmash of a poem; it was Hans Sachs, their precious Sachs. "He palmed it off on me!" That is the last of Beckmesser; he storms away and is lost in the crowd.

"This poem by Sachs? Is it possible? What a scandal!" Sachs picks up the sheet which Beckmesser has hurled at him and quietly answers: "No. This song is not by me. I cannot boast of having created so good a poem. The fault lies in the way in which Herr Beckmesser has treated it. Let me try to prove this to you. Let us have the song sung properly. Let me call a witness in my defense, one who not only will prove that the song is worthy of being called a Master Song but that he is its author."

Sachs turns the manuscript over to the Mastersingers so that they may read it. Walther steps forward, ascends the mound, and begins the Prize Song.

Wagner here found himself in a difficult situation. It is necessary that Walther repeat what we have already heard in the preceding scene; yet exact repetition, he was a good enough dramatist to see, would result in an anticlimax. He solved the problem ingeniously. When Walther reaches the sixth line of the poem, Kothner, overcome with emotion, drops the sheet of paper to listen more intently. Walther perceives this and now departs from the original version of the song. He improvises. In doing so, he improves the song, driving it at greater intensity, enhancing it, as it were at the inspiration of the moment, with new vitality. The change in the music preserves us from being wearied by the song, the more so as Wagner rings yet another change in its presentation: he supports it at the end with the full chorus, the people demanding that the prize be awarded to this skillful singer.

Walther is led to the steps of the platform. Eva crowns him with a wreath of laurels, singing as she does so a marvelously beautiful coda: "No one knows how to woo as charmingly as you." Here again the chorus joins in, Eva's voice floating above it.

"Well," concludes Sachs, "I think I chose a good witness." The Mastersingers, not to be outdone in generosity, turn to Pogner and ask him to confer masterhood on the young knight. The goldsmith takes the chain and, in the name of their patron saint, King David, is about to declare Walther a newly elected member of the Masters' Guild. But Walther turns away impetuously. A remnant of the hurt he experienced remains in his soul. He declines. The only reward he values is Eva's hand.

In perplexity everybody looks at Sachs, who advances toward Walther, takes him by the hand, and reads the young man a little sermon: "*Verachtet mir die Meister nicht!*"—"Do not disdain the Masters, and honor their art."

The sermon, meant for the audience, is a bit of proselytizing which has strayed in here from one of Wagner's essays. Sachs speaks of "the holy German art" which could save what is fine and true in the German soul, even if the land itself were to be conquered by foreign kings. We know that when Wagner was completing the score, he planned to end the opera with the Prize Song and its joyful acclamation by the people. Sachs' final speech, he realized, was not really an integral part of the story, and though its text had been written, he now proposed to eliminate it. Cosima, however, pleaded against this, and eventually he gave way to her. Between two and three o'clock one night, after she had been talking to him the whole day about the conclusion of the work, he composed the speech in the form in which it now stands. It would have been better in this case had Wagner not listened to Cosima, for Sachs' lecture at the end of the long work is wearying, its patriotism somewhat maudlin.

Sachs' admonition has the desired effect on Walther: he consents to accept his victory. Eva takes the laurel wreath from Walther's brow and places it on Sachs'. Sachs in turn takes the chain from Pogner's hand and places it around Walther's neck. He embraces the happy couple as all the participants join in a tribute to the real protagonist of *Die Meistersinger*, Hans Sachs.

THE MORAL OF DIE MEISTERSINGER

Some of the most beautiful music to be heard in opera house or concert hall is sounded in Wagner's Nuremberg. What more can we wish for than this music with its seemingly inexhaustible inspiration; now contemplative, now jocose; now ardent, now satiric; now of gossamer texture, now sturdy; now almost as simple as a shepherd's tune, now so imaginatively constructed that we can still marvel at its daring? What more? Wagner wants more. He hands out an artistic lesson, propounds a moral.

Curiously, the moral is not drawn in the original concept of the drama. It developed later. It so to speak drew itself as the work ripened and Wagner's concept broadened. We have spoken of the opera's genesis in some detail to observe that a difference exists not only in detail but in philosophy between Wagner's first plan and his final accomplishment. *Die Meistersinger* started out as a comedy which was to satirize art hidebound by tradition, or, more specifically, music bound by tradition, or, still more specifically, the kind of operas against which Wagner's works were then competing in vain. Wagner wished to sweep from the stage "Grand Opera," the products of Meyerbeer and the early Verdi. (To the end of his life he knew almost nothing of Verdi and did not understand him —but that's beside the point.) He wished to topple "traditional opera," the *Robert le Diables* and *Les Huguenots* and *Nabuccos* and their German imitations which were then all the rage in European theaters. He wanted to replace them with a nobler form in which various arts were to be combined in a new and original way. The first sketch of *Die Meistersinger* demands that the old be overthrown. In this sketch Sachs' third-act soliloquy, which was later to become the *"Wahn"* Monologue, is "a petulant jeremiad about the decadence of poetic art in Germany." When he wrote it, Wagner was, if not an angry young man, at least a revolutionary young man.

Then he changed, for the great artist is never wholly a revolutionary. The final work does not say that tradition must be broken. It does not, except lightly and good-naturedly, mock the keepers of tradition. And it does not deny the necessity of establishing artistic laws. Between the two frontier lines, the old—that is, Kothner and his ilk—and the new—that is, Walther—now stands the philosopher who understands the necessity of bringing both lines together.

Wagner used Hans Sachs as his spokesman. As Sachs' character developed, so did the moral become clarified. In the *"Flieder"* Monologue Sachs speaks of the song that sounded so old and was yet so new. He is conscious of the continuity of art. "The merit of originality is not novelty," Wagner might have read in Carlyle's *Heroes and Hero-Worship*. Only that art is valid which builds on tradition, but grows beyond to blossom forth with new thought or —equally important—old verities freshly presented. To arrive at such art, a mastery of the Masters' rules is required. As Hans Sachs explains to Walther in the first scene of the third act, rules help an artist to give shape to his emotions. Without shape, without design, without "order," art is impossible. It is the combination of the old and the new, it is the inheritance that the new artist draws from all who have preceded him, joined to laws and rules he first learns, then himself casts in new form serviceable to his particular needs, which denotes progress. Like Walther, one may rebel against superannuated rules or laws become rigid. One may moan over the inability of the conservatives to hear a new tune. But one may not set aside inheritance.

The moral itself is old. It is an artistic precept recognized since time immemorial, and practiced in fruitful periods. Only in our times has the moral been challenged, perhaps with disastrous results. "In art that which is wholly new quickly withers away or grows stale," wrote Cecil Gray in *A Survey of Contemporary Music*.

Wagner expresses the moral not in words alone, but in music. Walther rails furiously against the crusty pedants and their *"Tabulatur."* Yet—when he creates his Prize Song, he observes the *"Tabulatur,"* though with some freedom. The song follows traditional forms, with its orderly strophes (*"Stollen"*) and "aftermelody" (*"Abgesang"*).

Not only in the Prize Song but in other defined parts of the opera, traditional forms are not cast aside but newly interpreted. Many of Wagner's contemporaries could not understand this (the critics less than the public). We are sufficiently removed from it to be able to appreciate not only the marvelous originality of this "long, exact, and serious comedy," but its indebtedness to previous music.

DER ROSENKAVALIER

COMPOSER: Richard Strauss

LIBRETTIST: Hugo von Hofmannsthal

FIRST PERFORMANCE: January 26, 1911
Royal Opera House, Dresden

RECEPTION: Success

CHARACTERS:

The Marschallin, Princess von Werdenberg	Soprano
Baron Ochs of Lerchenau	Bass
Octavian, a young gentleman of noble family	Mezzo-soprano
Von Faninal, a rich merchant, newly ennobled	High baritone
Sophie, his daughter	High soprano
Marianne, duenna of Sophie	High soprano
Valzacchi, a man of affairs	Tenor
Annina, his partner	Contralto
Commissioner of Police	Bass
Major-domo of the Marschallin	Tenor
Major-domo of Faninal	Tenor
The Princess' Notary	Bass
Landlord	Tenor

Singer	High tenor
Scholar	
Flute Player	
Hairdresser	
His Assistant	
A Widow of Noble Family	
Three Orphans of Noble Family	Soprano
	Mezzo-soprano
	Contralto
Milliner	Soprano
Vendor of Animals	Tenor
Four Footmen of the Princess	2 Tenor, 2 Bass
Four Waiters	1 Tenor, 3 Bass

A Little Black Boy, Footmen, Couriers, Haiduks, Cookboys, Guests, Musicians, Two Watchmen, Four Little Children, Various Personages of Suspicious Appearance

DER ROSENKAVALIER
(INTERNATIONALLY SPEAKING)

Two months after the premiere of *Der Rosenkavalier*, Hofmannsthal, writing to Richard Strauss, drew a retrospective estimate of the work on which both of them had spent the intensive labor of the past two years. Hofmannsthal wrote that now that he understood more intimately the nature of Strauss' music, he hoped to accomplish a new large work in which the text and music would be better mated;[1] *Der Rosenkavalier* did not entirely satisfy him. Still, he the poet liked the text. He liked the whole opera. And he dared to hope that this opera would retain its place on the stage for several, perhaps for many, decades. At least, that is, on the German stage; the reception of *Der Rosenkavalier* at La Scala had been anything but encouraging. "It is true," wrote Hofmannsthal, "that my libretto contains the *heavy* defect that much which goes to make up its individuality and its charm disappears in translation." It was, then, as a German opera on German stages that Hofmannsthal envisioned the future of the work.

To be sure, of the two collaborators Hofmannsthal was the more modest. Yet even the confident Strauss could, in 1911, hardly have foreseen the extent of the *international* success of the comedy, the one opera of his not only most often performed within but outside Germany, part and parcel of the standard repertoire, which shuttles between London and Buenos Aires and San Francisco.

[1] The work was *Die Frau ohne Schatten*, to be considered after the project of a "thirty-minute opera for chamber orchestra, *Ariadne auf Naxos*."

Yet logic—a nearsighed guide on the road of art—could trot out several reasons why *Der Rosenkavalier* cannot be, and never will become, popular in foreign lands. The first and strongest of these reasons lies in language. Much of the opera's fun, its wit, its irony is verbal. What is entertaining about a joke you don't understand? The language used, or rather the several languages used, by Hofmannsthal are gradations of German, ranging from the precious candy-box language of the aristocrats, liberally interspersed with French, to the Viennese street dialect of the suburban tradesman. Unlike *The Marriage of Figaro*, to which the *Rosenkavalier* has often been compared—a comparison which is absurd and unfair to Strauss' work—the jokes are frequently found in the turn of a phrase rather than in the turn of a melody. Ochs' lecture on his amatory prowess in Act I, only lightly punctuated by music—is it not a verbal piece of humor? So is the scene between Ochs and the Notary (descendant of a long line of stuttering legal pedants). So is Faninal's rage after the Baron is pinked, the comic rage of a talkative *nouveau riche*.

Not only the wit, but also the thought content which gives this remarkable text its body and fullness, make it necessary that we understand. Octavian's self-centered, self-assured thoughts of youth need language as much as music for their expression. The philosophy of the Marschallin, her animadversions on the passage of life and the inconstancy of feeling, lose the subtler part of their savor if the words remain incomprehensible, eloquent though her music undoubtedly is. At its best the music of *Der Rosenkavalier* is poetic and the poetry is musical. What happens if one of the two partners speaks a "foreign" language?

How very much to the past does this language belong! It was written by a poet whose skill lay in the exquisite tooling of a phrase, in the romantic sheen of expression, in the lambent coloring of verse. He belonged to a group of artists who delicately analyzed their own souls, souls which, if I may so express it, swayed in the wind and swayed most effectively when the wind blew mildly on a late summer day. The mood of the moment could make and unmake. All was transient. Grace was the one essential. (There were exceptions, of course: Hofmannsthal's *Elektra* is one of these.)

In present-day theater gentle self-examination has given way to the harsh cut into the ego and psychiatric dredging. The silver mirror has been replaced by a surgical lance. Hofmannsthal's plays, such as *The Fool and Death* (*Der Tor und der Tod*) or *The Theater of the Little World* (*Das Kleine Welttheater*) or *Christine*, are now out of fashion, even in Austria. Aside from the texts he did for Strauss, only his reworking of the old morality play *Everyman* is to be found on the stage, rather on one stage, that of the Salzburg Festival.

The Austrian dramatists at the turn of the century, the Hofmannsthals and Bahrs and Schnitzlers, have now passed into a limbo which seems laid in faraway, almost fabled history, as the Austro-Hungarian Empire in which they lived seems faraway history. To an edition of Schnitzler's *Anatol* Hofmannsthal wrote some dedicatory verses which characterize not only Schnitzler but his own works:

> Thus we play theater,
> Play-act our own feelings,
> Ripe before their time,
> Tender and triste,
> The comedy of our soul. . . .

> A few listen but not all,
> A few dream, a few smile,
> And a few sip a sherbet. . . .

> (*Also spielen wir Theater,*
> *Spielen unsre eignen Stücke,*
> *Frühgereift und zart und traurig,*
> *Die Komödie unsrer Seele. . . .*

> *Manche hören zu, nicht alle,*
> *Manche träumen, manche lachen,*
> *Manche essen Eis. . . .*)

Does not this sound *vieux jeu*? It is yesterday's theater, yesterday's sentiment.

Finally, we are up against the social structure of *Der Rosenkavalier*, which, one would think, is to modern audiences well nigh incomprehensible. The action of the opera takes place a little earlier than *Figaro*'s, that is, before the French Revolution, in the

reign of Queen Maria Theresa. But *Figaro* seems timeless and inde-
pendent and indefinite in locale, while *Der Rosenkavalier* is closely
linked to Vienna's court politics, degree and rank of Hapsburg
hierarchy. It is specific in locale and so archetypically Viennese as
to appear parochial. That Hofmannsthal was able to create so vivid
a reproduction of eighteenth-century Vienna is an advantage for
spectators who know their history and know the glamorous city
on the Danube. But what about those who have never been to
Vienna?

Yet all this counts for nothing. The objections are invalid, the
logic does not apply. *Der Rosenkavalier* continues to be one of the
half-dozen most beloved comedies of opera. Part of the explanation
for its world-wide preferment lies in the simplicity of the fundamental plot. It *is* simple, with all its sophistication and complication. When Hofmannsthal broached the subject and when Strauss
feared that it would be "a little too fine for the mob," he replied:
"The action is simple and understandable even to the most naïve
public: a fat old arrogant suitor favored by the father of the bride
is bested by a young and handsome one—isn't that the *non plus
ultra* in simplicity?"

A more important reason can be defined by the word used by
Hofmannsthal in the letter quoted above: "charm." The play has
charm. Charm need not be understood. Indeed, it can be said of a
comedy what Barrie said of a woman's charm: "If you have it,
you don't need to have anything else; if you don't have it—it
doesn't matter what else you have."

What are the ingredients of this charm? Of the several which
may be delineated, the readiest is the liveliness of the characters of
the comedy. They are all filled with life; not one of them, not even
a minor character, is pallid. Most of them are thoroughly enjoying
themselves, transmitting that enjoyment to us. And the best time
is had by that tourist from the hinterland, Baron Ochs auf
Lerchenau.

When Hofmannsthal and Strauss began the work, they conceived of the big bad bouncing Baron as the central character. For
a long time the title of the opera remained *Ochs*. In the beginning
the other protagonists were subordinated to the fat provincial
whose visit to Vienna and *mariage de convenance* were to be the
main action. Hofmannsthal and Strauss wanted to create another

Falstaff:[2] at least, Falstaff's name crops up in the correspondence. Hofmannsthal worried about the casting of the part, protesting that if the role were to be played by a thin, "specter-like" actor instead of an expansive, "comfortable" interpreter, it would mean the death of the opera. He wanted it done in *buffo* style and, if need be, a foreigner, an Italian, was to sing it. (Hofmannsthal mentioned Pini-Corsi, a surprising choice, for how could an Italian have handled the Austrian dialect? Carl Perron, a German, played the role at the Dresden premiere in 1911; But Strauss' and Hofmannsthal's favorite Ochs was Richard Mayr.)

Ochs is of course no Falstaff. He is not only not that witty in himself but does not produce that much wit in other men. Still, he is a funny creation, being a double spoofing of the chaser who thinks himself irresistible and the boor who thinks himself a diplomat. He turns out to be one of those "villains" of the theater whom, though he combines in himself a list of traits we dislike, we end up liking. He is, as Octavian describes him (though in a moment of fury), "a *filou*, a dowry hunter, an out-and-out liar, a dirty peasant, a fellow without decency or honor." Octavian might have added that he is a coward, stingy, a snob, and, like most snobs, subservient to those who outrank him. He comes from "up north," presumably near Bohemia. That is a local Austrian joke: the ignoramuses hail from Bohemia. So Ochs is the hayseed who is shown up in the big city, with his airs, his ignorance, his bad German, and his worse French. Yet he is so expansively and rotundly drawn that we laugh at him with easy tolerance. He even shows one good trait: he is something of a good fellow; as he says, he is "no spoilsport never." We are not at all sorry that he loses his bride but wouldn't have minded if he had captured her dowry.

Octavian, with his seventeen years and two months, is the dashing hero of the opera, romantic from his white wig to his satin shoes, carrying with him in well-born poise all the attractiveness

---

[2] The young Richard Strauss sent Verdi the score of his first opera, *Guntram*. He wrote to Verdi: "I cannot find words to express to you the impression which the extraordinary beauty of your *Falstaff* made on me. I cannot ever thank you adequately for this pleasure." Verdi answered promptly that, though he had not found time to read the whole score, the portions he did peruse convinced him that it was a work "written by a knowing hand. Too bad that I cannot understand the text. Not that I wish to pronounce expert judgment (that I would not dare to do), but rather so that I might better be able to admire and to be glad for you." How characteristic of Verdi!

that only unprincipled youth can bestow. He is obviously modeled on Cherubino, though he lacks Mozart's mystery. Octavian is predictable. But that does not make him any less attractive. Not only to Sophie and the Marschallin but to the audience that attraction is largely a physical one. Octavian does not say anything very witty or profound. He bears a light heart in a lithe body—that is more than enough. He makes love well, differently to the older than to the younger woman; Hofmannsthal writes these scenes with a delicate difference. Octavian is courageous, as he has been brought up to be. He is headstrong; that is to be expected from somebody who must have been everybody's favorite. The poet named him Rofrano and tells us that the Rofranos were a very noble family. It is not a Viennese name and, I believe, Hofmannsthal meant to suggest that in Octavian's character some volatile Italian traits can be found. At any rate, he acts impulsively—and loves play-acting. He does the part of "Mariandel" to perfection, and we can guess that the elaborate scenario in the inn was his idea.

Sophie is a product of the eighteenth-century equivalent of a finishing school for young ladies: she comes "fresh from the convent." Nothing much need be said about her except the all-important fact that she is young and pretty and innocent. Her excessive innocence is relieved by a certain amount of spunk. She stands up for herself, convent or no convent. The playwright Hermann Bahr criticized "the ordinariness" of Sophie's speech. But Hofmannsthal replied that her way of expressing herself—a mixture of what she had learned in the convent and the jargon of her father—is consistent with her character, a girl like a dozen others. In that lies the irony of the situation: Octavian falls for the first "nice" girl of his own age who comes along. Sophie has to be as she is, says Hofmannsthal, if she is not to detract from the dominating figure of the Marschallin.

Marie Therese, Princess of Werdenberg, wife of the Field Marshal of the Imperial Austrian Army, grew to be the central character of the opera as the work progressed. We mentioned that it was not so planned in the beginning; but even fairly late in the development of the scheme we find her still merely one of the protagonists, not the unique personality which she was to become. She became central and dominant almost by accident, as if she had a life of her own which pressed and enlarged the boundary of the poet's and the composer's imagination. (This is not a unique phenomenon in art, though it is usually the work itself, not just one character, which grows beyond the plan. Thomas Mann's *The Magic Mountain* was planned as a short story. *Die Meistersinger* began as a "short, light opera." *Der Rosenkavalier* itself, when Hofmannsthal first proposed it, was to be "extremely terse, playing time two and a half hours, that is, half as long as *Die Meistersinger*." Perhaps the fascination which Hofmannsthal felt for the Marschallin contributed to the final length of the opera, which is, in fact, only an hour shorter than *Die Meistersinger*.)

However it happened, the Marschallin turned out to be one of the loveliest, most individually endowed, most human of the human beings of operatic literature. She has offered a never-ending challenge to a score of singing actresses (in this role of all roles the acting is as important as the singing), a challenge which none but Lotte Lehmann has fully met.

It is easy to become sentimental about the Marschallin, to call her, as several critics have done, the female Hans Sachs. We need no such fulsome comparison. She is an experienced, wise, and understanding woman, but she is certainly not all wise, devoid of foible or vanity. More important, she is certainly not beyond the pale of life, beyond error and passion, looking back from a vantage point of tranquillity. Strauss himself has told us that the Marschallin should be "a pretty young woman, no older than thirty-two years. True enough, in a bad humor she calls herself an 'old woman' in comparison to the seventeen-year-old Octavian, but surely she is not David's Magdalena, who by the way is likewise portrayed too old. Octavian is neither the first nor the last lover of the beautiful Marschallin, and she must not act the closing of the first act too sentimentally, as tragic farewell to her life, but must retain some measure of Viennese grace and lightness, with one mournful and one joyous eye."

Those "thirty-two years"—we must take them in eighteenth-century terms (see Jane Austen, where a woman of thirty is considered almost beyond marriageable age), not in terms of a twentieth-century life span. At thirty-two, which might be the modern equivalent of forty or forty-five, she has learned her lesson that time cannot stand still, nor can love. She knows that Octavian must be passed on to one who is "younger and prettier." Undiplomati-

cally she tells him so, though he chases the thought away, only to
make it come true a day later. She has clear eyes and she knows
"when a thing has come to an end." She isn't going to spoil those
eyes by weeping, however. Even when she is sad she refuses to become lachrymose. One tear, perhaps, and then on to the next experience. It is her humor, her sense of life played as a game—serious now and then but still a game—which endears her to us. If
we are not quite dealing with a Viennese masquerade, as the Marschallin calls the affair in the last act, neither are we dealing with
a triangle in which she becomes a point of tragedy. Some of us do
not understand this and we feel more sorry for this wonderful
woman than we ought to feel.

What other traits can we discern which account for the Marschallin's having so strong a hold on the audience that the comedy,
originally entitled *Ochs,* could in the end be entitled *Marie Therese*
—and this in spite of the fact that she is absent for one whole and
one-half an act? She belongs to the loftiest aristocracy, the Field
Marshal's office being one of the highest in the realm. She takes
her social position for granted. She possesses the elegance of simplicity; she is naturally gracious in all she says and does, equally at
ease with the bourgeois Faninal and the suburban policeman. We
can be sure that her staff of servants are devoted to her. Her genuine kindness is part of her elegance. How we would like to be
like her!

Der Rosenkavalier moves in a richly romantic milieu. Costumes
and scenery add to the total effect, as do the minor characters;
each of them, from the Italian singer to Annina to the aforementioned worthy policeman, contributes to the general charm of the
comedy.

Der Rosenkavalier is a comedy, not a burlesque. The difference
between burlesque and comedy was described by Joseph Addison in
the *Spectator:* "The two great branches of ridicule in writing are
comedy and burlesque. The first ridicules persons by drawing them
in their proper characters, the other by drawing them quite unlike
themselves." "Proper characters," full-dimensional characters—
that is why the play continues to hold our interest. Curiously
enough, Hofmannsthal considered calling the work "Burlesque
Opera." Strauss squashed the title peremptorily: " 'Burlesque Opera'

is impossible. There is nothing burlesque in it." They then settled on the final "Comedy for Music."

Thus far we have spoken mostly of Hofmannsthal, of the play, adducing proof that a successful opera needs a good libretto and that Hofmannsthal's libretto, in spite of seeming obstacles and difficulties, is one of the very best. We must now turn to Richard Strauss and note, obvious though it is, that the most important reason, the all-important, the decisive reason for the popularity of the work lies in its music. In this opera the magician from Munich is at his most joyful, most ebullient, most brilliant, and, so to speak, at his most natural. That the orchestration is fascinating—that we expect from Richard Strauss! Orchestral effects such as those in the Prelude to the first act, the philosophic scene between Octavian and the Marschallin, the close of the act, the beginning of Act II with the backstage chorus, the scene of the Presentation of the Rose, the scoring of the final trio and the duet, and many, many more such moments prove that all Strauss learned, assimilated, thought about, and originated in the handling of the orchestra in his symphonic tone poems has been put to service in the opera. One constantly marvels at the sheer virtuosity with which Strauss manipulates the apparatus. It is a huge orchestra, so pliantly used that it ranges from chamber music intimacy (the first monologue of the Marschallin) to the grandest grand opera exaltation (the trio in the third act). But what is more important, the musical substance of the opera is of first quality, rich in singing melodies, original and bold in harmony. The music blooms, luxuriates, flourishes. In its thrall the listener is suffused with the glow, the sense of participation, the concern for what happens next, the bond of sympathy with the characters, which mark the vitality of musical drama.

The romance is there in full; nothing in the music sounds middle-aged. If we speak of charm in the text—the music has it, and in what abundance! The waltzes, which have been so highly praised and which help to give the opera its popularity, while excellent as waltzes, do not seem to me to represent the musical pinnacle of the work. The high points, rather, are to be found where they properly belong, in the ecstatic moments, the scenes of tension and resolution, culminating in the finale of the last act, from the moment on when the Baron and the mocking crowd have departed.

Strauss' humor has triumphed in two of his works. One is *Till Eulenspiegel,* the other *Der Rosenkavalier.* For even *Ariadne,* which in the first act is a masterpiece of humor, loses that sense in the second act, with its German charade in Greek costume. Strauss' sense of the romantic, while never absent in his music (he was the last of the nineteenth-century Romantics, notwithstanding his twentieth-century innovations), is at its freshest in two of his works. One is the tone poem *Don Juan,* the other *Der Rosenkavalier.*

It is curious that Strauss, a most intellectual and analytical craftsman, was a poor critic of his own music. The good fairies standing at his cradle, who gave him so much, failed to give him a blue pencil. Many of his works, even those composed before his gift flagged, are marred by banal stretches. Some of them, notably *Also Sprach Zarathustra* and *Ein Heldenleben,* are marred by an excessive egocentricity, a taking of oneself too seriously, an attempt to write a treatise. *Der Rosenkavalier* is not so handicapped. It is never overblown; the philosophy it contains remains light and airy. That is not to say that the opera stands altogether on a high level. Even here there are moments of banality, spots of mere noise, passages in which the inspiration sinks, the orchestra coasts. All the same, on balance, the result is joy.

ACT I

The Prelude begins with an upward leap, a bold, simple motive which characterizes Octavian. Once the young man is introduced, the orchestra suggests his ardor, a somewhat inexperienced and wild ardor, the music flaying about in a purposefully exaggerated manner. Strauss notes that this section of the Prelude is to be played as if it were "a parody." Then, after the helter-skelter, the orchestra quiets down; the change of mood brings us a lyric motive which is to be associated with the Princess in her serious moments. As the Prelude nears the end, the love of Octavian and Marie Therese is expressed in a beautiful round theme, an ecstatic sigh enclosed in a ring of melody.

The scene is the boudoir of the Princess of Werdenberg. The

Marschallin is lying in bed,[3] Octavian is kneeling before her. It is morning. The sun is streaming into the room. The song of the birds is heard in the garden.

Octavian indulges himself in an amorous apostrophe on the subject of "You and I becoming one." "It is I and I alone who know your real self," he boasts. The Marschallin teases him: would he prefer that it were common knowledge?[4] No, indeed he would not. He is divinely happy. Yet in his transport, as his hand seeks her hand, his lips her lips, is he not in danger of losing his identity? What will become of him? To this high-flown nonsense, the Marschallin answers simply that she loves him. They embrace, and the love theme which ended the Prelude is heard once more.

Octavian protests against the day. Why must it be daylight, during which his mistress belongs to society and the world? He jumps up and closes the curtains so that he may prolong the night. The Marschallin laughs, for she knows there is no escaping reality. Her ears, accustomed to the sounds of the household, have heard a discreet tinkling of a bell from afar. Nobody is to enter, Octavian decrees. But the Marschallin bids him hide himself quickly behind the screen, for she knows that the sound denotes nothing more ominous than her little Negro servant bringing the morning chocolate. With an elaborate tripping ceremonial—set to a motive which reminds one of a parody of the Hunding motive in *Die Walküre*—the page boy places the silver salver on a small table, bows, and trips out again.

How can he be so careless as to let his sword lie around in a lady's bedroom? the Marschallin wants to know. Octavian answers that if she dislikes his lack of experience in such matters, then what does

[3] Thus in the original stage direction. When *Der Rosenkavalier* was first given, the German theater directors were shocked by such frankness. Hofmannsthal and Strauss agreed to have the first scene played on a sofa in the foreground of the stage. That is how the scene was staged at the Metropolitan as well, until recently, when the original direction was adopted.

[4] Right here we have a nuance which slips by the non-German spectator, though even most Germans may not be aware of it. In eighteenth-century German three forms of address were used, only two of which remain in the language. There was the familiar *"du"* used between lovers or very good friends. There was the formal *"Sie."* There was also a third form, *"er,"* which was used by a person of higher rank speaking to one below him, or by distant relatives, etc. When the Marschallin teases Octavian, or when she is annoyed by him, she uses this third form. In her tenderer moments (one such follows shortly), she reverts to the *"du."*

she see in him? No philosophizing, begs the Marschallin, not now, at breakfast. Everything in its proper time.

They sit down to take their chocolate together, to the accompaniment of a waltz which is as sunny as the morning. He calls her by her nickname, Bichette, and she him by his, Quinquin.[5] "How lucky I am!" Octavian exclaims. "The Field Marshal is off somewhere in the Croatian forest, hunting bear and fox, while I—" A shadow flits over the Marschallin's beautiful face. "Do not mention the Field Marshal. Last night I dreamt of him." Octavian is shocked. "Last night you dreamt of your husband?" "One cannot control one's dreams. I dreamt he was home again. There was a tumult below of horses and servants, and I got so frightened I woke up. Isn't it curious? I still hear the noise. I can't get it out of my ears. Don't you hear it?"

Octavian hears it, but tries to reassure Marie Therese. The Field Marshal is far, far away. Marie Therese is not convinced. "Even if he is far away, the Field Marshal travels quickly. It happened once that—" She interrupts herself. "What happened once?" Octavian demands angrily. "Never mind," says the Marschallin. "You don't have to know everything." This is no time for jealous caprices. The situation is serious. No stranger would dare to create such a hubbub so early in the morning. "Quinquin, it *is* my husband."

The orchestra, at this announcement, darts in all directions as Octavian runs toward the right door. No, he cannot pass there, for there the morning visitors and half the servants are assembled. Then through the little door which leads to the antechamber of the boudoir. Too late! The Field Marshal is already in the antechamber. Octavian must hide in the alcove as best he can. Now deeply worried, he asks: if he is discovered, what will become of her? The Marschallin assures him that she is capable of remaining mistress of the situation. Nobody is going to search her boudoir. It is her battlefield and she is no "Neapolitan general" (meaning that the Neapolitans always gave way on the battlefield).

But what does she hear? The voice outside—it is not the voice of her husband. It is the voice of a stranger. They call him Herr Baron. "Quinquin," she sings jubilantly, "it is a visitor." And by

5 "Bichette" is an actual French term of endearment, meaning literally "little deer." "Quinquin" means "baby" in a dialect used in the north of France.

way of showing relief the orchestra bursts into another waltz. And what a waltz!

Who is this visitor? Suddenly the Marschallin recalls that five or six days ago, as she sat with Quinquin in her carriage, a letter was handed to her. It was a letter from a relative, a distant cousin from the country, Baron Ochs von Lerchenau. Being much too occupied with Quinquin, she did not open the letter; now she has not the faintest idea why the Baron is coming to see her at this unseemly hour.

The Major-domo's voice is heard in the antechamber, begging the visitor to wait in the gallery; to which a coarse voice replies that a Baron Lerchenau is not accustomed to being detained in an antechamber. Octavian has disappeared behind the alcove. As the Marschallin inquires what in the world he is up to, he pops out— dressed as a serving maid in a skirt and a short jacket, his head covered with a kerchief.[6] "Your Highness will please excuse me, I have only just entered your Highness' service," Octavian pipes in broadest Viennese dialect. It's not a bad plan; he'll escape disguised among the Princess' retinue. Marie Therese approves and Octavian makes for the door.

Just as he reaches it the door is forced open and the Baron bursts in, being restrained in vain by the lackeys. Octavian (in the way prescribed by comedy) bumps smack into the Baron. At once the Baron's interest is aroused. "I beg your pardon, my sweet child! I didn't hurt you, did I?" But before he can pay further attention to this appetizing young "maid," he must perforce perform his greeting to the lady of the house. He bows three times in the Parisian manner, and in answer to a cool "How-do-you-do?" from the Princess, he proclaims to one and all that it is obvious that Her Highness is very glad to see him. Why not? What does the early hour matter among persons of rank? Did he not time and time again pay his respects to the Princess Brioche as she sat in her bath —with nothing but a little screen separating her from him? He is really astonished that he has been kept waiting. The Princess excuses herself: she was suffering a migraine headache this morning. (The orchestra comments on this social lie by repeating a little of the love music.)

---

[6] Where does Octavian find these clothes? How is it that they were lying about in the boudoir? Hofmannsthal does not explain.

The Baron's attention is torn between the necessity of discussing with the Marschallin the business which has brought him to Vienna and the desire not to let the serving minx out of his sight. His two-way monologue, half-politeness, half-lechery, is punctuated by the Princess' questions, and is later joined by Octavian to form a trio. It all glides along to insouciant music. Strauss matches his wit to the poet's.

The Princess still hasn't the faintest idea to what she owes the honor of Ochs' visit. Pretending that she did read his letter, but drawing him out, she learns that the Baron is about to choose a bride. Indeed, he has chosen her already. She is a certain Mlle. Faninal, the family, he must confess, bourgeois Viennese. But father Faninal has been newly appointed to the nobility by His Majesty; he has the contract for supplying the army stationed in the Netherlands. He is very rich, being the owner of twelve large houses, not to mention a palace in the most elegant part of town. What is perhaps most fortunate, his health is reputed to be not of the best. The girl is young, fresh from the convent, and an only child. Well, if this be a misalliance, if the Baron is marrying beneath his station, what does it matter? His own body contains sufficient blue blood to serve for two.

At this point Octavian makes another attempt to escape, carrying the breakfast salver toward the door. The Baron, observing this, quickly confesses to the Princess that he has not had time to stop for breakfast. The Princess is constrained to observe the amenities and orders "Mariandel" to serve the Baron.

It is the custom of his family, Ochs continues, that a silver rose belonging to the founder of the Lerchenau dynasty is to be presented to the bride of each Lerchenau, an ancient and solemn tradition. We hear here the charming theme of the Silver Rose, which is developed and used with great effect during the second act. He, Ochs, begs the Princess to suggest to him some member of the family who could serve as a deputy, as bearer of the silver rose.

Very well, the Princess will consider the matter and let him know her choice on the morrow. How else can she be of use to him? One thing more: he needs a good notary to handle the legalities of the marriage contract. Her notary often calls in the morning, says the Marschallin. Will Mariandel find out if he is here? The Baron won't hear of sending the "delicate child" away.

At this moment the Major-domo enters and confirms the fact that among the people waiting for an audience the Notary is to be found.

While the Princess instructs the Major-domo in the duties of the day, the Baron grasps the opportunity to make headway with Mariandel. Has she, he asks her, ever supped with a cavalier? Tête-à-tête? No? Then she has quite a thrill in store for her. His question is put to the tune of yet another waltz, one a lot more seductive than is the Baron himself. (The waltz is to be used again in the third act.)

The Princess has observed the Baron's technique and now chides him for conduct unbecoming to a bridegroom. Unbecoming? Not at all. Being a bridegroom does not turn him into a "lame donkey." He is a hunter by profession, his quarry the female of the species. It is capital sport, this hunt, and it is to be regretted that the Princess can only be familiar with—how shall he put it?—its defending strategy. Then Ochs launches into a eulogy of his own prowess, with much vivid description of the various things in skirts that he pursues, the milkmaids and the peasant girls, the naïve and the sly, the girls who want to be coaxed and those who do the coaxing, the rebellious ones and those overcome by awe—and so on, and so on. His patron saint is Jupiter. He would like to be like Jupiter, adopting a thousand disguises; he'd have use for every one of them. Hofmannsthal runs away with this speech, making it overlong for stage purposes. Nor is the music as funny as all that. (It is usually shortened in performance.)

Both the Princess and Mariandel smile over this unique rogue, who then caps the climax by asking the Princess to give him Mariandel, "the little monkey," as part of his future wife's retinue. Speaking as a connoisseur, it appears to him that Mariandel has a drop of good blood in her. He finds it quite in order that persons of rank surround themselves with servants of "back-door" aristocratic origin. He himself is waited on by a "son of his caprice," his personal valet, who will in a moment or two bring the Princess the silver rose.

This gives the Princess an idea. She bids Mariandel fetch a medallion, Octavian's portrait. It is this young Count Rofrano whom she proposes as the bearer of the silver rose. The Baron, the moment he sees the portrait, is much struck by the resemblance between Mariandel and Octavian. He supposes that the serving maid has the same parental history as his own valet. At any rate, he is happy to accept the noble Count as his "Cavalier of the Rose."

The Princess, having satisfied Ochs' request, now proceeds to receive her morning visitors. As they stream in, Octavian finally makes good his escape. This *"levée,"* based on an eighteenth-century social custom, is a colorful scene, in which both librettist and composer combine various incidents into an entertaining whole, the music being vivid and descriptive. Pictorially, the scene is inspired by Hogarth's painting in his *Marriage à la Mode* series. The staging of the scene was first suggested by Max Reinhardt.[7]

Among the people who wait on the Princess are her chef who, aided by an assistant, hands her the choice of the day's menus; a French milliner, offering the latest styles in hats; an animal dealer, with dogs which are "tiny but housebroken"; a scholar with a folio; the Notary; the Marschallin's hairdresser and his assistant, who enter with a great flourish; a singer, sent to entertain the Princess, with a flautist to accompany him; and two dubious Italian characters, Valzacchi and Annina. Among the morning's callers there appears as well an old aristocratic widow who has come down in her fortunes, with her three daughters. These three supplicate the Princess' aid with a ditty-like tune, as if they were used to repeating that plea regularly. They are rewarded by a gift. The two Italians slink toward the Princess and offer her "the black scandal sheet," containing all the latest scandal of Vienna. This the Princess resolutely refuses.

While the hairdresser performs his ministrations,[8] the singer, in true tenor-like fashion, preens himself and, after much preluding by the flautist, begins his song. He sings an Italian aria, one which

[7] During the rehearsals for the premiere in Dresden, Strauss and Hofmannsthal became aware that the regular Dresden stage director was hopelessly inadequate for the task of staging this new comedy. They insisted that Reinhardt be called. At first Reinhardt was not permitted to go up on the stage, and he directed from the auditorium. Whether the reason for this nonsensical arrangement was the attempt to assuage wounded feelings or —as Strauss implied later—because Reinhardt was a Jew is not known. The following day Reinhardt took complete command.

No doubt both Hofmannsthal and Reinhardt were familiar with Hogarth's painting in London's National Gallery.

[8] There is a little byplay: The Marschallin receives a note, presumably a *billet-doux*. The hairdresser's curling iron is too hot. He looks around for a piece of paper to cool it. The Marschallin smilingly hands him the letter. All this originates in Hogarth's painting.

Strauss wrote in the most *arioso* of styles, as if to prove that if he wanted to write Italian opera he could do so with the best of them.

After the singer has finished the first stanza, there is an interruption caused by the servants of Baron Ochs, led by the valet, who lumber into the room. In dress, manner, general unkemptness, and the plump music which accompanies them, they betray their yokel origin.

The singer is waiting to begin the second strophe, but there is a further delay caused by the Baron's and the Notary's very audible discussion of the details of the marriage contract and the dowry. What Ochs wants, among other things, is the return of a castle and of property that his family once owned; he wants the gift free and clear as "*Morgengabe*," a gift to be given the morning after the nuptial night. The stuttering Notary (notaries always stutter in opera) raises what seem to the Baron pedantic difficulties. A *Morgengabe* may be bestowed by a husband upon a wife, never by a wife upon a husband. Such is the law. "Nonsense!" objects the Baron. Laws and prescripts have to recognize an exception when they deal with somebody as exalted as a Baron von Lerchenau. The tenor has grown tired of waiting and has begun the second stanza while the argument continues, the Baron's temper rising until he loses it altogether and screams, "As *Morgengabe*," causing the singer to break off in the middle of his last mellifluous phrase.

All this—the noise, the Baron's raucous voice, the people pressing around her, the shock she experienced at the early hour—could not have failed to pinch the Marschallin's nerves, though she is too seasoned a diplomat to explode like a Baron Ochs. It is as a woman that she betrays her irritation: surveying herself in the mirror, she does not like what she sees. "My dear Hippolyte," she murmurs tonelessly, "today you have made an old woman of me." Hippolyte lunges once more at her coiffure—with no better result. The Marschallin declares the *levée* terminated. As a final episode, the two Italians slink over to the Baron and offer their confidential detective service. The Baron marvels at all the curiosities that Vienna offers, and to try them out asks whether they know a Mlle. Mariandel. Valzacchi and Annina haven't of course the faintest notion who Mariandel is, but this does not prevent them from swearing that they will deliver her.

The Baron then beckons to his valet to hand the silver rose to the Marschallin. She bids him leave it in its case and, still remaining urbane, finally manages to dismiss the intruding relative. With a bow as elaborate as that with which he entered, he departs.

Marie Therese is now left alone with her thoughts. There goes this arrogant Baron; he will get what he is after, a pretty young girl and a mess of money. Yet he fancies it is he himself who is conferring a favor. But why does she think this strange? Is it not the way of the world? Does she not remember that as a young girl, fresh from the convent, she herself was ordered into marriage? Where is this girl now? she asks as she looks at herself in the mirror. One may as well find the snows of yesteryear. And yet how is it possible that a long time ago she was "little Resi" and that one day she will be "the old lady, the old Princess"? How does such transformation come about? Is she not, deep within herself, still the same girl, the same "little Resi"? And if it is needful that change must run its course, why is it that God forces her to be conscious of it, why does He compel her to be so clear-eyed an observer? There is no answer. One is born to bear the enigma, and *how* one bears it, ah, there lies the difference. On the word "how" the orchestra resolves the monologue on a consoling chord.

The meditation is expressed in the gentlest of music, in sadness that is not pallid, in regret that is not tragic. Strauss never forgets that, even at her most serious, his Marschallin is blessed with grace and lightness.

The door opens and Octavian returns, dressed in his riding costume. At once the lover's eye perceives that his mistress is in a pensive mood. He is familiar with these moods, half-merry, half-sad. He ascribes her present state to the concern she felt—for him! —when she thought her husband was returning. But it was no husband, it was just a comic cousin.

Octavian is quite ready to resume the lover's play which had been interrupted earlier. But now he finds that it is a different Bichette who is sitting before him. She is a changeling, he complains. For Marie Therese cannot shake off the reflective sadness which encumbers her heart. She feels the futility of fulfillment, the impossibility of holding fast, the illusion of possession. Life slips through one's fingers; that for which one reaches proves ephemeral.

Octavian puts a young boy's interpretation on the Princess'

philosophy: she no longer loves him. He bursts into tears. The Marschallin, perhaps further irritated by this childish display, observes quietly, "Now I must console the boy for the fact that sooner or later he is going to leave me flat." "Sooner or later?" "Yes, if not today, then tomorrow. It is not important when. But it will happen, in time. Time is inexorable." As she says this to Octavian, the strains of the little ditty the three poor girls sang at the *levée* run underneath her words. Time, Marie Therese continues, is unfathomable. From day to day, time is nothing. But suddenly one feels time all around one, deep within one. One feels nothing but time. Time shows up in the face in your mirror; time trickles in your veins. Even between her and her lover time is flowing, silently, like the sand of an hourglass. (One hears this flow in the orchestra.) No power she can command can arrest the flow, though once in a while she gets up in the middle of the night—and stops all the clocks.

Having arrived at this standstill pause (one of the musical highlights of the first act), the Marschallin shakes her head and concludes, "There is no use being afraid of time. It too is a creation of God." Octavian tenderly asks her whether she wants to make herself sad on purpose. But she cannot let be. She repeats to him, as she has told herself, that today or tomorrow or the day after he will give her up—for someone who is younger and (here Strauss writes the direction "a little hesitatingly") prettier than she. That day will come by itself. Octavian, soaring to the summit of protestation to the motive of their love, does not want to think of so awful a day. Why does she plague him and herself? She replies: Not to torture him, no, but to state what is true and inevitable, and to accept that truth lightly. With a light heart and a light hand one must take and surrender. Those who cannot learn this lesson are punished by life, and God, God has no pity on them.

Does that mean that he can no longer kiss her and make love to her? Not now. Now it is time for her to go to church. Later she will pay a visit to her uncle, who is old and paralyzed, and take lunch with him, just to please the old man. In the afternoon she will send him a messenger. Perhaps she will go riding in the Prater. If she does, and if he is so inclined, he may come to the Prater and ride next to her carriage. This is all she says, though the orchestra makes it clear what the invitation implies.

Now he is to go. "As you please, Bichette," answers Octavian with a quick bow, and is gone.

No sooner has he disappeared than the Marschallin starts up. "I did not even kiss him good-bye!" She rings the bell. Four footmen hurry in. She bids them run after the Count and ask him to return for a moment. The lackeys, however, are unable to find Rofrano. He has galloped away.

The Marschallin dismisses them and asks for Mohammed, her little Negro page. She orders him to take the case with the silver rose to— The little boy turns to go and she says, "Wait, you do not know where to." But of course he does know, a charming touch by the poet. "Take this to Count Octavian and say that it contains the silver rose. The Count will understand."

Once more alone, the Marschallin seats herself in front of her dressing table and remains in silent thought. The closing of the act is taken over by the orchestra; it reminds us of the motives associated with the Princess and Octavian, passing the themes in retrospect while a solo violin adds its own sweetness to a clear, still mood of "It has passed."

From the moment of Ochs' departure to the fall of the curtain, Strauss is at his greatest. The music guides us through not one but two philosophical speeches; this music freshens and quickens the thoughts of the Marschallin and makes them seem profound and universal reflections, when coldly examined they might appear as middling wisdom—a certain felicity of expression notwithstanding. In the creation of the character of the Marschallin both Strauss and Hofmannsthal are equivalent collaborators—but it is Strauss' special merit, an achievement almost unique, to have succeeded in portraying through music melancholy garbed in gay colors, sadness lightened by intelligence. Is it possible that music can smile ruefully? It seems so. Certain it is that the shifting of the Marschallin's animadversions is subtly yet clearly expressed by the music.

Few scenes in the theater and few in opera can compare in sensitivity to the latter half of this act.

ACT II

The scene is laid in Faninal's town palace, a room as sumptuous as is to be expected in the house of a man who has recently amassed a fortune. There is a large window on the right; the main entrance is at the back of the stage.

Faninal is about to depart, for it is customary for the father of the bride to meet the bridegroom at a little distance from the house and personally to conduct the groom into the presence of his bride. Faninal is being instructed in etiquette by his Major-domo, who warns our *bourgeois gentilhomme* that he may not be present when the bearer of the silver rose enters.

Sophie and her duenna, Marianne, listen to these last-minute instructions. They can hardly contain themselves in the general excitement. Marianne goes to the window to describe the departure of Faninal's carriage. Sophie, standing by herself, attempts to marshal her thoughts "in this solemn hour." Is she worthy of the honor that is about to be bestowed on her? Will she be able to meet the responsibilities of this marriage? The solemnity of the young girl gives way soon enough before the bustle which penetrates into the room through the open window. Octavian's couriers in the street below are heard calling out "Rofrano," as he himself draws nearer. The musical material consists mainly of reiteration of Octavian's theme, now charged with an imposing and stately force.

Sophie promises herself that she will never become overbearing or marriage-proud, but will remain humble. And yet—and yet she cannot help feeling elated. This moment of all moments—it is too thrilling not to feel pride.

The music comes to a magnificent climax as the center door is flung open and Octavian, dressed entirely in white, enters. He is accompanied by a number of his own servants dressed in their liveries of white and pale green. He carries the silver rose in his right hand. With a noble grace, yet not without a trace of young shyness, he advances a step toward Sophie. As the orchestra subsides into a *pianissimo* and we hear the music associated with the silver rose, he begins his little ceremonial speech: "Mine is the honor to present to the high and well-born bride the rose which is the token of my cousin's love, the Baron of Lerchenau." Sophie answers equally ceremoniously that she is "obliged to His Grace unto eternity." Then they both stand confused. We hear through this a series of chords of a strange timbre produced by a mixture of flutes, harps, violins, and the celesta, the whole conveying a silvery sound. Sophie stammers out that the rose seems to exude a strange perfume, like a living rose. Octavian tells her that it contains a drop of Persian attar. She calls it a rose of Paradise, not one of this earth, a greeting from heaven. Lost in admiration and wonder, one for the other, knowing but imperfectly what is happening to them, Sophie and Octavian begin a duet, first shy then soaring to ever greater intensity, and still accompanied by the strange harmonies of the silver rose. "Where was it and when was it, once before, that I was so happy?" They do not know. They know only that they seem to wing their way, the two together, high above the roof of Faninal's town palace.

Then, with a sudden break, they are brought back to earth. Marianne takes the rose from Sophie's hand, the servants of Faninal bring in chairs, and Sophie and Octavian know that they are expected to "make conversation." The orchestra, too, leaves the higher region and sets their conversation to a slow waltz tune. Sophie tells Octavian that she knows quite well who he is. She has looked him up in *The Mirror of Austrian Nobility*.[9] She takes the book to bed with her to study her future relatives. She knows how old he is and all of his first names, which she promptly proceeds to reel off. And, she adds, she knows still another name, Quinquin, the name by which he is known to his good friends and to beautiful ladies.

Sophie confesses that she is glad she is going to be married. A man is a man, but a woman needs a man to become herself. She hopes that though she is marrying into nobility and is herself of humble birth, no one is going to snub her. As she prattles on, Octavian observes to himself, "How beautiful and good she is!" and assures her with a smile that no one would dream of slighting her.

"Are you making fun of me?" she asks. "You may do so. For I have never met a man whom I have liked as well as I do you."

It is high time for their scene to be cut short. To the accompaniment of a staccato motive, Faninal enters, formally conducting the Baron, who in turn is accompanied by his servants. Sophie is presented to him. The Baron takes one look at her and is pleased by what he sees. He kisses her hand and notes that she has a fine wrist; one doesn't often find such a wrist among the bourgeoisie. He rudely waves away the duenna to greet his *Rosenkavalier*. Sophie, her pride at once offended by the behavior of a man who

---

[9] A book similar to *Burke's Peerage*.

judges her as if she were a filly to be purchased, wants to know if this fiancé of hers is a horse dealer. He certainly acts like one. She finds him repulsive and ill-bred and pockmarked in the bargain.

But all this is lost on the Baron, who is deep in conversation with Octavian. It is remarkable, he observes, how much Octavian looks like a certain young person he has seen, a cute little trick. There is no reason for Octavian to feel ashamed that his father, the Marquis Rofrano, once sowed his wild oats. Who is guiltless? Certainly not he himself.

Faninal, overjoyed at the whole situation—all this aristocracy in his house retailing gossip!—now serves a glass of Tokay. "Bravo!" the Baron applauds. "Serving a glass of old wine with a young girl —I am satisfied with you, Faninal." Turning to Octavian, he seeks commendation for his treatment of Faninal. After all, one has to show these people with their green patent of nobility that they do not really count. One needs to employ a bit of condescension. Octavian answers with sarcasm lost on Lerchenau that his manners are as sophisticated as those of an ambassador.

The Baron proposes now that he'll converse a little with his bride, just to see whether she's got any brains in her head. Crossing over to where Sophie stands, he asks what it is that she is looking forward to most in marriage. He attempts to draw her on to his lap. Sophie, in disgust, tries to break away, while the fatuous Faninal compliments himself on his own shrewdness in arranging the august marriage, and Octavian tries to suppress his fury.

The Baron compliments Sophie on her good looks. She is too thin yet and has shoulders like a chicken—but with a white sheen which he finds appetizing. By all that's holy, he has the luck of the Lerchenaus. Near to tears, she asks him how he dare speak to her in this manner. What is he to her? To which the Baron replies in a *gemütlich* tone that she will find out soon enough what he is to her. Just as the song has it, that little song which is his favorite. Does she know it? He begins to hum the tune: "With me, with me, no chamber too small. Without me, without me, every day too long. With me, with me," (loud and coarsely) "no night too long."

The Notary has entered, and the Baron is now needed to sign the contract. Leaving Sophie for the moment, he whispers to Octavian that it might not be a bad idea if he, Octavian, were to flirt a little with Sophie. She is as yet quite unawakened, like an unridden horse. If Octavian were to warm her up a little—well, eventually the husband would benefit.

Faninal, the Notary, and the Baron repair to the adjoining room, leaving Octavian, Sophie, and Marianne once more together. At once he hurries to the young girl and whispers, "Are you going to marry this horror?" "Not for anything in the world! If I could only ask you to help me. But how can you, since he is your cousin?" "I call him a cousin only by courtesy. I never saw him before yesterday."

At this moment a great commotion startles everybody. Faninal's female servants rush in pursued by Ochs' lecherous lackeys: like master, like servant. The Major-domo implores the duenna's help to restore order. Marianne runs out of the room. (The incident serves as a rather lame dramatic device to contrive privacy for the young people.)

Left alone, Octavian and Sophie realize that they are in love. He tells her that from this moment they must stand together, must act one for the other. Sophie takes his hand and bends to kiss it; instead, he kisses her lips, and begins the declaration of love which forms the duet. It is a good enough duet, but it lacks the ethereal sweetness of the music of their first meeting, in my opinion. As they stand there, close together, oblivious of their entanglements, the two Italians, Valzacchi and Annina, creep from the corners of the room and in the traditionally stealthy manner of spies steal up behind the lovers. Suddenly Valzacchi grabs Octavian while Annina holds Sophie fast; both of them loudly call for their employer, the Baron.

He enters. Folding his arms and quite enjoying the situation, he turns to Sophie. "*Eh bien*, Mademoiselle. What have you to tell me?" The frightened girl is unable to answer; Octavian becomes the spokesman. He informs the Baron that the proposed marriage is off, because, to put it bluntly, Fräulein Sophie cannot abide him. Ochs waves that little objection away. Sophie is to follow him immediately to sign the marriage document. Octavian suggests that rather than bother with the contract, the Baron would oblige him by meeting him behind the house, where there is a convenient garden. Thick-skinned Ochs refuses that challenge, so Octavian is forced to act more plainly. He draws his sword and hurls every insult he can think of at his pusillanimous adversary. Ochs utters a loud whistle, summoning his servants, but all of them together are no match for the infuriated young boy. The Baron most reluctantly draws his sword, they duel—and one, two, three, Octavian nicks him in the arm. "Murder! Murder!" howls the Baron. "Help! A doctor! A bandage! Police! Help!" The whole place is in an uproar. Faninal's servants, male and female, pour in. The Baron's servants suggest that the clothes of the younger and better-looking of Faninal's maids be used for bandages. But this suggestion is rendered unnecessary by the appearance of the duenna, who returns with bandages and a basin. Finally Faninal re-enters to survey the situation.

Poor Faninal! So scandalous an incident, and it has occurred in his house! What is more, the miscreant is not one on whom he can take revenge: it is the noble Rofrano himself. His daughter is standing there, close by the boy! Faninal surmises that something has gone wrong with the marriage plan. He knows instinctively too that while it is possible that Sophie may be betrothed to a Baron Ochs, Rofrano's social status is too lofty for any aspirations toward an alliance. The boy has spoiled everything and yet he must be treated with the deference due to an aristocrat. (It is a difficult point for the actor playing Faninal to get across.) All Faninal can do is first to vent his rage on his own servants, none of whom has had the presence of mind to call a doctor; then, turning to Sophie, to demand to know what this is all about. To Sophie's answer, "The gentleman over there did not behave himself as he should have," Faninal replies, "Of whom are you speaking? Of your future husband?" Sophie declares, "I do not regard him as such."

The doctor has entered, examines Baron Ochs, who has been made comfortable, and pronounces the wound not dangerous.

"You are going to marry him," yells Faninal at his daughter. "And if he does not survive, you will marry his corpse." But Sophie has found her courage. Under no circumstances will she concede, though Faninal, in further rage, threatens to shut her up in a convent—for her whole lifetime. Octavian has time still to whisper to her, "I will send you word!" before he finds it prudent to leave.[10]

---

[10] In present-day staging, Valzacchi and Annina approach Octavian as he turns to go and in pantomime offer their services. Struck by an idea, Octavian beckons to them to follow him. There is no authority in the score or the book for such business, which spells out what the audience had better guess.

Ochs is weary of Faninal's repeated protestations of friendship, his abject apologies, and his litany of the dire punishments proposed for Sophie. He demands to be left alone. Gradually the stage empties, only the Baron remaining in the company of his yokels. Having imbibed a copious draught of wine, Ochs' mood changes for the better. Things are not so bad as they look. The wound appears to be somewhat less than mortal. But it is curious what can befall a man in wicked Vienna! While the Baron reflects on what he still considers a temporary setback to his marriage plans, the Lerchenau servants, very brave now that Octavian has disappeared, sing a chorus, the burden of which is that they'll cut Octavian, that "Italian dog," to ribbons, if they catch him.

The scene from the duel to the final soliloquy of the Baron, while dramatically a little too long (it is almost always abbreviated in performance), is set to delightfully comic music. What is particularly adroit is the transition from the tumult and the excitement to the alcoholic calm of the Baron.

There he lies, then, a little tired, a little spent, but with his optimism gradually getting the upper hand. Two hours still remain before dinner is to be served. He sends the doctor to prepare a bed for him, a bed entirely upholstered in down. In the meantime he is entertaining himself by humming his favorite ditty. The comfortable waltz is heard again, while Annina enters bearing a letter. It is a confidential missive, to be read only by the addressee. Since the Baron hasn't his spectacles handy, she reads the contents to him. The letter is from Mariandel, who confesses that she has succumbed to the Baron's charm, though she dared not give an inkling of her feelings in the presence of the Marschallin. Tomorrow night she would be free, provided the Baron still cared. She is waiting for an answer. The identity of the writer is made clear to the knowledgeable listener because Octavian's motive accompanies the reading of the letter.

"She is waiting for an answer." Well, this is something more like it! Vienna is not so different from home, after all. The luck of the Lerchenaus still holds. Ochs commands Annina to bring pen and paper to his room, where he will dictate his reply. Ignoring her hint for a tip, he is all fire as he anticipates the coming adventure. The orchestra takes over to intone his favorite song in an exaggeratedly "*schmaltzy*" style, a style that would undoubtedly suit the Baron's musical taste. As the curtain falls slowly, he repeats as a coda the proposition that "with me, with me, no night can be too long."

ACT III

The Prelude is, in spite of the tempo indication "As fast as possible," an overlong introduction. There is a hurrying and a scurrying in the orchestra which means to convey that something eerie is about to happen. But the music is not very effective. Before the Prelude ends, the curtain rises and we get a clearer idea of what that something is.

The scene is a little private room of a run-down restaurant in a suburb of Vienna. At the right, a table is set for two. At the left, separated from the main room by a curtain, there is an alcove in which stands the bed which is essential equipment for such a *chambre separée*. One window opens onto the street, but in addition there are several blind windows or apertures set in the back of the wall. The illumination is furnished by candles; at present only a few of these are lit, so that the room is in semidarkness.

Annina is here, dressed in widow's weeds. She is studying a piece of paper, the part she is to play. Valzacchi is putting the finishing touches to her masquerade. Presently Octavian enters, disguised as Mariandel. He surveys the room and pays off the two Italians. Then he disappears to wait for the Baron.

Valzacchi now beckons to a few disreputable individuals whom he has employed. He assigns them to their posts. One is hidden in a trap door near the little table, the others being placed behind the various apertures. His men in position, Valzacchi claps his hands for a quick rehearsal; the men appear and disappear. Everything is ready for the trick that is to be played on the Baron; it has become obvious that he is to be scared out of whatever wits he may possess, at a crucial point in his attempt to seduce Mariandel.

The scene is played in pantomime. Musically it could be dispensed with, at least until the moment when from somewhere behind the stage we hear a waltz. To its strains the candles are lighted by serving boys. Valzacchi hurries to the entrance, opens the door, and, bowing deeply, admits the Baron, who enters escorting Mariandel on his left arm since his right is in a sling. The Baron is closely followed by his valet. Valzacchi discreetly shows the Baron the lay of the land. Ochs is highly satisfied with the arrangements, except that he promptly proceeds to extinguish most of the candles. The more candles, the higher the bill. What about the music which is still playing the waltz behind the scene? He hasn't ordered a band. The proprietor of the inn has appeared with a quite numerous troupe of waiters. The Baron doesn't want them around; food is to be served by his valet, the wine he will pour himself.

Ochs suggests that Valzacchi help him chisel a discount on the bill, in which case the Italian may keep the difference as his tip.

Then the Baron and Mariandel are left alone. They sit down at the table and the Baron urges Mariandel to have a glass of wine. But this she refuses. "No, no, no, no! I won't drink wine," she sings to a languishingly sentimental tune (*schmachtend* is the expressive German word for it), a tune typical of the Viennese songs one hears at the *Heurigen* in Grinzing. Octavian plays his part perfectly: he is the coquettish little baggage. As such, she takes fright and runs, seemingly not knowing what she is doing, toward the alcove, tears the curtains apart, and sees the bed. "Who sleeps here?" Mariandel wonders, wide-eyed. . . . "You will find out."

As the Baron draws her again to the table and becomes amorous, she protests, "Oh, you mustn't! You, a bridegroom—" "Forget that boring word," Ochs rejoins. "Here in this room we have no bridegrooms and no chambermaids. Here there are only a lover and his pretty girl about to partake of supper."

The moment for the first kiss seems propitious. But as the Baron draws near to Mariandel he is once again struck by the extraordinary resemblance between this girl and "that accursed boy." The irritation passes, however, to be followed by worse. The man under the trap door mistakes his cue and appears too soon. The Baron recoils in terror: "What is that?" But Mariandel assures him that it is nothing, nothing at all. He must be seeing things. It must be so, he concludes, his amorousness getting the better of his common sense.

The valet arrives with the supper. Once more we hear the backstage orchestra. This time they are playing the Baron's favorite ditty. Such music makes Mariandel very, very sad. How useless is life! When she hears music she must shed tears. For music reminds her that nothing is permanent, the hour must pass, and like everybody else the two of them will fade away, gone with the wind.

Mariandel, pretending to be drunk, gives out her bibulous philosophy to another insinuating waltz strain, the orchestral setting of
which bears some relationship to the Marschallin's serious thoughts
on the passing of time in the first act. It is as if Octavin remembers
and as if the composer were mocking himself.

"Does wine always have this effect on you?" the Baron wants to
know. "Perhaps it is your corset which is pressing on your heart."
As he prepares to remedy this difficulty, Ochs is beginning to feel
rather warm. He doffs his wig. As he does so, he notices a face
staring at him from the alcove, then another, then another. The
effect is all Octavian could have wished for. Frantic with fear,
Ochs grabs the bell and shouts for help. Annina appears within the
frame of the blind window, and pointing at the Baron with a gesture of the Tragic Muse, exclaims, "It is he, my husband!"

The avalanche has come. Annina and four young children who
shout, "Papa! Papa!" (while a child's rattle is heard in the orchestra), the waiters, the proprietor, Valzacchi—they all crowd in,
causing bedlam. (The horseplay is a little overdone and is carried
on for longer than necessary.)

The Baron now loses his head altogether. He opens the window
and screams for the police. It is the least prudent course that he can
adopt, for in no time at all—proving that the security forces of
eighteenth-century Vienna were on their job—there enters a Constable of the "Moral Police" (*Sittenpolizei*) with his men. "No one
is to stir," is the sharp command. "Excellent!" observes the Baron.
"Get these people off my neck." To his great shock he finds that
his wish makes not the least impression on the policeman. Who is
this bald fellow with an arm in a sling? The Constable isn't even
impressed when he is told that this is the Baron Ochs von Lerchenau. Can the Baron identify himself? Ochs appeals for identification to Valzacchi, but the wily Italian declines to say yes or no.
The Constable next inquires who the girl is. Ochs tries to pass her
off as his fiancée. The name? "Fräulein Faninal, Sophia Anna Barbara, legitimate daughter of the well-born Herr von Faninal."

"Present!" exclaims a voice. It is Faninal himself, who has pushed
his way through the crowd. How did he get here, in the name of
the Devil? the Baron wants to know. "What a stupid question!"
Faninal replies. "Didn't you break my doors in with messenger
after messenger begging me to come and help you out in an awk-

ward situation?" (Obviously these messengers had been sent by Octavian.)

Well, then, if this is the father, does Faninal acknowledge the girl standing there in the corner as his daughter? That is the Constable's next question. "What!" cries Faninal, apoplectic with rage. "That washrag? Certainly not! My daughter is downstairs in the carriage. Let her come up."

Faninal now perceives what kind of man it is to whom he has promised his daughter. Here are this disreputable girl, as well as a woman who claims to be Frau Baron, and four little children in the bargain. And the bridegroom has the gall to summon him, Faninal, to a dirty dubious locale to witness the scene. An incredible mess! Sophie has arrived, just in time to hear Faninal moan that his good name has been blackened forever. The mortification proves too much. The poor old fellow faints and is carried into the next room with Sophie fussing over him.

By this time the Baron has recovered his wig; with it some of his habitual self-assurance has returned. But he cannot be let off lightly. The Constable still has some awkward questions to pose. Mariandel, who has remained silent throughout, suddenly turns to the policeman and says, "I have something to testify, but the Herr Baron must not hear it."[11] Mariandel disappears into the alcove, and presently from behind the curtain there are thrown, one after the other, pieces of female clothing. The Constable looks on and, understanding the joke, begins to laugh uproariously, while the Baron, who doesn't understand the joke, protests volubly and struggles to get free of the two burly policemen who hold him.

Suddenly the door bursts open and the innkeeper, quite out of breath with excitement, announces, "Her Serene Highness, the Marschallin."

In the midst of general astonishment, Marie Therese enters, looking her most beautiful. Why has she come? For what reason does her presence grace this shoddy inn? How did she learn about the whole affair? It is possible that some time between Octavian's exit from Faninal's house in the second act and Mariandel's rendezvous with the Baron, Octavian told her about the prank he intended to perpetrate. But it is clear that he had not wished her to play a part

---

11 These words are spoken, not sung.

in this hoax. For he says to her explicitly, "Why are you here? We had agreed on a different plan, Marie Therese." Searching for a plausible explanation for the Marschallin's presence, we find but a slight indication: During the scene of the harassment of the Baron, his valet "seems to be struck by a helpful idea and disappears suddenly through the center door." This stage direction in the score does not, however, appear in the text book and seems to have been added as an afterthought. Perhaps—as Ernest Newman has suggested—Hofmannsthal and Strauss realized later, possibly during the rehearsals, "that in the original text the visit of the Princess to the inn had been left quite unexplained." Even if the valet's summoning of the Princess is part of the original plan, the plan is inadequate dramatically. In the first place, the spectator can hardly be expected to notice so slight an incident as the disappearance of the valet during a general upheaval nor draw the proper conclusion therefrom; in the second place, there would not have been enough time for the Marschallin to order her carriage and travel from her palace to the suburb. Indeed, there would not have been enough time for a woman like the Marschallin to put on her hat. We are left, then, with the feeling that Hofmannsthal and Strauss brought back the Marschallin for no better reason than that they wanted to bring her back.

But here she is, this handsome *dea ex machina,* and we are very glad to see her; for with her entrance the horseplay ends, the farce terminates, and we are back in the realm of high comedy.

The Baron, obtuse to the last, interprets her visit as a personal favor to him. The Constable, who recognizes her—the wife of the Field Marshal would hardly need identification—pays his humble respects. She knows him as well: he turns out to be a former orderly of the Field Marshal. So the police withdraw to the back of the room, satisfied to leave the affair in her capable hands.

Sophie appears at the door with a message. Octavian is still half-hidden behind the curtain. But the Marschallin has not failed to notice him nor his embarrassment. "I find you a little *empressé,* Rofrano" (she now addresses him by his formal title). "I can imagine who the girl is. I find her *charmante.*" Sophie's message to the Baron is short and sharp. The marriage is called off and her father wishes to convey to him the admonition that he is not to show his nose within a hundred paces of their town house. The

Baron protests noisily against this insult, until the Marschallin takes
a step toward him and taps him on the shoulder. "Let it go," she
says, "and disappear at once. . . . For if you are able to preserve
bonne mine à mauvais jeu,[12] you may still remain a person of
quality." Turning then to the Constable, she explains, "You see, the
whole thing was a farce, and nothing more." That suffices; he and
his helpers disappear. The explanation and all it implies touches
Sophie to the quick. Has she merely been used as an actor in a
comedy? She repeats sadly to herself, "The whole thing was a farce,
and nothing more."

The Baron is still unwilling to acknowledge defeat. It is only
when the Marschallin feels it necessary to give Ochs a broader hint,
calling to her aid Octavian, who now appears fully dressed with his
sword at his side, that Ochs begins to understand that he shall have
to return home *sans* bride, *sans* money. Not being altogether inexperienced in such matters, he guesses the identity of that "Mariandel" who moved so freely in the Princess' boudoir early in the
morning and whose double now stands glowering at him. As he
puts it with an attempt at finesse, "I don't know what to think
about this whole *quid pro quo*." To which the Marschallin answers,
"You are, if I am not mistaken, a cavalier. Therefore you are not
going to think anything at all."

He has his marching orders. "Can't you understand when a
thing has come to an end?" commands the Marschallin. "Your
marriage, the whole affair, and everything connected with it, is at
this moment over and done with."

The Baron has no choice but to call for the bill. All the super-
numeraries who have taken part in the masquerade—the proprietor,
the waiters, the musicians, the coachmen, the candle boys, the
children—all rush in to demand money. And amid this general
hubbub we see the last of Ochs von Lerchenau.

The three principals of the triangle remain. Sophie, broken-
hearted because she believes that Octavian's love is "over and done
with" as well, is standing at the extreme right; the Marschallin is
sitting near the center of the stage; while Octavian, awkward and
ill at ease, hovers between them. What is he to do next? The
Marschallin instructs him. "Go and do what your heart dictates."

[12] The Marschallin employs French phrases possibly because she is speaking in the
presence of the Constable and his aides.

But when he turns to Sophie in search of a "friendly word," he finds no ready consolation.

Here begins what is the climax of the opera, the trio in which, as it is customary in opera, each of the three gives voice to separate thought. As is Strauss' way, the ensemble begins quietly, then swells to a river in which the currents of his orchestra flow and swirl with the voices, all at floodgate tide. In the art of voice writing as well as orchestration this trio is charged with magic. If with it we return to old-fashioned opera, the set number in which music takes over while the action is suspended, who would complain?[13]

The recitative leading up to the trio is poetic and delicate, both in its words and in its musical setting. The Marschallin remembers the covenant she has made with herself: that today or tomorrow or the day after, this fate was to be expected and that she, like every woman, must learn to live with it. Octavian is torn between his new love for Sophie and his attachment for Marie Therese, a feeling in which the remains of love, admiration, and a little guilty conscience are intermingled. Sophie, in her simple but intuitive way, knows that the Princess is giving Octavian to her; on whatever terms, she is grateful for that gift.

As the Marschallin recalls her vow made so often—"to bear it with a light heart"—she rises and, not deigning to look at Octavian, goes over to where the girl is standing. "So quickly have you learned to love him?" she asks. Sophie blurts out that she has no idea what Her Highness means by the question. "Your pale face gives me the answer." Sophie protests in voluble chatter of embarrassment that her pallor is caused by her concern over her father's malaise and the Baron's treachery, but the Marschallin cuts her words short. "Don't talk too much, you are pretty enough. As for your father, I know a remedy that may cure him! I'll go to him and invite him to return home in my carriage. . . . As for your pallor, perhaps my cousin here knows the right medicine."

With deep emotion Octavian stammers, "Marie Therese, how kind you are! I don't know—" She answers enigmatically, "I don't know either. I know nothing." Silence. Then a chord by the orchestra. Then the main melody of the trio, sung by the character

---

[13] This trio bears a relationship, in construction and position, to the third-act quintet of *Die Meistersinger*. This too is a set number which, though it runs counter to Wagner's theories, we would not exchange for a theory.

who has taken command of the composer's imagination: "I have promised myself," sings the Marschallin, "to love him in the right way, even to loving the love he feels for another." Octavian and Sophie join in; step by step their voices rise, carried upward in the fullness of their feelings, finally to culminate in the most passionate climax of the opera. The Marschallin's epilogic words are: "There stands the boy. And here am I. And with this new love he will be happy, at least as happy as men understand happiness. God's will be done." That is her coda. Then she is gone, having quietly disappeared into the next room.

The lovers do not even notice it. They fly into each other's arms. Accompanied by the motive of the Silver Rose, they sing a very simple, almost naïve duet. It serves as a contrast to the "adult" trio, and it is noteworthy that Strauss' setting of the duet is a Bellinian accompaniment, as against the trio's polyphonic complexity.

The door opens, and Faninal, escorting the Marschallin and now quite restored to equilibrium, enters. He sees the two lovers; with paternal benevolence, he pats his Sophie on the cheek. "It is the way of young people," he observes. The Marschallin answers a quick, almost inaudible "Yes, yes," leaving it to the orchestra to hint at her true feeling with a reminiscence of the closing moments of the first act. These monosyllables are a poignant example of understatement in opera. Faninal's little speech is musically accented on the word "young." Marie Therese, with her "Yes, yes," separates herself from youth.

Sophie and Octavian, left alone for a brief moment, repeat their duet in dreamy ecstasy. Then they embrace and run off into the night.

The stage remains empty. The door opens to admit the little Negro page. Candle in hand, he searches for a handkerchief which Sophie has dropped. He searches here, there, in this corner and that, finds the handkerchief, then trips away triumphantly. The curtain falls.

Did Strauss and Hofmannsthal mean to indicate by this final touch that the whole thing was indeed a "Viennese masquerade," a once-upon-a-time story not to be taken too seriously? We do not know. All we do know is that the final touch is like the last exclamation point ending a long, long love letter.